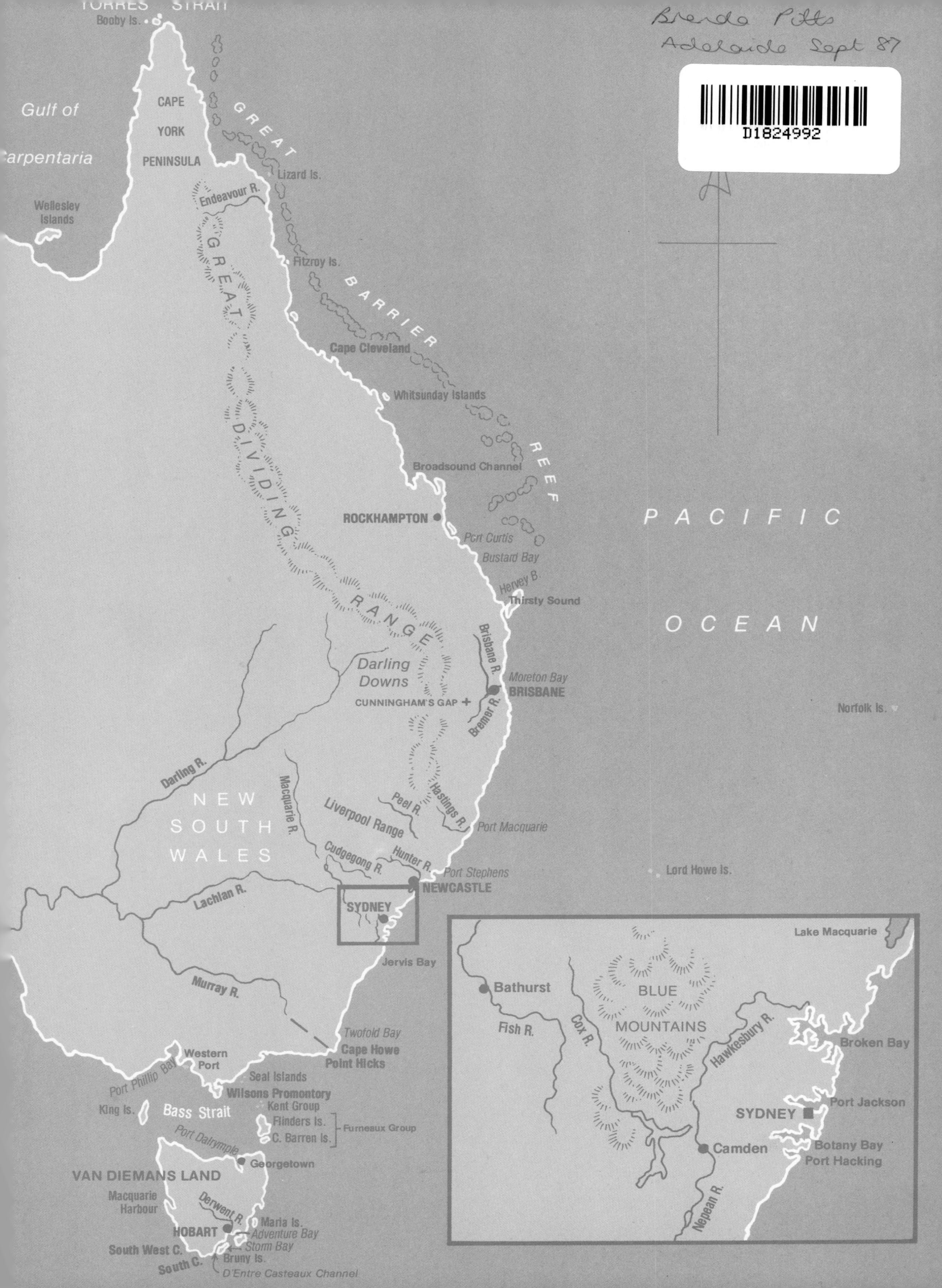

TORRES STRAIT
Booby Is.

Gulf of
Carpentaria

Wellesley
Islands

CAPE
YORK
PENINSULA

Lizard Is.

Endeavour R.

Fitzroy Is.

G R E A T

B A R R I E R

R E E F

Cape Cleveland

Whitsunday Islands

Broadsound Channel

G R E A T   D I V I D I N G   R A N G E

ROCKHAMPTON

Port Curtis

Bustard Bay

Hervey B.

Thirsty Sound

Darling
Downs

CUNNINGHAM'S GAP

Brisbane R.

Moreton Bay

BRISBANE

Bremer R.

P A C I F I C

O C E A N

Norfolk Is.

Darling R.

N E W
S O U T H
W A L E S

Macquarie R.

Liverpool Range

Peel R.

Hastings R.

Port Macquarie

Cudgegong R.

Hunter R.

Port Stephens

Lord Howe Is.

Lachlan R.

NEWCASTLE

SYDNEY

Murray R.

Jervis Bay

Twofold Bay
Cape Howe
Point Hicks

Western
Port

Seal Islands

Port Phillip Bay

Wilsons Promontory

King Is.

Bass Strait

Kent Group

Flinders Is.

C. Barren Is.

Furneaux Group

Port Dalrymple

VAN DIEMANS LAND

Georgetown

Macquarie
Harbour

Derwent R.

Maria Is.

Adventure Bay

Storm Bay

HOBART

South West C.

South C.

Bruny Is.

D'Entre Casteaux Channel

Lake Macquarie

Bathurst

BLUE
MOUNTAINS

Fish R.

Cox R.

Hawkesbury R.

Broken Bay

Port Jackson

SYDNEY

Camden

Botany Bay
Port Hacking

Nepean R.

To Sail Beyond The Sunset
NATURAL HISTORY IN AUSTRALIA 1699-1829

TO SAIL BEYOND THE SUNSET
NATURAL HISTORY IN AUSTRALIA 1699-1829

C. M. FINNEY

RIGBY

For Denise

National Library of Australia
Cataloguing-in-Publication entry

Finney, C. M. (Colin Michael), 1950–
   To sail beyond the sunset.
   Bibliography.
   Includes index.
   ISBN 0 7270 1881 7.
   1. Natural history—Australia.
   I. Title.

508.94

RIGBY PUBLISHERS • ADELAIDE
SYDNEY • MELBOURNE • BRISBANE • PERTH
NEW YORK • LONDON • AUCKLAND
First published 1984
Copyright © 1984 C. M. Finney
Wholly designed and typeset in Australia
Printed by Everbest Printing Co. Ltd, Hong Kong

Some work of noble note, may yet be done,
Not unbecoming men that strove with the Gods.
The lights begin to twinkle from the rocks:
The long day wanes: the slow moon climbs: the deep
Moans round with many voices. Come, my friends
'Tis not too late to seek a newer world.
Push off, and sitting well in order smite
The sounding furrows; for my purpose holds
To sail beyond the sunset, and the baths
Of all the western stars, until I die.

Ulysses
Alfred, Lord Tennyson

Contents

Preface

In writing the history of any subject, an author is immediately faced with a dichotomy. One can either trace events in a chronological manner or deal with events by subject matter. Both approaches have their limitations. The chronological style is often disjointed; although the several separate strands of the rope of history must be interwoven, it can not always be done successfully. Contrariwise the description of historical events by topic suffers the disadvantage that events are difficult to view in the context of time and place, perspective is narrowed to the immediate subject.

For this record of the early years of natural history in Australia I have chosen the former approach. The chronological strategy allows a more intimate feel for the monthly, or, where the historical record is incomplete, the yearly activities of the individuals involved in the quest for knowledge of natural history. This concentration on individual involvement is deliberate. Much of the early work on the Australian flora and fauna was purely descriptive. While a certain amount of comparative anatomy and reproductive physiology was carried out on kangaroos and platypuses to determine their taxonomic status, descriptive natural history was still at its zenith. Other than detailed descriptions promulgated at the time of an organism's discovery, very little was known about individual plants or animals. Hence the development of Australian natural history is better characterised by its practitioners rather than by their subjects. Concomitantly, events of significance to Australian natural history must be placed in perspective, their relationship defined in terms of other activities; in the colony the exploration of the continent and the occasional interference that the naturalist suffered from political factors; abroad, especially important was the response of the European naturalists and public. For most of the initial years of the colony in New South Wales, the European demand for specimens and curiosities was the primary stimulus behind efforts made in natural history.

Concentration on placing events in perspective has led to the inclusion of examples of natural history art in the text. The often crude early sketches and paintings of the flora and fauna of Australia reflect the uncertainty about the subjects from the artist's point of view. There was no tradition of knowledge about animals such as kangaroos or wombats, and the early draughtsmen's attempts to come to terms with their lack of familiarity with the organisms often resulted in caricatures of the animals. As the years passed artistic representation of the animals grew increasingly more sophisticated, an artistic tradition of representation developed as the animals lost their strangeness. The Australian flora had always been easier to illustrate; depictions of plants were in general much better for they were visually less curious than the animals of the continent. These pictorial representations often give clues to the way that the draughtsmen, and indeed, the naturalists, saw the organisms.

In general I have tried to avoid the use of anecdotal material. Too often anecdotes have been formulated for amusement rather than accuracy. A case in point is the tale of Samuel Stutchbury's purported discovery of the 'living fossil' species of bivalve, *Neotrigonia*. Long known as a fossil species from Europe, tradition has it that the first live *Neotrigonia* was obtained by Stutchbury while dredging in Sydney Harbour in 1826. Stutchbury immediately recognised it as a specimen of the genus *Trigonia* but unfortunately, before he could scoop it up, it 'leapt' overboard. Amusing the story may be, accurate it is not. Live *Neotrigonia* had been obtained twenty-four years earlier in 1802, when François Peron on the French expedition of Nicholas Baudin dredged *Neotrigonia* in the vicinity of Bruny Island off the coast of Tasmania.

Many people were of assistance to me in the preparation of this manuscript. The librarians of the Australian Museum, Sydney; of the Royal Botanic Gardens, Sydney; and especially of the Mitchell Library, Sydney patiently suffered my constant demands for rare or obscure books. Dr D. Griffin, Director of the Australian Museum and Dr L. Johnson, Director of the Royal Botanic Gardens allowed my photographers John Fields and Kate Lowe to photograph illustrations from their collections. Deanne Thomas typed the final manuscript. Both the Literature Board of the Australia Council and the Division of Cultural Activities, New South Wales Premier's Department, provided me with funds to help with completion of the manuscript. Gilbert Whitley's seminal work on the history of Australian zoology provided a starting point for much of the work in the manuscript. Those who provided great help in establishing the currently valid taxonomy of various species include J. Anderson, K. Aplin, W. Boles, E. Cameron, P. Colman, T. Flannery, R. King, J. Mahoney, and D. McAlpine, while both Jack Mahoney and my editor at Rigby, Diana Hill, immensely improved the text with their criticisms. Any inaccuracies of fact remaining in the text remain my responsibility. Lastly, Denise Rennis contributed so much to the manuscript that without her help it would never have been written. To all these individuals and organisations my most grateful thanks.

Note: Throughout this book the current scientific names of identifiable species appearing in the illustrations can be found at the end of the accompanying caption.

Introduction

More than 30,000 years ago, small groups of individuals first walked then rafted their way southward out of the Asian landmass. Over numerous generations they passed through an island archipelago until their unguided journey finally brought them to a vast new continent. During their long tenure of this land they wrought many changes upon its face: they increased the frequency of fires rampaging across the grasslands, they introduced new species of animals such as the dingo to the continent, and they may have contributed to the decline and extinction of certain animal species either alone or in conjunction with the dingoes. Great as these changes may seem, they were applied over thousands of years, as the Aborigines lacked the technology necessary for drastic change. Perhaps more importantly they lacked a theology that empowered them with dominion over the plants and animals, that taught them that the earth and all its riches were theirs to tame and subdue. So the Aborigines learned from nature and co-existed with it—but their hunting and food-gathering lifestyle was ultimately to contribute to the end of their guardianship of the land. Not only did their nomadic existence leave them open to the ravages of natural disasters, disease, and famine, but it left them ill-equipped to meet the onslaught of encroaching societies. Societies which, unlike the isolated Australian Aborigines, had developed technology that not only could change man's perception of the environment but dramatically change the very face of the land.

Tens of thousands of years after the initial invasion of Australia by the Aborigines, the scouts of another society arrived off the coast. In small, fragile ships they crossed thousands of kilometres in search of new countries, and having found them, drew maps, made reports and drawings of the peculiar flora and fauna, and collected specimens to carry home. In spite of their unfavourable reports of *Terra Australis*, which they often described as the most bleak and desolate of lands, a colony was founded, and increasingly large numbers of convicts and settlers came to eke out a meagre existence. Within a few years of their arrival, the colonists had managed to replicate an approximation of the English society that had spawned them.

With the arrival of the first groups of convicts and their warders was laid the foundation of natural history in the formalised European sense, natural history which then included zoology, botany, and mineralogy. While a formidable reservoir of knowledge about the plants and animals of the land existed in the minds and lore of the Aborigines, with the exception of a few individuals who sought to tap this knowledge the development of Australian natural history for the Europeans and their descendants began anew. Early exploratory seaborne expeditions carried naturalists and natural history draughtsmen, as well as amateur naturalists and artists, among the officers and crew. Their journals and diaries, some published, others hidden away in Admiralty archives, were filled with the curious and bizarre: animals that carried their young around with them in pouches hanging from their stomachs, birds of gaudy plumage, and plants like none ever seen before. With a permanent colony on New Holland, the savants of Europe could now expect to receive a regular flow of these specimens. Among the convicts and the administrative personnel of the new colony, a surprisingly large proportion of amateur naturalists and artists found time to collect and sketch, despite the constant struggle for survival amid shortages of food and most other necessities of life. The early administrators of the colony forwarded reports to England of amazing animals, animals that did not fit into the classificatory schemes worked out on the basis of European, American, and Asian species. Specimens, alive and preserved, were dispatched to England to confound the learned and general public alike.

By 1800, when the colony had overcome the initial struggle for survival, a second group of naturalists had begun to arrive. While the assemblages of plants and animals made prior to 1800 were collected mostly by convicts assigned to colonial officers such as William Paterson and John White, after 1800 there arrived in the colony several free men who were employed by the leading European naturalists to procure specimens. Better trained and often with considerable artistic ability in illustrating the plants and animals, George Caley, John Lewin, Robert Brown, and Allan Cunningham were also able to contribute to the analysis of their collections. Robert Brown in particular was an extremely competent taxonomist, fitting his discoveries into the existing Linnaean classification and extending it. The accompanying natural history art took on a more polished appearance, overcoming the rather stilted and less-than-lifelike look of the earlier work.

During the first two decades of the nineteenth century the British Admiralty, often in response to the French scientific expeditions formed to investigate the Pacific region and New Holland, sent a number of major expeditions to survey and chart the coastline of the continent. At least one naturalist was normally included in the complement of the vessels, although usually in the capacity of a surgeon. Voyages that gave rise to a number of Australian folk heroes such as Matthew Flinders and Phillip Parker King carried competent naturalists with them: Robert Brown and Allan Cunningham respectively. Naturalists in Europe were inundated with new species from these voyages, so much so that the natural philosophers began to give up the widely held belief that natural history would soon have described all the plants and animals existing on the face of the earth. As a result of these numerous expeditions the natural history of Australia was better recorded than that of many regions much closer to Europe but less accessible to seaborne investigation.

The French expeditions that touched on the shores of New Holland, or 'Australia' as it was increasingly being called, considerably extended the knowledge of the flora and fauna of the continent, not so much with the large, obvious marsupials and birds that preoccupied the British settlers, but with the marine invertebrates that proliferated along the subtidal margins of the continent. Carrying qualified naturalists and natural history draughtsmen, and having adequate printing facilities back in France, the newly won knowledge from these expeditions was published in portfolios complete with lavish colour illustrations of zoological and botanical specimens. The voyages of *La Recherche*, *Le Naturaliste*,

L'Uranie, and *L'Astrolabe* set a standard to which the resident naturalists and artists could aspire. With the English professional collectors under the influence of Sir Joseph Banks almost wholly concerned with botany, and the amateur naturalists of the colony mesmerised by the large marsupials and diverse birds, it was left to the French to record most of the more 'mundane' species of the colony. The French went about this in an immeasurably more scientific manner than did the resident naturalists.

By the late 1820s a change was overtaking the pursuit of natural history in Australia. During the first thirty years of the fledgling colony's existence, naturalists merely collected their specimens for shipment to Europe where they were studied by naturalists such as John Hunter, Everard Home, George Shaw, and James Edward Smith. Natural history in Australia owed its existence to and received its stimulus from Europe, and when that interest waned, it suffered accordingly. However, by the late 1820s Australia was beginning to establish its own institutions for the study of natural history: a Botanic Garden, a Colonial Museum, and various scientific societies which, although short-lived, proved that the foundations were being laid for a significant Australian contribution to the study of its flora and fauna. Whereas initially naturalists spent several years collecting in the colony before returning to Europe, a resident population of naturalists gradually formed, not of the calibre of the European visitors, but certainly competent enough to add a local stimulus to natural history. The ever-increasing numbers of Australian-based naturalists were to lay the foundations for a new, more scientific trend in the continent's natural history studies.

The outstanding question about natural history in Australia during the early years is why it existed at all? Why did a considerable portion of the population of the nascent colony devote so much of their time to natural history? While it may be expected that the first colonists would scour the countryside to obtain whatever native fruits, vegetables, and animals were available as food, most of the First Fleet diarists disappointedly noted that there was a dearth of edible plants in the neighbourhood of Port Jackson and that the animals comprised mainly kangaroos and birds. Certainly there was little call for an extensive knowledge of the natural productions of the country to satisfy the appetite of the colony, which much preferred the sustenance gained from European crops.

The answer seems to lie in the popularisation that natural history was undergoing in Europe during the nineteenth century. In the years when the colony of New South Wales was conceived, natural history was transformed in Europe, removed from the domain of isolated eccentric collectors to the realm of the wealthy upper class. In 1789 Gilbert White published *The Natural History and Antiquities of Selborne* which aroused interest in natural history and also provided a model for future volumes on the subject. *The Natural History and Antiquities of Selborne* was published at a time when a handful of wealthy naturalists and patrons, Joseph Banks and James Edward Smith to name but two, were already deeply interested in natural history, and their interest made the pastime socially acceptable. The upper classes of England took to this new diversion with great enthusiasm, amassing endless collections and libraries. Thus led, could the less wealthy classes be far behind?

As the passion for natural history gained momentum, the clergy supplied a rationalisation for the new craze. Natural history was cast in the role of 'rational amusement', an edifying activity that exercised both the mind and the body. In this period, natural theology, a clerical device which utilised the wonders of nature to demonstrate the existence of God, gained popularity. Natural history provided the clergy with moral lessons—the industry of the bee and the parental care of birds soon peppered the sermons trumpeted from the pulpit. By the 1820s natural history had been claimed by the masses in England as a national preoccupation. Museums, botanic gardens, and zoological parks had all been opened to cater to the population's curiosity. It was this adoption of natural history, first by the upper

classes, later by the less wealthy, that was the driving force during the initial foundation of Australian natural history.

The development of natural history in Australia has been intimately connected to the history of the exploration of the continent. The initial contact by the Dutch, Spanish, and Portuguese resulted in very little in the way of records of the flora and fauna, indeed, there were few extant reports from these voyages at all. Later sea voyages to reach the continent, such as those of William Dampier in 1688 and 1699 and of James Cook in 1770, were to leave more evidence— voluminous in the case of Cook, who had the scientific entourage of Joseph Banks aboard.

While the naturalists aboard ships worked the coastal margin of Australia, the inland exploration parties came to be dominated by the explorer naturalist. The incentives for inland exploration were generally twofold: the first, the discovery of new land suitable for agriculture, was generally successful, while the second, the quest for an inland sea or continental river, was less so. The well-developed rivers of Europe as well as the Mississippi and Amazon in the Americas and the Nile in Africa, left no doubt in the minds of early geographers that such a continent-spanning river must exist in Australia. Even Sir Joseph Banks found it impossible to believe that the land was not pierced to the heart by navigable rivers. The Murray River, even when traced, would not satisfy the geographers, and so natural history became all the richer for the numerous attempts to find the fabled inland waterway.

Military officer-explorers formed the other major group to extend the geographic knowledge of the colony, and while many of these officers had an interest and a certain amount of expertise in natural history, especially geology, they also had access to a number of handbooks written for collectors of natural history specimens. James Lee, a botanical acquaintance of Joseph Banks, offered a pamphlet: *Rules for collecting and preserving seeds from Botany Bay*, before the colony's survival was even assured. In 1817 Bullock's Museum issued its own instructions for the collection and preservation of specimens, and by 1825 J. Mawe's *The Voyager's Companion* had gone through four editions. The latter offered advice to travellers on the type of specimens wanted by natural history collectors and dealers as well as hints on the preservation of specimens; sections were included on shells, which formed Mawe's principal interest, insects, birds, reptiles, quadrupeds, plants, and minerals—all of which fell into the purview of the natural historian. These handbooks, although fairly rudimentary, offered the traveller the possibility of making observations and collections while contributing to the interest that natural history generated, not only in European academic circles but also in potential amateur naturalists working in remote colonies and collecting sites. This interest was hardly limited to Australia as the interiors of Africa and Asia were concomitantly being opened to the dubious benefits of European imperialism.

The development of natural history in Australia was inextricably connected to political machinations, due to both the colonial aspirations of the European powers and the interplay between resident governors and the colonial administration in England. Many of the early surveys and exploratory voyages of the British and the French, which offered unrivalled opportunities for the naturalists aboard, had their origins in the colonial imperialism of both countries. The French expeditions, especially in the early years of discovery, considered the potential of the Australian continent for future French settlements, while the British expeditions sought to extend British dominion over the entire continent to preclude any such French claims. The local administrators in New South Wales and later in Van Diemens Land were not slow to recognise the importance that natural history could assume in their relations with the Home Office in London. The dispatches of the early governors often concluded with the news that seeds of native Australian plants so much in demand by the virtuosi of Europe had been sent to the secretary of the Home Office, to the Royal Gardens at Kew, or to Sir Joseph Banks. Banks, prior to the foundation of the colony of New South Wales, had assumed the presi-

dency of the Royal Society as well as becoming an unofficial adviser to King George III. His influence, during the period from 1780 to 1820 in terms of organising many of the British exploratory expeditions, choosing the personnel to embark on such expeditions, and evaluating the results brought back, cannot be underestimated. Banks was the major influential force in many areas of British science, particularly in the field of botany, and the governors of the colony were well aware that the collection and dispatch of seed and plant specimens to him could only benefit the Home Office's perception of their administration.

What of the men who carried out the early natural history studies in Australia? Who were these men that sought a newer world beyond the sunset? There was one obvious dichotomy regarding the naturalists residing in New South Wales and Van Diemens Land— the separation of the amateur naturalist from what might be called the semi-professional.

Curiously enough, the amateur naturalist tended to be the better educated of the two. Most were either military officers, such as William Paterson, or were military or colonial surgeons, prime examples being John White and George Bass. Surgeons especially had the practical experience and training which could be directly translated into work in the description and anatomy of the animals they found in the colony, although they were just as likely to be drawn to botany, as was Robert Brown. The problem remained that most of the surgeons could spare only occasional time for the pursuit of natural history; their medical duties, especially in those first few years when dysentery and scurvy were rife, left little time for zoological or botanical discovery.

The second group, the semi-professional naturalists, were, during the early years of the nineteenth century, exclusively botanists—the influence and wealth of Joseph Banks saw to that. Almost all acquired their status and expertise in the same fashion: they were trained as gardeners, usually in the employ of wealthy gentlemen or at the Royal Gardens at Kew. Given that their training was much narrower than that of a naval surgeon, these individuals all lacked the theoretical background necessary to achieve more than the mere collection and dispatch of specimens to authorities in Europe. The exception to the list of practical gardeners was Robert Brown, but his case was very different; a military surgeon, the period he spent in Australia was limited to the duration of the *Investigator* cruise and a short time after. He subsequently returned to Europe to take up the position of Joseph Banks' librarian, one of the few paid positions open to a botanist at the time.

It is curious that the botanists dominated the early years of Australian natural history, for although the flora of the continent was in many cases unique, it was the fauna that attracted the attention of the public. The earliest explorers of the west coast of Australia recorded the presence of 'cats', 'rats', and 'racoons', all of which later became recognised as a coherent group, the marsupials. That the marsupials did indeed form a consistent group was recognised as early as the eighteenth century in the work of John Hunter and Everard Home, two of the pre-eminent anatomists who studied the Australian fauna from specimens returned to Europe by the transports of the First Fleet. Hunter, and later Home, recognised that the kangaroos and native cats had certain affinities with the opossums which had been brought to Europe from North America as early as 1500. Although the marsupials were clearly mammals, denoted by the presence of mammae and the covering of fur on their bodies, there was considerable uncertainty about their exact taxonomic position. For instance, the French zoologists Geoffroy and Cuvier in 1795 placed the opossums and the dasyurids (native cats) in a separate order, Pedimanes, falling taxonomically between the Carnivora and the Rodentia, while the kangaroos they included within the Rodentia itself. By 1816, the French physician-naturalist Henri de Blainville recognised that the marsupials were set apart from the other mammals by their reproductive anatomy but included the recently discovered platypus and echidna among them. The marsupials are now considered to be closer to the placental mammals that occupy much of

the rest of the world than to the more primitive egg-laying Monotremes as exemplified by the platypus. If the kangaroo and the native cats were to give the taxonomists problems with their position in 'the great chain of Being', the Monotremes, particularly the platypus, were to mystify them. During the early 1800s, the platypus was described as having affinities with the birds and the reptiles, as well as with the mammals. Although its external covering of fur seemed to ally it with the mammals, its reproductive anatomy and ostensible lack of mammary glands, an obvious necessary feature of mammals, threw its taxonomic position into doubt until the 1830s when the English officer Lauderdale Maule recorded the flow of milk from teats. These were but a few of the taxonomic problems that the vast faunal treasury unearthed in Australia caused for the descriptive naturalists, but these instances gave rise to the most speculation because of the spectacular nature of the organisms.

The preoccupation of the naturalists with taxonomy and the increasingly empirical approach to natural history was not to the liking of all. George Shaw, in his introduction to *Zoological Lectures* published in 1809, defended natural history against the Philistines, among them a French author whom Shaw quoted as writing:

> How can it happen that men of any sterling sense should spend their time in endeavouring to reduce into geometrical divisions the beautiful gradations of Nature, and to be slaves to arbitrary and petty arrangements, which rise and perish, like so many mushrooms, and which appear to be of no other effect but to disgust and fatigue those who are doomed to study them? When shall we see a stop put to that inundation of new and barbarous words and terms which deform and disgrace almost all our new works on Natural History, and which threaten to reproduce the scholastic jargon of the ages of darkness?[1]

There were many who adopted the romantic attitude that natural history was degrading the beauty of nature; France was not alone in such authors. In Australia,

Barron Field echoed these same sentiments. While for some the denigration of the romance of nature by scientific investigation was a trend to be disparaged in itself, others had a different motive for the debasement of natural history, foretelling the impending clash between the established church and natural historians that was to reach the scale of open warfare in 1859. W. Wood, in his work *Zoography* published in 1807, noted:

> How many examine the different objects of the three natural kingdoms, not as if they were created for any good or particular purpose; not as if a designing Providence had any share in their formation; but as matters of idle curiosity that are to be seen to-day, and are forgotten tomorrow.[2]

This was an attitude that was to be further embellished in the Reverend William Paley's *Natural Theology* and to culminate in the writings of the Reverend William Buckland in the 1820s and 1830s.

Paley's argument rested on the fact that nature appeared to be contrived; the analogy he used was that of finding a watch on a heath. Just as the integrated parts of the watch indicated that it had been contrived by some hand, so the infinitely greater integration of nature revealed the hand of the ultimate contriver, God. Surely the 'bag of the opossum' was a mechanical contrivance, enabling the opossum and kangaroo to transport their young, designed for that purpose by the Deity. Paley, in fact, anticipated the argument that was later to be used by biologists in the controversy of evolutionary debate with the minor inversion of cause and effect. Paley argued that the fact that animals and plants were so wonderfully suited and proportioned for their various stations on earth reflected the intervention of the Deity in creating them. Rather than the advantage to be gained by swimming (the cause) producing the webbed feet of ducks (the effect) the reverse was true: God gave ducks webbed feet (the cause) so that they could swim (the effect) and the fact that webbed feet were designed so well for a duck's

purposes revealed that only God could have created the webbed feet. Many of Paley's arguments were directed at refuting the inroads made by the pioneer French biologist Jean-Baptiste Lamarck, who, despite his subsequent fall from grace at the hands of the Darwinians, had formulated an early evolutionary theory in the latter part of the eighteenth century.

Paley's theological successor, the Reverend William Buckland, published *Geology and Mineralogy: considered with reference to Natural Theology*, the theologians' last defense of the biblical domain of geology before it passed into the realm of science, a transfer that geology was to complete more than forty years earlier than biology. Since the 1660s when Archbishop Ussher calculated, by the addition of the chronology listed in Genesis, that the earth was created in 4,004 B.C., the overriding problem for geologists was to determine how rock strata could be laid down in such a short period. By the 1800s, the 4,004 B.C. date was recognised as inconsistent with geological fact, and Buckland's answer was to reinterpret the six days of creation to be six periods of indefinite length. These indefinite periods allowed sufficient time for geological processes to take place but pushed natural history perilously close to the limits of heresy. Buckland's work represented the last attempts of the minister-geologists to shore up the crumbling framework of biblical cosmology, and Buckland's and Paley's ideas were not without relevance to New South Wales. They found a strong advocate in the geologist, the Reverend Charles Wilton, who in many ways argued for a stricter interpretation of the Genesis myth than Buckland did. However these arguments touched only a small minority of the colonists in Australia. Few had the background to participate in the debate, even fewer had the inclination.

The use of illustrations in natural history developed concurrently with the growth of natural history in the Australian colonies. At the same time as the early explorers were recording rudimentary descriptions of the flora and fauna of the western Australian coastline during the 1600s, natural history art was also making its first tentative steps toward maturity in Europe. In the 1600s the Royal Society of London had advocated draughtsmanship for navigational purposes; later they were to expand the field to the depiction of the plants and animals found on foreign shores. The following century brought Mark Catesby's illustrated *The Natural History of Carolina, Florida and the Bahama Islands*, a seminal link between art and science. The connection blossomed with Joseph Banks' interest in Australia. When Banks accompanied James Cook on the voyage of the *Endeavour* in 1768, he brought in his scientific retinue both a botanical draughtsman and a landscape artist. Hundreds of illustrations were prepared on the voyage and although most of these figures were not published until long after the death of Banks, the illustrations demonstrated to Banks the value of pictorial records.

Twenty years later, when the colony of New South Wales was established, the art of natural history received another boost. The artistic output of the convicts and early administrators, which flourished under the auspices of the governors and especially the surgeon-general of the colony, John White, was huge. George Raper, John Hunter, John Doody, and particularly Thomas Watling produced hundreds of sketches and paintings which White shipped back to England for inclusion in serial natural history volumes. Works such as *Naturalist's Miscellany*, and the less successful *Specimen of the Botany of New Holland* and *Illustrationes Florae Novae Hollandiae* began to be published in the 1790s and 1800s, severely glutting a market, which, because of their cost, could support only a few such lavish portfolios. To an extent disproportionate to either the specimens' uniqueness or rarity, the Australian flora and fauna dominated many of these serial volumes. Largely this can be attributed to the availability of the numerous paintings of Australian natural history. A tradition of natural history art was established in Australia that was to carry on through John Lewin and Ferdinand Bauer until its culmination in the middle of the nineteenth century with John Cotton, Elizabeth and John Gould, and George French Angas.

The French scientific expeditions of the late eighteenth and early nineteenth centuries contributed significantly to the pictorial representation of the Australian flora and fauna. The French draughtsmen were to take the art of zoological illustration to an early zenith. Concentrating primarily on marine invertebrates, the zoological and botanical atlases resulting from these voyages were notable for their distinctive bright colouration and fine detail. Deprived of any background, the illustrations strove for accuracy in delineation of detail rather than the fluid grace that could be ascribed to sympathetically portrayed living specimens.

Australian natural history was uniquely fortunate. The discovery and exploration of much of the continent occurred at a time when natural history enjoyed a vogue which was to greatly facilitate the study of Australian organisms. This interest was often not apparent to the collectors toiling in irksome conditions in the colony itself, but without the European stimulus, the development of natural history in the colonies would have been much impoverished. Debate on the central problems of biology may often have bypassed the colonies for lack of competent theorists, but the specimens that returned to Europe from the 'fifth continent' contributed greatly to debates in all three Linnaean Kingdoms: zoology, botany, and geology.

Chapter One

Early on the morning of 1 August 1699, a small vessel, the *Roebuck*, tacked back and forth over the shoals off the western coast of New Holland awaiting daylight and the sight of land. Having suffered a long journey from Brazil, Captain William Dampier sought a harbour on the coast to replenish his dwindling supplies of water and fresh vegetables for his malnourished crew. Making landfall on that August morning, he was unable to locate a sheltered anchorage, and consequently sailed north for five days until he could drop anchor in a sound he was later to name Shark's Bay due to the abundance of sharks his men caught with hook and line.

Accompanying his men ashore during their fruitless searches for water, Dampier observed and noted in his journal the plants and animals of the area.

> There were also besides some Plants, Herbs, and tall Flowers, some very small Flowers, growing on the Ground, that were sweet and beautiful, and for the most part unlike any I had seen elsewhere.[1]

During the next five weeks, as the *Roebuck* coursed northward in search of water on that bleak and desolate coast, Dampier had a number of opportunities to observe the flora and fauna of this vast unknown land. Plants that were, to his limited botanical knowledge, very different from those he was familiar with, were collected and pressed between the pages of books to dry. Having little knowledge of preservation techniques for animals, Dampier had the birds and fish that were caught, as well as the plants, sketched for him by a member of the crew. These sketches he coupled with verbal descriptions in his journal. A plate taken from his published journal illustrates four of the many birds he found on the north-west coast of New Holland.

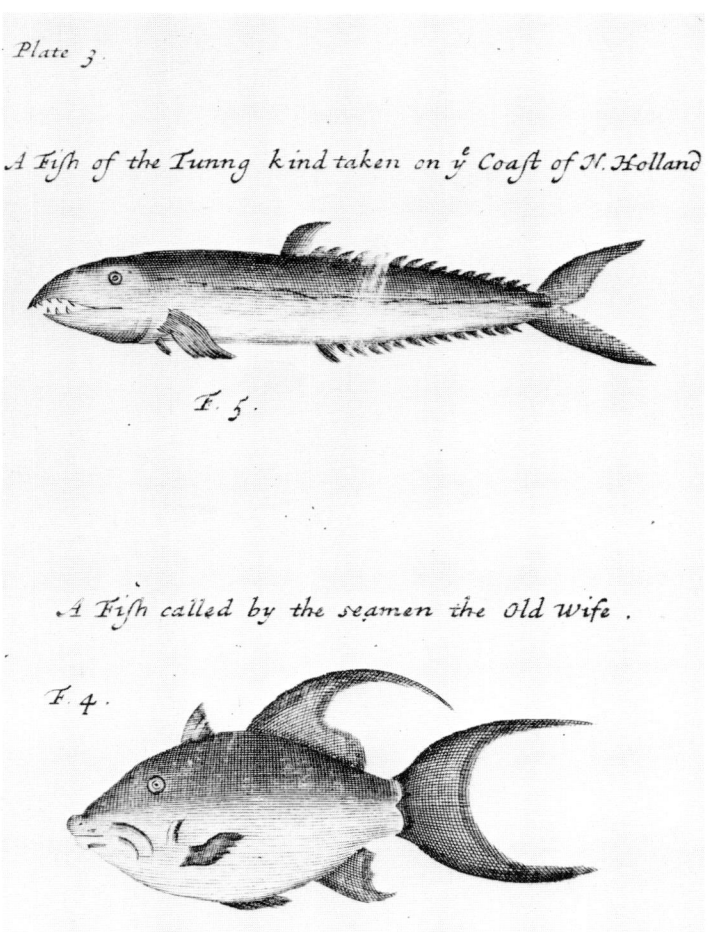

'Fish of New Holland'
Dampier. *A Voyage to New Holland*. 1703.

These have since been identified as the red-necked avocet *Recurvirostra novaehollandiae*, the oystercatcher *Haematophus ostralegus*, the bridled tern *Sterna anaethetus*, and a 'common tern', probably *Anous stolidus*.

Of the land animals Dampier complained that there were few to be seen. The description of those he did observe was usually accompanied by an evaluation of their gastronomic merit, for most organisms that fell prey to his gun were considered as food. Lizards,

'Birds of New Holland'
Dampier. *A Voyage to New Holland.* 1703.

'Black swans'
Valentijn. *Oud en Nieuw Oost-Indiën.* 1724–26.
Cygnus atratus

snakes, 'beasts like hungry wolves' which were
undoubtedly dingoes were seen, and

> . . . a Sort of Racoons, different from those of the West
> Indies; chiefly as to their Legs; for these have very short
> Fore-Legs; but go jumping upon them as the others do . . .[2]

Thus Dampier recorded the first kangaroos or
wallabies he saw; whether they were the banded hare-
wallaby *Lagostrophus fasciatus*, or some other
marsupial such as the dama pademelon or tammar,
Macropus eugenii, remains unknown. The credit for
the first sightings of these animals cannot go to
Dampier however, for wallabies had been seen by
earlier visitors to the western coast of New Holland. In
1629 the Dutch seaman merchant Francisco Pelsaert,
while rescuing survivors of the merchant ship *Batavia*
wrecked on Houtman Rocks off the western coast of
New Holland, recorded a description of what was
probably the tammar, the first manuscript record of a
wallaby or kangaroo. After describing the animal
Pelsaert hypothesised that the young grew out of the
nipples of the mammary gland located in the pouch,
thus inaugurating a myth that was to continue for

hundreds of years. In 1658, the short-tailed pademelon
or 'quokka', *Setonix brachyurus*, was mistaken by the
Dutchman Samuel Volckertsen for a cat, and forty
years later by his compatriot, Willem de Vlamingh, for
a large rat. De Vlamingh named the island on which he
found these 'rats' 'Ratsnest Island', or 'Rottnest' Island
in Dutch. Later still the earliest picture of a wallaby, or
as it was called a 'Filander', was published by the
Dutchman Cornelis de Bruijn in his *Travels into
Muscovie* in 1698. This wallaby, *Thylogale brunii*, was
not, however, from New Holland but is native to the
Aru Islands and New Guinea and presumably taken
from either locality to Java where de Bruijn drew it.

Many of the mariners who chanced upon the shores

drawings of two shells found in New Holland by de Vlamingh. Parts of the letter were published in the *Philosophical Transactions of the Royal Society* of October 1698:

> The soil of this country is very barren and like a desert; no freshwater rivers have been found, but some of saltwater; no quadrupeds, except one as large as a dog, with long ears, that lives in the water as well as on the land. Black Swans, parrots, and many sea-cows were found there.[3]

In his *Noord en Oost Tartarije* Witsen wrote of rats as large as cats with a pouch under their throat into which you could place your entire hand. The purpose of this pouch eluded Witsen.

Despite his complaints about the scarcity of sightings Dampier also found his share of animals. Among the more remarkable entries Dampier recorded in his journal was that of the head and bones of a hippopotamus found in the stomach of a shark. Presumably these were the bones of a dugong or seacow, *Dugong dugon*, animals Dampier found further north. The ocean provided not only entries for his journal but also sustenance for his crew:

> In the Night while Calm we fish'd with Hook and Line, and caught good Store of Fish, viz. Snappers, Breams, Old-Wives and Dog-fish . . . We caught also a Monk-fish of which I brought Home a Picture.[4]

The monkfish or angel shark, *Squatina australis*, has the appearance of being an intermediate form between sharks and rays.

Finding little water and no edible vegetables on the coast of New Holland, Dampier was forced to sail north to Timor for replenishment. He continued to the north around the top of New Guinea before sailing for England in 1700.

Upon his return to England, Dampier published a narrative of his voyage entitled *A Voyage to New Holland* in which he included illustrations of some of the plants and animals he had encountered. The voyage and the subsequent account of it were remarkable for the emphasis that Dampier placed on natural history. His journal with its sketches represented the first published attempt to record the plants and animals of New Holland in graphic form. As early as 1665, the Royal Society had encouraged drawings and sketches to be made by travellers or explorers: in preparing a set of instructions for mariners, the Royal Society suggested that drawings would be a valuable aid to verbal descriptions. While these instructions were meant to aid the clarification of navigational data, they applied equally to natural history. However, with few exceptions, the Royal Society's advice was largely ignored.

of New Holland during the dawning of European knowledge of the continent had noted the types of animals encountered there (although generally their concern was strictly limited to whether the animals were edible). An early sketch from the 1697 Dutch voyage of Willem de Vlamingh by the expedition's artist, Victorszoon depicts black swans, *Cygnus atratus*, in the Swan River estuary, and may claim precedence as the earliest illustration of an Australian animal by Europeans. De Vlamingh's men caught several of the swans to send back to Holland in order to confound the European savants who denied the existence of such an aberration as a black swan; but the swans survived only to Batavia, Java. Nevertheless, news of the swans travelled quickly back to Europe, for Nicholaas Witsen, a former manager of the Dutch East India Company, wrote to the English physician-naturalist Dr Martin Lister in London about the voyage and included

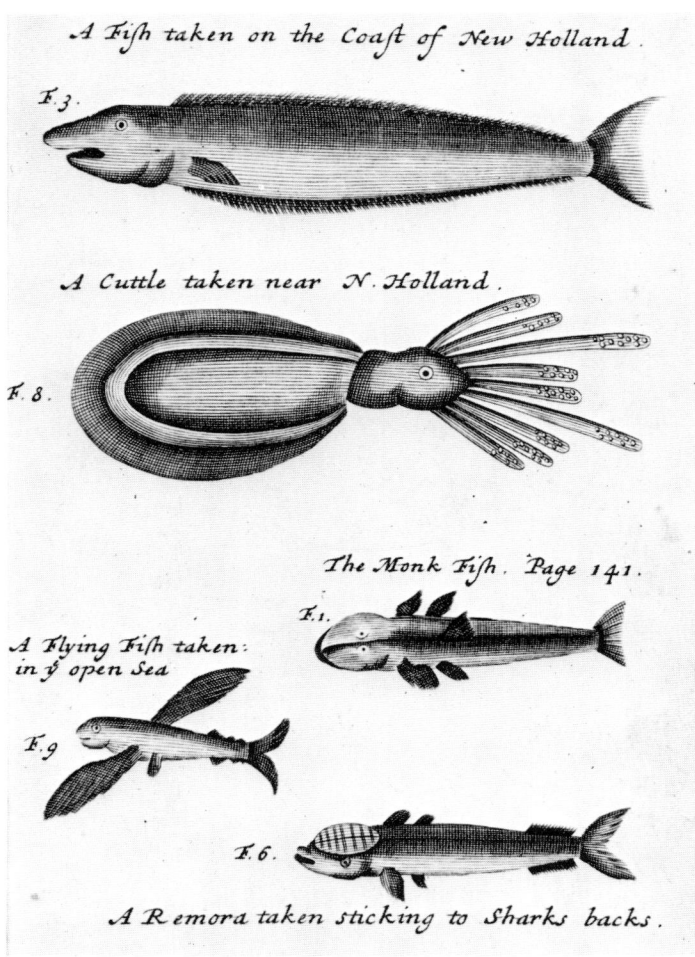

A Fish taken on the Coast of New Holland.
F.3.

A Cuttle taken near N. Holland.
F.8.

A Flying Fish taken in y^e open Sea
F.9.

The Monk Fish. Page 141.
F.1.

F.6.

A Remora taken sticking to Sharks backs.

'Fish of New Holland'
Dampier. *A Voyage to New Holland*. 1703.

Victorszoon's black swans in the Swan River estuary formed only a minor part of the sketch, not the central focus. In any case, this picture was not published until 1726 when it appeared in François Valentyn's *Oud en Nieuw Oost-Indien*.

A Voyage to New Holland was not Dampier's first experience with travelling or with natural history. As a young man Dampier had explored much of the world. While in the West Indies he had joined a group of privateers, an action he later justified by stating 'the further we went the more knowledge and experience I should get, which was the main thing I regarded'. By fits and starts he completed a circumnavigation of the world, including a landing on the northern coast of New Holland while a member of a privateering expedition on the vessel *Cygnet* in 1688. In 1697 Dampier published an edited version of his journal entitled *A New Voyage Round the World* which met with immediate success and brought him to the attention of many influential people, including members of the Royal Society and the Earl of Oxford, first lord of the Admiralty. After his literary success he went on to secure a scientific reputation with the volume *A Discourse of tradewinds, Breezes, storms,*

seasons of the Year, Tides and Currents of the Torrid Zone throughout the World thus establishing himself as a hydrographer and an expert on the Pacific Ocean. These qualifications, rather than his fitness for leadership, led the Admiralty to offer Dampier command of the *Roebuck* for a voyage to New Holland. Despite the many Dutch voyages to the area, which had charted not only much of the coastline from the Gulf of Carpentaria to Cape Leeuwin but parts of Van Diemens Land as well, the East Indies were virtually unknown to the English. The wealth from spices and tales of a land of gold lured the Admiralty into bestowing command on an individual whose only experience was in a subordinate capacity on a privateer. Predictably, Dampier showed little aptitude for command and suffered rebellion from his officers. Before the *Roebuck*'s voyage ended at Ascension Island (where the vessel foundered from old age), Dampier had laid grounds for two courts martial against himself. Yet, while Dampier took pains to record in his journal a plethora of observations on natural history and topographic features, all in accurate detail, little of the narrative of the voyage, his troubles with the officers and crew, or the daily life on board ship entered into his writings. This was fortunate for natural history; his journal was to be of significant value to the scientific community of the time. Possessed of an insatiable curiosity, yet never camouflaging the facts with his own beliefs, Dampier managed to comment dispassionately on the environment he saw. Although all his work was descriptive, lacking as he did a framework for theoretical explanations, no better scientific observations were made on a sea voyage until the expeditions of Cook one hundred years later.

As was often to be the case in the early years of New Holland, Dampier used the services of a draughtsman without crediting him by name. Dampier mentions in the preface of *A Voyage to New Holland* 'having now had in the Ship with me a Person Skill'd in Drawing' but nowhere is there a record of that individual's name. The drawings, and indeed the whole journal, were lucky to survive the journey back to England for when the *Roebuck* sank off Ascension Island in February of 1700, Dampier only managed to salvage his journal because he kept it in a bamboo holder with the ends closed by two pieces of wax.

On his arrival in England Dampier turned the botanical specimens over to Dr John Woodward, a member of the Royal Society, who in turn gave them to John Ray, a botanist then working on his *Historia Plantarum*. Ray included a two-page Latin description of the specimens in an appendix to the third volume of the work, and it is a translation of this description that forms the basis of the 'Account of Several Plants' found in Dampier's *A Voyage to New Holland*.

Dampier's specimens were later acquired by the English botanist William Sherard and eventually by

'Plants of New Holland'
Dampier. *A Voyage to New Holland*. 1703.

Oxford University where seventeen specimens from New Holland along with others he collected elsewhere during the voyage still exist today. Dampier's name was enshrined in botanical literature when in the early 1800s Robert Brown collected and named the genus *Dampiera* for him.

The specimens that Dampier brought back from his voyage were classified by John Ray in a polynomial system, a scheme that was little more than a verbal description of the plant. During the 1600s there was no set format for zoological or botanical descriptions, resulting in almost as many classificatory schemes as there were classifiers, with obvious attendant problems for comparative studies. In the period between Dampier's return to England and the next major voyage to New Holland, there was to be an upheaval in the way organisms were classified, brought about mainly by one individual, Carl von Linné, known as Linnaeus. In 1753 Linnaeus introduced the concept of binomial nomen-clature where each plant and animal was given just two names, a generic and a specific name, a distinct advantage over previous systems.

If the crude sketches done by the artist on Dampier's voyage were the inauspicious beginnings of the European style of natural history art of New Holland, a subsequent English voyage was to put it on a much surer footing. Early in 1768 HMS *Endeavour*, under the command of Lieutenant James Cook, put to sea from Plymouth for the ostensible purpose of observing the transit of Venus across the face of the sun. Observations of the transit would allow astronomers to calculate the distance of the sun from the earth with far greater accuracy than ever before. Anticipating the possibility of cloudy or otherwise inclement weather during the observation period, the Royal Society proposed sending parties to widely separate locations: Hudson Bay on the east coast of North America, North Cape, and the island of Tahiti recently discovered by Samuel Wallis in the mid South Pacific. The Royal Society prevailed upon the Admiralty to supply a vessel for the voyage to the South Pacific, to which the English authorities consented, as they had other plans for such a voyage. Subsidiary orders issued to Cook instructed him to traverse the Southern Ocean in search of the 'Great South Land' which geographers of the day insisted must exist.

The presence of a Great South Land stemmed from the belief that an amount of land equal to that in the Northern Hemisphere must exist in the Southern Hemisphere, otherwise the planet would be unbalanced and turn over. Problems with the determination of longitude on previous voyages to the Pacific had resulted in erroneous reports of extensive land in the South Pacific which further reinforced the idea that there existed a vast continent in southern latitudes. Inspired by fables of gold and fabulous wealth, most European countries sent expeditions to locate the continent, which, if inhabited by barbarians, would be plundered of its riches or, if inhabited by a civilised people, would promise wealth in the way of trade and alliances. That Tasman had already circumnavigated the only habitable continent to be found was not appreciated until a succession of voyages had criss-crossed that vast ocean.

When news of the proposed expedition to the South Seas became known, Joseph Banks, then only a newly elected member of the Royal Society, requested that the society obtain leave for him to take a scientific party of eight on the voyage. Permission was granted, and Banks set about organising his party and equipment, of which, as a condition of the Admiralty's permission, he bore the entire cost. Joseph Banks could well afford the expense as he was receiving a substantial return each year from his estates. Though still a young man of twenty-five, Banks possessed all the right qualifications for advancement in scientific circles in the eighteenth century. Educated at Harrow, Eton, and Oxford, he had little necessity for earning a living and was thus able to indulge in his passion for botany. In 1766 at the age of twenty-three, he had accompanied HMS *Niger* to the eastern coast of Canada where he spent several months collecting plants in Labrador and Newfoundland. On his return, his collections were illustrated by the German artist Georg Ehret. This same year saw him elected a fellow of the Royal Society. He subsequently planned another voyage, this time to Lapland, but, on hearing of Cook's intended voyage to the Pacific, sought permission to accompany that expedition instead.

Pre-eminent in Banks' retinue of eight was a botanical acquaintance of his, Dr Daniel Carl Solander, favourite student of Linnaeus, fellow of the Royal Society, and at the time working at the British Museum from which he was granted special leave to accompany Banks. The other members of the party were less august: Herman Spöring, a sometime doctor and naturalist employed by Banks as a secretary; Sydney Parkinson, botanical draughtsman; Alexander Buchan, landscape artist; and four personal servants for the party who doubled as collectors. Also included at the Royal Society's expense was Charles Green, an astronomer.

Recognised artists, or natural history draughtsmen, were a relatively new addition to exploratory voyages, as indeed was the inclusion of a 'professional' scientific party. Anson's voyage around the world in 1739 had been seminal in this process; Banks carried it to fruition. Banks and his immediate circle of botanically minded friends could afford the luxury of employing trained botanical draughtsmen to illustrate either their written works or their collections. It was more than a luxury, though, for the primitive techniques of preserving botanical, and, primarily, zoological specimens, made illustrations of living organisms vital, especially when specimens were collected on long sea voyages to the tropics. There the twin ravages of high temperature and high humidity, together with the inevitable destruction by insects and mould, rendered specimens useless in a short time. Nevertheless, it seems that Banks was able to bring back some bird skins from the voyage, for prominent British ornithologist John Latham in his *General Synopsis of Birds* (1781–1805), described New Holland birds based on specimens in the collection of Joseph Banks.

Of all the artists on Cook's first voyage, least can be said of Alexander Buchan. Known to be an epileptic, he survived only until the expedition reached Tahiti where he suffered a fatal epileptic attack.

Sydney Parkinson was also to die on the voyage, but not until the *Endeavour* had left Batavia on the island of Java where he, as well as most of the rest of the crew, contracted dysentery. Before he died, Parkinson

was to draw or paint more than 1,300 works, a good number of which were executed while the *Endeavour* was charting the east coast of New Holland. Parkinson had, at an early age, attracted the attention of wealthy botanists, among them Joseph Banks, for the high quality of his botanical draughtsmanship. Banks, on the recommendation of James Lee of Hammersmith, invited Parkinson to participate in the proposed voyage to the Southern Ocean for which he would receive the sum of £80 per annum. Parkinson, like many of the young men of his time who had little money but plenty of talent and enthusiasm for natural history, found it convenient to attach himself to a wealthy patron. In Banks he found one who also had a taste for adventure, which, as Parkinson was ultimately to learn, imposed high risks.

Herman Spöring, also fated to die after the debilitating stop in Batavia, was impressed into contributing to the pictorial record of the voyage. Like most naturalists of the time, he was a reasonably competent artist, almost a necessity in the days before photography. Initially employed as Banks' secretary, Spöring was taken into service as a draughtsman after Buchan's death left Parkinson with an overload of work.

The *Endeavour* weighed anchor on 26 August 1768, and left Plymouth astern. After a brief stop-over in Brazil, she rounded Cape Horn and entered the South Pacific with Banks and Solander collecting and describing specimens at every landfall. By April 1769 the vessel had arrived at Tahiti and commenced preparations for the requisite astronomical observations. It was here in Tahiti that Buchan died, leaving Parkinson to bear the entire burden of keeping a pictorial record. The transit of Venus observed, Cook pushed on through the Pacific following the Admiralty's orders to look for the Southern Continent. Finding no land larger than island archipelagos in the lower latitudes, Cook turned southward where, after circumnavigating and charting much of New Zealand, he continued westward towards the east coast of New Holland. Apart from New Holland, another continent did exist in the Southern Ocean, and Cook was to sail close to it during a subsequent voyage, but it lay much further south amid the ice- and snow-shrouded peaks of the Antarctic.

The east coast of New Holland was sighted on 19 April 1770, just to the south of Cape Howe. Sailing north along the coast, a large bay was sighted and entered on 29 April. While parties were out searching for a source of fresh water or charting the bay, Banks and Solander made collections of the plants and animals they came across, and Parkinson sketched furiously. Banks had noted in his journal the discipline they maintained at sea:

> We had a suitable stock of books relating to the natural
> history of the Indies with us; and seldom was there a

storm strong enough to break up our normal study time, which lasted daily from nearly 8 o'clock in the morning till 2 in the afternoon. From 4 to 5, when the cabin had lost the odour of food, we sat till dark by the great table with our draughtsman opposite and showed him in what way to make his drawings, and ourselves made rapid descriptions of all the details of natural history while our specimens were still fresh.[5]

With the exception of Banks' and Solander's excursions ashore to collect specimens, life was probably little different from this description for Banks' associates during much of the time spent in the bay. Originally called Stingray Bay, Cook later changed the name to Botanist's Bay and finally to Botany Bay. Lest anyone should forget exactly which botanists Cook had in mind, he then named the two headlands enclosing the bay Cape Banks and Cape Solander.

Banks and Solander collected continuously; most of the botanical specimens from this virgin territory were undescribed genera and species. More than 3,500 plants of 240 species were procured, including the specimens which were to become the basis of the description of the genus *Banksia*, first described in the younger Linnaeus' 1781 supplement to his father's *Species Plantarum*. With so many new species to illustrate, Parkinson fell behind in the preparation of finished drawings of the plants and so resorted to the device of making quick sketches, colouring only representative portions, and making notes that would allow him to complete finished drawings later. Spöring contributed by drawing a number of the rays which had given the bay its original name.

The animals that were caught or shot at Botany Bay were relatively few. A variety of birds were seen as Sydney Parkinson recorded in his posthumously published journal: '. . . a great number of birds of a beautiful plumage; among which were two sorts of parroquets and a beautiful loriquet'.[6]

They also saw ravens, quail, and cockatoos. Before leaving Botany Bay, a Polynesian, Tupia, who had accepted passage to England with Cook, obtained a rainbow lorikeet, *Trichoglossus haematodus*, which was kept alive until the *Endeavour* reached England. There it was given to Marmaduke Turnstall in whose possession it was when Peter Brown painted and published a colour engraving of it under the name of the 'blue-bellied parrot' in his *New Illustrations in Zoology* in 1776.

On 7 May the anchors were hoisted and the *Endeavour* sailed out of Botany Bay and northward along the coast; Port Jackson was noted but not investigated. By 12 May, Parkinson had finished ninety-four sketches of plants. The specimens had been kept in tin chests with damp cloths to preserve them in as fresh a condition as possible until the artist's pen could record

'Blue-bellied parrot'
Brown. *New Illustrations in Zoology*. 1776.
Trichoglossus haematodus

them. The next landing was made at Bustard Bay, so named for the bustards they encountered there. As well as eating the bustards, Solander wrote a detailed description of them under the name 'Otis australis', but the description was left unpublished; in 1829 Griffith applied the name *Eupodotis australis* to the species in his *Animal Kingdom*.

As in many of the inaugural exploratory voyages to distant parts of the globe, it was impractical to bring back living plants, and therefore much effort was put into devising methods to secure seeds. If seeds of an interesting species could be found, if they could be transported back to Europe without deterioration, and finally if appropriate conditions for their germination and growth could be maintained, then botanists and perhaps nurserymen would benefit accordingly. Linnaeus spent a good deal of his time on the problem and in 1758 wrote to John Ellis, a London merchant, of his experiments:

Seeds may be brought from abroad in a growing state if we attend to the following method. Put your seeds into a cylindrical glass bottle and fill up the interstices with dry sand to prevent their lying too close together and that they may perspire freely thro the sand. Then cork the bottle or tie a bladder over the mouth of it. Prepare a glass vessel so much larger than that which contains the seeds, that when it is suspended in it there may be a vacant space on all sides about 2 inches distance between both glasses for the following mixture: 4 parts nitre, one-fifth part in equal parts of common salt and sal ammoniac.[7]

During the first voyage of Cook, Banks also tried various methods of preserving viable seeds, methods which were to stand him in good stead when in future years he sent out plant collectors to all parts of the world to collect for him.

Short landings were made at a number of other sites along the coast, usually to search for fresh water. At Thirsty Sound, the scientific party found on the branches of trees 'ant nests, made of Clay, as big as a bushel' probably constructed by termites of the *Eutermes* genus. Many of the insects collected on the voyage were later described by Johann Fabricius. Fabricius, another of the students of Linnaeus, journeyed to London to catalogue the insects after the return of the expedition. When he published his *Systema Entomologiae* in 1775, he included 212 insects from New Holland: beetles, ants, bees, butterflies and moths, mantids and flies, most from the Endeavour River region. During the voyage northward, seabirds, especially frigatebirds, gannets, and shearwaters were frequently sighted. Banks and Solander during the weary days spent at sea also collected marine plankton with nets and fish with hooks. Somewhere along the coast a native cat was caught; it was described by the German zoologist Eberhard von Zimmermann in 1777 as '*Dasyurus quoll*' (*D. viverrinus*) from John Hawkesworth's narrative of the voyage.

On the night of 10 June, while sailing northwards amid the myriad reefs of the Great Barrier Reef, disaster struck—the *Endeavour* ran on to a reef, holing herself. Action by the crew prevented the vessel sinking immediately, and they managed to get her off the reef. Limping north-east with all hands taking a turn at the pumps, the *Endeavour* reached a river mouth and was beached on the southern side of what was to be named the Endeavour River. With the *Endeavour* careened on its side to effect repairs, Solander and Banks found that the bread compartment in which they had stored much of their material was flooded and most of their specimens ruined. In the seven weeks it took to complete repairs to the *Endeavour*, Solander and Banks set about rectifying their losses and obtaining new specimens. While most of the collecting seems to have been done by both Banks and Solander, Solander carried out the bulk of the work involved in maintaining the specimen catalogues and preparing descriptions of the plants. Banks limited himself to supervising the drying

'*Myristica cimicifera*'
Britten. *Illustrations of the botany of Cook's voyage round the world in HMS Endeavour.* 1900–05.
Myristica muelleri

and storage of the botanical specimens, probably using the labour of his servants. Pages of Milton's *Paradise Lost* which Banks had managed to acquire unbound in large quantities before the outset of the voyage were used in pressing the specimens—Banks' choice of paper was to be prophetic for the Aboriginal societies inhabiting New Holland. Over 200 species of plants were obtained at Endeavour River, and preliminary sketches of 190 of the specimens were made by Parkinson.

Shortly after careening the *Endeavour*, seamen out hunting to vary their diet of salted provisions reported sighting peculiar creatures; first came a tale of an animal '. . . as large as a grey hound, of a mouse coulour and very swift'[8] as well as an animal 'as large and much like a one gallon cagg (keg), as black as the Devil, and had 2 horns on its head'.[9] Banks was to see both these animals at a later date; the first was a kangaroo or wallaby, the second apparently a fruit bat, *Pteropus* sp. Although Banks and Solander collected various animals, aside from having Parkinson prepare some

'Kangaroo'
Hawkesworth. *An account of the voyages undertaken by the order of His Present Majesty for making discoveries in the Southern Hemisphere.* 1773.

sketches, little was done with them. These included, in Sydney Parkinson's words:

> Of quadrupeds, there are goats, wolves, a small red animal about the size of a squirrel, a spotted one of the viverra kind; and an animal of a kind nearly approaching the mus genus, about the size of grey-hound, that had a head like a fawn's; lips and ears, which it throws back, like a hare's; . . . Mr Banks found, in the woods, an Opossum (This creature has a membraneous bag near the stomach in which it conceals and carries its young when it is apprehensive of danger) with two young ones sucking at her breasts.[10]

The species of the kangaroo, Parkinson's animal 'approaching the mus genus', was to become the subject of much academic debate over the years, although at the time Banks was at a loss: 'To compare it to any European animal would be impossible as it has not the least resemblance of any one I have seen'.[11]

The initial scientific description of the kangaroo by German naturalist P. L. S. Müller in 1776 was based on the description and plate of the kangaroo published in Hawkesworth's account of Cook's voyage printed three years earlier. Müller gave the animal the name '*Mus canguru*'. The plate in Hawkesworth was engraved from a painting by George Stubbs who used Parkinson's sketches as his model.

Zimmermann, in 1777, working from the same illustration named the animal '*Yerboa gigantea*', and that same year German naturalist J. C. P. Erxleben proposed the name '*Jaculus giganteus*'. However, in 1790 George Shaw first used the generic name *Macropus*, accepted for many years as the correct scientific name. John Gould assumed that Cook's party had seen *Macropus major*, while others have concluded that the party may have caught more than one species of kangaroo; suggestions include the eastern wallaroo, *Macropus robustus* and the great grey kangaroo, *Macropus giganteus*. Solander wrote a description of the animal, but it provides little help in deciding which species the kangaroos belong to.

While camped at Endeavour River, numerous birds were observed or caught. Parkinson sketched a red-tailed black-cockatoo, *Calyptorhynchus magnificus*, the only bird of New Holland he was to draw. Some confusion arose over this bird's species. Latham, in

1781, considered that it was probably the same as the black cockatoo of Ceylon, but by 1787, in figuring the Banksian cockatoo, which he named 'Psittacus magnificus' in the first supplement to his General Synopsis of Birds, Latham saw that it was clearly different from the Ceylon species. Latham also recorded a 'crested parrakeet' said to have been brought back from New Holland by Banks.

Sharks and rays found in abundance at Botany Bay were also plentiful at Endeavour River. Solander wrote descriptions of 'Squalus oculatus' (Hemiscyllium ocellatum), 'Raja rostrata' (Aptychotrema rostrata), 'Raja fasciata' (Trygonorrhina fasciata), and 'Raja testacea' (Urolophus testaceus).

Having finally managed to repair the Endeavour, Cook set out to wend his way through the tortuous Barrier Reef and sail north to Torres Strait. Short visits were paid to Lizard Island, appropriately named by Cook, and later to Booby Island in the strait itself, also named for its dominant fauna; the Endeavour then sailed out of the waters of New Holland.

When they called at Batavia in Java, many of the crew contracted dysentery. Banks, Solander, Parkinson, and Spöring all fell sick, Parkinson and Spöring fatally so. The fatalities due to malaria and dysentery picked up in Batavia were also a constant problem for later ships. However, with the prime illness of long sea voyages, scurvy, Cook had no problem. There were no deaths on the Endeavour from scurvy, a most unusual occurrence which may be attributed in part to Cook having two competent botanists on board able to identify edible vegetables.

What of the scientific results of Cook's first voyage? Much of the descriptive work was completed on the voyage itself; the lengthy periods at sea allowed Solander to describe and classify many of his specimens. Using Linnaeus' 'sexual' classification scheme, Solander was able to organise the plants into existing genera or to set up new genera. He meticulously described the specimens on small cards which were then filed; by the end of the voyage there were to be twenty-five volumes of these cards for botanical specimens and twenty-seven volumes for zoological specimens. Parkinson had finished drawings of many of the specimens collected prior to the Endeavour's arrival in New Holland, but after Botany Bay and until his death he had time only for representative sketches.

From the voyage as a whole came 110 new genera and approximately 1,300 new species. Solander prepared a number of manuscripts for publication on the botany of the voyage which awaited only the preparation of illustrations. Banks therefore employed a number of well-known botanical draughtsmen to complete the finished drawings from Parkinson's sketches; these draughtsmen included Frederick Nodder, John and James Miller, and John Cleveley.

From the drawings executed in England and the drawings that Parkinson finished before he died, copper plates were engraved, but for the quantity of sketches brought back to England, over 950, this task required years to complete. Meanwhile, expectations rose in the scientific community awaiting the publication of the voyage's results. Linnaeus wrote of 'the matchless and truly astonishing collection, such as has never been seen before, nor may ever be seen again', though he fretted that the specimens would fall prey to insects or mould before completion of the work.[12] Linnaeus had been promised by Solander a share of the botanical treasures of the voyage but he waited in vain; to his great sorrow he was never to receive any plant specimens derived from the voyage.

Soon after Cook's return, plans began to take shape for a second voyage; after all, the Southern Continent had still not been located. Banks immediately threw his energies into the planning of the voyage, in the mistaken belief that he would accompany it. This division of his time unduly prolonged the process of readying the material from the first voyage for publication, much to the dissatisfaction of many naturalists, Linnaeus included, who preferred that the first voyage be disposed of before the second was begun. By 1778, 500 plates had been engraved, but the final work was expected to feature twice that many. That same year, Banks was elected president of the Royal Society, a position which began to draw heavily on his time. Four years later, only 200 more plates had been engraved and the impetus was lost. Carl Solander died in May 1782, and with him the grand botanical design died. The final engravings were never realised, for Banks had too many other interests and by now he may have felt that it was all too late. The work was never to be published; the disparate parts were to remain in the British Museum which obtained many of Banks' collections on his death.

James Edward Smith, Banks' colleague and disciple, attributed the delay and final deferment of publication to Banks' attention to his duties as president of the Royal Society and to the 'dissipation' of Solander in London society. In view of the number of manuscripts Solander completed except for the illustrations, this was hardly a fair evaluation, though perhaps Solander was not the most energetic of individuals. In 1900, the British Museum, which had retained the copper engravings, published a portfolio of the illustrations. Of the 412 sketches of New Holland plants by Parkinson, 362 had been rendered into finished drawings and 340 of these were actually engraved; 318 were printed in the 1900 publication.

Despite the fact that Solander's work had remained unpublished, the specimens and Solander's manuscripts were freely available to any botanists wishing to consult them. Some of the material was thus published in the works of other naturalists. James Edward Smith

'Grand Martin-Pêcheur de la Nouvelle Guinée'
Sonnerat. *Voyage à la Nouvelle Guinée*. 1776.
Dacelo gigas

established several new genera from the material; the
younger Linnaeus consulted and included material from
the collection in his *Supplementum Plantarum* (1781);
and Joseph Gaertner the German physician-botanist
was also to use some material in *De Fructibus et
Seminibus Plantarum* (1788–1805), as did Robert
Brown in *Prodromus Florae Novae Hollandiae*. Not
everyone was as scrupulous as these individuals in
acknowledging the source of their specimens. William
Aiton, the gardener in charge of the Royal Gardens at
Kew, also consulted Banks' collection. In his *Hortus
Kewensis* he included extracts from Solander's
manuscripts without acknowledging their originator.

Botanists were not the only individuals guilty of
usurping specimens given them. In 1776 when the
French adventurer-explorer Pierre Sonnerat published
his *Voyage à la Nouvelle Guinée* he included a sketch
of the kookaburra, *Dacelo gigas*, erroneously reporting
it as a native bird of New Guinea. The specimen was
probably collected by Banks in New Holland and, on
the return voyage from New Holland, given to
Sonnerat at the Cape of Good Hope. Latham recorded
that Banks had skins of *Dacelo gigas* in his collection by
1782 so it seems likely that Sonnerat obtained his

specimens from Banks. Sonnerat borrowed freely from
naturalists other than Banks. The French naturalist
Philibert Commerson, for example, also suffered at his
hands.

The first of Cook's voyages was an expedition that
had set forth with the highest of hopes— John Ellis had
written of it to Linnaeus:

> . . . No people ever went to sea better fitted out for the
> purpose of natural history, nor more elegantly. They
> have got a fine library of natural history; they have all
> sorts of machines for catching and preserving insects; all
> kinds of nets, trawls, drags, and hooks for coral fishing;
> they have even a curious contrivance of a telescope by
> which, put under water, you can see the bottom at a
> great depth, where it is clear. They have many cases of
> bottles with ground stoppers, of several sizes, to preserve
> animals in spirits. They have the several sorts of salts to
> surround the seeds, and wax, both bee's wax and that of
> the Myrica, . . .[13]

Yet it ended with most of the information gathered
remaining unpublished and unavailable to all but a
select few.

Other than the plant specimens, possibly the best
collection resulting from Cook's first voyage was
mollusc shells, simply because there were no problems
involved in their preservation. The officers and crew of
the *Endeavour* filled their cabins with shells picked up
from the beaches of the lands they visited in the certain
knowledge that they would find a ready market for
them from collectors on their return to England. Lists
of shells brought back from New Holland later
appeared in the collections of Joseph Banks, of Dr John
Fothergill, the physician-botanist who obtained Sydney
Parkinson's collection, and of the Duchess of Portland,
possessor of one of the finest shell collections in
Europe. Her collection included a wide variety of
species from edible molluscs such as the Sydney rock
oyster, *Saccostrea commercialis*, and the mud oyster,
Ostrea angasi, to bubble shells, *Bulla botanica*, and
giant clams, *Tridacna* sp. Carl Solander not only
curated the plant collection of Joseph Banks but also
worked on the mollusc collections of both Banks and
the Duchess of Portland. From the extensive descriptions Solander wrote of most of the organisms he
encountered on Cook's voyage, it may have been
possible that he contemplated publishing a complete
natural history of the voyage.

Shortly after Cook's voyage, two French expeditions
landed on the shores of New Holland, one under
Marion du Fresne, which, on 6 March 1772, anchored
for a few days close to the site on Van Diemens Land
where Abel Tasman had raised the Dutch flag. The
other was led by François de Saint Allouarn who sailed
up the western coast of New Holland that same year.

19

Neither ship carried naturalists and both spent little time in New Holland.

Almost exactly a year after the return of the *Endeavour*, HMS *Resolution*, and HMS *Adventure* left Plymouth on Cook's second voyage. Alexander Dalrymple, the chief British advocate of the Southern Continent theory, was not dismayed by the negative evidence that Cook had brought back and pointed out that there were still vast unexplored areas of the ocean. The Admiralty resolved to send another expedition to complete the task. Banks had barely unloaded and transported his specimens from the *Endeavour* to his New Burlington Street home before he became involved in the planning of this subsequent expedition at the invitation of Lord Sandwich. This time, Banks began gathering a scientific party of twelve to accompany the expedition. Feeling space on the *Resolution* to be inadequate, Banks prevailed on the Admiralty to build additional accommodation and plant-cabins on the deck. These were found to alter the trim and sailing ability of the *Resolution*, and Cook refused to command the unseaworthy vessel. The alterations were torn down, and Banks withdrew from the voyage in a huff, as did Dr James Lind, and also Solander, who had been appointed naturalists to the expedition. The rest of Banks' intended party, including John Zoffany, a portrait painter, John and James Miller, natural history draughtsmen, and John Cleveley, marine draughtsman, also withdrew. These last three draughtsmen were instead employed to render Parkinson's sketches into finished drawings.

After Banks' withdrawal from the expedition, and mindful of the advantages of having a naturalist on board, the Admiralty engaged Johann Reinhold Forster as naturalist and his seventeen-year-old son George as natural history draughtsman. Forster was a member of the Royal Society and, although a rather prickly personality at times, was a competent naturalist. Joseph Banks, despite his irritation with the Admiralty over his treatment, still contributed to the proposed expedition; the Forsters were in fact his nominees.

The complete scientific party on board the *Resolution* included the two Forsters; William Hodges, a landscape and topographic artist; William Wales, an astronomer; and the Swedish botanist Anders Sparrman, another student of Linnaeus, engaged by the senior Forster to join the *Resolution* at Cape Town. HMS *Adventure*, commanded by Tobias Furneaux, a veteran of Wallis' discovery of Tahiti, was without a naturalist, carrying only William Bayly as astronomer. The voyage was insignificant in terms of either the exploration or natural history of New Holland. After separating from the *Resolution* in the icefields of the Antarctic, *Adventure* put into Van Diemens Land for five days to obtain water and repair the ship's rigging. The bay in which Furneaux anchored was given the name

'An opossum of Van Diemen's Land'
Cook's voyages round the world. Plates. 1804.
Pseudocheirus peregrinus

Adventure Bay, and while there they saw:

> . . . a bird like a Raven; some of the Crow kind, . . . some Paroquets . . . Duck, Teal, and the Sheldrake, . . . about the size of a large Kite, of the Eagle kind. As for the beasts we saw but one which was a Possum . . .[14]

Two birds were killed, and the skins taken to New Zealand. There George Forster drew the two specimens and his father described them, one being the grey groshawk, *Accipiter novaehollandiae* described by Latham in 1781 in his *General Synopsis of Birds* as the 'New Holland Eagle' and in 1788 given the Latin name '*Falco novaehollandiae*' by Gmelin; the other being the penguin, *Eudyptes chrysolophus*, caught on a small island at the entrance to Adventure Bay, which was consequently given the name Penguin Island. In Sir

Joseph Banks' library there was also a painting by an unknown artist of a tawny-crowned honeyeater, *Phylidonyris melanops*, described by Latham in 1801 and said to have been caught in Van Diemens Land during the second voyage of Cook.

On the return of the *Resolution* and *Adventure* to England, Banks and James Smith bought items from the Forsters, Banks acquiring most of the drawings sketched on the voyage, Smith buying duplicate herbarium specimens they had collected. The Forsters, never the easiest of individuals to know, proceeded to antagonise both Banks and the Admiralty. In 1776 the Forsters published *Characteres Generum Plantarum*, and in 1786 George Forster published *Prodromus* and *De Plantis Esculentis*, all of which drew heavily on the Solander/Banks' material from the first voyage. Despite containing almost verbatim material from the Solander manuscripts, there appears little acknowledgement of Solander's contribution to the work. When the *Resolution* returned to England, a gunner's mate, John Marra, who had perseveringly collected shells during

the voyage, wrote to Banks offering him the collection. Banks must have refused the offer, for the bulk of the collection was later bought by the natural history dealer George Humphrey, whose son was to become the first government mineralogist in New South Wales.

Banks had, in 1773, become the unofficial director of the Royal Gardens at Kew. His interest in and encouragement of the Royal Gardens did much to increase their collections, which in turn allowed Banks to send more collectors abroad for new specimens.

On Cook's last, fateful voyage, his scientific party was principally composed of crew members. William Anderson served a dual role as both surgeon and naturalist; the surgeon's mate, William Ellis, was an unofficial draughtsman for the expedition; David Nelson, a Kew gardener, had been put aboard by Banks to ensure that his and the Royal Garden's botanical interests were well cared for; and an official artist, John Webber, was included as a landscape artist, having been recommended for the position by Carl Solander.

The voyage left Plymouth in July of 1776 with Cook

again in command of HMS *Resolution* and accompanied by HMS *Discovery* under Captain Charles Clerke. The *Resolution* put into Adventure Bay from 26–30 January 1777, on its way to the Pacific. During this brief time, Nelson, with the assistance of Anderson, spent his time collecting plants including the seeds and specimens of the tree that L'Heritier later used to describe the genus *Eucalyptus*. Both Anderson and Ellis painted birds; among the subjects of Ellis' brush was the green rosella, *Platycercus caledonicus*. Latham saw this bird from Van Diemens Land in Banks' collection and mistakenly placed its origin in New Caledonia; Johann Gmelin, the German physician-botanist, later accentuated the error when he gave it the specific name *caledonicus*. Many of the published descriptions of the animals from the late eighteenth century were based not on preserved or live animals, which were too difficult to keep on long sea voyages, but from either paintings or sketches made by amateur or professional artists. It has already been indicated that the original description of the kangaroo was based on a painting derived from one of Sydney Parkinson's sketches, and some of the birds painted on this voyage provide other examples of this practice.

Anderson, in his journal, comments at length on the 'natural productions' of Adventure Bay. He despaired that there were no edible plants to be found but thought that some of the *Eucalyptus* trees might be useful for ship repairs. Among the numerous other plants Anderson noted was *Melaleuca squarrosa* which Nelson brought back alive to England for the Royal Gardens at Kew. Otherwise he noted a possum, probably *Pseudocheirus peregrinus*:

> The only animal of the Quadruped kind we got was a sort of Opossum about twice the size of a large cat and liker that than any other creature. It is of a dusky colour above tingd with a brown or rusty cast and below it is whitish: about a third of the tail towards its tip is white and bare underneath, by which it probably hangs on the branches of trees as it climbs these and lives on berrys.[15]

Before sailing from Adventure Bay to the death that awaited him in the Hawaiian Islands, Cook liberated a male and female pig which he hoped might reproduce if they could avoid the Aborigines, and directed the planting of some vegetables and fruit seeds.

Chapter Two

Upon the return of the last Cook expedition to England, there occurred a hiatus in the exploratory voyages touching on the shores of New Holland. The next major impetus in the chronicling of the natural history of this still largely unknown land was to be the establishment of a colony on the eastern coast which would begin the continuous occupation by European stock. However, this was still ten years in the future.

During this hiatus, the unusual animals brought back from New Holland began to find their way into published works and therefore into the popular imagination. Dampier's books had had little in them to fire the public's conception of the land, but published journals of Cook's voyages, both official and unofficial, with their descriptions of possums, kangaroos, and a multitude of harlequin parrots, whetted the public's

'Superb warbler'
Latham. *A General Synopsis of Birds*. 1781.
Malurus cyaneus

imagination. In 1781, John Latham began publication of his multivolume *A General Synopsis of Birds*. Latham, the most eminent British ornithologist of the late eighteenth century and a medical practitioner who had studied under John Hunter, was a fellow of the Royal Society and probably a close associate of Joseph Banks. His intent in *A General Synopsis of Birds* was to include all the birds known to natural history, and many of the birds brought back from New Holland found their way into this mighty undertaking. The first volume, published in 1781, included the 'New Holland white eagle', communicated by Dr George Forster; the 'blue-bellied parrot', recorded by the English painter Peter Brown in his *Illustrations*; a 'crested parakeet' in the possession of Joseph Banks; the 'black cockatoo' mentioned by Sydney Parkinson; and the 'crow' found by Dampier on the coast of New Holland.

Later volumes included the superb warbler, specimens of which found their way to Joseph Banks' collection as well as the Leverian Museum, along with the 'New Holland thrush', 'red neck plover', 'pied oystercatcher', 'sooty tern', 'black-backed gull', and 'wood ibis'. In a supplement to the *General Synopsis of Birds*, published in 1787, Latham included the 'crimson winged parrot', the 'pennantian parrot', and other birds from the collections of the English naturalists Thomas Pennant and Joseph Banks, or described by Anderson on Cook's third voyage.

In 1788, Johann Gmelin edited the thirteenth edition of Linnaeus' *Systema Naturae*. Gmelin included organisms from all the published works he could locate, incorporating those which embraced New Holland species. Many of Latham's species from *A General Synopsis of Birds* were assimilated and given Latin names, particularly the parrots which became, in *Systema Naturae*, 'Psittacus moluccans', 'P. novaehollandiae', 'P. erythropterus', 'P. caledonicus', and 'P. elegans'. Since Gmelin conferred the Latin names on the birds, he is given the credit for their description rather than Latham who actually wrote the descriptions.

Those in England interested in the fauna of distant

Bankian Cockatoo.

lands did not have to content themselves simply with illustrated volumes. By the 1780s several large collections of specimens existed, the most important belonging to Joseph Banks which, although available for the use of botanists or zoologists, was of limited access to the general public. A more accessible collection was the museum of Sir Ashton Lever set up circa 1760 in Lancashire. By 1775 Lever had moved the expanded museum to London, having been able to obtain many items from New Holland for exhibition. Joseph Banks gave Lever items collected on his voyage with Cook, while John Latham contributed specimens he had obtained. From William Anderson, Lever also gained specimens collected on Cook's third voyage. The acquisition of specimens and their upkeep unfortunately proved a constant drain on Lever's finances, so he offered the British Museum the opportunity of purchasing the collection. The museum, however, was not interested, so in 1788, after petitioning Parliament for permission, Lever organised a lottery, the winner of which would gain the entire museum. A London surgeon and dentist, James Parkinson, discoverer of Parkinson's Disease, won the lottery and continued to display the collection.

By the late 1780s England was again demonstrating an interest in the Pacific region. On his third and last voyage, Cook had chosen as master of the *Resolution* a young man who was to become as well known as Cook himself, although under very different circumstances. On that voyage, William Bligh had ample opportunity to hone his navigational skills under the finest navigator extant in the British navy. Bligh's skills were not found wanting; he prepared many of the charts of that third voyage. As the *Resolution* put in briefly at Adventure Bay, he was able to familiarise himself with the anchorage, an asset during the subsequent voyages he made to the area.

Both Dampier and Cook had brought back to England specimens of the plants that they encountered in the Pacific. Among these was the breadfruit, accompanied by reports that the Pacific islanders were able to subsist on the plant for many months of the year. These reports reached the ears of large plantation owners in the West Indies who plied King George III with requests for the introduction of the plant to the West Indies as a cheap staple for the diet of their slaves. In 1787 the request was approved and a voyage was proposed to obtain breadfruit from Tahiti and transport it to the West Indies. Sir Joseph Banks put forward the name of William Bligh as the commander of the expedition, a recommendation that the Admiralty accepted. Banks, then the president of the Royal

Society, considered it an interesting scientific proposal and took a personal concern in the selection of an appropriate vessel and the alterations necessary to accommodate the breadfruit plants. This included turning the main cabin into a conservatory, the floor of which was lined with lead that drained into pipes and then to tubs so that the limited freshwater supplies carried on board could be recycled. David Nelson, employed as a gardener on Cook's last voyage, was appointed botanist and charged with caring for the breadfruit on the journey. Banks issued Bligh and Nelson with a set of guidelines for the collection and care of the plants and also recommended an assistant for Nelson named William Brown, but was hesitant about entrusting Bligh with too much botanical responsibility: 'As to Bligh learning the gardener's trade, I earnestly hope he will not attempt it as I have seen so much mischief done by dabblers.'[1] Nelson was advanced money by Banks to acquire an outfit for the voyage, and his equipment included: paper, drawing cartridge, pens, pencils, ink, India ink, brushes, colours of all kinds, drawing instruments, paddle, spade, pins, wire, chests, trunk, insect box, tin specimen box, a lead box for preserving seeds, flower pots, bottles and vials, camphire, flytrap, knives, cloth, gun, powder, shot, flint, books, and trinkets for the natives.

Bligh's original orders prescribed a route around Cape Horn to Tahiti, but before he left the orders were amended to allow him the choice of the Cape of Good Hope should the weather at Cape Horn preclude a safe passage. This proved to be the case so Bligh rounded the Cape of Good Hope then sailed across the Indian Ocean to Adventure Bay, Van Diemens Land, where the *Bounty* anchored on 21 August 1788. Bligh went ashore accompanied by Nelson, who set about collecting botanical specimens for Banks and the Royal Gardens at Kew. While there, Nelson planted a number of fruit trees which had been brought from the Cape of Good Hope for that purpose, but Bligh despaired of the trees surviving the twin ravages of fire and the Aborigines. Two weeks after its arrival, the *Bounty* sailed for Tahiti and the mutiny that was to sully Bligh's reputation forever.

The mutiny may have cost Australia some early sketches of the fauna of Van Diemens Land, for when set afloat in the *Bounty*'s launch, Bligh was denied a box which included charts, drawings, and comments made on the present and previous voyages. During the two weeks at Adventure Bay, Bligh, who was a competent artist, may well have sketched animals and plants as he was to do on a later voyage. Nelson, who had survived Cook's last voyage and was one of the men to accompany Bligh on his open boat journey, tragically died soon after the party reached safety on the island of Timor. Brown, the gardener's assistant, sided with the mutineers and eventually died on Pitcairn Island.

'Banksian cockatoo'
Latham. *A General Synopsis of Birds*. First Supplement. 1781.
Calyptorhynchus sp.

On his return to England, Bligh convinced both Banks and the Admiralty of his lack of culpability in the mutiny and was given command of another vessel, the HMS *Providence*, for a second attempt to deliver bread-fruit to the West Indies. The *Assistant*, a small brig under the command of Nathaniel Portlock, was to accompany the *Providence* as a tender. Once again Banks devoted his attention to fitting out the voyage and overseeing the appointment of two gardeners, James Wiles and Christopher Smith, to care for the breadfruit and collect rare specimens for the Royal Garden. The entire aft cabin was reserved for the bread-fruit which increased the already cramped conditions on board. Those recruited for the voyage included a young midshipman named Matthew Flinders and a newly promoted lieutenant, George Tobin, a distant relative of Lord Nelson.

Once again Bligh's route took him first to the Cape of Good Hope and then to Adventure Bay before proceeding to Tahiti. At Adventure Bay, he found that of the trees planted in 1788 only one apple tree had survived until this voyage in early 1792. Once again he had his gardeners plant fruit trees as well as straw-berries, pomegranate, rosemary, oak, fir, apricot, and peach seed. When La Billardière, naturalist with the French scientific expedition of d'Entrecasteaux, put into Adventure Bay one year later, he stated:

> We saw three young fig trees, two pomegranate trees and a quince tree they had planted, which had thriven very well: but it appeared to us that one of the trees they had planted in this country had already perished, for the following inscription, which we found on the trunk of a large tree near, mentions seven:—Near this tree Captain William Bligh planted seven Fruit Trees, 1792. Messrs. S. and W. Botanists.[2]

Bligh also turned loose a cock and some hens, hoping that they would survive and breed and thus supply food for future visitors to the area.

While his crew loaded fresh supplies of wood and water, Bligh and Lieutenant George Tobin spent much of the ensuing two weeks sketching and painting the flora and fauna of Van Diemens Land. Originally an artist had been included in the expedition but had with-drawn before departure due to ill health. Tobin, like many young officers of his day, was a keen amateur naturalist and artist; as well as completing many paintings of the New Holland fauna, he kept a journal in which his notes on natural history were recorded, but as he wrote:

> I can tell you the colour of a bird, a fish or an animal, as well as their shape and size, but exactly of what species, or to what genus they belong I am in the dark.[3]

Nevertheless, Tobin left accurate portrayals of the animals he encountered both pictorially and verbally:

> The only animals seen were the Kangaroo and a kind of sloth, about the size of a roasting pig, with a proboscis two or three inches in length. On the back were short quills like those of the Porcupine. This animal was roasted and found of a delicate flavour.[4]

and

> Of Birds there are a great variety, both land and aquatic . . . A parrot in a wild state was quite a novelty, nor until there was 'ocular demonstration of it' could I suppose their flight was so rapid. I speak particularly of a small kind of which there are abundance in these woods. When convocated on a high tree a 'confusion of tongues' frequently attracted our attention. A few of the smaller birds are singularly beautiful in their plumage and not without a pleasing note.[5]

Fish also became the subjects of Tobin's watercolours.

'Animal of Adventure Bay'
Tobin. Unpublished. Courtesy of Mitchell Library.
Tachyglossus aculeatus

'Fish of Adventure Bay'
Tobin. Unpublished. Courtesy of Mitchell Library.
Aracana aurita

Bird of Van Diemans Land. About three fourth its natural size — GT 1792 — Page 99

WB

Bird of Van Die mans Land. Nearly as large as life — GT 1792 — Page 99 —

WB

'Birds of Van Diemen's Land'
Tobin. Unpublished. Courtesy of Mitchell Library.
Malurus cyaneus, Petroica rodinogaster

Bligh presented a much clearer sketch of the animal that Tobin described as a sloth:

> . . . seventeen inches long, and a small flat head connected so close to the shoulders that it can scarce be said to have a neck. It has no mouth like any other animal, but a kind of a duck bill, two inches long, which opens at the extremity and will not admit anything above the size of a pistol ball. It has four legs, and on each foot are very sharp claws; it has no tail but a rump not unlike a penguin's on which are quills of rusty brown.[6]

Although later variously described as a platypus or anteater by people reading the description, it was an echidna, *Tachyglossus aculeatus*. When Bligh returned to England, a description of the animal was published by Everard Home who referred to

> Another species of *Ornithorhynchus*, of the same size as the Hystrix was shot at Adventure Bay, Van Diemen's Land by Lieutenant Guthrie in the year 1790, a drawing of which was made by Captain Bligh and sent to Sir Joseph Banks, who has allowed me to annex a copy of it to this paper.[7]

Home included the animal in the genus *Ornithorhynchus* because it had in common with the platypus such characteristics as the spurs on the hind legs of the males, the tongue having horny processes instead of teeth, and the beak being smooth while the rest of the animal was covered with hair. Home was aware that the echidna was not really in the same genus as the platypus for he finished his paper thus:

> When more of this extraordinary tribe of animals, which, although quadrupeds, are not Mammalia, shall have been discovered, and naturalists thereby enabled to divide them properly, the two which I have described will doubtless be arranged under different genera; till then, I have thought it best to consider them as species of the same genus, rather than encumber science with an additional name or attempt to frame generic characters from one species only.[8]

Bligh was also to paint a number of pictures of the birds of Van Diemens Land and in his journal mentioned various other animals, including kangaroos, fish, lizards, and birds. He also corrected a mistake he had made in his published journal of the *Bounty* voyage:

> I have said in the accounts of my former voyage that the

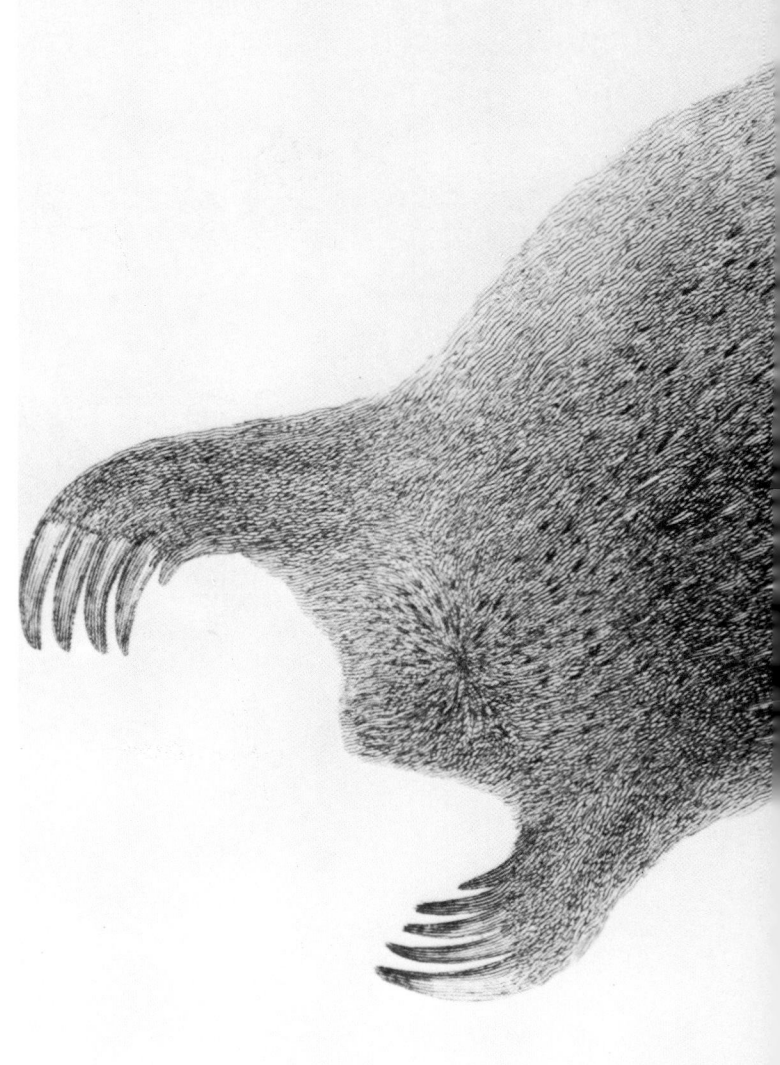

'Ornithorhynchus'
Home. *Philosophical Transactions of the Royal Society*. 1802.
Tachyglossus aculeatus

29

trees shed their bark every year and said it principally on the authority of Mr. Nelson, the botanist, but it appears to me at this time not to be the case.[9]

The idyllic two weeks were soon over and Bligh and Tobin returned to the business at hand—the voyage to Tahiti to collect the breadfruit. The vessels arrived in Tahiti without incident after the seven month voyage and the crew loaded 2,000 breadfruit on board the *Providence*. Bligh decided to return westward, stopping first at Fiji and later passing through the Torres Strait. Tobin continued his painting and had a fine portfolio of Tahitian fish and birds to add to those he had completed in Van Diemens Land. In Torres Strait he found time to finish further paintings of birds.

As Bligh left no pictorial record of the Torres Strait, it appears that he was too busy navigating the numerous reefs and islets to devote his attention to artistic endeavours. There were also several confrontations with the Torres Strait islanders to occupy his thoughts.

The breadfruit were eventually delivered to the West Indies successfully, though as a staple for the West Indians, they proved a failure. Smith and Wiles managed to collect plants on the voyage which they returned to England including *Banksia* and *Metrosidera*. Bligh sailed to England where his departure from his vessel was a far cry from that of his previous voyage—his crew lined the rails to cheer him. George Tobin commented:

> . . . that in the Providence there was no settled System of Tyranny exercised by him likely to produce dissatisfaction. It was in those violent Tornados of temper when he lost himself. Yet when all, in his opinion, went right when could a man be more placid and interesting? For myself I feel indebted to him. Let our old Captain's frailities be forgotten and view him as a man of Science and excellent practical Seaman.[10]

The splenetic Bligh was never to be remembered as either of these by most people, but he was elected to the Royal Society for his services to navigation and botany. As Sir Joseph Banks remained his lifelong friend and was president of the Royal Society at the time, even this may have depended less on perceived merit than on politics.

As with so many of the early exploratory voyages, the next expedition to New Holland was the result of English fears that another country would establish a claim on territory that they believed should rightfully be theirs. In the late 1780s, Spain claimed the north-west coast of North America on the strength of first discovery and proceeded to harass British trading vessels. Early in 1790, the British Admiralty commissioned a vessel, HMS *Discovery* under Captain

'Seabird, Possession Island, Torres Strait'
Tobin. Unpublished. Courtesy of Mitchell Library.
Sterna anaethetus

Henry Roberts with George Vancouver second in command, to make the British presence felt on that coast. Both Roberts and Vancouver were veterans of the Cook voyages to the Pacific and so were familiar with problems of sailing those waters. The *Discovery* did not sail until April 1791, and then with Vancouver in command, as Roberts was no longer involved in the enterprise. The everpresent Banks was involved in the scientific end of the cruise and Vancouver states:

> Botany, however, was an object of scientific inquiry with which no one of us was much acquainted; but as, in expeditions of a similar nature, the most valuable opportunities had been afforded for adding to the general stock of botanical information, Mr. Archibald Menzies,

res Straits — about two thirds the size of life — GT. 1792 — Page 268

a surgeon in the royal navy, . . . was appointed for the specific purpose of making such researches.[11]

John Melville had been the original choice for surgeon-naturalist on board the *Discovery* but due to illness was replaced by Archibald Menzies. Menzies was appointed on the recommendation of Joseph Banks, with whom he had maintained a botanical correspondence for several years prior to his assignment on the *Discovery*. He was instructed to investigate the various minerals and the nature of the soil, to collect specimens of the plants he saw, and to observe and describe the animals.

The Admiralty issued no specific instructions for a course to bring Vancouver to the north-west coast of America so he chose to round the Cape of Good Hope rather than chance the foul weather of Cape Horn. Then: 'I resolved in our way to the pacific ocean to visit the sw part of New Holland and endeavour to acquire some information of that unknown, though interesting country.'[12]

Vancouver, in HMS *Discovery*, accompanied by the tender *Chatham*, left Falmouth on 1 April 1791, and, sailing somewhat south of Dampier's earlier track, was off the coast of New Holland by 26 September. Due to the debilitating effects of dysentery which many of his crew had contracted at the Cape of Good Hope, Vancouver sought the first harbour he could find. Sailing eastward along the coast, he came to a large, well-protected embayment which he called 'King George the Thirds Sound'.

Landing, he took possession for Britain of the area from the Sound to as far as he might explore, which turned out to be no more than about 500 kilometres. To counter the effects of scurvy, Menzies sought out green vegetables and was able to find a bountiful supply of wild celery; meanwhile the crew found such an abundance of oysters in an inlet that Vancouver named

it Oyster Harbour. Later an expedition inland from
Oyster Harbour was organised to acquire information
and specimens of natural history. Menzies, participating
in this excursion, found a new species of duck, one
which possessed a wattle below its bill causing Menzies
to name it 'Anas carunculata' in his journal. His journal
description remained unpublished and the duck was
described as 'Anas lobata' by Dr George Shaw who
examined it following the expedition's return to
England; it has since been renamed Biziura lobata. The
duck exuded a very distinct musky odour which
permeated the entire ship and gave rise to its common
name, the musk duck. During the sojourn at King
George Sound, Menzies had time to collect a number of
new species of plants, and several species of marine
algae which were later described by the English botanist
and antiquary Dawson Turner, but only one quadruped—
the carcass of a dead kangaroo—was seen. Among the
birds noted in the journals of Vancouver and Menzies
were black swans, hawks, parrots, pelicans, owls,
penguins, and a variety of small birds. Menzies also
wrote scientific descriptions of the southern boobook,
or boobook owl, the red-capped parrot, and the western
rosella, although none of these were formally named
until specimens were examined which were collected
during a later voyage led by Matthew Flinders. The
seine was hauled frequently to supply the crew with
fish, allowing Menzies the opportunity to obtain and
describe several species.

As one still does today, Menzies found a profusion of
wildflowers in the area of south-western Australia. His
collection included numerous species of plants
including Banksia and Eucalyptus. In common with
most of the expeditions sent out under the auspices of
Joseph Banks, provision had been made for a plant-
cabin to be erected on the quarterdeck of the vessel.
Here were kept live specimens for the Royal Gardens at
Kew, although the survival rate of the plants was often
minimal, especially on voyages such as Vancouver's
which were destined to penetrate the far north Pacific.
Seeds stood a far greater chance of survival, and so
were diligently collected to be sent back to Kew for
germination. Menzies and Vancouver also observed the
soil and tested it chemically for characteristics such as
effervescence in acid and vitrification under heat; some
samples they thought might be suitable for porcelain.
Before leaving King George Sound, Menzies planted
vine cuttings and watercress, as well as seeds of
almonds, lemon, orange, and pumpkin. On 11 October
the vessels departed from the sound and touched briefly
at two other points on the southern coast of New
Holland—Doubtful Island and Termination Island,
before sailing for New Zealand and the north-west
Pacific.

On his return to England, Menzies brought back with
him specimens of the fauna and especially the flora of

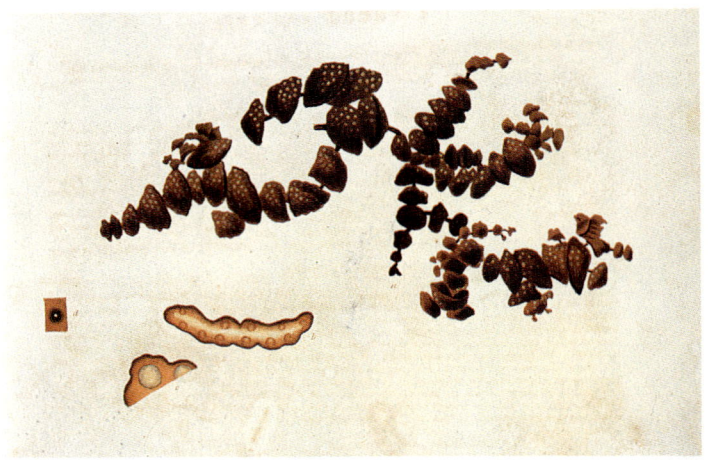

'Fucus radiatus'
Turner. *Fuci.* 1808–19.
Ecklonia radiata

New Holland. Although he described a new species of
sucking fish and several other animals, many of his
specimens' descriptions were never published, thus
leaving the credit for others.

Other expeditions equipped with scientists or
naturalists ventured to the shores of New Holland at
this time. During the late eighteenth century, a
scientific renaissance began in France. Individuals such
as Pierre-Simon Laplace in astronomy, Antoine-Laurent
Lavoisier in chemistry, Georges Cuvier in palaeontology,
and Bernard de Jussieu in botany exemplified this
tradition. Concurrent with the development of
theoretical paradigms for science, the naturalists among
them turned to new horizons for the acquisition of
specimens to support and extend their theories.

To this end a French expedition, sponsored by King
Louis XVI of France, left France in 1785 under the
command of Jean-François de Galaup, Comte de la
Pérouse. The French sailed into Botany Bay shortly
after the First Fleet had dropped anchor, much to the
consternation of the British officers. Aboard *La
Boussole* and *L'Astrolabe* were the naturalists Abbé
Mongès and Father Louis Receveur. Lasting evidence of
their visit to New Holland is the grave on the foreshore
of Botany Bay of Receveur, who died of wounds
received in the Pacific Islands. The expedition left no
records or illustrations of the organisms of New
Holland, for shortly after leaving New Holland both
vessels were wrecked in the Santa Cruz Islands leaving
little trace of their passing. Their demise was unknown
to the French government—or the world, for the
wrecks of La Pérouse's ships were not located until
Irish captain-adventurer Peter Dillon found wreckage
on Vanikoro Island in 1827, forty years later.

'Fucus banksii'
Turner. *Fuci.* 1808–19.
Hormosira banksii

Three years passed after La Pérouse's departure from Botany Bay, and having received no word of him, the French National Assembly authorised another expedition to search for La Pérouse as well as to carry out the scientific and geographic work originally assigned to that expedition. The vessels were placed under the command of Joseph-Antoine de Bruni d'Entrecasteaux. He commanded two ships, *La Recherche*, under his immediate command, and *L'Espérance* under Captain Huon de Kermadec. Both vessels carried a full complement of scientists; on board *La Recherche* were three naturalists, La Billardière, Deschamps, and Ventenat; a geographer, Beaupré; a draughtsman, Piron; and a gardener, Lahaie. *L'Espérance*'s complement numbered two naturalists, Riche and Blavier; an astronomer, Pierson; a geographer, Jouvency; and a draughtsman, Ely. It is primarily La Billardière and Claude Riche who dominate the saga of the journey, for La Billardière subsequently wrote a narrative of the voyage as well as publishing a seminal work on the botany of New Holland.

Jacques-Julien de La Billardière had studied medicine and botany at Montpellier. Finishing his medical training in Paris, he journeyed to England where he met Joseph Banks and probably James Edward Smith, two of the foremost botanists in England. On La Billardière's return to France, and at the instigation of the botanist, Le Lemonnier, he was assigned a governmental mission to Asia Minor. Back in France, La Billardière published the botanical results of the journey and was then invited to participate in d'Entrecasteaux's proposed voyage as a botanist. La Billardière was primarily interested in 'vegetables', or more accurately the botany of the voyage, but his narrative ranges freely over botany, zoology, geology, and anthropology, even down to a study of the insects which were to be found in the ship's biscuits. La Billardière was undoubtedly a naturalist with a reasonable knowledge of the plant, animal, and mineral kingdoms, but much of his zoological and geological information would have come from his colleagues in the scientific party. Principal among those fellow workers was Claude Riche, one of the zoologists assigned to the voyage. Riche's main interest was entomology; however, he failed to write up any significant results from the journey, and seems to have been primarily a collector.

The vanished La Pérouse's intended plan after leaving Botany Bay had been to visit many of the Pacific islands, then pass through Torres Strait, the Gulf of Carpentaria, and round the west coast of New Holland as far east as Van Diemens Land. This was approximately the course that d'Entrecasteaux was to follow in his efforts to locate La Pérouse. After rounding the Cape of Good Hope, however, d'Entrecasteaux deviated from his itinerary, deciding to head for Adventure Bay, Van Diemens Land, instead.

Arriving off the south-eastern coast of Van Diemens Land, (or Cape Van Diemen as La Billardière called it, for it was not known whether Van Diemens Land was connected to New Holland), on 25 April 1792, the expedition entered Storm Bay sixty-four days after leaving the Cape of Good Hope. The crew soon had fishing lines over the side to replenish their larder and caught some two-metre sharks, '*Squalus cinereus*' (*Heptranchias perlo*). La Billardière reasoned that the sharks remained close to the bottom as they were never seen at the surface and did not seem to bother the Aborigines who dived for shellfish. The vessels proceeded further into Storm Bay to an inlet they called Port d'Entrecasteaux, and here the scientific party set about making comprehensive collections and investigations. Ashore, La Billardière and Lahaie encountered several species of *Banksia* and *Epacris*, as well as various species of eucalyptus, one of which John White

'*Banksia repens*'
La Billardière. *Voyage in search of La Pérouse*. 1800.
Banksia repens

had named *Eucalyptus resinifera* in his *Journal of a Voyage to New South Wales*, published in 1790.

In a later excursion La Billardière described the collection of:

> A bird that . . . surprised us very much by the singularity of its plumage. It was a new species of the swan, of the same beautiful form, but rather larger than ours. Its colour was a shining black, as striking in its appearance as the clear white of ours . . .[13]

La Billardière apparently had no knowledge of the black swan which had been named by Latham, '*Anas atrata*', in 1790 and by the French naturalist Abbé Bonnaterre as '*Anas novae-hollandiae*' in 1791. Yet the black swan was no longer a complete novelty to naturalists; it had been recorded as early as 1636 by the Dutchman Antoine Caen, and illustrated in Valentijn's book in 1726. On the same excursion La Billardière killed specimens of *Motacilla* as well as some parrots, amongst which was the species that John Latham had called the parrot of New Caledonia. Latham's parrot of New Caledonia was a specimen of the green rosella, *Platycercus caledonicus* killed by William Anderson on Cook's third voyage at Adventure Bay and named by Gmelin as '*Psittacus caledonicus*' in 1788.

La Billardière recorded a constant flow of new plant species, among them *Scleria*, *Epacris*, *Erigeron*, and *Eucalyptus*. In addition, La Billardière noted and named a new species of parsley, *Apium prostratum*, an important find for sailors heartily sick of salt pork and biscuits.

One of the crew shot a kangaroo which:

> As he goes in quest of his food more in the nighttime than during the day, nature has provided him with the membrane termed by zoologists *membrana nicitans*, situated at the interior angle of the eye, which he can extend at pleasure over the whole ball. His stomach was full of vegetables and divided by three very distinct partitions, which seem to approach him to the class of the ruminant quadrupeds.[14]

While the scientific party was engrossed in collecting specimens, the surveying parties found that Tasmans Head and Adventure Bay were part of an island separated from Van Diemens Land, a fact that none of the previous mariners had noticed.

La Billardière had filled his personal cabin with drying specimens and then moved his plant presses into the great cabin of *La Recherche*, bringing him into conflict with the naval officers who thought that he was encroaching upon their territory. It appears that the French officers were much less inclined to give up their cabin for the sake of a few plants than British officers. Another complaint, from the naturalists this time, was that they were allowed none of the freshly caught meat obtained on the collecting trips inland and had to make do with salted meat and biscuits, the usual ship's fare. On this French scientific expedition there was an

'*Banksia nivea*'
La Billardière. *Voyage in search of La Pérouse.* 1800.
Dryandra nivea

'Black swan'
La Billardière. *Voyage in search of La Pérouse.* 1800.
Cygnus atratus

'*Diplarrena moraea*'
La Billardière. *Voyage in search of La Pérouse*. 1800.
Diplarrhena moraea

'*Eucalyptus globulus*'
La Billardière. *Voyage in search of La Pérouse*. 1800.
Eucalyptus globulus

undercurrent of antagonism between the naval officers and the naturalists, a tension that was also to plague future French voyages to the region.

At Adventure Bay, La Billardière located a new species of eucalyptus, *Eucalyptus globulus*, which he thought might be useful in shipbuilding, especially for masts and spars. Later use was made of this tree for repairs to *La Recherche*'s launch.

Before leaving the first anchorage, the gardener sowed a variety of European seeds, matching the efforts of Bligh's gardeners the previous year. The scientists continued to collect along the eastern coast of Van Diemens Land and encountered a new genus of plant that La Billardière named *Richea* after the zoologist of the expedition.

They also caught a *Merops* which White had called a wattled bee-eater, and 'a quadruped of the size of a large dog . . . This animal which was of a white colour spotted with black had the appearance of a beast of prey.'[15] This was possibly a Tasmanian devil; if so this would be the earliest record of the animal.

La Recherche and *L'Espérance* then left the New Holland coast and sought traces of La Pérouse in the Pacific Islands. Later, after rounding the north coast of New Guinea, they continued first to the south-west then south-east.till they encountered the south-west coast of New Holland on 6 December 1792. The months at sea brought new tribulations—La Billardiere

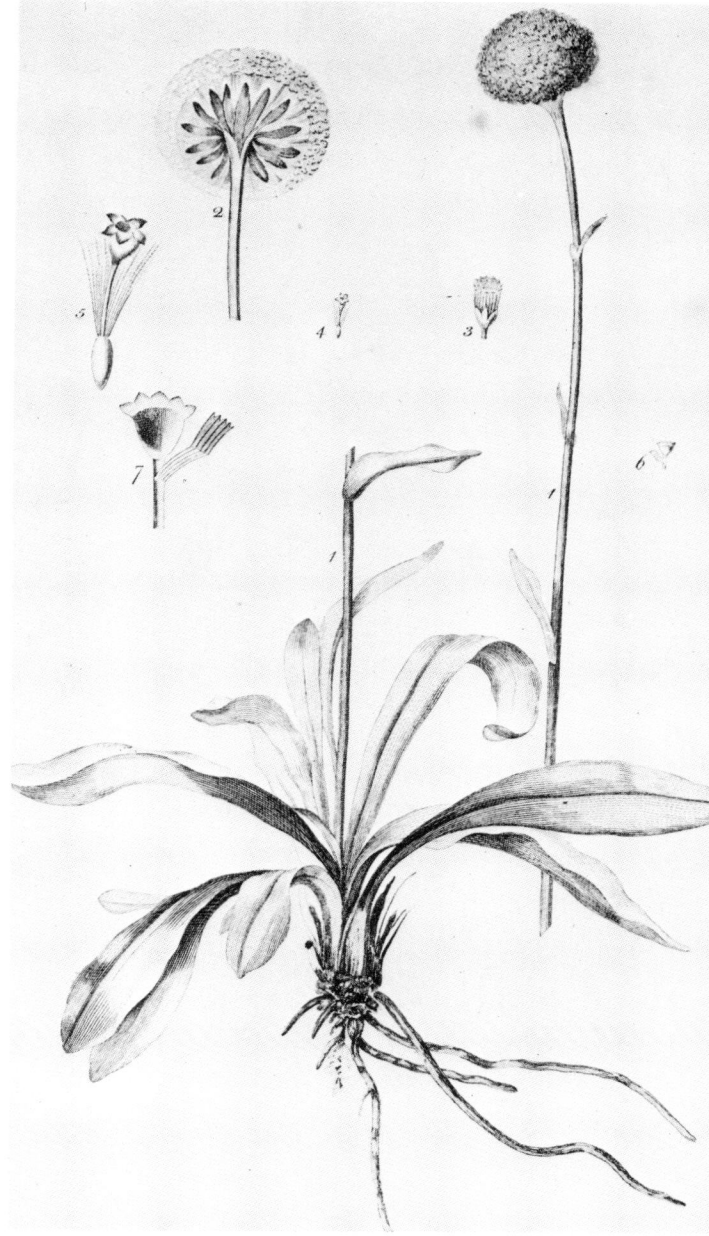

'*Richea glauca*'
La Billardière. *Voyage in search of La Pérouse*. 1800.
Craspedia glauca

botanical specimens to be collected, and La Billardière found several new species. During one of the daily collecting trips, Riche became separated from his companions, and La Billardière was among the group sent to search for him. La Billardière seems to have spent at least as much time looking for specimens as he did looking for Riche for during the search he recorded three new species of plants and the 'red crested cockatoo', '*Psittacus moluccensis*'. Riche was eventually found after two days despite La Billardière's preoccupation with the flora and fauna.

The French vessels continued to sail along the barren coastline until lack of fresh water forced them towards Van Diemens Land. Noting the strength of the current on the western side of Cape Van Diemen, La Billardière speculated that a strait existed between the Cape and New Holland, thus anticipating Bass and Flinders by several years. On the passage to Cape Van Diemen, La Billardière saw what he thought to be a new species of cetaceous fish (now known to be mammals), possibly a *Delphinus* species. They were easily distinguished by a large white spot behind the dorsal fin. The upper part of the body is of a blackish brown and the belly white.'[16]

The two vessels doubled South Cape of Cape Van Diemen and entered a small inlet of Storm Bay which they named Rocky Bay. Here La Billardière and his colleagues were surprised at the number of new species to be found despite having been in the general area only twelve months previously. Of the garden that Lahaie had planted the year before, only some cabbages, potatoes, radishes, cress, endive, and sorrel survived, and these in a poor condition. The botanists found a species that La Billardière named '*Ficiodes*'; it appeared to be similar to the common fig tree that they were familiar with, and they noted that the Aborigines relished its fruit.

While searching for new plants, La Billardière and his companions killed a parakeet upon which he conferred the unwieldy title of the 'black spotted parakeet of Cape Van Diemen'. Green in colour, spotted with black, and moving constantly among the grasses, the bird did not perch in trees. This was the 'ground parrot', '*Psittacus formosus*' (*Pezoporus wallicus*), which Latham had named in 1790 from a specimen sent to him from New South Wales.

The two ships left Rocky Bay on 14 February 1793. Prior to sailing, a male and female goat were released in the hope that these would multiply and supply food for future mariners visiting these shores. Before leaving Van Diemens Land altogether, they put into the same bay as Bligh had and found the inscriptions carved into tree trunks by Smith and Wiles in February of 1792. A last haul was made with the seine and it produced a new species of sea hedgehog (puffer); then *La Recherche* and *L'Espérance* sailed out of New Holland waters—but certainly not out of troubled waters.

began to find the insects on board to be a problem. A species of *Tinea* not only devoured the food on board but also his linen, paper, and even the ink in his inkwell if he left it uncovered. Running along the southern coastline, the two ships were brought to anchor in the Archipelago de la Recherche to wait out inclement weather. On one of the myriad islands, La Billardière caught some large birds that he thought to be swans but which were almost certainly Cape Barren Geese, described as *Cereopsis novaehollandiae* by Latham in 1801. They also encountered the dove that John White had called the 'golden winged pigeon' *Phaps elegans*, and the penguin Cook had reported from New Zealand, '*Aptenodyta minor*' (*Eudyptula minor*). There were new

Black Spotted Parroquet of Van Diemen's Land.

Pub.^d by I.Stockdale, Piccadilly. 15.th April. 1800.

'Black spotted parroquet'
La Billardière. *Voyage in search of La Pérouse.* 1800.
Pezoporus wallicus

Having finished their surveying and scientific tasks, the two vessels put in at Java, but by this time the long voyage had taken its toll; both d'Entrecasteaux and Huon, the leaders of the expedition, had died leaving d'Auribeau in command. In Java the expedition received word of the French Revolution and of the war that had broken out between revolutionary France and Holland. Rather than allow the two French vessels to sail home to France and be placed into the service of the republican government now in power, d'Auribeau and the other senior naval officers, all staunch monarchists, turned the vessels over to the Dutch authorities in Java. At d'Auribeau's instigation, all the avowed republicans on the vessels, including La Billardière, Riche, and the artist Piron, were imprisoned. D'Auribeau soon died in the less-than-healthy climate of Batavia, further depleting the chain of command, and then de Rossel, who had assumed command, confiscated all the natural history collections, charts, and journals and set off for Amsterdam in a Dutch East India Company ship in 1795. However a state of war existing between Holland and Britain resulted in the vessel's interception and capture by HMS *Spectre* off Saint Helena in June of 1795. The spoils of war, including the natural history specimens, were turned over to the Admiralty.

During the eighteenth and early nineteenth centuries, France and Britain were engaged in hostilities so often

that in time, the scientific communities came to circumvent, if not entirely ignore, the restrictions imposed upon their communication. Scientists exchanged visits during most of the intermittent wars. Although science produced advances in navigation, medicine, and even weapons, natural history was not considered to be directly influential upon the fighting and therefore was exempt. In 1745 a British naturalist collected plants in North America and sent them back to England with a note attached to the effect that if the specimens were captured by the French, the plants should be sent to the French botanist Bernard de Jussieu. During this time, scientists on both sides were frequently able to intercede and obtain the release of specimens captured by their respective governments.

When Cook left on his third voyage in 1776, Benjamin Franklin, then American envoy to France, issued a passport to Cook asking all American ships and their commanders not to detain or plunder Cook's vessels as he was undertaking a voyage to increase the knowledge of science and geography for the benefit of mankind. The French and Spanish issued similar instructions to their ships, stating that Cook was to be treated as a neutral.

Not all scientific travellers were so fortunate. La Billardière was to suffer not so much at the hands of a foreign power but from his own countrymen. When La Billardière was interned by the Dutch in 1794 and his specimens seized and brought to London, the collection was placed at the disposal of the exiled King Louis XVIII, then in England. Louis subsequently presented the collections to the queen of England who sought Sir Joseph Banks' advice on their dispersion. Banks inspected the collections and suggested that he make a selection of items for the Royal collection. He had little sympathy for the predicament of La Billardière, labelling him the principal troublemaker, responsible for the trials that had plagued the expedition, but at least praised the effort and industry that went into the collection of the specimens.

La Billardière had previously written to Banks lamenting the loss of his collection; he now wrote again to both Banks and James Edward Smith inveighing their help with the return of his specimens. Banks was still not particularly sympathetic, but Smith had recognised La Billardière's contribution to botany and named a genus after him, the genus *Billardiera*. The republican French government also made a formal request for the return of the specimens, which placed the British government in a predicament, as it had already given the specimens to Louis XVIII. Following his release from Java, La Billardière returned to Paris where he took up the position of director of the Botanical Gardens of Paris. Banks had by this time changed his opinion of La Billardière's character and was making efforts to have the collections forwarded to Paris in order that La Billardière could finish his descriptions and publish his observations. With Banks as president of the Royal Society and the king's adviser, his opinion could scarcely be ignored and he was successful in gaining the specimens' release and return.

After La Billardière was eventually released by the Dutch in Java, and had returned to Paris and secured the return of his impounded specimens, he set about writing up descriptions of the new plants. His *Novae Hollandiae Plantarum Specimen* was published in 1804 and contained descriptions of the new plants and marine algae, some 265 species. By the time that La Billardière completed much of the work on *Novae Hollandiae Plantarum Specimen* a subsequent French scientific expedition, the expedition of Nicholas Baudin in 1800, had also collected in New Holland. La Billardière acquired and described specimens in his book obtained on Baudin's voyage. One problem with La Billardière's volume is the confusion that has arisen from the mislabelling of specimens—a number of plants attributed to Van Diemens Land are endemic to the western coast of Australia and would appear to have been incorrectly labelled by either La Billardière or others. La Billardière, a true Linnaean in his classification of the plants, followed the artificial classification based on sexual characteristics. In a few years' time, this system was to be supplanted by the 'natural affinity' system pioneered by Bernard de Jussieu and Robert Brown. *Novae Hollandiae Plantarum Specimen* was illustrated by 265 black-and-white engravings, including those made on the voyage

itself by Piron and others completed back in Paris by various botanical draughtsmen. D'Entrecasteaux's voyage collected over 4,000 specimens of plants; duplicate sets of specimens were sent to Robert Brown, James Edward Smith, and Antoine-Laurent de Jussieu. The zoological collections of the voyage were described piecemeal in French publications. Seeds brought back by La Billardière and his colleagues were germinated and later graced the Empress Josephine's garden at Malmaison.

One of the interesting incidents on d'Entrecasteaux's voyage was the surreptitious signing of a woman into the crew. La Girardrin signed on as a purser on *La Recherche* and for many months successfully mas-

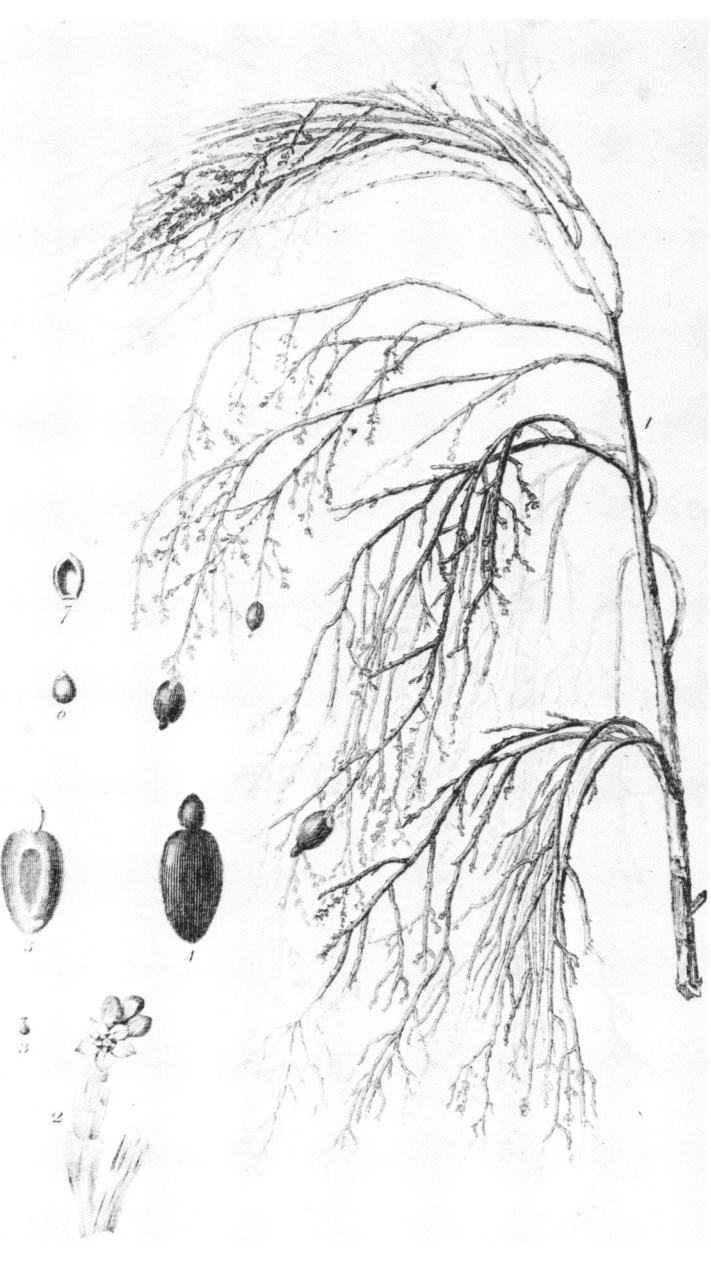

'*Exocarpos cupressiformis*'
La Billardière. *Voyage in search of La Pérouse*. 1800.
Exocarpos cupressiformis

queraded as a male. On one occasion, when unwittingly being teased for her effeminate face, she challenged her tormentor to a duel and was wounded in the arm. Her ruse unmasked in Tahiti, she continued with *La Recherche* to Java where she died of fever.

'*Eucalyptus cornuta*'
La Billardière. *Voyage in search of La Pérouse*. 1800.
Eucalyptus cornuta

Chapter Three

ESTABLISHMENT OF THE BRITISH COLONY, THE INITIAL YEARS: 1788–92

The proposal to establish a colony in the antipodes was neither radical or new in the 1780s: suggestions to this effect by both the Frenchman Charles de Brosses and the Scottish antiquary John Callander had been published in 1756 and 1766 respectively. In 1776 events in another British colony brought things to a head, for no longer could England's undesirables be banished to the other side of the Atlantic. A long-term solution to the problem was temporarily avoided by the use of prison hulks to accommodate convicted criminals, but the demand soon outstripped the availability of condemned vessels. By 1779 a House of Commons' Committee considered evidence on the advantages of transportation and possible sites for a place of servitude.

Joseph Banks, considered by many to have the greatest knowledge of the Pacific region, appeared before the committee and advocated the use of New Holland, specifically Botany Bay, for the proposed penal colony. Banks enumerated several points that New Holland had in its favour: sufficient fertile soil to support a sizable population, an indigenous population of little consequence and likely to be less antagonistic than the people of other locations considered such as New Zealand, adequate water and timber, and the possibility of a fishing industry. When questioned about the material benefits England would reap from the settlement Banks was vague, but concluded that in such a vast tract of land there was certain to be something of value. This attitude was in marked contrast to a section in his journal of 1770 which he entitled 'Some account of that part of New Holland now called New South Wales'. Written while Banks was actually on the antipodean coast, it described the coastline as barren except for occasional bays clothed in mangroves, while inland the country was little better, water was too scarce, the timber too hard, no edible vegetables existed, and there was a dearth of other useful plants. Banks stated:

> Upon the whole New Holland, tho in every respect the most barren countrey I have seen, is not so bad but that between the productions of the sea and Land a company of People who should have the misfortune of being shipwreckd upon it might support themselves, even by the resources that we have seen.[1]

Perhaps Banks viewed any proposed penal colony as less demanding on the resources of the land than the requirements of the survivors of a shipwreck.

The question of the increasing number of malefactors in England had still not been resolved in 1785, and the prisoner population had become an acute problem. In August 1786 the *Heads of a Plan for effectually disposing of convicts, by Establishment of a Colony in New South Wales* was promulgated and preparations were begun for the selection of vessels, crew, and supplies.

In early 1787 Captain Arthur Phillip was appointed to command the voyage to New Holland and subsequently to take control of the establishment of the penal colony. The fleet, made up of two Admiralty vessels, six convict transports, and three storeships, sailed from England on 13 May 1787 and touched at the Canary Islands, Rio de Janeiro, and the Cape of Good Hope before arriving off Van Diemens Land on 7 January 1788. From there it was another two weeks before the vessels were anchored in Botany Bay. During their calls at ports en route, seeds and plants were taken aboard the transports, plants which were considered suitable for the new colony: coffee, cocoa, cotton, bananas, oranges, lemons, guavas, tamarind, and prickly pear at Rio de Janeiro; fig, bamboo, sugar cane, quince, apple, pear, and strawberries at Cape Town.

Less than a week after the arrival of that first fleet at Botany Bay, the crews and convicts were incredulous at the news that two sails were to be seen trying to round the head of Cape Solander. After some initial confusion it was determined that the vessels were French, the exploratory expedition of La Pérouse. At Botany Bay it was apparent that Banks' 1770 assessment of the area had been accurate. As a result of finding little fresh water, no suitable farmland, and an exposed anchorage in Botany Bay, Phillip led the British vessels north to Port Jackson where conditions were found to be more advantageous. The convicts soon disembarked and were employed in organising the rudimentary camp that was later transformed into the town of Sydney. Although scurvy had been virtually absent during the voyage out to New Holland, it put in an appearance soon after arrival. Wild celery, 'Apium australe' (Apium prostratum), spinach, 'Tetragonia expansa' (Tetragonia tetragonioides), and parsley, 'Apium tenuifolium' (Apium leptophyllum), were used by the naval surgeons to combat the disease but with little success, although the native currant, Leptomeria acida, known also as the acid berry proved a partial anodyne.

Almost immediately the strange fauna of the land ensnared the attention of the individuals with sufficient time and training to look about them, primarily the ship's surgeons. Some of the animals, notably the kangaroo and opossum, were familiar from the prints and engravings resulting from Cook's voyages, while others were totally new.

Arthur Bowes Smyth, surgeon on the convict transport the Lady Penrhyn, commented in his journal for 21 January 1788:

> There are great Nos. of Kangaroos but so extreamly shy that 'tis no easy matter to get near enough to them even to shoot them . . . As there is a most exact print of this uncommon Animal in Capt. Cook's Acct. of this Country I shall not take the trouble to describe it.[2]

'Vulpine opossum'
Anon. The voyage of Governor Phillip to Botany Bay. 1789.
Trichosurus vulpecula

Nevertheless Smyth sketched a copy of the kangaroo print from Hawkesworth's volume of Cook's voyages and included it in the fair copy of his journal along with other sketches of the fauna. At the end of February an emu, Dromaius novaehollandiae, the 'New Holland Cassowary' of John White and the 'ostrich' of Phillip, was shot and brought back to the nascent town.

A sketch of the animal was prepared by Lieutenant Watts, after which the bird was skinned, and the skin preserved in spirits until it could be shipped back to England as a present from Governor Phillip to the Home-Secretary Lord Sydney. Lord Sydney exhibited the skin to Joseph Banks through whose offices it was eventually deposited in the collection of the anatomist and naturalist, John Hunter. By the time that Arthur Smyth left the settlement in a returning vessel of the First Fleet in April of 1788 after a stay of three months in New South Wales, he was able to list the following animals known in the colony: kangaroos, dogs, rats, opossums, flying squirrels, lizards, snakes, emus, many species of birds, and eight to ten species of ants. Smyth was an avid entomologist which accounts for his particular interest in the insects. On his departure, Smyth took with him to England several young kangaroos preserved in spirits.

While the settlement was being constructed, Phillip took two small boats up the coast to investigate Broken Bay and later walked along the coast north to Dee Why Lagoon. Here on 15 April they caught their first sight of the black swan, although the surgeon-general of the colony, John White, was not convinced:

> Our frequent firing, however, caused them to take wing, . . . Had we not raised them, we should certainly have concluded that they were black swans; but their flight gave us an opportunity of seeing some white feathers, which terminated the tip of each wing; in every other part they were perfectly black.[3]

John White, although lacking any formal training in natural history, was to become a diligent collector during the early years of the colony. At the behest of Thomas Wilson, a friend of White's in London and an amateur naturalist, White kept a diary of the daily life in the new colony in which he included his observations on natural history, and it was this diary, edited by Wilson, that was to become an important source of information on the first few years of New South Wales.

On the same journey to Dee Why Lagoon, the party came across a bird which White called the 'great brown King's Fisher' later to become more widely known as the kookaburra, Dacelo gigas. In addition, White saw a bird he mistook for the Banksian cockatoo, several 'blue bellied parrots', (Trichoglossus haematodus or rainbow lorikeet); the 'anomalous hornbill', (Scythrops novaehollandiae or channel-billed cuckoo); the 'wattled bee-

'Cassowary'
White. *Journal of a voyage to New South Wales*. 1790.
Dromaius novaehollandiae

'Blue-bellied parrot'
Anon. *The voyage of Governor Phillip to Botany Bay.* 1789.
Trichoglossus haematodus

eater', (*Anthochaera carunculata* or red wattlebird); and the 'gold winged pigeon', (*Phaps chalcoptera* or common bronzewing).

White and the other surgeons had increasing problems with scurvy and dysentery spreading among the warders and convicts, and this necessarily had a more urgent claim on their time than did their natural history interests. Both White and Denis Considen, the assistant-surgeon of the transport *Scarborough*, laid claim to the discovery that the gum from certain indigenous trees, especially the 'red gum', *Angophora costata*, proved efficacious against dysentery. This initiated the first dispute over scientific priority only a few months after the colony had been founded. Phillip wrote in his journal:

> In the dysentery, the red gum of the tree which princi-
> pally abounds on this coast, was found a very powerful
> remedy. The yellow gum has been discovered to possess
> the same property, but in an inferior degree.[4]

Samples of the yellow gum were sent back to England where Dr Blane at St Thomas' Hospital used the gum in the cure of 'fluxes' such as dysentery and other diarrhoeic disorders.

Considen, in a letter to Joseph Banks, claimed the discovery of the medicinal powers of the gum as well as that of the native sarsaparilla. Native sarsaparilla, *Smilax glyciphylla*, was referred to by the colonists as 'sweet tea' and was much sought after to relieve the tedium of their preserved provisions, for its taste bore a resemblance to liquorice. In his journal White noted its use as a medicine and antiscorbutic, but again his claim to its discovery was disputed by Considen.

While the convicts struggled to build a town out of the wilderness, one of the earliest actions of Phillip was to send a party of convicts and a detachment of marines to settle Norfolk Island. Here the British Admiralty hoped to obtain supplies of masts from the Norfolk Island pines *Araucaria heterophylla* and sailcloth and cordage from the flax that Cook had reported growing there. Cook had sighted and named Norfolk Island on 8 October 1774 while aboard the *Resolution* on the second of his voyages to the Pacific. The vessel *Supply* left Sydney Cove for Norfolk Island on 14 February 1788 and was back again on 19 March bearing reports of magnificent pines and luxuriant soil. Although unable to visit Norfolk Island himself, Phillip heard the reports:

> The woods are inhabited by innumerable tribes of birds,
> many of them very gay in plumage. The most useful are
> pigeons, which are very numerous, and a bird not unlike
> the Guinea fowl, except in colour (being chiefly
> white) . . .[5]

'Norfolk Island Petrel'
Anon. *The Voyage of Governor Phillip to Botany Bay*, 1789.
Pterodroma melanopus

The then-numerous pigeon was probably *Hemiphaga novaeseelandiae*, now extinct on the island.

On the outward passage to Norfolk Island, Lieutenant Henry Ball, in charge of the *Supply*, discovered and named Lord Howe Island on 17 February but was unable to land for lack of a good anchorage. On the return trip, he and his crew were able to effect a landing and explore the island. A profusion of turtles as well as a number of bird species were found. The white gallinale, *Porphyrio albus*, endemic to Lord Howe Island was seen; this bird is now extinct, most having been killed for food by hungry sailors, as was the Lord Howe Island pigeon, *Columba vitiensis*.

On 5 May 1788 the convict transport *Lady Penrhyn* left Port Jackson to return to England. Having heard of Ball's discovery, she called at Lord Howe Island on the passage and Lieutenant Watts recorded:

> The inhabitants of this island were all of the feathered
> tribe, and the chief of these was the ganet, of which
> there were prodigious numbers, and it should seem that
> this is the time of their incubation, the females being all
> on their nests: these are places simply hollowed in the
> sand, there not being a single quadruped that could be
> found upon the island to disturb them . . . Very large
> pigeons were also met with in great plenty; likewise
> beautiful parrots and parroquets; a new species,
> apparently, of the coote, and also of the rail, and magpie;
> and a most beautiful small bird, brown, with a yellow
> brest and yellow on the wing; it seemed to be a species of
> hummingbird . . .[6]

LEFT: In flower   ABOVE: In fruit

'*Banksia serrata*'
White. *Journal of a voyage to New South Wales.* 1790.
Banksia serrata

The next vessel to leave the colony was the transport *Alexander* which sailed from Port Jackson on 13 July 1788 bearing dispatches from Governor Phillip to the Colonial Office in England. Despite pressing problems in setting up the colony, Phillip found time to comment on the botany of the region in his dispatches and included samples of seeds, red gum, yellow gum, flax, and emu feathers to be sent to Joseph Banks. Phillip complained in a letter to Banks that he would have sent him a much larger consignment of seeds but that the person employed to collect them had not done so at the proper time and it was now winter. He requested that Banks share some of the seeds with Lord Sydney and Mr Nepean, the powers in the Home Office.

In his dispatch to Lord Sydney, Phillip noted:

> . . . and here, my Lord, I must beg leave to observe, with regret, that being myself without the smallest knowledge of botany, I am without one botanist, or even an intelligent gardener, in the colony; it is not therefore in my power to give more than a very superficial account of the produce of this country, which has such variety of plants that I cannot, with all my ignorance, help being convinced that it merits the attention of the naturalist and the botanist.[7]

In addition to sending Lord Sydney the emu skin and seeds, Phillip also enclosed a preserved kangaroo and forwarded some birds from Lord Howe Island to Lady

'White fulica'
White. *Journal of a voyage to New South Wales.* 1790.
Porphyrio albus

Chatham.

Some of the seeds that Phillip sent to Banks ultimately found their way to James Lee, a nursery owner and well known botanist. Co-owner and principle botanist of the Vineyard Nursery, Lee had in 1760 published *An Introduction to Botany* which was largely a translation of Linnaeus' *Philosophia Botanica*. When Lee and his silent partner, Lewis Kennedy, established their nursery, they almost immediately started introducing foreign plants to England, marketing them to the landed gentry who dabbled in botany. *Hortus Kewensis* lists among the plants that Lee introduced into England in 1788: *Banksia oblongifolia*, *B. serrata*, *Fabricia laevigata*, *Lambertia formosa*, and *Melaleuca armillaris*, all of which must have come from the seeds sent by Phillip to Banks. The saw-leaved banksia was the first plant to be successfully raised from this batch of seeds.

When the colonisation of New Holland had first been proposed, James Lee compiled a pamphlet entitled *Rules for collecting and preserving seeds from Botany Bay* in which he recommended the following:

> In a country where all the plants are new to a European Botanist, and unknown to the Collector, the best method is to select the most beautiful, or those that are known to be of use in dying, mechanics, food, or physic. Trees and shrubs are more particularly wanted; and herbaceous plants for their beauty or the sweetness of their flowers.
>
> The Collector should observe every seed be perfectly ripened before it is gathered, and well dried, before it is folded up in the paper where it is to remain; every kind should be kept to itself . . .[8]

Lee went on to recommend the use of alternate layers of oakum in packing the seeds to protect them from the ravages of insects, and suggested enclosing the entire parcel in oilskins to keep out moisture. Since flax was of special interest to the Admiralty, he suggested that it be planted in boxes of earth lined with oyster shells and with holes placed in the bottom to promote good drainage.

By July 1788 the settlers were not only shooting the local fauna for food but also domesticating them as pets. A young dingo obtained from Aborigines was brought to the settlement and attempts were made to tame it. Young kangaroos were occasionally brought back after hunting expeditions and these the settlers tried to rear but without success, lacking adequate food for the animals. White continued to add to his collection of birds, and in the following month he obtained specimens of a knob-fronted bee-eater, *Philemon* sp., as well as the sacred kingfisher, *Halcyon sancta*.

In August of 1788 Phillip, White, and several others examined the coastline between Manly Cove and Broken Bay. White was able to collect twenty-five species of plants on the return journey as they trouped down the shore. The specimens were forwarded to Thomas Wilson in England in due course.

The next set of dispatches to be sent to England left on the *Golden Grove* on 19 November. Phillip enclosed for Joseph Banks samples of the Norfolk Island flax and a supposed pepper plant that had also been collected from the island, as well as a mineral sample thought to contain lead, and a vial of eucalyptus oil. Phillip again complained to Banks that he would have been able to send a wider variety of seeds to him except that the man he had employed for the work had sold the seeds to people returning on the convict transports. In the coming years the trade in seeds, live plants, and animals assumed huge proportions. Phillip wrote to Banks about the problem again while the Judge-Advocate David Collins lamented that there were convicts who could always be found collecting plants and animals to sell to those embarked on the returning convict transports.

Even naturalists sent out by Banks to collect in the colony feared that their shipments of specimens bound for England would be pillaged of the best samples. Such was the demand that when the potted plants died during shipment, eager nurserymen carefully cultivated the soil in the hope of germinating a few seeds that might have remained buried there. Phillip promised Banks that he would renew his efforts to supply him with seeds but suggested that Banks should send his botanical collector at the Cape of Good Hope, Francis Masson, to New South Wales. Phillip felt that the variety of plants

'Norfolk Island Flying Squirrel'
Anon. *The Voyage of Governor Phillip to Botany Bay*. 1789.
Petaurus norfolcensis

48

in the colony far exceeded the number that might have been found in other countries.

On the recommendation of Abbé Mongez, the naturalist who had accompanied La Pérouse's expedition, Phillip included a sample of clay thought to be suitable for china with the same dispatches of 19 November. Banks in turn forwarded the sample to Josiah Wedgwood, who confirmed its fitness for porcelain. Not only was the clay adequate for china, but after a number of chemical tests on the sample Wedgwood considered that he had discovered a new mineral in it, a mineral that he promptly named sydneia. Wedgwood subsequently published a paper 'On the analysis of a Mineral Substance from New South Wales' in the *Philosophical Transactions of the Royal Society* detailing his chemical analysis of the substance. The mineral sample was to be widely distributed by Banks to various people: the British scientist Joseph Priestley, who, when his laboratory was destroyed in the anti-liberal Birmingham riots of 1791, was offered replacements of sand and clay from Sydney by Banks; Stanesby Alchorne, the assay master of the Royal Mint, who solicited a sample for his own collection; and Johann Blumenbach, a German naturalist who had engaged in correspondence with Banks since the early 1780s and who later described and named the platypus. By the year 1798 the existence of sydneia had been disputed by the German chemist Martin Klaproth, who failed to find it in a second sample, but the English scientist William Nicholson defended his friend Wedgwood's analysis with the suggestion that the two original samples were different. That same year the English chemist Charles Hatchett repeated Wedgwood's analysis on the remainder of the original sample and concluded that Wedgwood had been led astray by impurities in his analytical reagents; there was no such mineral as sydneia. Later in 1801 another sample of sand from New Holland given by Banks to the Irish chemist-mineralogist Richard Chenevix did yield a new mineral, menaccanite, a variety of ilmenite.

Before the year 1788 was out, Banks was again sent specimens from New South Wales, this time from Denis Considen. Considen sent nine stuffed birds, a preserved flying squirrel, kangaroo skins, two live opossums, two live parrots, one of which was a present for Banks' daughter, samples of red and yellow gum, and flower seeds. Considen desired to become a supplier of natural history curiosities to Banks and offered to send him seeds at every possible opportunity. Phillip also sent off more specimens, but to the Admiralty this time. Although there was by now disillusionment with the Norfolk pine as a source of Royal Navy masts, Phillip forwarded more spars for Admiralty testing.

In 1789 Gilbert White, a close friend of Banks, published his *The Natural History and Antiquities of Selborne*, a seminal work in natural history literature.

The Tabuan Parrot, Female

Although there was already a market for the published journals of exploratory voyages and the natural history contained therein, it existed among the upper strata of society. With the publication of White's book the day of the popular natural history volume had arrived, and this popularisation provided the impetus for the publication of a number of natural history works on New Holland.

Another publication with a large market among the scientifically inclined was the 1789 edition of Linnaeus' *Systema Naturae* which first mentioned some of the novel animals to be found in New Holland, those obtained on the voyages of James Cook. Also in 1789, George Shaw, one of the prominent naturalists of the day, began publication of his *Naturalist's Miscellany*, a massive undertaking that was to eventually involve twenty-four volumes and over 1,000 colour plates illustrated by Frederick Nodder. In the first volume in 1789 was a plate and description of '*Motacilla superba*', said to have been painted from a specimen brought back from a recent voyage to New South Wales.

On 27 April 1789, Joseph Banks wrote to the under-secretary of the Home Office proposing that the *Guardian*, a transport and storeship bound for New South Wales, be fitted with racks of pots to enable agriculturally valuable plants to be sent out to New Holland. The return journey would in turn bring live plants back to England to grace the Royal Botanic Gardens at Kew. A positive response must have been forthcoming, for on 7 June Banks was writing to William Grenville, head of the Home Office, indicating his agreement in helping with the arrangements to send live specimens of those plants that could not be taken as seeds to New South Wales. Banks now suggested that a small 'coach' or greenhouse be erected on the *Guardian*'s deck to protect the plants. Grenville readily agreed to this plan, and in turn recommended to the Admiralty that one or two gardeners be assigned to the *Guardian* as superintendents of the convicts and to provide the botanical skills Phillip had requested in earlier dispatches. As the gardeners were to remain in the colony, they were to teach a sailor how to care for plants; this impressed student of botany would then assume responsibility for the plants destined for Kew on the return journey. Two gardeners were appointed to the position of superintendents, James Smith and George Austin, both having acquired their training at the Royal Gardens at Kew. Banks, as he was prone to do throughout his life, gave very specific instructions to Smith and Austin, ranging from the care of the plants to moralistic homilies inveighing against drunkenness. Banks' usual injunction against collecting for others beside himself and Kew was ignored by Austin who informed Smith

'The Tabuan Parrot'
White. *Journal of a voyage to New South Wales*. 1790.
Alisterus scapularis

Top:
'Pennantian Parrot'
White. *Journal of a voyage to New South Wales*. 1790.
Platycercus elegans

Bottom:
'Poto Roo'
White. *Journal of a voyage to New South Wales*. 1790.
Potorous tridactylus

during the voyage that he had several orders to send seeds to nurserymen back in England. Austin expected to make a great deal of money out of this arrangement and tried to induce Smith to join the scheme. Smith refused to break faith with his employer and wrote to Banks of Austin's intentions and preference for the sailors' company to that of the plants, much to the detriment of the specimens in his charge.

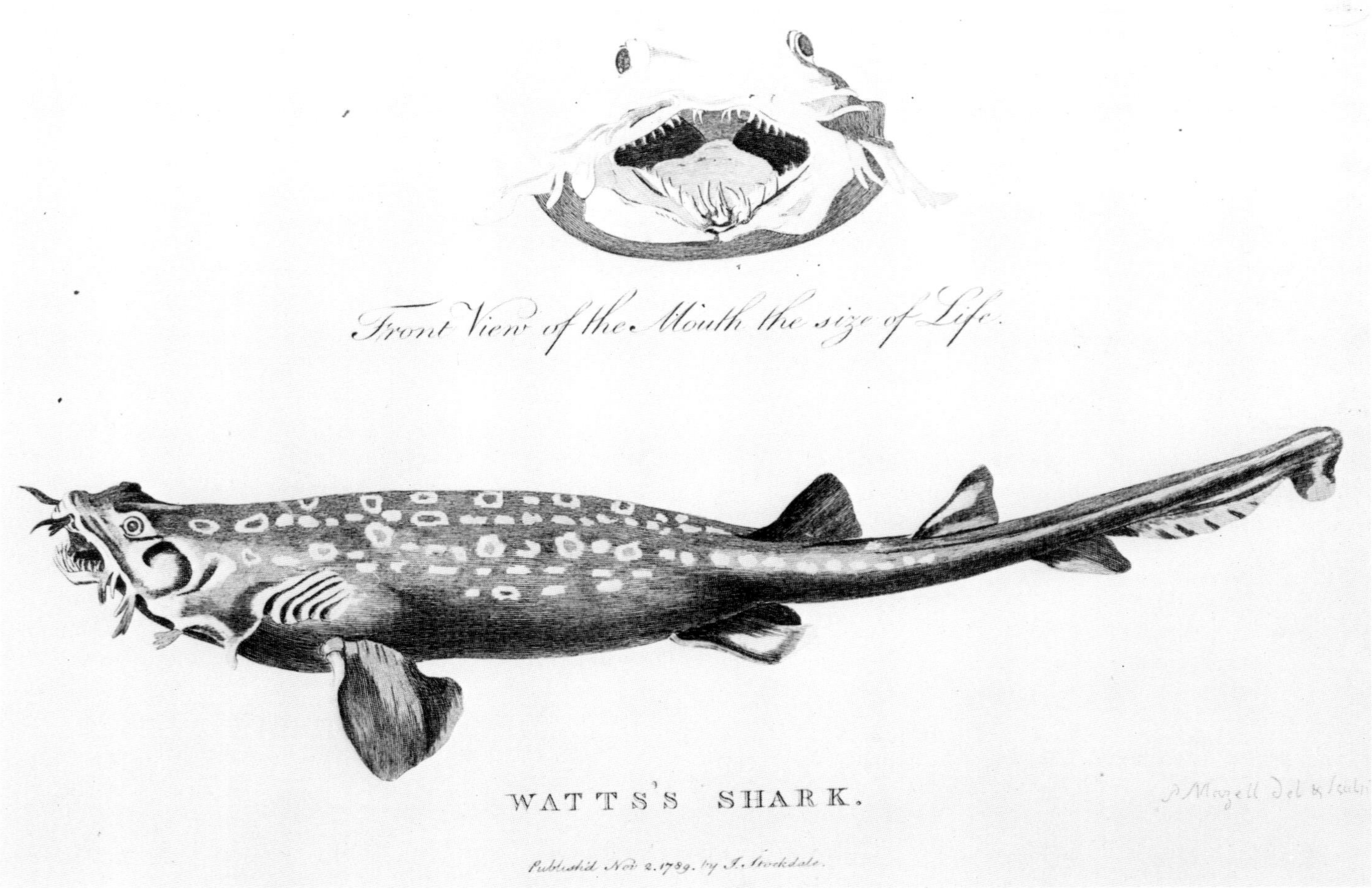

Front View of the Mouth the size of Life.

WATTS'S SHARK.

P. Mazell del & sculp

Published Nov 2. 1789. by J. Stockdale.

Austin's abdication of his responsibilities was to be of little consequence as the name of their vessel, the *Guardian*, was to prove a misnomer. On 23 December, while trying to round the Cape of Good Hope, the *Guardian* struck an iceberg; the two gardeners abandoned ship in a small boat and were never seen again. The *Guardian* was not mortally wounded and managed to limp back to the Cape where she was beached and abandoned. The other superintendents, none of whom were gardeners but who had remained with the vessel, eventually took passage to New South Wales in another ship. Phillip was not to receive his botanist or gardener for some time.

Toward the middle of 1789, the first of several volumes that described the journey of the First Fleet and the initial period of the settlement of New South Wales was published. Written by Watkin Tench, a captain of the marines sent to superintend the convicts, the volume, *A Narrative of the Expedition to Botany Bay*, contained a chapter on 'The Face of the Country; its Productions, Climate, &c.' which summarised Tench's observations on the natural history of the land. Tench held an ambivalent view of the botany of New Holland, but he, too, added a plea for a botanist to be sent to the colony:

> In those places where trees are scarce, a variety of flowering shrubs abound, most of them entirely new to an European, and surpassing in beauty, fragrance, and number, all I ever saw in an uncultivated state . . . The species of trees are few, and, I am concerned to add, the wood universally of so bad a grain, as almost to preclude a possibility of using it . . .[9]

But about the fauna he was more enthusiastic:

> To the naturalist this country holds out many invitations. — Birds, though not remarkably numerous, are in great variety, and of the most exquisite beauty of plumage . . . but the bird which principally claims attention is, a species of ostrich, approaching nearer to the emu of South America than any other we know of . . . Of the quadrupeds, except the kangaroo, I have little to say. The few we met with are almost invariably of the

opossum tribe, but even these do not abound. To beasts of prey we are utter strangers, nor have we yet any cause to believe that they exist in the country . . . Of the natural history of the kangaroo we are still very ignorant. We may, venture to pronounce this animal, a new species of opossum . . .[10]

Whether the colonists had a copy of published journals from Cook's first voyage is unknown. Tench did mention that he and the commander of the French exploratory expedition, La Pérouse, compared a kangaroo with the plate in Hawkesworth's volume and found it suitable for giving a general impression of the animal but inadequate for a scientific portrayal, hardly surprising since the English artist, George Stubbs, had to depend on Sydney Parkinson's sketches as the model for his painting. It seems probable that somewhere in the First Fleet there was a volume of Goldsmith's *History of the Earth, and Animated Nature*, published in 1774, for Tench made reference to it. Goldsmith's book, although treated with disdain by savants of the late eighteenth century, was one of the popular volumes that dealt with natural history.

Tench's journal was not the only published description of the colony's early months. An anonymous editor at the publishing firm of Stockdale compiled a volume from a variety of sources but primarily from Governor Arthur Phillip's dispatches to England. This volume, also published in 1789 under the title *The Voyage of Governor Phillip to Botany Bay* was released soon after Tench's book. Unlike Tench's volume which was presumably written by Tench while in the colony, the Phillip volume had the benefit of several sources, some of the leading artists of the day to illustrate it, and the expertise of such naturalists as Joseph Banks and John Latham, both of whom were acknowledged by the publishers as having supplied drawings and descriptions for the volume.

The Phillip volume contained two chapters dealing with the fauna of New South Wales, each page of description usually accompanying an illustration of the animal. The plates were engraved either from drawings sent from the colony or in many cases from the specimens that were beginning to accrue in private collections in England. Included in the list of plates were mammals such as the native cat, drawn from a live specimen in England, the brushtail possum, and the squirrel-glider. Descriptions of the birds in the volume relied predominantly on those that had already been described in Latham's *General Synopsis of Birds* and included Latham's discussions from those volumes. Numbered among them were the rainbow lorikeet, the Australian king-parrot, the crimson rosella, the superb fairy-wren, and the sacred kingfisher, all of which were caught in the Port Jackson area. A later chapter appended at a subsequent stage in the compilation

The Peppermint Tree.

London, Published Dec: 29, 1789, by I. Debrett.

contained descriptions and plates of the red-tailed black-cockatoo, swift parrot, emu, purple swamphen, kookaburra, dingo, greater glider, and the wobbegong shark.

By the time of publication of *The Voyage of Governor Phillip to Botany Bay*, the list of specimens from New Holland, both alive and preserved, in England was large. As well as specimens of most of the above-named species, there were also said to be specimens of lizards and blue frogs in private collections, although the blue frogs appear to have been specimens of the green tree frog, *Litoria caerulea*, which had undergone a colour change while they were being preserved. To the live opossums and parrots that had been shipped back to Banks by Denis Considen, there had now been added at least two live dingoes and a pair of kangaroo rats.

Before the year was out, still another work was published which contained figures of various organisms collected from New South Wales. The specimens in this case were not collected by the colonists but originated from the various private collections that had grown up around the voyages of Byron, Wallis, Cook,

and other explorers of the Pacific. Thomas Martyn was inspired to publish his book *Universal Conchologist* by a collection of shells purchased from the crew of the returned vessels. Martyn hired young boys to hand-colour the plates in each volume, and after some preliminary training the acolytes toiled away in Dickensian fashion. The ensuing two-volume sets contained eleven species gathered from sites along the coast of New Holland.

For geology, or the mineral kingdom of natural history as it was then termed, the late 1780s were times of exciting speculation. Two opposing theories of geology which were to dominate the field for the next thirty years and find proponents even in the distant colony of New South Wales were first published during this time.

In the 1780s the German geologist Abraham Werner proposed a theory of the formation of the earth's surface dependent on all geological strata having been laid down by crystallisation from a universal ocean. Werner's theory, termed the 'neptunian model', postulated that before any living creatures appeared on the earth's surface the entire globe was covered by a deep ocean. From the elements contained in solution in the water, the first minerals crystallised out as granite which Werner visualised as forming the base rock of all other strata. Subsequent to the crystallisation of the granite, the level of the ocean fell, the water decomposing into hydrogen and oxygen and thus forming the earth's atmosphere. As other minerals crystallised out

FACING PAGE:
'Peppermint tree'
White. *Journal of a Voyage to New South Wales*. 1790.
Eucalyptus piperita

BELOW:
'Hepoona roo'
White. *Journal of a Voyage to New South Wales*. 1790.
Petaurus australis

C Catton Jun Delin

of the water they formed strata of gneiss, clay, and slate at different levels. Local chemical differences in the falling waters accounted for the inclusion of deposits of other rock types such as limestone that appeared within rock strata. In order to account for the various reworking and uplifting of geological formations that were evident to everybody, Werner was forced to postulate that the world ocean had not fallen once only but had risen and fallen several times, these fluctuations distorting the way the strata were laid down and nicely accounting for the trapping of organic fossils in rock and the deposition of sea shells on mountain tops. The all-encompassing world floods earned Werner's theory the title of catastrophic, but truly violent catastrophes such as volcanoes Werner dismissed as minor occur-rences attributable to the presence of vast underground beds of coal which, when set afire, melted the covering basalt to force eruptions.

The opposing theory of the formation of the earth's surface, propounded by the English physician-naturalist James Hutton, was called the vulcanist theory because it postulated the formation of minerals primarily through the action of fire and high temperatures. Hutton rejected the supposition that all minerals had crystallised out of solutions for he reasoned that not all minerals were soluble in water. Although agreeing with the first premise of Werner, that mineral strata had originally been deposited as unconsolidated material under water, in direct contrast to the Wernerian theory Hutton believed that fusion by heat had modified the minerals into their present state. This same heat also produced an expansion of the rock which elevated the strata to their present positions. Hutton envisioned the temperature-mediated process of the change from unconsolidated material on the ocean floor to solidified rock to be a continuous process, undergone over immeasurable periods of time; this led to his theory being called 'uniformitarism'.

Geologists for the next quarter of a decade were to divide themselves along the lines of neptunians and vulcanists, and advocates of both theories, as will be seen, carried the debate to New South Wales and used geological evidence from the colony to further their views.

In 1790 yet another journal appeared, this time that of the surgeon-general of the colony, John White. White's journal had been sent to England in November of 1788, there to be edited by Thomas Wilson who was able to enlist the services of several naturalists to polish the natural history sections of the journal which were added as an appendix to the main work, *Journal of a Voyage to New South Wales*. James Edward Smith contributed excerpts on different species of banksias; the tea-tree; the sweet tea plant, *Smilax glyciphylla*; the red gum, *Eucalyptus resinifera*; the yellow resin tree, *Xanthorrhoea resinosa*; and the peppermint tree,

Eucalyptus piperita, which White named for the oil he was able to extract from its leaves. White sent a bottle of this oil to Thomas Wilson, claiming that he found it to be beneficial in the treatment of 'cholickly complaints', more so than the oil of the English peppermint. Smith recognised that the peppermint tree of White was of the same genus that the Frenchman, L'Heritier, had described in his *Sertum Anglicum* under the name *Eucalyptus obliqua*, a plant being grown in English greenhouses.

Wilson was able to command the services of George Shaw and John Hunter to describe the zoological specimens. Shaw described the birds, reptiles, and fish although Wilson should perhaps have left the birds to John Latham as Shaw made a number of mistakes in assigning them to genera, but this would have been a difficult task for anyone working with unknown genera on the basis of inadequately preserved bird skins.

Dr John Hunter described the following mammals in the appendix: the brushtail possum, the dingo, the brushtail phascogale, a marsupial mouse, the quoll, which Hunter considered the same as the brushtail phascogale, a rat kangaroo, the greater glider, which Hunter correctly surmised to be able to glide similarly to the North American flying squirrel, and the kangaroo. The kangaroo somewhat baffled Hunter concerning its affinities to other animal groups as in reproductive anatomy it appeared similar to the possums, but in other respects was very different.

The illustrations in White's published journal also received expert attention; generally they were done by either Sarah Stone or Frederick Nodder. Nodder was already involved with George Shaw in the preparation of *Naturalist's Miscellany*, and Shaw may have suggested the utilisation of his talents. The plates were drawn from specimens sent by White to Wilson, either as preserved whole animals or as skins. After the specimens had been painted or sketched, they were deposited in the Leverian Museum.

Naturalist's Miscellany continued its publication run, and in 1790 both the kangaroo, '*Macropus giganteus*', and the red-tailed black-cockatoo, '*Psittacus magnificus*' (*Calyptorhynchus magnificus*), represented the New Holland fauna in this serial publication. Although other earlier names for the genus exist, *Macropus*, nominated in 1790, has been sanctioned by scientific nomenclature as the generic name of kangaroos. The French, however, were partial to the name '*Kangurus*' until the middle of the nineteenth century.

In March of 1790, Lord Grenville wrote to Arthur Phillip with the news that the Admiralty was fitting out an expedition to the north-west coast of North America. It was expected that the expedition would put into Port Jackson and unload stores before continuing on through the Pacific. Grenville also informed Phillip of the mutiny on the HMS *Bounty* under Lieutenant

Bligh and the possibility that a vessel sent to capture the mutineers might call at Port Jackson. Vancouver, the captain of the first ship referred to, did anchor off Van Diemens Land but bypassed Port Jackson; however HMS *Pandora*, the vessel which captured a number of the *Bounty*'s mutineers, did return to New Holland on its homeward passage if only to be wrecked trying to pass through the Great Barrier Reef at Pandora Passage.

On 19 April the disheartening news arrived that HMS *Sirius* had been wrecked on the shores of Norfolk Island. The loss of the *Sirius* was a terrible blow for the colony, for although no lives were lost it left Phillip with the *Supply* as his only vessel. Lieutenant Fowell, the second-lieutenant of the *Sirius*, lost not only his ship but also a collection of stuffed birds that he had been preparing for his father. If Norfolk Island proved treacherous to approaching vessels, other difficulties arose for the settlement there. A letter from an anonymous writer foresaw some of the problems that were to plague agriculture both there and on the mainland:

> Yet it (Norfolk Island) has its evils, three in number vizt., Blights, Grubs, and Paroquets . . . the Grubs, whose unlimitted Numbers and Mischief are beyond account . . . Paroquets make vast havoc, devouring the Seeds of all Grain.[11]

Yet not everyone was disillusioned with the country. Towards the end of July, Captain W. Hill, second-captain of the New South Wales Corps, wrote back to England from Sydney about his posting:

> Here is an ample field for the botanist and naturalist, the most beautiful shrubs, and the greatest variety of any in the world. The plumage of the birds is uncommonly beautiful, some of which (as I am informed) are a new species, or rather nondescripts . . . I shall collect various seeds, birds, plumage . . .[12]

Arthur Phillip was also using collections of the natural curiosities of New South Wales to mollify persons of influence in England, this time it was a pair of pigeons sent to Lady Chatham. The shipment of prize specimens of both living plants and animals to friends and patrons was to become a recurrent theme throughout the correspondence of the early governors of the colony of New South Wales.

In October of 1790, one David Burton made arrangements to sail on the storeship, *Gorgon*, for New South Wales. Sent out as a superintendent of convicts, Burton had higher aspirations than the mere direction of convict labour. Before embarking on the *Gorgon*, Burton corresponded with Joseph Banks requesting a letter of recommendation to Governor Phillip. Burton was afraid that in his position as superintendent he would have no occasion for the collection of plant specimens and asked Banks to intercede for him to be allowed time to collect natural history specimens. Primarily employed to direct convict labour, Burton obviously misunderstood his position for in a letter sent in January of the following year he wrote: 'I understood all along that I was to be authorized to collect for His Majesty's Royal Botanic Garden . . .' and concluded that the salary of £50 per annum provided by his wardenship would hardly keep him in necessities.[13] Banks replied curtly that there was never any expectation of Burton being employed as a collector for Kew; Banks, however, was willing to employ Burton as a private collector at a rate of £20 a year in addition to his salary as a super-intendent. Burton accepted the offer which Banks amended to stipulate that Burton would be expected to collect for Banks and Banks alone, a less-than-subtle reminder that Burton was not to collect for his relative through marriage, James Lee of the Kennedy and Lee Nursery. Despite Banks's injunction, Lee may also have employed Burton while he was in New South Wales, for certainly during the next few years the Kennedy and Lee Nursery continually added to their stock of New Holland plant species. In 1790 they introduced such plants as *Crowea armillaris*, *Grevillea buxifolia* and *G. sericea* to England, but as these specimens were added to their catalogue were all well before Burton arrived in New South Wales, they were probably grown from seeds sent by White, Phillip, and others.

Natural history in the colony in the early part of 1791 was concerned very much with the flora and fauna of Norfolk Island. After the vessel *Sirius* foundered in mid–1790 while landing supplies on the island, the crew was stranded there for some months. George Raper, a midshipman from the *Sirius*, along with others of the crew and officers put their enforced stay on the island to good use. Raper had sailed out on the *Sirius* with the First Fleet and during his free time was able to exercise his talent for painting. Much of his subject matter included the plants and animals of the new land, especially the birds. While on Norfolk Island he continued his watercolours, leaving a number of paintings that have become valuable to ornithologists as they represent the only illustrations of bird species such as the Lord Howe Island pigeon, *Columba vitiensis*, that have since become extinct.

The large numbers of birds that annually nested on Norfolk Island attracted the attention of Raper and others. Captain David Blackburn of the *Supply* wrote to a friend, R. Knight:

> . . . it being the season when Immense Quantities of Birds Resort to the Highest part of the Island to Deposit their Eggs which are as large as a Goose's I am Informd that upwards of 5000 birds have been taken in one night.[14]

'Crinum'
Raper. Unpublished. Courtesy of Mitchell Library.

'Clematis'
Raper. Unpublished. Courtesy of Mitchell Library.

During the year 1791 a new occupation evidenced itself along the coasts of the colony. Vessels returning to England had brought word of sizable schools of whales to be found off the southern shores of New South Wales. American and British whalers were quick to capitalise on these reports and soon vessels originally bound for the west coast of North America were calling at Port Jackson. Although they also sighted large pods of whales, the ventures were not always successful due to the great wastage involved—for example, of seven whales struck by two vessels only two of the whales were landed.

In late September the vessel bearing David Burton arrived in Port Jackson and the colony had its first 'professional', if part-time, naturalist. December saw another round of letter writing by the colonial officers. Phillip in a private letter to Grenville indicated that:

. . . an animal known in England by the name of kangaroo had been put aboard the Supply, as I presumed that so uncommon an animal might not be judged improper to be sent to his Majesty.[15]

A second kangaroo was later put on board the returning *Gorgon* should the first not survive the voyage back to England, which indeed was the case. If Phillip wrote terse dispatches to his superiors at the Home Office, his letters to Joseph Banks were both longer and more informative. By the returning *Gorgon*, Phillip sent a letter to Banks which covered a range of natural history. He acquainted Banks with the fact that there were sixty tubs of live plants on the *Gorgon* for him containing 221 mature plants as well as seeds. Most of the plants had already flowered in the pots so that they were in good condition, although the long exposure to salt air on the voyage to Europe would change that. Realising the necessity of not seeming to ignore his superiors, Phillip asked Banks to forward a few seeds in his name to Lord Sydney, Mr Nepean, and Mr Rose of the Treasury, while the skin of a black swan was to be forwarded to Mr Pitt, and the kangaroo already mentioned to be presented to the king. Phillip commented that the newly arrived Burton would be useful in obtaining collections and closed with the statement that he was sending Banks a drawing of a 'war-ret-tah', (*Telopea speciosissima*), some plants of which were included in the tubs. Since the First Fleet had arrived in New South Wales, Phillip had ordered that drawings be made of the plants and animals of the colony; by now some 200 had been completed. These illustrations were probably done by a variety of artists, including George Raper, John Hunter, and an unknown artist usually referred to as the 'Port Jackson painter'.

Also on board the *Gorgon* was a letter from David Burton to Banks. Whether the plants that the vessel carried were collected by Burton or somebody in Phillip's employ, both implied that they were responsible for the shipment. If indeed the plants had flowered in their tubs, it is unlikely that Burton had collected them as he had only been in the colony but a few months at this point. Burton enclosed a list of the specimens and promised to replace any damaged en route. He could hardly have been happy in his position as an overseer of the convict population for in this same letter he implored Banks' help in obtaining the appointment of surveyor-general to the colony, as the previous incumbent was considering retirement.

In the year 1791 in England, the second volume of *Naturalist's Miscellany* was completed, the initial sections having been published the previous year. Included were four animals from New Holland: '*Psittacus glorious*', the splendid parrot; '*Chaetodon armatus*', the long-spined chaetodon; *Petaurus australis*, the 'flying squirrel' or yellow-bellied glider; and '*Lacerta platura*', the broad-tailed lizard.

In March of that year a review of John White's *Journal of a Voyage to New South Wales* appeared in the Monthly Review. The reviewer noted the spate of publications dealing with New South Wales since the colony's foundation but considered White's journal to fill a need, especially with regard to natural history.

By 1792 the situation of the colony had started to ease in comparison to the first desperate years. Ship-loads of convicts and much-needed supplies had arrived and agricultural attempts were beginning to meet with limited success. In his dispatch of 19 March 1792, Governor Phillip wrote to Henry Dundas of the Home Office that he had had the quality of the soil around the colony assessed by one of the convict superintendents who had been brought up as a gardener. This, of course, was David Burton; in a report to Phillip dated

24 February, Burton wrote:

> . . . I have attended to the land at and round Parramatta, . . . the land is excellent. It is a black rich light soil, . . . I beg leave to observe here that where the different species of red gum-trees grow the earth has a great portion of oils mixed with it, and unless the ground is properly worked and turned over to meliorate and dissolve those oils, the first crop will come to little account.[16]

Concurrently Burton also wrote to Banks about his recently completed report on the soil of the colony noting that Banks would be able to evaluate the quality

Top and Bottom:
'Plant'
Doody. Unpublished. Courtesy of Mitchell Library.

of the soil himself from the quantity contained in the pots in which live plants were shipped to him. Burton had collected more specimens for Banks but was unable to include the fifty tubs on board the *Pitt* due to restrictions of space on that vessel. He was able to send the stalled shipment on the subsequent returning vessel, the *Atlantic*, along with seeds and insect specimens.

The plant tubs for the live shipment of specimens usually consisted of boxes approximately 1·25 metres by ·5 metre by ·5 metre, which, if half filled with soil, could conveniently be carried by two men by the rope handles attached to the sides. Board hoops were often nailed to the sides of the boxes, arching over them, and either twine or a canvas cover was tied to the hoops to form a protective webbing against seabirds and the various pets carried aboard ship. The boxes were normally carried on the poop deck of the vessel, or if the collector could prevail on an indulgent captain, the plants gained the protection of the ship's great cabin. The canvas covers on the deck-housed boxes had to be kept on the majority of the time to ward off saltwater spray, but on occasion had to be removed to allow the plants access to direct sunlight. If, as was so often the case, there was no botanically minded person aboard, the plants were often ignored for extended periods of time rendering their chances of survival slim: frequently less than one in a hundred plants survived the voyage. Seeds stood a better chance of survival which accounted for the great importance placed on them by both the myriad suppliers and receivers.

During the 1790s, James Lee was still receiving a steady flow of seeds either directly from Burton or indirectly from Banks; throughout this period his nursery was able to keep up a steady introduction of new exotics from New South Wales, including *Sowerbaea*. Another of Lee's suppliers was Colonel William Paterson who regularly corresponded with Lee and sent him samples both of the silky emboth, *Grevillea sericea*, and the slender-stemmed pogonia.

In April of 1792 the career of the first naturalist sent out to the colony came to an abrupt end just over six months after it had commenced. In Collins' account of that month he reported:

> Mr. Burton, in order to have a better view of them (ducks), got upon the stump of a tree, and, resting his hand upon the muzzle of his piece, raised himself by its assistance as high as he was able . . . By some motion of this unfortunate young man the piece went off, and the contents, entering at his wrist, forced their way up between the two bones of his right arm . . .[17]

The accident occurred on 7 April and Burton was to die from the wound six days later. Despite the short period Burton had spent in the colony, he obviously

'The Pompadour Parrot'
Shaw. *Museum Leverianum*. 1792.
Prosopeia tabuensis

impressed many individuals there. Phillip in his correspondence wrote that he could not replace Burton; David Collins echoed these sentiments when he stated:

> This young man, on account of the talents he possessed as a botanist, and the services which he was capable of rendering in the surveying line, could be but ill spared in this settlement.[18]

Among Burton's effects were to be found the accoutrements of an early collector: a thermometer, insect collecting apparatus, specimen boxes, a drawing book, paints and some sketches, and of course the many specimens of plants and insects that Burton had accumulated but not yet forwarded to Banks.

In late 1791 Colonel William Paterson had arrived in New South Wales, a member of that bastion of free enterprise in the colony, the New South Wales Corps. On his arrival he was assigned to command the detachment of troops on Norfolk Island, where to occupy his time, he continued an earlier interest in natural history. Paterson had established his credentials as an amateur naturalist over ten years previously when he sent plant specimens to Joseph Banks while stationed in Madras,

'*Psittacus splendidus*'
Shaw. *Museum Leverianum*. 1792.
Platycercus elegans

India. Before embarking for New South Wales,
Paterson requested Banks to obtain for him
membership in the Royal Society, but Banks suggested
that Paterson's application would be more successful if
he waited until he had furthered the cause of natural
history somehow. Paterson was eventually to gain the
coveted prize of membership, but not until 1797.

   After his arrival on Norfolk Island, Paterson began
his natural history collections and in May of 1792

dispatched a consignment of plant specimens to Banks.
Paterson indicated that a number of the specimens were
probably undescribed and although his health had not
been very good he ambitiously hoped to send a
specimen of every plant on the island by the next vessel
to return to England. Included with the first shipment
of plants were a number of drawings of Norfolk Island
plants which appear to be the work of John Doody, a
convict assigned to Paterson as a servant and who
accompanied him to Norfolk Island in 1791.

   Paterson's written descriptions of the plants revealed
that he was familiar with the terminology of botany and
taxonomy; however, Paterson's interest lay not in

botany alone, but in the entire field of natural history as evidenced by the concluding paragraph of his letter to Banks:

> In continuing my collection I have now begun to make my observations on the stratas and formation of the Island, some of the drawings will be found curious, after that is finished I shall give some account of the birds and fishes that frequent this place. I shall also continue my observations on the climate, soil, and carefully watch the progress & success of the ensuing crop.[19]

Philip Gidley King, then the commandant of Norfolk Island, praised Paterson in a letter to Banks for visiting everywhere on and under the island in search of specimens for Banks, this despite Paterson's ill health. King felt that before Paterson left the island Banks would have a fairly complete account of the natural history of Norfolk Island. Paterson continued to serve on Norfolk Island until 1793, making collections which were dispatched to various acquaintances in England. During this time he acquired the reputation as the foremost naturalist in the colony.

In this same year, 1792, a convict arrived in the colony who was to become one of the better known artists of the early colonial era, Thomas Watling. Trained as a landscape artist, and a painter of no little talent, Watling had been charged with forging Bank of Scotland notes, an apparently common recourse of penurious draughtsmen. Rather than face the court charge and possibly the rope, for forgery was a capital offence, Watling requested transportation. He was sentenced to fourteen years in the ill-reputed colony of New South Wales. After tasting life in the prison hulks and the journey as far as the Cape of Good Hope, Watling must have regretted his decision, for there he managed to escape from the convict transport the *Pitt*. He was recaptured after the *Pitt* had continued her voyage and so enjoyed the dubious hospitality of Dutch gaols while awaiting the next transport, the *Royal Admiral*, in which he completed his voyage to New South Wales. He arrived at Port Jackson on 7 October 1792 and was assigned to the surgeon-general, John White, as a hospital clerk. White, who quickly recognised Watling's artistic talents, soon had him employed in painting the birds, fish, and plants of the colony.

By the latter part of 1792, several more English volumes concerned in part with the natural history of New South Wales were published. George Shaw continued to edit illustrated books on biological novelties, this time from the collection of Ashton Lever in a volume entitled *Museum Leverianum*. The first volume published in 1792 contained three New Holland birds: the 'splendid parrot', '*Psittacus splendidus*'; the 'southern brown parrot', '*P. australis*'; and the Pompadour parrot, '*P. atropurpureus*'.

Shaw, with his usual illustrator, Frederick Nodder, was still engaged in the production of further volumes of *Naturalist's Miscellany*; the third volume of that serial work came out in 1792. As well as more illustrations of the New Holland parrots which were becoming quite commonplace by this time, Shaw included a lizard, the emu, the black swan, and the animal now known as the echidna, *Tachyglossus aculeatus*, which was described for the first time. Notes accompanying the illustration of the animal which Shaw had received from John White stated that it had been caught upon an anthill. This, with the lack of obvious teeth and its extensible tongue, led Shaw to the conclusion that the animal might be a member of the genus *Myrmecophaga*, the central and south American anteaters, so Shaw named the animal '*Myrmecophaga aculeata*'. Ten years later Everard Home recognised the echidna's affinities with the platypus and so removed it to the genus *Ornithorhynchus*, although Home added the proviso that when sufficient information was known about the species, it would probably be removed to a genus of its own, as was suggested by Cuvier in 1795.

Robert Kerr's *Animal Kingdom*, a translation and revision of Linnaeus' *Systema Naturae* was also published in 1792, and in this Kerr included a number of New Holland animals. The taxonomic heading 'Ferae' was created, defined as animals having six incisors in the upper jaw and a single canine on either side of both the upper and lower jaws. Kerr included in this the dingo, which he named '*Canis antarcticus*', noting that it was on the whole a very elegant animal but fierce and cruel; 'the spotted fichet', which corresponded to the 'spotted martin' of Phillip; the 'New Holland opossum', which he labelled '*Didelphis caudivolvula*'; and five members of the genus '*Didelphis*' including the kangaroos. Two of these species, the kangaroo and the rat kangaroo, he placed in the division Ferae on the authority of Gmelin, but Kerr himself felt that they should probably be placed in the next division, 'Glires'. Glires were defined as animals which did not have a tusk on either upper or lower jaws, and to this division he assigned the flying squirrels. The ornithological section of *Animal Kingdom* went on to list many of the various birds that had been described from New Holland up to the year 1792.

December saw the close of the initial period of settlement of New South Wales. Arthur Phillip had requested leave from his position as governor of the colony, and late in 1792 permission was granted. Phillip sailed from Port Jackson for England in December of 1792 leaving Francis Grose, lieutenant-governor and member of the New South Wales Corps, in charge of the colonial government.

Chapter Four

By 1793 a new maturity had developed in the approach to natural history of New Holland, a maturity in line with the increasingly prevalent idea of the empirical observation of nature that was taking hold in Europe. No longer content to merely describe the multitude of plants and animals strewn across the globe, the philosophers of nature now sought relationships between the hierarchical groupings of animals and plants. Linnaeus' work which had stood unchallenged for many years was being scrutinised and amended.

In March of 1793 a paper on the reproduction of the kangaroo was read before the Royal Society of London by Everard Home. The opossum tribe, of which Home believed the kangaroo to be a member of, he felt to be very different from other quadrupeds—their mode of reproduction was halfway between animals such as birds and reptiles, in which the foetus is detached from the parent as an egg, and quadrupeds in which the foetus remains attached to the parent by a placenta. The semi-independent status of the foetus in the pouch of the opossum seemed to Home to be a compromise between the two. How the foetus came to be in the 'false belly' was a matter of much interest, with speculation centering on the foetus growing out of the nipple or the occurrence of an internal passage between the abdomen and the pouch. Home discarded both of these ideas and concluded that the mouth of the false belly must be brought close to the opening of the vulva allowing the transfer of the foetus, an idea closer to the truth than the other hypotheses. After his paper had been read before the Royal Society, Home asked Denis Considen to read a copy of it and Considen, who had lately returned to England from New South Wales and had performed a number of dissections of kangaroos while in the colony, agreed with Home's conclusions. The paper was eventually published in *Philosophical Transactions* in 1795. In his paper Home mentioned that Dr John Hunter had also worked on the problem of kangaroo reproduction but had died before he could resolve the problem. There has been speculation that Home came into the possession of many of Hunter's papers, and that much of the work on kangaroo reproduction had already been done by Hunter. Claims that Home utilised some of Hunter's information without crediting him must be weighed against the many other publications that Home produced over the years on unrelated subjects.

March of 1793 saw the arrival in Port Jackson of a foreign scientific expedition consisting of two Spanish vessels under the command of Alejandro Malaspina. The *Descubierta* and the *Atrevida* had been constructed specifically for the expedition, and the Spanish government had paid particular concern to the outfitting of the two ships. Prior to the departure of the vessels, Malaspina wrote to various European savants inviting their suggestions for types of research to be undertaken by the expedition. Joseph Banks was one of these correspondents, and it may be assumed that Banks advocated botanical endeavours. The expedition sailed from Cadiz on 30 July 1789 and spent much of its time in South America and the Pacific Islands before entering Port Jackson on 13 March 1793. Here the crew rested, replenished their stocks of food and wood, and obtained supplies of fresh water while the scientific party explored the immediate neighbourhood of Sydney and Botany Bay. The botanists Luis Nee and Thaddeus Haenke accompanied David Collins and John White on a collecting excursion upriver to Parramatta. By the time the expedition was ready to sail a month after arrival, Nee had collected close to 1,000 species, including seeds which were germinated on the expedition's return to Spain. There the specimens were eventually turned over to Antonio Canvantilles who described many of them in his *Icones et Descriptions Plantarum*, published from 1791 to 1801.

Attempts to penetrate inland were becoming more

'*Platilobium formosum*'
Smith. *Specimen of the botany of New Holland*. 1793.
Platylobium formosum

'*Goodenia ramosissima*'
Smith. *Specimen of the botany of New Holland*. 1793.
Scaevola hispida

prevalent. In March William Paterson was transferred from Norfolk Island to Port Jackson and wrote to Banks mentioning a journey to the Blue Mountains with Major Grose that he intended to undertake. Paterson included for Banks' collection a specimen of the destructive fly of Norfolk Island which he termed a 'locust', along with a request that Banks obtain and send to the colony some wide-mouthed glass bottles for the shipment of flower specimens back to England. The trip to the Blue Mountains was completed in September; David Collins noted in his journal that while the explorers had been unable to fare very far up the Hawkesbury River by boat, Paterson as a botanist had been amply rewarded by the discovery of several new species of plants.

In November, James Edward Smith read a paper before the Linnean Society of London on two new genera of plants from New South Wales, *Goodenia* and *Platylobium*. The species had been given to Smith by Thomas Hay and John Fairburn from samples they had earlier received from the colony.

Late in the year Banks was sent a number of specimens of the flax plant of Norfolk Island by Philip Gidley King. The production of canvas and cordage

that the Admiralty hoped could be manufactured from the plants suffered numerous delays before a start could be made. Little was accomplished until several Maoris, possessing a knowledge of processing the flax into cordage, were brought from New Zealand.

In 1793 three new publications directly concerned with New South Wales and partially with its flora and fauna became available. John Hunter, Captain of the *Sirius* and not to be confused with the English anatomist of the same name, published *An historical journal of events at Sydney and at sea*. Although Hunter was a competent artist and made a number of drawings and paintings of the fauna of New South Wales, the only natural history illustrations in the volume were of three undescribed shells from New South Wales.

As was usual in such diaries, Hunter described the animal productions of the country including the dingo, kangaroo, parrots, emu, and the black swan. He commented on the similarity that New Holland animals bore to each other; in fact he went further:

It would appear, from the great similarity in some part or other of the different quadrupeds which we find here,

64

'Buccinum'
Hunter. *An historical journal of events at Sydney and at sea.*
1793.

that there is a promiscuous intercourse between the
different sexes of all those animals. The same observation
might be made also on the fishes of the sea, on the fowls
of the air, and, I may add, the trees of the forest. It was
wonderful to see what a vast variety of fish were caught,
which, in some part or other, partake of the shark: it is
no uncommon thing to see a skait's head and shoulders
to the hind part of a shark, or a shark's head to the body
of a large mullet, and sometimes to the flat body of a
sting-ray.[1]

This paragraph strongly echoes similar statements in
John White's earlier journal in which he wrote of
'fish . . . like the animals in some degree resembling the
Kangaroo, partake of the properties of the shark.'[2]
White, with a more substantial knowledge of natural
history, was not prepared to state that 'promiscuous
intercourse' occurred between species, but Hunter
appears to have thought that it was relatively common.
Earlier in 1788 Daniel Southwell had written:

Most of the Quads of this place are handy with their paw
and tho not to be pronounced of the Monkey kind, they
are monkey-ish in their manners, and were it not that we

meet with no regular Gent of that Class sho'd suspect
there was a dist. Grad'n as links in the Chain which
Naturallists affirm is insensibly continued from one
Order to another.[3]

It is doubtful that each individual arrived at these
conclusions independently, especially as they all tend to
use the same examples. The idea of the strong affinities
between many of the animals was probably hit upon
soon after the arrival of the First Fleet and remained in
common currency for some time thereafter.

Whoever was responsible for its origin, the idea of
the intermingling of species defied the then-current
dogma of the philosophers of nature. No idea was more
central to the natural philosophers and theologians of
the day than that the created species of God were for all
time immutable. Linnaeus himself had firmly believed
in the constancy of species, and this constancy was
accepted by the leading naturalists all over Europe with
the exception of a few radicals such as Lamarck, who
was disparaged as a dilettante. It remained for the poet
philosopher, Erasmus Darwin, grandfather of Charles
Darwin, to elaborate upon the implications of the
'promiscuous' animals of New South Wales. In
Zoonomia, or the Laws of Organic Life published in
1794, Darwin used the idea of this promiscuity as the
basis for his theory that all life derived from primeval

filaments, such promiscuous intercourse between different filaments giving rise to the extant species of animals. In *Zoonomia* Darwin reproduced Hunter's paragraphs on the subject almost exactly.

Watkin Tench published a second journal in 1793 to supplement his 1789 *A Narrative of the Expedition to Botany Bay*. The second volume was entitled *A Complete Account of the Settlement at Port Jackson* and included a much more comprehensive description of the plants and animals than his first volume had been able to give. Tench still remained unimpressed with the indigenous vegetables and was not very optimistic about the ability of the soil to produce crops of cereals. In discussing a period of very hot weather, Tench was to be prophetic: he thought that the origin of the hot dry winds that descended upon Sydney each summer must be immense deserts situated to the north-west of Port Jackson. In later years when speculation abounded about the possibility of an inland sea, these words of Tench were forgotten.

Of the animals of the country, Tench noted that the generic term kangaroo could now be divided into at least three species, the grey kangaroo, the red kangaroo, and one with a head resembling an opossum. Tench listed other animals but dealt briefly with them, pleading ignorance as a naturalist.

The third volume published that year was James Edward Smith's *Specimen of the Botany of New Holland*. Originally intended to be an ongoing serial publication it ceased to appear after the first volume. The preface included the information that the figures were from coloured drawings sent by John White to Thomas Wilson, so Wilson, who lent the drawings to Smith, was the vital link in still another publication, having already been associated with John White's *Journal*. In addition to sending the drawings, White had also included specimens of the plants so the English engravers were able to compare the two for an accurate representation of the plant on the final plate. Plants depicted in the illustrations included *Billardiera scandens*, named for La Billardière; the waratah, Smith's choice for the best of the New Holland flowers; *Eucalyptus robusta*; and the Christmas bush, *Cerato-*

66

4

Banksia spinulosa.

'*Embothrium speciosissima*'
Smith. *Specimen of the botany of New Holland.* 1793.
Telopea speciosissima

petalum gummiferum, which Smith felt had such
botanical characters as to render it difficult to classify
satisfactorily.

The majority of the plants illustrated and described in
Smith's work had been successfully germinated in
English hothouses; exceptions to this were the waratah
and the silky embothrium. Some further plants from
New South Wales cultivated in the greenhouses of Kew
were illustrated two years later in *Exotic Plants
Cultivated in the Royal Garden at Kew* by Francis
Bauer. The original seeds and specimens for that work
had been sent to Kew by Arthur Phillip.

Previously, Joseph Banks had tried to convince the
Admiralty to outfit a vessel to send plants of agricultural benefit to the New South Wales colony. The plan
was thwarted when the *Guardian* struck an iceberg
rounding the Cape of Good Hope. In April of 1794
Banks renewed his requests and petitioned the
Admiralty to send out plants in pots on HMS *Reliance*
under Captain Waterhouse. The *Reliance* was not to
sail for another year, but Banks' plans were successful
this time.

In July Banks received a letter from Philip Gidley
King informing him that King had now established flax
plants in pots which he would send to Banks at the first
opportunity. This came in November when King
forwarded ten boxes of flax and other plants to England.
Another letter came from William Paterson and was
accompanied by other specimens. Paterson asked Banks
to recommend a gardener who would be willing to
emigrate to the colony and undertake to collect
botanical specimens in addition to horticultural
activities. A second request of Paterson was that Banks
send him some specimen paper as he lacked anything
suitable for drying his plant specimens. For the early
collectors in the colony there were very real problems
with storing their specimens, and paper of any kind was
extremely difficult to obtain.

Paterson, in the time that he was stationed on
Norfolk Island, had begun to assemble a "Natural
History of Norfolk Island". Letters to Banks from
Paterson and King followed the development of the
manuscript, and in a letter to King earlier in the year,
Banks offered his assistance in publishing the manuscript. Paterson's recall to Port Jackson deprived him of
the time and specimens needed to complete his work,
particularly the sections on the birds and fish of
Norfolk Island. The botanical section was already in the
possession of Banks, and Paterson now sent a folio of
drawings to accompany the text. The illustrations were
the work of John Doody, Paterson's convict servant.
Paterson inquired of Banks whether he thought the
botanical text and illustrations were worth publishing,
since he would be unable to complete the full "Natural
History". On the strength of the manuscript, Paterson
solicited Banks' help in becoming a fellow of the Royal
Society, and on his return to England in 1797 his
election to the Royal Society was successful.

'The Flora of Norfolk Island', the manuscript that
Paterson submitted to Banks, was never published. A
hand-written copy exists in the Mitchell Library,
Sydney, but the handwriting does not appear to be that
of Paterson. The text is really nothing more than an
amalgamation and amplification of Paterson's letters to
Banks, often copied verbatim from them. The text deals
not only with the descriptions of the plants but also
with the climate of the island and the problems of
agriculture. There is, in fact, a sizable amount of
horticultural information contained in the manuscript.
The text also lists the quadrupeds and birds recorded on
the island, the only quadruped being a rat probably
brought by the first vessels to the island. Of the birds,
there were pigeons, doves, parrots, curlews, and the
'Mount Pitt bird', a species of petrel which was the
main source of food for the convicts during the initial
years of settlement of the island.

Banks was not the only recipient of Paterson's
largesse. In the records of the Society for Promoting
Natural History, later to merge with the Linnean
Society of London, there are letters from Paterson along

with acquisition records of specimens such as ferns from Norfolk Island. Other New Holland items were received by the society from John White. Both Paterson and White, as well as Archibald Menzies and George Bass, were elected honorary members of this society.

On the vessel that carried Paterson's letter to Banks were two other people who had been involved with natural history in the settlement. Edward Laing, a surgeon's mate of the New South Wales Corps, collected and explored with Paterson around the environs of Sydney and had been entrusted with the care of specimens for Banks. More importantly, John White, who had supplied so many of the specimens and illustrations of the New South Wales flora and fauna, sailed on the *Daedalus* on 16 December, having obtained leave to return to England.

Thomas Watling, John White's purported hospital clerk, had not ceased his productive painting throughout the time he was assigned to White. Watling was less than pleased with his situation in life; in a letter to his aunt he querulously noted of his painting: 'The performances are, in consequence, such as may be expected from genius in bondage, to a very mercenary sordid person.'[4]

Whether the aspersions cast upon White were justified, Watling continued with his prodigious output of over 500 paintings, commenting on the plants and animals that he drew:

> Should the curious Ornothologist, or the prying Botanist, emigrate here, they could not fail of deriving ample gratification in their favorite pursuits in this luxuriant museum. Birds, flowers, shrubs and plants; of these, many are tinged with hues that must baffle the happiest efforts of the pencil.—Quadrupeds are by no means various; but we have a variety of fishes, the greater part of which, are dropped and spangled with gold and silver, and stained with dyes transparent and brralliant as the arch of heaven.[5]

Watling in his distinctive prose also commented on the common thread that seemed to run through the plants and animals of the colony:

> In short, from the savage native in the animal, and the towering red gum in the vegetable, every thing indigenous to this colony, approaches or recedes by a very striking and singular gradation of proximity.[6]

Remaining in the colony after White's departure, Watling continued to serve his original sentence of fourteen years transportation. His affranchisement came quickly; he was granted a conditional pardon in September of 1796 and an absolute pardon eight months later. Watling left the colony and eventually made his way back to England, but his eight years of penal servitude may have done nothing to improve his character, for in 1806 he was again charged with forgery, although this time the Crown's case was not proven and he escaped punishment.

John White seems to have controlled the dispersal of the majority of Watling's artistic output. Not all the paintings were originals; there were several other artists in the colony and they appeared to have freely copied each other's work or even made multiple copies of their own work. This duplication presumably occurred because much of the painting was intended to illustrate specimens, and White sent the illustrations to a number of different people. Much of Watling's output was not used directly for publication but served as initial sketches that English artists used as models for their final paintings. John Latham employed some of Watling's paintings as his 'type' specimens for the descriptions of New Holland birds in his *General Synopsis of Birds*. Latham was to be subsequently criticised by the English naturalist William Swainson for this use of drawings in describing species. Many of Watling's paintings were gathered together by James Lee, the English horticulturist who specialised in New Holland plants; this collection later came into the possession of the British Museum.

John White, upon his return to England, considered writing another book to follow up his *Journal of a Voyage to New South Wales*. He corresponded with Aylmer Bourke Lambert, a well established botanist and secretary of the Linnean Society, about possible publication and some related drawings, but the manuscript was never published. On his return to England, John White disappeared from the pages of Australian history. As with many others like him he was not a man of particular importance and it was only the events that he had been caught up in which made him of any consequence at all.

In 1794 George Shaw began publication of the *Zoology of New Holland* which was very much along the lines of J. E. Smith's *A Specimen of the Botany of New Holland*. Many of the illustrations were figured by the naturalist-artist James Sowerby from specimens in collections in England, but some of the illustrations may be copies from paintings originally done by Thomas Watling and sent to England by John White. The animals listed in the first volume were: '*Psittacus eximius*', 'non pareil parrot'; '*Didelphis pygmea*', 'pygmy opossum'; '*Psittacus terrestris*', 'ground parrot'; '*Merops phrygius*', 'embroidered merops'; '*Columba antarctica*', 'antarctic pigeon'; '*Chaetodon constrictus*', 'constricted chaetodon'; '*Testudo longicollis*', 'long-necked turtle'; '*Cancer serratus*', 'serrated lobster'; '*Turdus punctatus*', 'spotted-shouldered thrush'; '*Coluber porphyriacus*', 'crimson-sided snake'; '*Didelphis sciurea*', 'squirrel opossum'; '*Didelphis macroura*', 'long-tailed opossum'.

Columba Antarctica

Paralleling Smith's *A Specimen of the Botany of New Holland* the demise of *Zoology of New Holland* occurred after just one volume.

Little new was added to the store of knowledge of the flora and fauna of New South Wales in 1795. David Collins, in his *Account of the English Colony of New South Wales* described William Paterson as the only naturalist to reside in the colony during this time.

In September of 1795, on board the vessel *Reliance*, two men arrived in the colony who were to do much during the ensuing years for both the exploration of the continent and the development of natural history of the colony. They were Matthew Flinders and George Bass. Flinders, a young master's mate on the *Reliance*, had previously accompanied William Bligh's second voyage to secure breadfruit for the West Indies. He had already served eight years in the Royal Navy and within a year was to become a lieutenant. George Bass had also served a number of years in the British navy as a surgeon, but, as he was later to admit, his passion was for exploration and natural history. When the chance of obtaining a berth on the *Reliance* arose, Bass immediately sought it, knowing that the vessel was bound for New South Wales, a land which offered innumerable opportunities for the pursuit of both his interests. On learning that Joseph Banks intended to construct a plant-cabin on board the *Reliance* for the transport of useful plants to the colony, Bass obtained a letter of introduction to Banks; however, on calling at Banks' Soho Square residence, he was informed that the owner was sojourning in the country for the summer. With the *Reliance* departing for the antipodes in a short time, Bass was forced to abandon his plans to meet Banks.

In Matthew Flinders Bass found a companion who shared his taste for exploration. When the two men arrived in the colony, the coastline of New South Wales had been roughly laid out on the charts but little was known of the area except for Botany Bay, Port Jackson, and Broken Bay. On 26 October, just seven weeks after their arrival in the colony, Flinders, Bass, and Bass' servant boy, William Martin, set off in a boat that Bass had brought from England to explore the Georges River from its outlet on the shores of Botany Bay. The craft, little more than a row boat, served them well, and when they returned on 4 November they were able to give Governor Hunter a report of the country that they had passed through and a chart of the river as far as they had explored it. On the strength of this report, Hunter explored the district himself and founded Bankstown. Before the year was out, Bass was to accompany Hunter on an exploratory journey inland toward Camden.

Bass and Flinders continued their exploratory

'Columba antarctica'
Smith. *Zoology of New Holland.* 1794.
Lopholaimus antarcticus

interests whenever they procured sufficient time away from the *Reliance*. In March 1796, in a slightly larger boat constructed in the colony, they explored as far south as Lake Illawarra. On the return voyage, they examined Port Hacking, which although but a few kilometres south of Botany Bay was then unknown. In June of that year, while Flinders was employed with duties about the *Reliance*, Bass with two companions set out to attempt a crossing of the Blue Mountains. For two weeks they tried to scale the mountain barrier but without success; however, the trip offered Bass an opportunity to observe the flora and fauna of the foothills east of the mountains. Having returned with samples of the vegetation from the area, Bass was able to apprise Hunter that the soil was good for up to 30 kilometres north-west of Mount Hunter.

August of 1796 saw William Paterson forced to return to England due to the aggravation of an eye inflammation. On the same vessel, Governor Hunter forwarded Under-Secretary King a cage of native birds which he requested be shared with Charles Middleton, the comptroller of the Royal Navy. Like Phillip before him, Hunter was not blind to the interest of the Navy and Home Office hierarchy in the novelties of the colony. Paterson, also mindful of the necessity of patronage, carried plant specimens for Joseph Banks on his return to England.

The second volume of *Museum Leverianum* appeared in 1796, four years after Shaw had published the first. Like the first, the second volume contained animals from New South Wales. Probably due to insufficient sales the series was abandoned after this volume, as were so many of Shaw's serial publications with the exception of *Naturalist's Miscellany*.

The year 1797 was to prove eventful for both the discovery of previously unknown animals and the continuation of George Bass' explorations of the coastline south of Port Jackson. Towards the end of March, Banks, replying to a previous query from Governor Hunter concerning another attempt to send a gardener out to New South Wales as a replacement for David Burton, wrote:

> When ever prosperity returns, I shall solicit the King to establish a botanist with you. The plants we have received, which are now tolerably numerous, make a most elegant addition to the gardens. I trust, good sir, that when you make your excursions, or when you send parties into new districts, you will not forget that Kew Gardens is the first in Europe, and that its Royal Master and Mistress never fail to receive personal satisfaction from every plant introduced there from foreign parts when it comes to perfection.[7]

Banks need not have feared. Hunter, like his predecessors, was well aware of the benefits of retaining Banks' patronage.

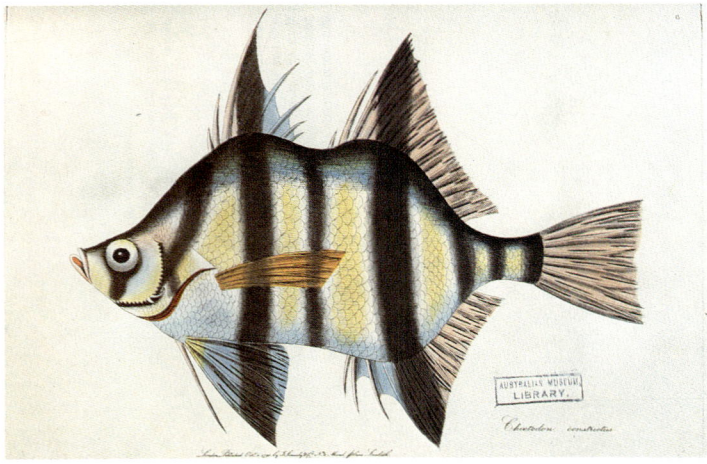

TOP:
'*Psittacus terrestris*'
Shaw. *Museum Leverianum*. 1796.
Pezoporus wallicus

ABOVE:
'*Chaetodon constrictus*'
Shaw. *Zoology of New Holland*. 1794.
Enoplosus armatus

RIGHT:
'*Columba chalcoptera*'
Shaw. *Museum Leverianum*. 1796.
Phaps chalcoptera

Banks in turn was mindful of the interests of the colony and was even then taking steps to send out the promised botanist. Banks was also not forgotten by Philip Gidley King, the lieutenant-governor of Norfolk Island. King, who returned to England that year as a result of illness, brought with him additional samples of the Norfolk Island pine and the waratah. Few of the plants survived, however, and only the pines reached Kew in acceptable condition.

In February of 1797, a merchant vessel, the *Sydney Cove*, bound from India to Port Jackson, had been wrecked on Preservation Island just to the north of Van Diemens Land. A party of survivors sailed one of the vessel's small boats to New South Wales, then trekked up the coast. Three of these survivors were spotted by a

72

fishing party close to Botany Bay and brought into Sydney. Matthew Flinders was dispatched in the colonial schooner, *Francis*, to recover the other survivors who had remained on Preservation Island. George Bass, told by the rescued men of a site where they had started a fire with coal found near the beach, opportuned Hunter for the chance to seek this valuable resource. Bass was given charge of a whaleboat and crew and on 5 August set out in search of the coal which was so much in demand in the colony. About 30 kilometres south of Botany Bay, Bass located a seam of coal which extended southward along the coast until it disappeared beneath the sea. He was also able to locate further veins of coal inland and presumed that the coal seams extended farther south than he was able to trace. After eight days of mineralogical prospecting, Bass returned to Port Jackson with bags of coal samples, having noted that the vegetation of the area was very different from that around Sydney. The area in which Bass located the seams was given the name Coalcliff and was to develop into one of New South Wales' largest coal mining centres despite David Collins' opinion that the coal was too inaccessible to be of use to the settlement then or at any other time. Samples of the coal were dispatched to Joseph Banks via the *Britannia*.

In September another advantageous mineralogical find was made when a group of convicts in the colony seized a small boat and fled northward along the coast. Two boats under the command of Lieutenant Shortland gave chase, but although unable to locate the escapees, Shortland did discover the mouth of a river to the south of Port Stephens which he named the Hunter. Along the banks of the river was located another stratum of coal, considerably more accessible than the site that Bass had located at Coalcliff. Samples of the coal were brought back to Port Jackson by the unsuccessful pursuit party.

By now natural history had begun to lose the aura of eccentricity that had surrounded colonial practitioners. In addition to a large library, Bass had the company of other individuals interested in the natural history of the colony. Paterson had left the colony to return to England, but the Reverend Thomas Palmer, one of the Scottish 'Martyrs', was interested in everything about the colony to which he was transported for 'seditious practices', including the curious plants and animals.

In November of 1797 another of these very curious animals was discovered. Described in David Collins' '*Account*' as an 'amphibious animal, of the mole species', it was of course, the platypus.[8] It astounded its

'Platypus'
Collins. *Account of the English colony in New South Wales.*
1798–1802.
Ornithorhynchus anatinus

The subjoined EN
by GOVERNOR HUN

OR

AN AMI

which Inhabits the

its fore feet are evide

feet having the Cla

ꟾNG is from a DRAWING made on the ſpot
.

ᴏRHYNCUS PARADOXUS.

ᴏUS ANIMAL of the MOLE KIND.

ꜱ of the freſh water Lagoons in New South Wales
eir principal aſſiſtance in Swimming & their hind
ding beyond the Web'd part are uſeful in burrowing

discoverers, for instead of the mouth that could be expected of a mammal it had the beak of a duck. The original specimen was found on the banks of a lake close to the Hawkesbury River, and Governor Hunter was quick to send a specimen of the animal to England to meet the disbelieving eyes of the naturalists there. Many thought the badly preserved original specimen a hoax, believing that some clever individual had sewn together the bodies of different animals. The 'Eastern Mermaid', an ingenious construction of the upper body of a monkey and the tail of a fish, had earlier been fobbed off on the European public by the Chinese.

Governor Hunter was among the first to see the platypus and wrote about its habits to Banks, who later transmitted both comments and a specimen to Dr Everard Home. Home, in a paper in the *Philosophical Transactions of the Royal Society*, refuted initial claims made by Johann Blumenbach that the platypus had no teeth. In the specimen he examined, Home noted teeth and concluded that the confusion of Blumenbach arose through his examination of a poorly preserved specimen.

On 3 December George Bass set off on another of his frequent exploring trips, this time on the voyage that was to place his name on the map of the colony. The wreck of the *Sydney Cove* in the Furneaux Islands had reopened the vexatious issue of whether a strait existed between Van Diemens Land and New South Wales. Among the proponents of this theory were Bayly (the astronomer of Cook's second Pacific voyage), La Billardière, and Captain Hamilton of the ill-fated *Sydney Cove*. Those who held the contrary opinion included Captain Furneaux, who maintained that the indentation in the coastline was merely a bay. Bass, with little to do while repairs were effected to the *Reliance*, was given permission by Hunter to take a whaleboat and six men to explore the coast to the south of Botany Bay. In an open boat almost 10 metres long, built of banksia and cedar, and provisioned for six weeks, the party sailed and rowed their way southward. By 2 January 1798, they had rounded Wilsons Promontory, named later by Hunter for the naturalist Thomas Wilson, and entered the long-hypothesised strait. Bass noted that petrels, gulls, and an abundance of seals inhabited the area.

Bass led his party farther west and explored Western Port before rerounding Wilsons Promontory en route back to Sydney. They paused briefly at an island they named Seal Island where they shot a number of seals to supplement their dwindling provisions, and this led Bass to consider the possibility of commercial sealing in the area. Closing his journal account of the voyage back in Sydney, Bass concluded with some general remarks: he had found several new species of plants during the trip but they had suffered badly from the continuous moisture in the open boat, and regarding animals there

was nothing new except the birds, which had a 'sweetness of note' not found in Sydney. Lacking sufficient knowledge of geology, Bass felt that he could make no pronouncements on the mineralogy of the area he had visited.

In January of 1798 another expedition was organised from Sydney, this time into the interior of the continent. It had long been rumoured among the Irish convicts transported to New South Wales that another colony existed about 600 kilometres to the south-west of Sydney where they would be able to throw off their bonds of infamy. Hunter, determined to put an end to this arcane rumour as it rendered the Irish unruly, had them choose four representatives to accompany an exploratory party to the area. Led by James Wilson, a former convict and experienced bushman, the party left Parramatta on 14 January. Within ten days of their departure the convicts, debilitated by penal rations and the rough life in the bush, had broken down and were unable to continue, and so returned to Parramatta with their soldier warders. Wilson and two companions, however, proceeded further, and on the day subsequent to the convicts turning back, the party shot a 'pheasant'. Wilson had earlier reported the existence of 'a bird of the Pheasant species' to the authorities in Sydney but no particular importance had been placed on the observation. As the unknown diarist of the expedition recorded, they saw

> . . . a bird about the size of a pheasant, but the tail of it very much resembles a peacock, with two large long feathers, which are white, orange, and lead colour, and black at the ends . . .[9]

Also recorded in the diary entry for that same day, 26 January, was the observation of the dung of several animals, one sample, Wilson told his companions, was from the 'whom-batt', an animal with the appearance of a badger; another from an animal that the natives called a 'cullawine', supposedly bearing some resemblance to the sloths of America. This appears to have been the first reference to the koala, *Phascolarctos cinereus*, by the European settlers of Australia. The three men continued south-west, observing 'pheasants' and rock kangaroos, although few fell prey to their guns. Fresh provisions were difficult to obtain, and they were forced to eat a rat and a cockatoo-like bird with a green, white, and lead-coloured body and a scarlet head, probably a gang-gang cockatoo. When Wilson and the others returned on 9 February after having travelled some 200 kilometres south-west of Parramatta, they brought with them one of the 'pheasant' species; David Collins recorded in his *Account* his notion that the bird was a variety of the bird of paradise, but it was actually the superb lyrebird, *Menura novaehollandiae*. Wilson also brought samples of salt deposits that they had located on their journey, an important find as salt was still being imported from England.

While Wilson and his companions were trudging southward and George Bass was returning northward on his whaleboat journey, Matthew Flinders was aboard the colonial schooner, *Francis*, sent south to Preservation Island a second time to collect what remained of the cargo of the *Sydney Cove*. While work was in progress removing the stores to the *Francis*, Flinders charted a number of the neighbouring islands. On 16 February he was on Cape Barren Island where a number of wombats were killed. The wombat, *Vombatus ursinus*, had originally been discovered by the shipwrecked men of the *Sydney Cove* in 1797 when it formed a part of their diet until they were rescued. The animal was not common around Sydney, for several Aborigines of that area to whom George Bass showed a specimen were unfamiliar with it. An Aboriginal from the Blue Mountains region, however, did recognise the animal.

Flinders recorded that the islands of the Furneaux Group were composed predominantly of granite interspersed with quartz that contained a significant proportion of tin. Many of the trees of the islands appeared to Flinders to be partially petrified. Of the animal kingdom, there were two kinds of seals, one of which Flinders noted, did not resort to the 'effeminacy of the beaches'; sooty petrels or shearwaters which burrowed into the ground like rabbits and fed their young with a 'gelatinous substance gathered from the waves'; penguins; a small reddish-brown species of kangaroo; the aculeated anteater, or echidna; Cape Barren geese, black swans, and the usual assortment of seabirds.[10] On his return to Sydney on 9 March, Flinders brought back a specimen of the wombat as a present for Governor Hunter, a specimen that was subsequently sent to Joseph Banks.

The same day that saw Flinders returning to Port Jackson bore witness to another expedition led by James Wilson setting off to again attempt the penetration of the country to the south-west. Again the party was unable to travel far inland but returned with additional specimens of the lyrebird, two of which were presented to Hunter who forwarded one to Joseph Banks and the other to Lady Mary Howe. The following year the specimen given to Lady Howe was seen by Major-General Thomas Davies who described the bird in a paper read before the Linnean Society in 1802. Included with the description of the bird, which Davies named 'Menura superba', was a colour plate.

Joseph Banks had not forgotten his promise to have a botanist sent to the colony. In May Banks wrote to Under-Secretary King about the possibility of sending a gardener to New South Wales. Banks already had in mind a young man who had approached him about emigrating to the colony, and as Banks was interested in fitting a plant cabin on to HMS *Porpoise* to transport

'*Menura superba*'
Davies. *Transactions of the Linnean Society*. 1802.
Menura novaehollandiae

much-needed plants, he thought that the gardener would also be able to care for the plants in transit. One of the plants in greatest demand in New South Wales was hops—for the production of beer. Concerned with the constant rumours of debauched and drunken behaviour in the colony, Banks considered that with a supply of locally brewed beer the colonists might be weaned away from unwholesome spirits such as rum.

The botanist Banks had in mind was more of a gardener than an explorer, so Banks also proposed that the British government employ Mungo Park to explore the interior of the continent. Park, a well known naturalist-explorer, had just returned to England from an expedition into the interior of Africa. Banks further suggested that as Park would have need of a decked vessel for his explorations, the best man to command such a vessel would be Lieutenant Matthew Flinders. While the Home Office pondered this proposal, Banks received official blessings for his enterprise of sending plants out via the *Porpoise* and so prepared the design of a plant cabin. Similar to that fitted aboard HMS *Discovery* in 1791, the cabin measured 1·8 by 3·6 metres. Within two weeks of gaining approval of the project, Banks had ordered mature hops and germinating seeds to be planted in pots. Banks also corresponded with George Aufrere about the terms under which free settlers such as gardeners could emigrate to New South Wales; the terms included a house built at the government's expense, a grant of 80 hectares of land, farming implements, two or more convict labourers, free passage out to the colony, and twelve months' provision of stores. In eliciting these terms, Banks had in mind George Suttor, who was to care for the hops on the sea voyage out to New South Wales.

George Suttor was anxious to emigrate to New South Wales. The son of a gardener who had studied with James Lee of Hammersmith, Suttor had become acquainted in 1796 with several officers who had served in the colony. Suttor was able to obtain an introduction to Joseph Banks through his uncle, and Banks offered him the chance he hoped for to go to New South Wales. In addition Banks offered to employ Suttor in a collecting capacity as the British government was determined to expand its collection of New South Wales plants. While Banks could grant no official remuneration for these services, there were substantial grants of labour and land to set Suttor up in the colony. Banks introduced Suttor to the Duke of Portland, then secretary of state for the colonies, who approved Suttor's application for emigration.

The year 1798 was to see the association of Joseph Banks with another young botanist bound for New South Wales. George Caley, a brash young man interested in botany, had sent specimens to Banks in 1795 asking him if he was aware of any positions available in assisting botanists. Banks replied that there was very little money to be made by way of botany but he would try to find Caley employment in one of the botanical gardens. Through Banks Caley obtained a job at Chelsea Gardens where he toiled as a gardener's labourer for two years. By 1797 Caley was again writing to Banks indicating his desire to be sent to New South Wales as a botanical collector, an offer which Banks declined. Caley was unhappy with his position at Chelsea so Banks managed to place him at Kew but at a lower salary. Caley lasted but a short time at Kew before returning home on the pretext of continuing his education. On hearing that Banks was sending Suttor to New South Wales, Caley again wrote to Banks asking why he, who was so admirably suited for the position, had been passed over. With notable forbearance Banks tolerated this and other diatribes the headstrong Caley directed at him.

In September of 1798 Mungo Park, the naturalist Banks thought to gain as an explorer-collector in New South Wales, declined the government offer citing as reasons the low wage offered and the haste with which he would have to depart England. Park, an explorer of the first rank, was a sad loss for exploration in New South Wales, and he later wrote to Banks of his depression at not realising his dream of settling in New South Wales. That depression was no doubt assuaged when he returned to Africa to pursue further exploration there. Banks then remembered the impetuous Caley and offered him the opportunity to go to New South Wales. Because the government had no wish to employ a collector, Banks was willing to hire Caley himself on a salary of fifteen shillings a week and a ration of government stores. In return Banks expected Caley to collect plants and seeds for both Banks' personal collection and the gardens at Kew, but Caley would also have the freedom to collect and sell specimens to other individuals. Caley accepted the offer with alacrity, and Banks arranged for his passage informing him that he would have only a few weeks to ready himself for departure on board the *Porpoise*.

The haste for Caley to be in London was unwarranted; the *Porpoise* was not to sail for some time due to problems with fitting out the vessel. One of the greatest of these problems was the weight of the plant-cabin which had been built on the deck under Banks' guidance. In a repetition of the problems with the *Resolution* on Cook's second voyage, it was found that eighteen plant boxes full of earth, weighing almost 4 tonnes, resulted in such a top-heavy ship that it was scarcely seaworthy. The proposed solution, the transference of the plant cabin between decks, caused a considerable delay in the departure of the *Porpoise*.

In New South Wales, Governor Hunter was able to move more expeditiously. Bass' explorations in the early part of the year had convinced Hunter of the existence of a strait between Van Diemens Land and the mainland, and Hunter was anxious to substantiate that belief by having a vessel circumnavigate the island. Hunter, in a dispatch of 3 September to Secretary Nepean indicated his intention of outfitting another expedition with Bass and Flinders in charge. The previous month Hunter had sent to Joseph Banks a number of specimens, including a cask containing a wombat preserved in spirits, a drawing of a platypus, two lyrebirds, and a lyrebird egg. This shipment therefore included samples of all three of the major zoological finds of the late 1790s.

By October Hunter had the means of proving the existence of the hypothetical strait between New South Wales and Van Diemens Land. The *Norfolk*, a 25-ton sloop constructed on Norfolk Island, was equipped, and Flinders was directed to pass through any strait he found and return round the southern coast of Van Diemens Land. The *Norfolk* was provisioned for twelve weeks and sailed on 7 October in company with a sealing vessel, the latter intent on reaping a profit from Flinder's earlier reports of quantities of seals in the area. The venture was to pay off handsomely: 9,000 seal skins and several tonnes of oil. With Flinders in command of the navigation on the voyage, George Bass was able to devote most of his attention to the natural history of the region and his observations were published in David Collins' *Account of the English Colony in New South Wales* in 1802.

The expedition first called at Twofold Bay where Bass described a species of *Eucalyptus* growing amid rocks that to Bass' mind resembled hardened clay. The *Norfolk* then sailed on to Preservation Island, site of the wreck of the *Sydney Cove*, and here Bass examined the petrified wood that Flinders had noticed earlier, testing it with acid to determine if the petrification was due to calcareous matter and how far it extended into the ground. Bass postulated that the trees must have been covered by a pond in which 'petrifying water' was contained; the pond had later disappeared leaving the trees stonily erect. The water supply of the island was tested and Bass concluded that it contained traces of arsenic leached from the rocks, a conclusion he thought might account for the ill-health of some of the survivors of the *Sydney Cove* while they awaited rescue.

Landing on Cape Barren Island, Bass compiled a detailed description of the wombat, still a relatively unknown animal in 1798, and remarked that the

'Wombat'
Collins. *Account of the English colony in New South Wales.* 1798–1802.
Vombatus ursinus

wombat was 'very economically made' and that it appeared quite tame when caught—until its legs were tied, at which time the animal's nature quickly changed from docility to ferocity. As well it might, for in the interests of science Bass dissected several of the wombats that he caught. On the island, Bass also found kangaroos, the 'porcupine anteater', as the echidna was called, a rat with webbed feet, parakeets, other unknown birds, fur seals, and a venomous black snake.

About the islands, Bass concluded:

> In point of animated life, nature seems to have acted so oddly with this and neighbouring islands, that if their rich stores were thoroughly ransacked, I doubt not but the departments of natural history would be enlarged by more new and valuable specimens than they ever before acquired from any land of many times their extent.[11]

Leaving the islands in Bass Strait, the *Norfolk* proceeded along the northern coast of Van Diemens Land with Bass making frequent excursions ashore. He found that while the vegetation of Van Diemens Land looked superficially very similar to that of New South Wales, it was quite different; among the peculiarities was a greater proliferation of scented flowers than was typical for the northern mainland. Grey kangaroos were common in the forest while the bush was the abode of a smaller black kangaroo. The parrots appeared dull in

colour in comparison to the gaudy plumage notable in New South Wales. Large concentrations of black swans abounded, 300 or more gathered in small areas, but of that number Bass estimated that only two-thirds could fly; the others were waterbound due to moulting. To both Bass and Flinders the swans seemed to exhibit a certain intelligence, for they were able to thwart the hunters at times by submerging their bodies almost completely in the water or by quickly swimming upwind.

Sailing further westward Bass and Flinders were astounded to see a huge flock of sooty shearwaters. With some rough calculations, Flinders amused himself by computing that the flock must have been composed of 151,500,000 individual birds which would require upward of 30 kilometres or more precisely '18¼ square miles' of burrows to house them.

On 9 December, Bass was ashore on an island they named Albatross Island for its vast flocks of albatross, and while there he wrote the first description of the white-capped albatross, *Diomedea cauta*. Later that day the object of the voyage was realised as the *Norfolk* rounded the north-western cape of Van Diemens Land, at last obtaining solid proof that the strait existed. They sailed south around the southern tip of Van Diemens Land, then north to Adventure Bay and the Derwent River. Here Bass almost fell foul of a venomous snake which he chanced upon. Determined to take the snake alive to test the effects of its venom on a hawk that he had captured, Bass tried to catch the snake but it died, causing Bass to surmise that the snake had inadvertently bitten itself and expired from its own poison.

Early in January the *Norfolk* sailed to Port Jackson bringing Hunter the welcome news of the strait. Bass brought north a number of specimens which he forwarded to Joseph Banks; these included plants, petrified wood, two skins and the skull of a wombat, a tin of metal ore, and two bird skins, one a pheasant shot near the Hawkesbury River, the other a 'banded runner' taken near the Derwent River. Bass informed Banks that he wished to write a scientific account of the wombat and the petrified wood when he returned to England, and he did indeed write up a paper on the wombat, much of it taken verbatim from his journal. However, it was never published and remained in Joseph Banks' voluminous files.

George Bass' explorations of the natural history and geography of New Holland were terminated by his increasing involvement in commercial interests. In later years he became associated with voyages to the Pacific islands to procure pork for the colony and finally disappeared on a voyage to South America which, among its other objects, included the importation of guanacos from Peru to New South Wales.

A consequence of the recent discovery of coal to the north and south of Sydney was a directive in December 1798 from the Duke of Portland for vessels carrying livestock to the colony to take on a return cargo of coal for the Cape of Good Hope. Portland suggested that timber from the colony might also make up a return cargo for the Cape. The initial attempts to export coal from New South Wales were delayed while repairs were effected to the vessels under consideration, but by September of 1799 a ship had sailed for India loaded with coal.

The *Transactions of the Linnean Society* continued to print papers dealing with the organisms from New South Wales or New Holland during 1798. Major-General Thomas Davies published a description based on specimens from Arthur Phillip and Nicholas Nepean of what he called a '*Muscicapa*' species, since reclassified as *Stipiturus malachurus*, the southern emu-wren. Shaw also examined the bird and named it '*Muscicapa malachura*', the soft-tailed flycatcher.

Also that year James Edward Smith published in the *Transactions* 'The Characters of Twenty New Genera of Plants' concerned with plants collected in New South Wales.

The initial publication of another serial natural history work which dealt partially with New South Wales was also on sale in 1798, an anonymously published work called *The Naturalist's Pocket Magazine*. In the preface to that work it was noted:

> By the favour of a few friends, long resident in distant countries, and particulary by the friendship of a gentleman who resided many years in a highly respectable official capacity at the British settlement in New South Wales, we have not only been enabled to present the naturalist with several non-descript articles in this our first volume but are qualified to promise, from the same source, a great variety of other rare productions, both in the animal and vegetable kingdoms.[12]

Volume one did indeed go on to illustrate such productions, many of them redrawn from a set of originals done in the colony. The 'gentleman' alluded to in the preface was probably John White, while the original drawings came from the pen of Thomas Watling. Unattributed, Watling seems to have been a major source of drawings and paintings from the colony, paintings which were later recopied by artists resident in England for inclusion in the various natural history publications. In the first volume of *The Naturalist's Pocket Magazine* were: *Banksia serrata*, honey flower of New South Wales; *Xanthorrhoea resinosa*, grass gum tree, 'This gum, when dissolved in spirits and water makes a pleasant beverage . . . The medicinal qualities of this Gum, which is the Resin Acaroides of the last London Dispensary, are not unknown in England . . .'; *Telopea speciosissima*, warre taw, 'is universally deemed the most superb flower of

'*Muscicapa*'
Davies. *Transactions of the Linnean Society.* 1798.
Stipiturus malachurus

New South Wales'; cassowary of New South Wales; '*Banksia pyriformis*'; black swan of New South Wales; '*Metrosideros lanceolata*', 'Many gardens in England, and most nurseries in the vicinity of the metropolis now boast possession of this beautiful shrub . . .'[13]

Also included were *Eucalyptus piperita*, peppermint of New South Wales; '*Banksia incognita*'; porcupine caterpillar of New South Wales; and the kangaroo:

> Pennant, who classes it with the opossums, calls it a Gerboid Kangaroo: and indeed, most naturalists seem inclined to consider it as a species of the Jerboa. Zimmerman, in particular, calls it the Jerboa Gigantea or Gigantic Jerboa.[14]

In early 1799, the *Porpoise*, long delayed in England with its passengers George Suttor and the new Governor of New South Wales, Philip Gidley King, still rode at anchor. Plants boxed and ready for the voyage since the previous September were aboard, and the new governor had also asked Banks to assemble a selection of seeds of vegetables, herbs, flowers, grasses, fruit, hops, and flax which he proposed to keep in his cabin during the voyage.

Caley did not arrive at the ship until February—only to find that a microscope that Banks had given to him had been lost. Meanwhile Banks had written to various acquaintances informing them of Caley's employment and requesting their assistance for him. To Dr William Roxburgh at the Cape of Good Hope he recommended Caley as a good fellow and an intelligent botanist; to Governor Hunter, Banks wrote that Caley was possessed of botanical knowledge beyond what his demeanour would lead one to believe. March came and the *Porpoise* remained in England; some of the plants that had been on board for six months were faltering, and Suttor

wrote to Banks enlisting his help in obtaining replacements for the weak or dead plants. A false keel was added to the *Porpoise* and her mast was shortened by a metre, but this increased her seaworthiness so little that she continued to be hardly more than a floating hostel and garden. Caley, without work to occupy his time as he shared no responsibility for the plants on board, frustrated by the long delay, asked Banks for an advance of money and permission to visit Chelsea. He received both and set off to walk to London from the anchorage at Portsea.

During this time, the Admiralty, following another suggestion from Joseph Banks, obtained boring equipment to be sent out to the colony for use in searching for coal at a more convenient distance to Sydney than Coalcliff or the Hunter River. Banks procured the necessary equipment for boring to 90 metres' depth and included it in the goods for shipment to New South Wales. Philip Gidley King in his new capacity was also interested in the production of coal, and before sailing to take up his post he suggested that two large water pumps be taken out to the colony for the removal of seepage water from the coal mines that he proposed to sink.

Another shipment of plants arrived for Suttor as replacements for those that had died; Caley brought the plants with him from London. After his return Caley attempted to learn the use of the sextant to equip himself for exploration, but the venture was less than a success. With the *Porpoise* still not ready in early June, Caley set off for the Isle of Wight. His excursion there resulted in nothing more than a plant specimen which he sent to Joseph Banks with the idea that it might be undescribed; however, the plant was well known. A fleet departed Portsmouth bound for the West Indies and still the *Porpoise* swung on her anchor chains, leaving Caley even more frustrated at the delay. He received from Banks a drawing of an animal which neither former Governor Phillip nor William Paterson were able to identify from their tenure in the colony. Presumably this was the drawing of the platypus that Hunter had forwarded to Banks in August of 1798. Banks, himself, must have had doubts about the animal's authenticity for he asked Caley once he had arrived in the colony to determine whether the platypus was a deception.

If Banks had reservations about the platypus so did one of the foremost naturalists of the day, George Shaw. In describing the animal in his long-running series *Naturalist's Miscellany* Shaw noted:

> Of all the Mammalia yet known it seems the most extraordinary in its conformation; exhibiting the perfect resemblance of the beak of a Duck engrafted on the head of a quadruped. So accurate is the similitude that, at first view, it naturally excites the idea of some deceptive

preparation by artificial means . . . nor is it without the most minute and rigid examination that we can persuade ourselves of its being the real beak or snout of a quadruped.

On a subject so extraordinary as the present, a degree of scepticism is not only pardonable, but laudable; and I ought perhaps to acknowledge that I almost doubt the testimony of my own eyes with respect to the structure of this animals beak.[15]

Shaw clearly hesitated to accept as valid the single specimen that had been brought to England and attempted to cover himself should it prove to be a deception.

In late August hopes were raised of the *Porpoise* sailing within a week. Suttor was happy with the state of the plants; although many of them had been aboard almost eleven months, it was only the herbs that had suffered badly, and Suttor hoped to have them replaced. Philip Gidley King, taking steps to improve on his unsuccessful attempts at the culture and processing of cotton while he was lieutenant-governor of Norfolk Island, embarked both cotton seed and cotton combs. The seeds of the fruit and vegetables that Banks had given King had been taken out to New South Wales in January, but King hoped to obtain a further supply at the Cape of Good Hope.

The *Porpoise* did indeed sail in September. After a number of minor accidents in weighing anchor and making sail, she left with a convoy on 6 September. By 17 September, however, she was back in port having badly damaged her steering gear. By now even the Admiralty was sceptical of the vessel, and it was decided to dispose of her and purchase another ship in her place. King and Caley were ordered to sail on the whaler, *Speedy*, while Suttor was left to transfer the plants to the replacement vessel and bring them out later. *Speedy*, living up to her name, sailed within a few weeks. Also on board was Francis Barrallier, a young Frenchman destined to become one of the early explorers of the interior of New South Wales.

By November of 1799, the whale fishery was well established on the New South Wales coast with nine vessels employed in whaling. The stormy weather often necessitated their removal to Port Jackson where they placed heavy pressure on the already limited resources of the colony. The seal skin fishery had also become established but was risky due to the often limited returns. In November Lieutenant-Colonel William Paterson returned to New South Wales from England.

In this the final year of the eighteenth century, there appeared a short pamphlet entitled *A Companion to Mr. Bullock's Museum*. Little is known about the antecedents of the museum of William Bullock, but it would appear to have been started around 1795 while Bullock was living in Sheffield. By 1799 he had acquired some 300 specimens, including pigeons collected during Captain Cook's Pacific voyages and parrots brought back by Joseph Banks from the first of those voyages; a portion of these specimens were from New Holland.

Naturalist's Pocket Magazine completed its first volume in 1799 having been published in parts, each part consisting of three coloured plates with the accompanying text. Twenty of these parts were then bound as a volume, and eventually seven volumes had been published by 1803 when the enterprise ceased publication. Of the forty-one illustrations of material from New South Wales, thirty-one were copied from drawings made in the colony, probably the work of Thomas Watling. An illustration of the kangaroo was copied from Hawkesworth's chronicle of Cook's voyages, and the spotted opossum was copied from John White's *Journal*. Although the initial parts were printed and distributed during 1798, the completed first volume was published in 1799. Volumes II and III were also completed in 1799 and included plants and animals from New South Wales such as: *Banksia serrata*, morron beetle, emperor moth, finger flower, yellow fragile flower, purple shell flower, scarlet woodbine, fern pine, '*Bomurro cammerral*' or 'potatoe apple fruit', '*Aster serrata*'.

Most of the illustrations had little or no information to accompany the drawings. Yet the anonymous author or authors indicated in part of the work that no country offered a wider field for botanical discovery than did the newly founded colony of New South Wales.

By the end of the eighteenth century, the penal colony in New South Wales was firmly established. For a region settled only twelve years earlier at a distance of six months' travel time from England, remarkable progress had been made in elucidating the flora and fauna of the country. The nineteenth century was to see the accretion of further knowledge as exploratory parties charted first the coastline, then the interior of the continent.

Chapter Five

For the first thirteen years of the colony's life, natural history had been characterised by the work of interested amateurs. Military officers, especially the surgeons possessed of medical training, were able to recognise that in New South Wales there existed a flora and fauna far different to that which they had encountered in Europe or any other part of the world. The competence of John White, William Paterson, and George Bass was such that they were able to make extensive collections of plants and animals, but they lacked the training to analyse the material, resulting in the shipment of new finds to England where the specimens were examined by the accepted authorities: James Edward Smith, George Shaw, Everard Home, or John Hunter. The local naturalists remained at best amateurs and collectors whose principal employment in the colony was other than natural history.

The dawn of the nineteenth century brought another breed of man to the colony. Like their predecessors they also had limited training in the emerging theoretical underpinnings of the sciences; often they possessed a more rudimentary knowledge than that which a naval surgeon could be expected to have, but they did differ in one important respect. These men saw themselves principally as naturalists; they expected to derive a substantial portion of their income from the pursuit of natural history. With their arrival in the colony began the hesitant rise of the professional naturalist in New South Wales.

The first decade of the nineteenth century saw an increase in the number of the seaborne scientific and exploratory expeditions to sail the uncharted waters of the colony. A portion of these expeditions touched the shores of New Holland only as they completed their circumnavigations of the globe. Other expeditions were directed entirely to outlining and exploring the unknown coastlines of the continent. Tentative steps were also taken towards inland exploration, but the forbidding mountain range behind the coastal flat on which Sydney lay, and the character of the land behind the mountain range, combined to severely limit the successes of these early probes inland.

In a dispatch of February 1798, the Duke of Portland informed Governor Hunter of a natural history painter emigrating to New South Wales. Hunter was to place the prospective settler on government victualling lists and afford him the other usual courtesies. This naturalist-artist was John William Lewin who arrived in Sydney on the vessel *Minerva* on 11 January 1800. Lewin was a son of William Lewin, author of *The Birds of Great Britain*, and a number of the plates from that work bore the signature J. W. Lewin, indicating that John Lewin gained an early apprenticeship in natural history and natural history draughtsmanship. During his efforts on his father's seven-volume work, which included illustrations of many birds' eggs, John Lewin would have come into contact with the Duke of Portland, for many of the figured eggs were drawn from specimens in the Duchess of Portland's collection. It was probably on this basis that Lewin secured the Duke of Portland's recommendation for emigration.

Before Lewin embarked on the *Minerva* for New South Wales, he gained the patronage of several other individuals. Dru Drury, a former silversmith, had in the 1790s retired to devote himself to the study of entomology and made a practise of financing naturalists embarking for exotic locations on the condition that they repay him with entomological specimens collected during their travels. The triumvirate of Drury, Thomas Mersham, author of *Entomologica Britannica*, and Alexander Macleay, secretary of the Linnean Society, advanced Lewin money to outfit himself for his journey. The items which Lewin purchased with this money included: a gun, shot and bullets, mahogany cabinet for insect specimens, compass, pocket magnifier, brass forceps, gold scales, collecting boxes, rope, crow quills, medicines, crucibles for fluxing, caterpillar boxes, sheet for collecting caterpillars, a number of pamphlets, boxes to breed insects, pins, vials, cork for pinning insects, fifty-three pieces of copper for engraving, small net for catching water insects, lead weights for bottom of a fish net, miscellaneous household goods.

This extensive list, although strongly biased toward the capture and preservation of insects, can be compared with the items carried by David Nelson four decades earlier.

When he arrived in Sydney, Lewin was about thirty years old and recently married. His marriage was to cause some initial problems since for some reason Lewin failed to embark upon the *Buffalo*, the vessel on board which he originally intended to travel to New South Wales. His wife, however, took passage aboard the *Buffalo* without him and was subsequently accused of imprudent behaviour with the second mate, one Mr Makin. On arrival in Port Jackson, a legal case followed which the Lewins eventually won after securing testimony from the Reverend Richard Johnson concerning the soundness of Mrs Lewin's character. The legal battle monopolised John Lewin's time for the first few months after his arrival in the colony.

In the early months of 1800, a potential rival to Matthew Flinders, with his desire to conduct the exploration of the shores of New Holland, emerged. Lieutenant James Grant was appointed to the command of the *Lady Nelson*, an experimental vessel designed with inshore exploration in mind. The *Lady Nelson*, a small 60-ton brig, had been fitted with three sliding keels enabling her to enter water as shallow as 2 metres when the keels were raised while still maintaining a seagoing capability when the keels were lowered. The *Lady Nelson* was directed to proceed to New South Wales, Joseph Banks having secured the position of commander of the vessel for Grant. In a letter of thanks to Banks, Grant indicated his interest in pursuing voyages of exploration; with much of the northern and southern coastlines of New Holland still uncharted, there was no lack of discoveries to be made. Before the *Lady Nelson* sailed from England, the astronomer William Bayly visited the vessel and supplied it with a chronometer.

Portland wrote to Governor Hunter informing him that he intended the *Lady Nelson* to prosecute the discovery and survey of the unknown parts of the coast of New Holland. On the outward journey to Port Jackson, Grant was directed to sail through the strait newly discovered by Bass and Flinders between New South Wales and Van Diemens Land. On his voyages Grant was to collect such specimens of seeds, plants, animals, and minerals as he thought likely to prove interesting to the naturalists of England. Grant was also to sow seeds of fruit trees and vegetables at locations where he went ashore for the benefit of future vessels.

The Admiralty apparently proposed to send a collector or naturalist on board the *Lady Nelson*, as they directed Grant to assist such a collector to the best of his ability. Any collections that such a naturalist made and any sketches or journals kept were to be turned over to the secretary of state for the Home Office or to be forwarded to the Royal Society—but they would invariably have found their way to Sir Joseph Banks.

On the 16th April 1800, the whaler, *Speedy*, passed through the heads of Port Jackson with the new governor of the colony, Philip Gidley King, and the naturalist George Caley on board. The two had already begun the confrontations that were to plague their relationship for the next several years. Having disagreed over Caley's collecting at the Cape of Good Hope, King concluded that Caley lacked discipline. Banks by this time may have become somewhat resigned to Caley's temperamental behaviour, but he could have hardly condoned it. By the beginning of May, with Hunter reluctant to hand over the control of the colony until he left, King employed himself in the organisation of the botanical affairs of the colony. Caley had been sent to Parramatta to commence collections of plants of the area and had been given the use of Government House there for the purpose of drying his specimens. Under the direction of William Paterson, a botanical garden had been laid out in Sydney.

By the end of September, Lewin had settled his marital affairs sufficiently to correspond with Drury. Living in Parramatta he had been able to gather a small collection of insects which he proposed to forward on the vessel returning shortly to England with the recalled Governor Hunter. At the same time Lewin had already opened his own collection of insects and had begun to sketch and paint the specimens. Along with the insect specimens, Lewin enclosed for Drury a painting he thought represented a new species of lily. Lewin suggested that Drury might wish to have the illustration published, but if not, to forward it to Dr Anders Sparrman. Sparrman, who had accompanied Cook and the Fosters on Cook's second voyage as a naturalist, by then had returned to his native Sweden.

John Hunter, reluctant to turn over the affairs of the colony to King, clearly intended to keep control of the colonial government until the day of his departure, but King was not idle. He employed a convict miner to bore for coal in the immediate neighbourhood of Sydney. At the head of Georges River where King thought there might be a better quality of coal than that at Coal River (Hunter River), the miner was set to work with the boring equipment Banks had procured for King. Simultaneously, King assessed the potential for shipment of coal from Coal River and Lake Macquarie where a seam

'*Cryptophasa pultenae*'
Lewin. *Prodromus Entomology*. 1805.

84

of coal had also been detected. In a letter to Sir Joseph Banks, King again complained about Caley and hoped that Banks was at least receiving some value from him in light of the abuse that King had to suffer. Caley had further aggravated King by becoming involved with a recently widowed woman. William Paterson was of the opinion that if Caley would marry the woman, a Mrs Wise, he would settle down, but King, so often the recipient of Caley's antipathy, was not convinced. If in fact Caley did marry the woman, and there is some evidence for it, it was not until a much later date. This was probably just as well for Banks wrote to King at the time:

> I did not hire him to beget a Family in NSW and if he is not more active than is compatible with a married life I must certainly get rid of him.[1]

Despite Banks' reservations, Caley was to be adequately diligent throughout his sojourn in New South Wales.

Along with the letters to Banks Caley sent several boxes of specimens, including the platypus which Banks had so desired as proof that the original animal sent to him had not been a contrived specimen. Other shipments contained two boxes of plant specimens from Caley, a box of minerals from the Coal River sent under the auspices of William Paterson, a type of fruit from Port Stephens, and two waratahs.

In October the first black swans to reach England alive were taken aboard the *Buffalo*. When they eventually arrived in London, they were given to Earl St Vincent who in turn presented them to the queen. That same month Caley wrote to Banks lamenting the tribulations of a botanist in the colony. He had no proper paper for drying his plant specimens, which not only seems to have prevented him from any collecting but also severely depressed him—the inactivity hurt when so many specimens had to be left on the tree for want of the drying paper. Specimens which he did manage to collect and send back to Banks Caley tried to apply names to, but he was afraid that many of the denominations he gave them would be inappropriate. Caley included some of the sought after seeds and advised that in his next shipment he would try packing the seeds in sugar, a technique recommended to him by Mr Sneyd, a friend of Banks. Other comments by Caley considered the abundance of minerals in the colony, the quantity of iron, the frequent finds of coal and the specimens of copper. Despite the fact that Caley considered that Englishmen tended to degenerate in New South Wales, he obviously did not feel that the same dissipation would apply to himself; he planned an ambitious programme of collecting not only for Banks but also for others in London.

Early in November 1800, the infamous *Porpoise*, or rather its replacement of the same name, finally arrived in the colony bearing George Suttor and his long-suffering plants. The majority were dead, the exceptions being only those few that Suttor had been able to replace at the Cape of Good Hope on the outward passage. These included: olives, apples, mulberries, willows, walnuts, chestnuts, oaks, pomegranates, plantains, mint, and several varieties of grape, a sorry representation of the extensive list with which Suttor had originally embarked. Most telling was the loss of the hops, without which there could be no hope of weaning the settlers and convicts from the demon rum.

King ordered that the plant cabin aboard the *Porpoise* be dismantled and packed away with the expectation that it could be re-erected and used to convey plants from the colony to the Cape of Good Hope when the *Porpoise* made a return voyage the following year. From there the plants would be trans-shipped to a vessel bound for England and Joseph Banks. King proposed that such plants as Paterson recommended would be started in pots five months prior to the *Porpoise*'s departure date to allow them sufficient time to root.

Caley in these months had managed to obtain some paper for drying plants, and also occupied his time in planting a garden to supplement his meagre ration from government stores. Offered the opportunity to journey to Norfolk Island, Caley was making preparations for the voyage when the *Lady Nelson* arrived in Port Jackson on 16 December, and Governor King suggested that the proposed voyage to Bass Strait would be of greater interest to him. The *Lady Nelson* was not to leave for several months so Caley took some time to write to his employer reiterating his usual complaints— the want of supplies and the misfortunes befalling the colony, most of which Caley attributed to the colonial administration. In his responses to these letters, Banks showed his usual patience with Caley's complaints and, despite the rather meagre return he had so far obtained from Caley's exertions, was even moved to increase his salary, optimistically noting that the raise was to 'prevent people from finding fault with you in the future'.[2]

The year 1800 saw a continuation of English scientific publications dealing in part with New South Wales. In the *Transactions of the Linnean Society of London* an article by George Shaw appeared in which he mentioned the 'New Holland Jabiru', *Xenorhynchus asiaticus*, a specimen of which had been obtained for the Leverian Museum. Also included was a description by James Edward Smith of *Sowerbaea juncea*, the vanilla plant, then frequently found in the nurseries of London, and a description of the marine algae, '*Conferva umbilicata*', sent from New South Wales by Governor Hunter.

Everard Home published a paper in the *Philosophical Transactions of the Royal Society of London* on the

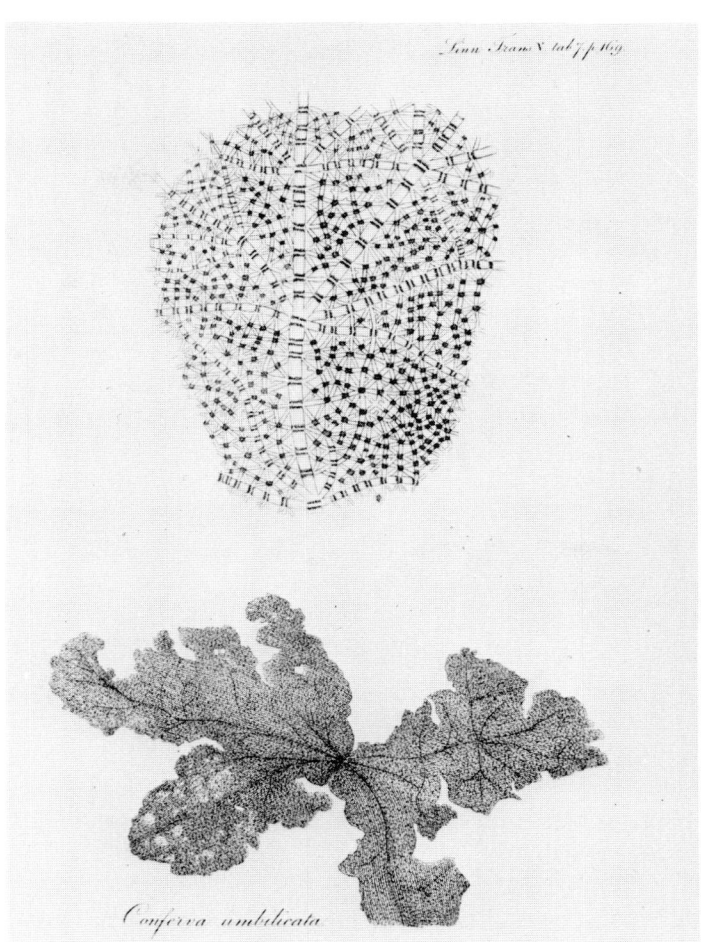

'*Sowerbea juncea*'
Smith. *Transactions of the Linnean Society.* 1800.
Sowerbea juncea

'*Conferva umbilicata*'
Velley. *Transactions of the Linnean Society.* 1800.
Microdictyon umbilicatum

platypus, *Ornithorhynchus anatinus*. Enough specimens of the platypus had made their way to Europe to convince the zoologists that the animal was indeed real and not the creation of some clever hands.

Much dissension remained about the taxonomic status of the platypus. George Shaw, in the first volume of his survey of animals entitled *General Zoology*—a serial work begun in 1800—placed the platypus in the lowest of the Linnaean mammalian orders, the Bruta, which included the anteaters and the sloths. The presence of fur convinced Shaw that the platypus was a mammal, but he could find no substantiation of the principal mammalian feature, the mammary glands. This inability to find mammary glands was to leave the question of the platypus' taxonomic position open for years. Speculation on the platypus' affinities ranged from the birds, as postulated by Everard Home, reptiles, (Illiger), and cetaceans, (Rexzius). Even the correct name of the animal was uncertain. In the original description published in the tenth volume of *Naturalist's Miscellany* in 1799, Shaw described the platypus under the name '*Platypus anatinus*'. In 1800 one of the specimens sent by Governor Hunter to Joseph Banks had been forwarded by Banks to Professor Johann

Blumenbach, a long-time correspondent of Banks, who on hearing of the new animal requested a specimen for his museum. Blumenbach, ignorant of Shaw's prior description, subsequently published his own name for the specimen, '*Ornithorhynchus paradoxus*', while Wiedemann, translating Shaw's original description into German in 1800, called it '*Dermipus anatinus*'. Blumenbach's generic name was eventually adopted as the valid scientific name because the generic name *Platypus* had been used seven years earlier for a genus of Coleoptera. The platypus therefore is formally known as *Ornithorhynchus anatinus*. Blumenbach continued to study the comparative anatomy of the platypus and later requested a second specimen from Banks; in return Banks received copies of Blumenbach's publications.

Also contained in *General Zoology*, of which only the volumes dealing with mammals were published in 1800, were entries on the echidna, which was still able to excite the interest of zoologists despite having been discovered about ten years previously. Shaw used the echidna to illustrate:

. . . a striking instance of that beautiful gradation, so

frequently observed in the animal kingdon by which creatures of one tribe or genus approach to those of a very different one.[3]

Here again is a reference to the fauna of New Holland illustrating gradations between species, a theme that was to reach major prominence fifty-nine years later with the publication of Charles Darwin's book *The Origin of Species*. Further entries in *General Zoology* included the dingo, eleven species of opossums (however these 'opossums' comprised a bandicoot, marsupial cats, and a wombat), the kangaroo rat, and the kangaroo. Although there was now appreciable evidence of a number of separate species of kangaroos, Shaw was wary of stating more than that the possibility might exist of several species or at least permanent varieties.

The Naturalist's Pocket Magazine, published anonymously but surely with the assistance of George Shaw, continued publication with volumes IV and V. New Holland flora was represented by the dandelion of New South Wales, *Banksia multiflora*, the everlasting pea, and the purple iris. An entry for the echidna, or aculeated anteater as it was often referred to, echoed Shaw's sentiments:

> . . . seems to form a connecting link, in the great chain of Nature, between the two very distant Linnaean genera of Hystrix, or the Porcupine, and the Myrmecophaga, or the Ant-Eater.[4]

Both the continuation of short-range explorations of the coastal zone of New South Wales as well as the initiation of a major expedition around the continent by sea occurred in 1801. In early March, Lieutenant James Grant, in command of the brig *Lady Nelson*, was given the opportunity for exploration he so earnestly desired. Governor King directed Grant to survey the south and south-western coast of New Holland. In his instructions to Grant, King named Bass Strait in honour of its discoverer, George Bass. As well as surveying the strait, Grant was further instructed to visit Western Port and the various islands in Bass Strait, and if time allowed he was to continue the survey as far west as King George Sound. Grant was to take possession of such territory as he found, note the fertility of the land, plant fruits and vegetables at any anchorages that might be favoured in the future by vessels, and collect whatever seeds, plants, minerals, and animals proved of interest for either their beauty or usefulness. To assist him with this last instruction and to supply the president of the Royal Society with plants, George Caley was to be allowed to accompany the *Lady Nelson*. Grant was to render Caley whatever assistance he needed. John Lewin also planned to accompany the expedition on the sloop, *Bee*, as did Francis Barrallier of the New South Wales Corps on the

Lady Nelson. At the termination of the voyage, Grant had orders to surrender all journals, drawings, and specimens to Governor King for transmission to the ministers back in England or to be forwarded to the Royal Society. The *Lady Nelson* and her consort, *Bee*, sailed from Port Jackson on 6 March, but unfortunately for Lewin, *Bee* was unable to keep pace with the *Lady Nelson* and was ordered back, Lewin with her.

While the *Lady Nelson* was away, life progressed in the colony. The miner John H. Platt, whom King employed to search for coal at Georges River, had, with the aid of convict labour, sunk a shaft of 10 metres and then continued boring for another 15 metres. Two thin layers of coal were found, and King entertained hopes of finding extractable coal close to Sydney. Merchants such as Simeon Lord and Joseph Underwood were already trading with Coal River where they were able to obtain small boatloads of coal for shipment to Sydney. Should his search for coal at Georges River prove inconclusive, King proposed to send Platt to Coal River to survey the deposits there.

King was informed by letter from Under-Secretary King of the Home Office that yet another botanist would be arriving in the colony, John Gordon, who was in the employment of J. A. Woodford of the War Office.

The *Lady Nelson* arrived back in Sydney on 14 May having accomplished only a small portion of her assigned tasks. Grant had broken the voyage at Jervis Bay on 11 March where he recorded seeing many black cockatoos and parrots, including a king-parrot, *Alisterus scapularis*, which Caley shot. Later that day, while further inland, Caley was able to collect some of his precious plants, including some obtained by Grant and Barrallier which Caley had never seen before. Grant noted that no country had a greater variety of insects than New South Wales. The following day was also spent in the district of Jervis Bay with Caley and Grant collecting further plants and seeing 'the Laughing Bird, so called from the noise it makes resembling laughter', an obvious reference to the kookaburra, *Dacelo gigas*.[5] Travelling farther around the coast, they landed on Churchill Island on 22 March, named by Grant for the gentleman who had supplied the seeds sown on the island for the benefit of future travellers. Here Caley continued to harvest undescribed plants but not to the extent he had envisioned, a disappointment he ascribed to the lateness of the season. They also observed a bellbird, *Manorina melanophrys*, were invariably saluted early in the morning by the kookaburra, and discovered a duck which made a distinctive whistling noise with its wings. Before they

'*Psittacus fimbriatus*'
Grant. *The narrative of a voyage of discovery performed in His Majesty's vessel, the Lady Nelson*. 1803.
Callocephalon fimbriatum

PSITTACUS FIMBRIATUS FRINGE CRESTED COCKATOO.
From New South Wales in the Museum of Major General Davies,
to whom this plate is respectfully inscribed by

left the island, Barrallier shot a rare cockatoo which was later painted by Major-General Thomas Davies from the specimen given him by Governor King. It is now known as the gang-gang cockatoo, *Callocephalon fimbriatum*.

One of the crew of the *Lady Nelson* was able to trap several cygnets, the young of the black swans, and one, which became quite tame by the end of the voyage, was presented to Governor King. Little in the way of the surveying tasks assigned to them by Governor King were accomplished before the *Lady Nelson* returned to Sydney in the middle of May. On the return voyage, Grant attempted to follow King's instructions concerning the confiscation of all journals and specimens but Caley would have none of it, refusing to give up the specimens in his possession—even those collected by Grant and Barrallier. Caley in a letter to Banks gave his version of the altercation:

> Because I would not give the captain everything I collected which he had not got he was afronted, and one day, because I would not give him a bird's skin, he told me he would have all I collected, for he had orders from the Gov. to seize everything . . . His Excellency, soon after we arrived in the colony, told me I must get him a duplicate collection of specimens of plants. To this I objected, and he never afterwards asked me for the like.[6]

King had apparently learned from prior confrontations that persistence was of little use in dealing with Caley. Caley went on to question the reason for King's demand for the surrender of the specimens, surmising that it must arise either from King's desire to use them as gifts or to have his name recorded in books on natural history.

Although the issue was apparently of great importance to Caley, for King it was minor irritation and received only a passing mention in a letter from King to Banks:

> I must not omit saying that Cayley behaved extremely well, and is much regarded by Lieut. Grant, to whom, with Mr. Barrallier, I am indebted for the few articles I send. As they all complain of Cayley's receiving everything they found, but would never give them up, nor part with a duplicate, I presume therefore you are sure of getting all he has collected.[7]

In June, King proposed another voyage for the *Lady Nelson*, this time north to Coal River to survey the entrance and report on the natural productions of the district. James Grant was directed to take with him the colonial schooner, *Francis*, and load her with coal for Sydney. Also assigned to the party were Ensign Barrallier, Lieutenant-Colonel William Paterson, Surgeon John Harris, John Lewin, and the miner John Platt. King was interested in determining whether the

soil of the Coal River region was fertile and whether coal could be procured with ease, as he had in mind the foundation of a settlement there. Grant, Paterson, Barrallier, and even Harris all wrote reports to King on the voyage. Coal was found in abundance with easy access for sailing vessels so Platt had little difficulty in loading the *Francis* with a cargo. Paterson and Harris trekked along the river every day, and one of these excursions resulted in Paterson reporting a new species of coconut, a tree between 12 and 15 metres high but with a smaller fruit than the palms found further north in the tropics. Paterson was able to collect a number of other plants that he thought to be undescribed including a hibiscus that the Aborigines used for constructing fishing nets. A collection of rare ferns made by Paterson was lost by misadventure; it was placed too close to a fire by Paterson's servant and suffered a searing fate. John Lewin considered that he had detected a number of new species of birds including a cockatoo whose feathers were a mixture of light brown and grey, probably the pallid cuckoo, but John Harris could not agree that the species was undescribed. Harris was also disappointed with the lack of shells, either alive or dead, on the beaches of the region. In his report on the area, Paterson commented favourably on the situation of Coal River. In many places the soil was fertile, coal was to be found in abundance, and salt was available, as were vast quantities of oyster shells that would be beneficial in the production of lime, an important consideration as a significant quantity of limestone had not yet been found in the colony. With an eye towards increasing the revenue of the government, King was quick to declare the timber and coal resources at Coal River the property of the Crown, imposing a licence fee and levy on the coal procured from the area. Shortly thereafter, a load of 150 tonnes of coal from Coal River was shipped to India.

The *Lady Nelson* had no sooner returned from the Coal River region than King again planned a voyage for her down to Bass Strait, both to investigate the prospects of a seal fishery and to continue her survey of the strait. Caley, who had complained of the dearth of plants encountered on his first excursion to the area, was not interested in participating in the second voyage to Bass Strait, so John Lewin was persuaded to undertake the voyage in Caley's stead. After the voyage Caley was to write to Banks that although Lewin was initially employed by Governor King for the job he refused it after a disagreement over the quantity of specimens expected from the voyage.

Further specimens had been shipped to Banks during the intervening time. From Governor King came a collection of birds obtained on the *Lady Nelson*'s initial trips to Bass Strait and the Coal River, included were a 'shell drake', 'sandpiper', and 'red headed cockatoo' from Western Port; and a 'musk duck', 'whistling-duck', 'widgeon', 'godwit', 'heron', 'tera', 'sparrow hawk', 'cuckoo', and 'pigeon' from Coal River. Towards the middle of the year, Banks also received specimens of a New South Wales lily from ex-Governor Hunter, who had resumed residence in England, and a box of waratahs from Governor King.

In September natural history in the colony almost suffered a grave loss. After an imbroglio concerning correspondence, Captain John MacArthur and Lieutenant-Colonel William Paterson fought a duel in which Paterson was wounded, although not severely. Both combatants were subsequently placed under arrest, and MacArthur was eventually sent back to England.

Of the three naturalists Banks had helped send to New South Wales in the early years of the 1800s, two were still actively working for him. In October, Caley started a series of journeys inland around the eastern slopes of the Blue Mountains, while the following November Lewin took passage to Tahiti on a voyage to collect for both Banks and Drury. Only Suttor appeared to take little interest in the myriad new organisms to be found in the colony, preferring instead the agricultural pursuits to which he had previously been accustomed. On the advice of Caley whom Suttor had befriended during the months they had awaited the departure of the *Porpoise*, Suttor had taken up a grant of 80 hectares near Parramatta and set about becoming one of the most industrious farmers and nurserymen in the colony. He was able to propagate a number of plants in the colony which until then had met with little success. These included orange seeds given to him by Paterson.

Specimens continued to arrive and accumulate at Banks' London house. Lieutenant William Kent of HMS *Buffalo* brought back samples of iron ore from New South Wales which when smelted produced a mediocre iron, although this may have been partially attributable to problems with the smelting process. Kent also brought live emus back from New Holland for Banks' pleasure.

Progress had now been made toward charting some of the coastline of New Holland, but it was still by no means certain that the Dutch-explored western coast and the British-colonised eastern coast were one and the same continent. Gulfs indenting the northern and southern coasts were known to exist and some European cartographers maintained that New Holland was a group of islands rather than a single continent, an idea that even Governor King alluded to in a letter to Secretary Nepean on 5 June 1801. William Bligh had written a proposal to Joseph Banks as early as 1791 suggesting a thorough survey of the coasts of New Holland, presumably with himself in command, but nothing further had been done with the idea until September 1800 when a young naval lieutenant wrote to Banks proposing a voyage to explore the coast of

'Mountain Eagle of New South Wales'
Collins. *An Account of the English Colony in New South Wales*. 1798–1802.
Aquila audax

New South Wales.

Matthew Flinders was already known to Banks through his surveying work with George Bass on the south-eastern coast of the continent. In 1800 Flinders had returned to England trying to find support for the extensive exploration of the coastline of the colony, addressing his proposal to Banks. Since his voyage with Cook in 1770, Banks had been considered the authority on New South Wales and had maintained a proprietary interest in the colony. President of the Royal Society, director of the Royal Gardens at Kew, scientific adviser to King George III, and friend of Earl Spencer—the first lord of the Admiralty, Banks ruled much of science in England as his own personal fiefdom.

Flinders had dedicated his *Observations on the Coasts of Van Diemen's Land* to Banks and in his proposal included the proposition that, 'a person or persons could be accommodated who should examine into the natural production of this wonderful country.'[8] Both items were designed, it would seem, to secure Banks' approval for his project. Banks was quick to appreciate the merits of the proposal and soon gained the Admiralty's approval. Banks' enthusiastic reception of Flinders' proposal may have resulted from its timing, coming soon after Banks' plans to send Mungo Park to the colony for exploration had come to naught. The Admiralty's approval of the project may have partially stemmed from the desire to forestall any discoveries by a French expedition, under Nicholas Baudin, which had recently been granted a passport for the exploration of the southern coast of the continent. Not only were there fears that the French might try to colonise the north-west coast of Van Diemens Land, but it was also thought that the colony in New South Wales would be useful for harassing French shipping in the Pacific in the event of renewed hostilities between France and England.

The Admiralty provided a vessel for the expedition, renamed HMS *Investigator*, and Matthew Flinders was appointed as her commander. Banks sought to place on board a full complement of scientists including a naturalist, natural history draughtsman, landscape artist, mineralogist, astronomer, gardener, and miner. As could be expected from Banks' botanical interests, the naturalist was to be primarily a botanist. Banks chose Robert Brown, a young botanist who had come to his attention the previous year. Brown had formerly studied medicine at the University of Edinburgh and was presently serving as an assistant surgeon with the army, but he showed both an aptitude and interest in botany, often utilising the vast resources of Banks' library and herbarium. On 12 December 1800 Banks offered Brown the position as naturalist on the voyage. Brown accepted, and with the major appointment settled, Banks could turn his attention to the other personnel needed. Ferdinand Bauer, a botanical draughtsman, was secured as the natural history artist. Bauer came from a family of painters: his brother was the chief botanical draughtsman of the Royal Gardens at Kew, and Ferdinand Bauer himself had gained acceptance as a botanical draughtsman after spending two years travelling with Dr John Sibthorp and illustrating the specimens they collected in Greece and the Levant for Sibthorp's *Florae Graeca*. For the position of landscape artist Banks approached first William Alexander, then William Daniell, but both declined so he finally settled on a young artist, William Westall, at the Royal Academy School. John Crosley was appointed astronomer and Peter Good, a young Scotsman, was given the position of gardener. Good had recently returned from a voyage to India with Christopher Smith, the botanist on the *Providence* under William Bligh, and so was cognisant of the problems involved with the seaborne collection and maintenance of plants. No mineralogist was appointed to the expedition, but by 20 January 1801 Banks had written to William Milnes of Derbyshire to secure the employment of a miner. From this correspondence, John Allen eventually signed on for the position. Banks clearly indicated that Allen was going in a subordinate

position under the direction of Robert Brown. Brown, a competent botanist, had reservations as to his abilities as a geologist and so was issued a set of instructions about mineral collecting by John Hawkins. Banks, however, cautioned Brown to pay attention to what he knew best, botany, and simply to return geological specimens to England for others to examine. The salaries to be paid to the scientific personnel were: naturalist, £420 per annum; draughtsman, £315; gardener, £105; miner, £105. The naturalist and the draughtsman were each allowed a servant.

While Banks assembled the scientific party, work was proceeding posthaste on readying the *Investigator* for the journey. Flinders felt that too much room was given over to the cabin of the captain and advocated a reduction in the size of his own cabin to make room for more specimens, a far cry from the attitude of the majority of naval officers. Banks once again designed and had built a greenhouse, which was stowed aboard the *Investigator* to be erected on the quarterdeck on arrival in New South Wales. Plants were to be collected during the circumnavigation of New Holland and housed in the greenhouse until the vessel called at Port Jackson, where the plants would be transferred to gardens to await transportation to England. Prior to embarkation, Robert Brown spent much of his time at Banks' house in Soho Square where he reviewed specimens previously brought back from New South Wales by Banks and Solander, as well as more recent collections acquired since settlement. Indeed, Brown obtained a small herbarium of New Holland plants and had already begun to write descriptions of them before the *Investigator* left England.

The extent to which Banks organised the expedition of the *Investigator* is revealed by the response to a memorandum written by Banks to the Admiralty on 28 April. Banks questioned if a proposal for an alteration in the purpose of the voyage had been approved and in reply Evan Nepean evidently wrote back that 'Any proposal you may make will be approved. The whole is left entirely to your decision.'[9]

By the middle of March, the *Investigator* was nearing readiness for the voyage; Flinders awaited only the appearance of a French passport to sail. Some months earlier Banks had been influential in gaining an English passport for the French expedition of Nicholas Baudin who proposed to touch on the shores of New Holland during his circumnavigation of the world. The passport which gave the French scientific and exploratory expedition freedom from harassment by British naval vessels had been granted and now the British Admiralty had cause to seek a similar French passport for their own exploratory voyage. The passport was granted but only after a lengthy delay, more from the lack of information about the *Investigator* included in the application than from any apparent desire of the French to give their own expedition a head start. Both the passport that the British granted Baudin and the passport that the French issued Flinders were later abrogated on purely technical reasons in which short-sighted nationalistic officers of each country interpreted their government's intentions to match their own whims.

During the time that the *Investigator* was awaiting the passport, Flinders married, thinking to take his bride with him as far as Port Jackson where she would remain while he was involved in the exploration of the coasts. Banks took a very dim view of Flinders' marriage, as marriages of his naturalists had already caused him considerable problems. Banks probably felt his opinion justified when, while Flinders was taking the *Investigator* from Nore to Spithead, a number of problems arose including the grounding of the vessel and the escape of a prisoner being transported to Spithead. Both Banks and the Admiralty attributed the mishaps to the poor discipline occasioned by the presence of Flinders' wife aboard. Flinders was suitably contrite and his wife left the vessel to spend many years in England waiting for her husband's return. With their imposed leisure caused by the delay in sailing, Brown and Bauer spent their time constructively roaming the Isle of Wight in search of plant specimens. Bauer, as well as being a competent draughtsman, was also an accomplished botanist.

The French passport was issued on 5 June, and finally on 18 July 1801 the *Investigator* was able to show its stern to Portsmouth. On the voyage south, Flinders commenced a series of measurements on the magnetic deviation of the ship's compass, records that were eventually to result in a paper read before the Royal Society. By 16 October the Cape of Good Hope was sighted, and here they spent the next eighteen days. John Crosley, the astronomer, left the *Investigator* at the Cape due to ill health, which placed the additional burden of undertaking the astronomical work on Flinders. By now it had become apparent that the timbers of the *Investigator* leaked badly, but Flinders, having obtained a vessel for his purpose, was determined to press on.

On 6 December 1801, landfall was made on the New Holland coast, close to Cape Leeuwin; two days later the *Investigator* rode at anchor in King George Sound. Here began the work of the scientific party, and the botanists were soon investigating the neighbourhood. Brown and Bauer were able to collect upwards of 500 species of plants in the King George district alone. Wood was taken aboard to construct garden boxes for the live plants that the botanists were returning to the ship. Among the plants collected by Brown was a species of pitcher plant which Flinders found intriguing in its ability to trap insects. Also obtained in the region were lizards, including the guano described by Dampier as having speckled yellow and black colouring, a large

and ugly head, and only a stump of a tail, which much resembled the head. Brown collected specimens of the red-capped parrot, *Purpureicephalus spurius*, and western rosella, *Platycercus icterotis*, both of which had been described by Menzies in his journal from Vancouver's voyage of 1791, but were not formally described until the German naturalist Heinrich Kuhl produced a description based on Brown's specimens in 1820.

After a month's refurbishment of the *Investigator*, Flinders set off to chart the south coast of New Holland, a task which Governor King had originally assigned to Grant in the *Lady Nelson*. To establish an accurate survey, Flinders attempted to stay within sight of land at all times, allowing Brown and his companions to go ashore whenever the *Investigator* anchored. Names such as Petrel Bay and Goose Island commemorate the birds that Flinders and the scientific party encountered at these anchorages. Flinders often stayed an extra day or two to allow the botanists more time for their work, a concession in which few other naval commanders were willing to indulge. At Lucky

'*Cephalotus follicularis*'
Flinders. *A voyage to Terra Australis*. 1814.
Cephalotus follicularis

Bay near Cape Le Grande, the *Investigator* remained at anchor three days while Brown and Bauer added 100 more species to their ever-increasing list. On nearby Mondrain Island they reported the first sighting of the Recherche rock-wallaby, *Petrogale lateralis*. Although Brown brought back many animal skins from the voyage, the majority were birds, the mammals had to await the Frenchman, Péron, of Baudin's expedition for their descriptions. Brown, however, was a traditional naturalist and considered botany, zoology, and mineralogy all within his purview. Throughout the voyage he not only paid attention to the soil where he uprooted his plant specimens but also brought back many minerals.

Progressing eastward, the *Investigator* anchored at Goose Island Bay where Brown collected another twenty-nine species of plants, twelve of them new to science. Here was sighted *Cereopsis novaehollandiae*, the Cape Barren goose, earlier noted by La Billardière, as well as the penguin, *Eudyptula minor*. The bight coast produced only 200 new species for Brown, a circumstance he attributed to the general sterility of the land and the unfavourable season. However, it was not until St Peter Island that Brown could remark that the land produced no item new to natural history. Species of kangaroos were taken on both St Francis Island and Flinders Island. Approaching the bodies of water that were later to be named Spencer Gulf and the Gulf of St Vincent, Flinders sailed northward, thinking that either might be the strait thought to divide New Holland from New South Wales. Such was not the case, for the land closed in on either side, and the gulfs ended only in swamps. At the head of Spencer Gulf, Brown, Bauer, and Westall took some days to climb a mountain upon which Flinders bestowed Brown's name. On Mount Brown the three climbers collected specimens of *Psephotus varius*, the mulga parrot, which was given the name '*Psittacus multicolor*' by Kuhl from the description that Brown wrote of it. After the disappointment of the gulfs, Kangaroo Island was surveyed and named by Flinders for the two apparently dissimilar kangaroos found there, *Macropus fuliginosus*, the western grey kangaroo, and *Macropus eugenii*, the tammar. Here the Kangaroo Island dwarf emu was first seen.

Sailing south-west a sail was sighted which proved to be the French vessel *Le Géographe* under Captain Nicholas Baudin. There existed a distinct element of rivalry between the two surveying-scientific expeditions, so the meeting was strained but cordial. Flinders and Brown went aboard the French frigate where they learned of Baudin's surveying efforts, mostly around Van Diemens Land, and in turn informed the French of their own efforts charting the bight between Cape Leeuwin and their present position. Flinders named the site of the meeting Encounter Bay. Péron, the naturalist aboard *Le Géographe*, was later to publish a narrative of the French voyage in 1807 which claimed that the whole southern coast had been discovered by the French, and placed the name '*Terra Napoleon*' on the map of the area.

With provisions in short supply, Flinders continued eastward entering Port Phillip where Brown, Bauer, and Good were given time to collect. The result was an additional ninety-six species of plants and animals which included a bird Brown described as the Banksian cockatoo but was probably *Calyptorhynchus funereus*, the yellow-tailed black-cockatoo, and an undescribed white-crested bird, '*Merops carunculatus*'. During the voyage Brown collected 217 bird skins and described 224 species of birds, the unpublished Latin descriptions of which remain in the British Museum.

Pressing on, Flinders passed through Bass Strait and on to Port Jackson where the *Investigator* arrived on 9 May 1802. In Sydney there followed a period of three months refitting the *Investigator* before she set off northward. All the live plants were taken ashore and planted in either Governor King's garden or in Caley's garden at Parramatta, despite the poor condition of most of the specimens. Ten boxes of these plants were to be trans-shipped to England the following February. Brown roamed over the Sydney district collecting plants and animals; he was able to collect almost 1,000 species in New South Wales during his various visits there.

While in Sydney Robert Brown wrote to Dr Jonas Dryander, the botanist who served both Joseph Banks and the Royal Society as librarian. Despite his large collections, Brown was reluctant to admit much success, a trait that he exhibited throughout the voyage. The number of plants Brown found was much less than he expected: of the 750 species he had already collected he thought only about 300 had not been collected by either Menzies, Banks, or La Billardière. Of special interest to Dryander, Brown had collected six species of the genus *Correa*, named for the exiled Portuguese botanist José Correa de Serra by James Edward Smith. Brown also collected twenty species of banksias at King George Sound and Lucky Bay. Echoing previous requests from George Caley, Brown requested Dryander to forward him some drying paper for plants as much of his had been ruined by the dampness that pervaded the *Investigator*. He also asked Dryander to send any recent botanical books such as La Billardière's work, if it had been published.

If 300 new species were but a small number to Robert Brown, it was proving a tremendous work load for the draughtsman, Bauer. He completed 350 sketches during the voyage from King George Sound to

'*Antiarus macrophylla*'
Bauer. *Illustrationes Florae Novae Hollandiae*. 1813.
Antiaris toxicaria

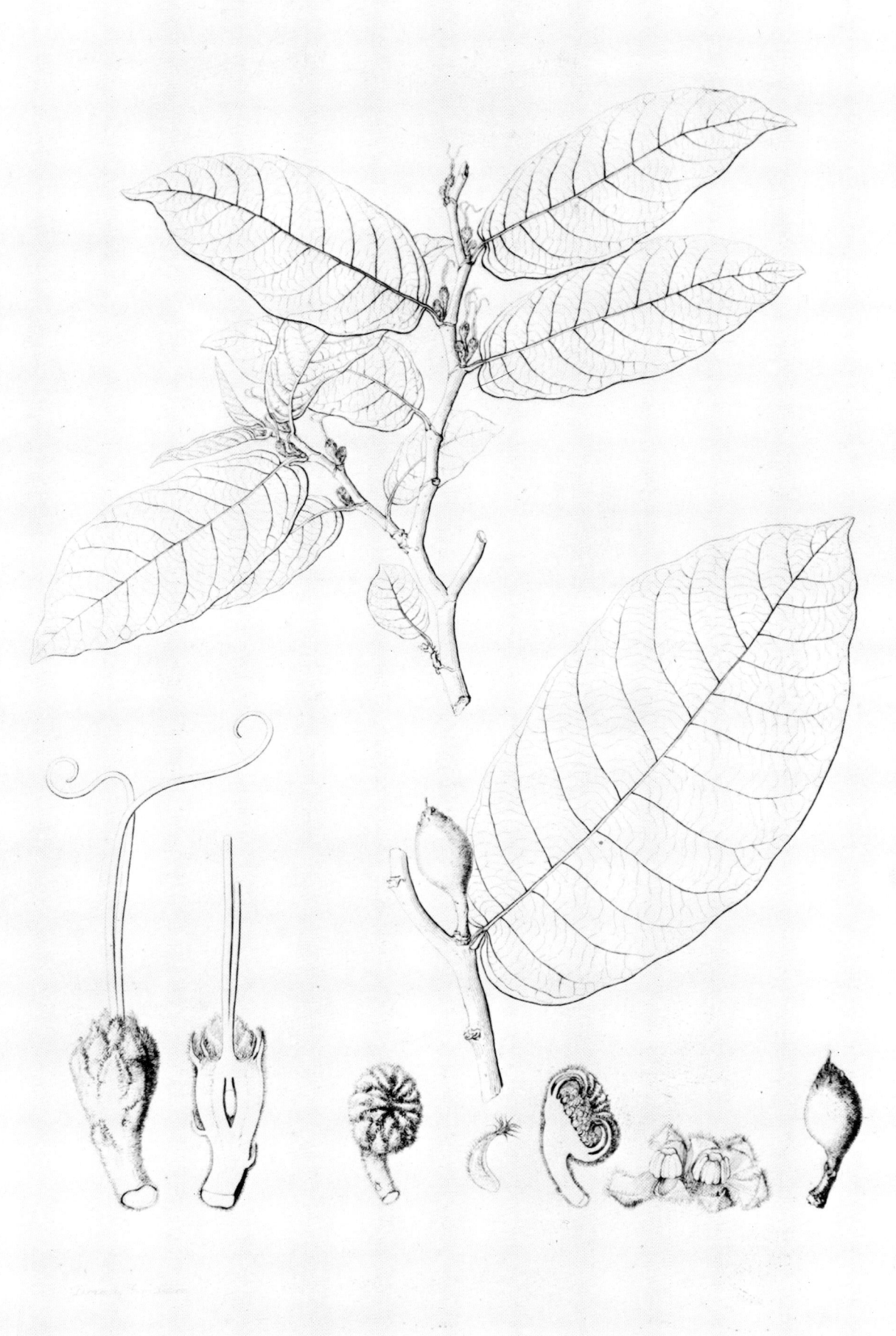

Port Jackson, 100 of them animals. Before the *Investigator* sailed northward, Bauer completed an additional 350 drawings, all of which were left with Governor King for safe keeping.

Robert Brown also corresponded with his patron Joseph Banks and sent him a box of seeds. Brown thought that of all the territory in New Holland that they had so far surveyed, by far the best in terms of new species was New South Wales. Unfortunately the time spent on botanical collections had so far limited his zoological and mineralogical efforts to superficial surveys. Brown commented on the Baudin expedition, suggesting that the greater and better part of the expedition's scientific personnel had either died or left the vessels at Mauritius, but he was complementary about the botanist, Jean-Baptiste Leschenault de la Tour, and eventually named a genus *Lechenaultia* for him.

When the *Investigator* arrived in Port Jackson, the second vessel of Baudin's expedition, *Le Naturaliste*, was there. Baudin had asked Flinders to instruct Captain Hamelin of *Le Naturaliste* to await him in Sydney, but Hamelin chose to sail for Mauritius instead; however he was soon forced back to Port Jackson by contrary winds. Baudin himself arrived off Sydney Heads in June but *Le Géographe*, rendered helpless by the wasted state of its crew due to scurvy, was unable to sail in through the heads. A boatcrew from the *Investigator* helped tow *Le Géographe* to an anchorage in the harbour. The French were treated with the usual courtesy, despite some feeling that their purpose might not be entirely scientific. This antipathy was later to be borne out when Péron and Freycinet, two of the scientific personnel, compiled a report on Sydney and its defences.

By 21 July the *Investigator* was again ready for sea; the collapsible greenhouse had been erected on the quarterdeck after some minor modifications. The next day she slipped down the harbour with the *Lady Nelson* in company as tender. Lieutenant James Grant was no longer commander of the *Lady Nelson*, as he had requested a return to England when it had been found that he lacked the surveying skills that were so necessary for exploratory voyages. Grant was replaced by Lieutenant John Murray. Sailing northward Flinders entered Hervey Bay, where Brown and his companions went ashore to seek specimens, and then on to Port Curtis where again Brown was given free rein. The *Lady Nelson* badly damaged one of her movable keels on the voyage and was sent back to Sydney; the *Investigator* continued to the north alone, stopping frequently while Flinders made his all important surveys. Although Brown noted in his botanical appendix to Flinders' narrative *Voyage to Terra Australis* that the scientific party was given frequent opportunities to collect, Brown complained to Banks that he did not have as

'*Flindersia australis*'
Flinders. *A voyage to Terra Australis*. 1814.
Flindersia australis

many chances ashore as he would have liked. Banks wrote back to Brown remonstrating that if he had had as many opportunities when on the voyage with Cook he would have been quite content.

From Broad Sound they progressed quickly up through Torres Strait, traversing it in three days, and then entered the Gulf of Carpentaria. Travelling down the eastern shore of the Gulf, Flinders continued his charting, correcting the 150-year-old Dutch surveys. While in the Gulf, Flinders found it necessary to careen the *Investigator* in an attempt to caulk some of the never-ending leaks. On inspecting the hull, his carpenters told Flinders that the timbers of the *Investigator* were so rotten that they could not be expected to last more than six months. The *Investigator* was repaired to the best of the carpenters' ability in the isolated circumstances, but Flinders now knew that the expedition was sailing on borrowed time. While repairs were carried out, Brown and Bauer sought more specimens in the Wellesley Islands, finding as usual several new species. Brown noted that neither of the commercial crops of the tropics, nutmeg and coconuts, were native to New Holland even in the tropical northern region, a dearth which was to reduce the economic viability of early settlements in the area.

'*Psittacus brownii*'
Donovan. *Naturalists Repository*. 1824.
Platycercus venustus

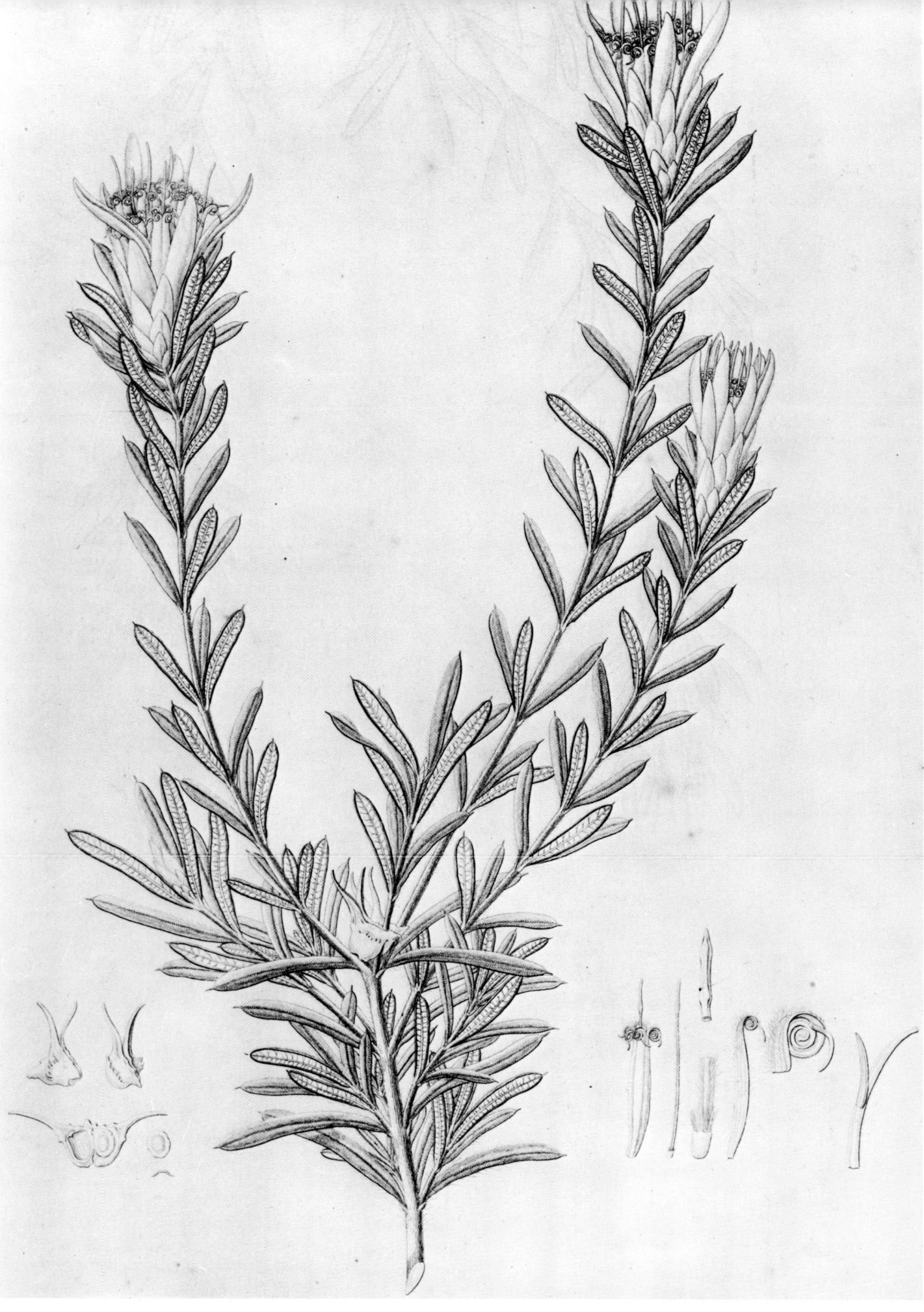

Flinders continued charting the Gulf—but with a new urgency. Near Melville Bay, a parrot of a species unknown at the time, was taken; the painting of it by Bauer reveals it to be the northern rosella, *Platycercus venustus*, later described by the Dutch naturalist Coenraad Jacob Temminck, who in 1819 dedicated the species to Robert Brown with the name '*Psittacus brownii*'. Kuhl in 1820 gave the species the specific name *venustus*, and due to delays in publishing the journal in which Temminck's description appeared, Kuhl's name has precedence.

By the beginning of January 1803, the expedition had reached Groote Eylandt where Brown found other plants to excite his interest including a species of nutmeg, although not the commercial species which had made the Molucca Islands the 'spice islands'. The 17 February saw the completion of the charting of the Gulf of Carpentaria, but by now Flinders had used three of the *Investigator*'s projected six-month life span. Cruising westward along the desolate coast, the *Investigator* came across an astonishing sight: six vessels lying close to a beach. These belonged to Malays who frequently crossed from their home islands to the northern coast of New Holland in search of trepang, the sea cucumbers much sought by the Chinese as delicacies. Soon after, Flinders was forced to break off his survey and run for Timor. Scurvy was now rife in his crew as well as partially laming Flinders, and both the vessel and crew were severely weakened. Finding little in the way of supplies at Timor and with the summer monsoons precluding a return trip through the Torres Strait, Flinders set a course back to Port Jackson via Cape Leeuwin. As was common on many vessels sailing the tropics, dysentery broke out soon after the *Investigator* left Timor which further added to the dismal health of the officers and crew. Making all possible sail, the *Investigator* raced for Port Jackson, its crew steadily weakening. A number of the ship's company did not survive that final run, or died soon after reaching Port Jackson on 9 June 1803. Peter Good, the gardener, was one.

In Sydney, after a survey of the *Investigator*'s timbers, the vessel was condemned from service. Most of the crew were paid off and returned to England. Of the scientific party, only Westall chose to leave New South Wales immediately. Allen, the miner, remained in Sydney for some time, while Robert Brown and Ferdinand Bauer considered that they could still be constructively employed with their botanical work in the colony.

Flinders attempted to obtain another vessel to take up the survey where the *Investigator* had left off, but no suitable vessels were available in New South Wales.

'*Lambertia formosa*'
Flinders. *A Voyage to Terra Australis*. 1814.
Lambertia formosa

Flinders then took passage in the *Porpoise* back to England along with the best specimens from Brown's herbarium and live plants and seeds for the garden at Kew. Bad luck continued to plague Flinders, for the *Porpoise* drove on to one of the barrier reefs much as Cook's *Endeavour* had done more than thirty years before. This time, however, the consequences were more severe: the *Porpoise* was abandoned. Flinders piloted a small boat back to Port Jackson to organise a rescue party for the rest of the *Porpoise*'s crew, but Brown's painstakingly collected plants were lost. Once again Flinders set off for England, this time on the small vessel *Cumberland*, but his luck deteriorated, for when the *Cumberland* put into Mauritius to reprovision, Flinders was detained by the French commander. War had again broken out between France and England, and the French governor of Mauritius, Charles De Caen, a rabid nationalist, interned Flinders on the grounds that although his passport was for the *Investigator* the vessel he had arrived on was the *Cumberland*. While Flinders was indeed a serving naval officer no longer on an exploratory voyage, his sequestration for several years on Mauritius was certainly a denial of the spirit of the passport issued to the *Investigator*.

In 1805, while still detained on Mauritius, Flinders wrote to the Admiralty proposing that the entire continent of New Holland, which he had indisputably shown to be connected to New South Wales, should be renamed *Terra Australis* or Australia.

Robert Brown and Ferdinand Bauer avoided the ill-luck of Flinders. They both collected extensively in New South Wales, around Sydney, the major rivers, and the Blue Mountains during 1804 and 1805, adding still another 1,000 specimens to their burgeoning collection. The collections were not limited to extant plants, they also collected fossil plants in the Hunter Valley.

Ferdinand Bauer took passage to Norfolk Island where he collected and illustrated plants until 1805, when he returned to Sydney. These specimens were given to the German naturalist Stephan Endlicher on Bauer's return to England and were formally described in Endlicher's *Prodromus Florae Norfolicae* published in 1833. One of the plants described, *Streblorrhiza*, is now extinct and is known only from Bauer's drawing.

During his time in the various parts of the colony after the termination of the *Investigator* voyage, Brown actively collected birds, writing descriptions of almost forty species including *Pezoporus wallicus*, the ground parrot, and a specimen he called '*Psittacus eximius*'. On his return to England, Brown took with him many bird skins, the majority of which ended up in the British Museum. Many specimens were also given by Brown to the Linnean Society. When Coenraad Jacob Temminck and Heinrich Kuhl visited London in 1819, they were able to study the parrots that Brown had given to the

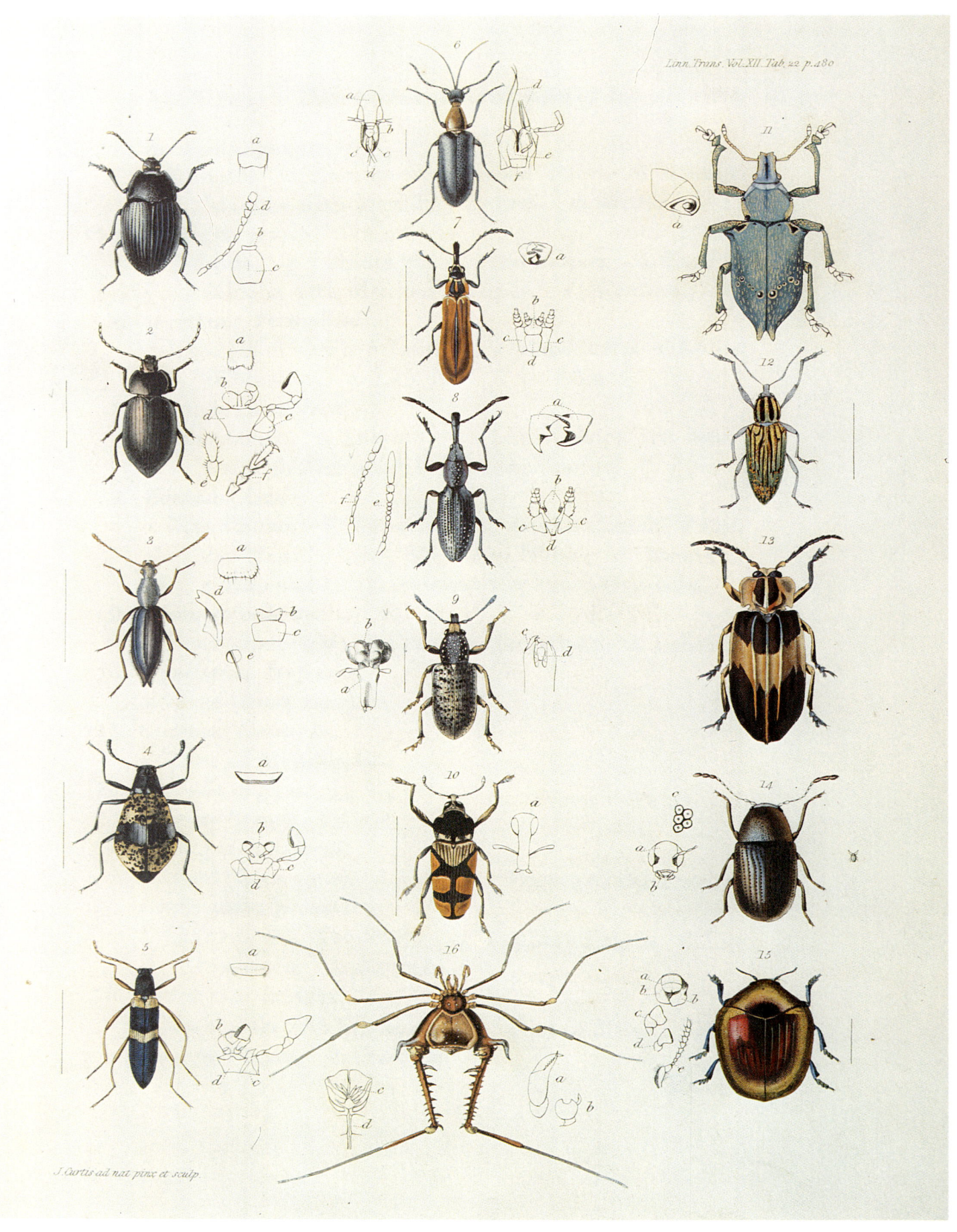

J. Curtis ad nat. pinx et sculp.

'Insects'
Kirby. *Transactions of the Linnean Society.* 1818.

'Insects'
Kirby. *Transactions of the Linnean Society.* 1818.

Aneilema crispata. Brown prod. fl. nov. holl. p. 271. n. 5.

Ferd. Bauer.

Linnean Society and publish their findings. Later still, in 1827, the English zoologist Nicholas Aylward Vigors and the American naturalist (resident in England) Thomas Horsfield described forty of these birds. A number of the insects collected by Brown while he was in New Holland were donated by him to the English naturalist Reverend William Kirby who published descriptions and illustrations of them in the *Transactions of the Linnean Society*.

By 1805 the formerly condemned *Investigator* had been repaired sufficiently to limp back to England, and Brown and Bauer took passage in her. The *Investigator*'s return voyage took five tedious months in which Brown was able to continue describing some of the 3,900 species of plants he had collected. Due to Brown's cautious duplication of the collected plants, he still retained specimens of those plants lost in the wreck of the *Porpoise*.

On Brown's return to England, Banks sought a salary for him from the government to continue his taxonomic work on the plant specimens. Banks wrote to Secretary of the Admiralty Marsden proposing that the government should continue to pay the salaries of both Brown and Bauer while they finished their manuscripts and sketches respectively, a task which Banks promised to oversee. Banks furthermore recommended that all the animal specimens be sent immediately to the British Museum, that Brown select a set of botanical specimens for the Admiralty and publish an account of the chosen specimens, that Bauer present his finished drawings or paintings to the Admiralty, and that Brown and Bauer publish a periodical work on the natural history of the voyage. Clearly Banks intended that a botany of New Holland such as had never been published after Cook's voyage would result from the journey of the *Investigator*.

By utilising specimens brought back from New Holland from voyages as far back as those of Dampier (1699), Banks and Solander (1770), Nelson (1777), Menzies (1791), Paterson (1791–1810), and Baudin (1802) as well as those supplied by George Caley, Brown was able to add another 300 species to his collection, bringing the total number of plant species from Australia to 4,200. In 1810 Brown published the first volume of *Prodromus Florae Novae Hollandiae* covering 2,000 of those species, the majority new to botanical science. Of a highly technical nature, the work was not a commercial success, and Brown withdrew it from sale without publishing the second volume. Nevertheless the first volume was well thought of by most of the respected botanists of the day, not only for its careful and competent documentation of much of the flora of New Holland but also because it

was one of the first botanical works to partially adopt the 'natural' system of classification espoused by Antoine-Laurent de Jussieu in his *Genera Plantarum secundum Ordinales naturales disposita*. Brown's problems with fitting his specimens into either system, the sexual system of Linnaeus or the natural affinity system of de Jussieu, led him to improve upon de Jussieu's classificatory scheme. Although the system of natural affinity led to classification hierarchies, the system was still held back by the belief in the 'perfection' and constancy of species, shackles that were not to be removed from taxonomy until the middle of the century.

Brown in his appendix, 'General Remarks, geographical and systematical, on the Botany of Terra

'*Banksia coccinea*'
Bauer. *Illustrationes Florae Novae Hollandiae*. 1813.
Banksia coccinea

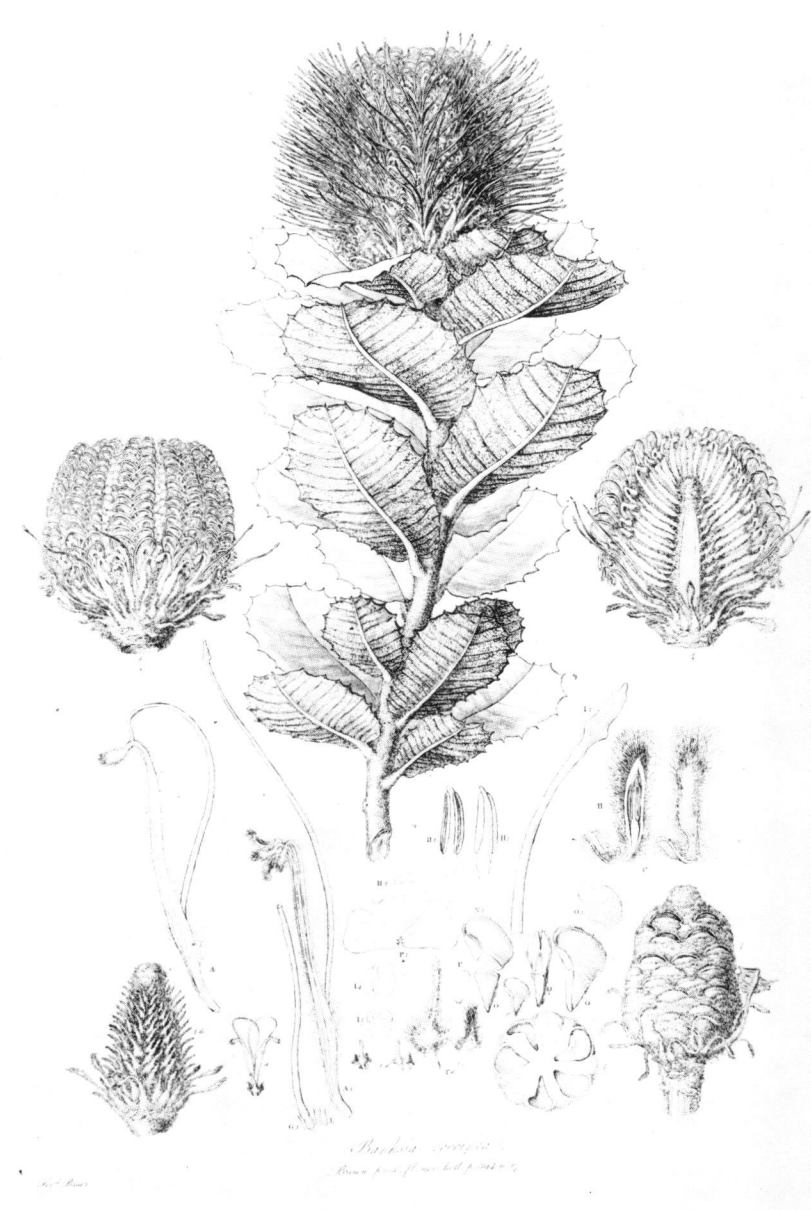

'*Aneilema crispata*'
Bauer. *Illustrationes Florae Novae Hollandiae*. 1813.
Pollia crispata

Australis' to Flinders *Voyage to Terra Australis* published in 1814 noted that:

> A methodical, and at the same time a natural, arrangement of these families is, in the existing state of our knowledge, perhaps impractible.[10]

The significance of Brown's work can be judged from the number of specimens that he collected in New Holland and treated to descriptions as compared with other contemporary works. In 1805 Jonas Dryander, compiling a catalogue of the plants of New Holland from published literature, listed some 370 species, while Brown, collecting at this same period, found 3,900 species. It must be noted that Brown had the advantage of collecting in New Holland itself while Dryander could only fossick through material returned to England. In 1860 Sir Joseph Dalton Hooker, himself a well respected botanist, said of the voyage of the *Investigator* and of Brown's work:

> . . . as far as botany is concerned, the most important in its results ever undertaken, and hence marks an epoch in the history of that science.[11]

Ferdinand Bauer, after his return to England, began in 1813 to publish a folio of his botanical drawings from the voyage under the title *Illustrationes Florae Novae Hollandiae*, but it was equally as unsuccessful in its sales as Brown's *Prodromus*, possibly because the market for lavishly illustrated and expensive productions on the flora and fauna of New Holland had been glutted. Bauer abandoned publication after the first volume of fifteen plates, and returned to his native Austria.

Chapter Six

In 1802 the *Investigator* arrived in Port Jackson after charting much of the southern coast of New Holland on the voyage from England to New South Wales. This year was also to see the advent of the other major expedition to the fifth continent during the first decade of the nineteenth century, that of the French under Nicholas Baudin. While these two expeditions drew the attention of the naturalists domiciled in Europe and produced a wealth of specimens, the naturalist-explorers resident in the colony continued their less-heralded work.

Charles F. Greville, in a letter dispatched to Robert Brown in January of 1802, wrote of Francis Barrallier collecting seeds for him and of the necessity for the resident collectors to continue to send specimens from New South Wales despite the attention paid to the exotic flora and fauna turned up by Brown and the *Investigator* party. The acclaim with which Brown was received in the colony was to spark the jealousy of Banks' resident collector, George Caley. Caley made several journeys inland to the Blue Mountains in the hope of penetrating that formidable barrier but met with little success in his explorations. He continued to ship seeds to England, some to Colville—a nurseryman in London—a practice of which Governor King strongly disapproved. King considered that all Caley's efforts should be devoted to the procurement of specimens for Banks. Under the terms of Caley's agreement with Banks, however, he was allowed to supply other individuals with material. Banks made arrangements for Caley to travel on the *Investigator*, if he so desired, when that vessel left Port Jackson to explore northward, but Caley turned down the opportunity. Apparently Caley was irritated by the botanical interlopers on the *Investigator*. Governor King later wrote to Banks that Caley was unhappy because King had supplied Brown with plant boxes for the *Porpoise* while refusing the same request from Caley. Caley felt that Brown was 'a labourer in the field that ought to be wrought by himself'.[1]

Toward the end of the year, both Caley and Barrallier set out on separate expeditions intended to delineate a path through the Blue Mountains. In October, while Caley was in the foothills of the mountains, King wrote to Banks expressing the hope that Banks was benefiting from Caley's labour, but having dealt first hand with Caley, the governor was not overly optimistic. On his return from yet another unsuccessful negotiation of the mountains, Caley himself wrote to Banks outlining his explorations, commenting on the undescribed plant species he had amassed, and disparaging Barrallier's contributions to inland discovery. Caley was as reluctant as ever to acknowledge the merits of others, especially those competing in Caley's field of endeavour, which he had now expanded from botany to geographical discovery. In future years of Australian exploration this was to become a common theme—naturalists yearning for the greater fame accorded to explorers—while the contrary was also evident, explorers occupying much of their time in the collection of natural curiosities.

Barrallier set off at approximately the same time as Caley, following his liberation from military duties with the connivance of Governor King. Despite his own earlier exploratory journeys, William Paterson was most reluctant to release one of his officers for inland discovery. King therefore claimed Barrallier as an aide-de-camp and then promptly sent him on an embassy to the 'King of the Mountains', a transparent artifice but one necessary for the undertaking of the exploration King desired. A few geological specimens were collected by Barrallier but nothing of great importance was discovered, probably much to Caley's great satisfaction. The specimens were subsequently forwarded to Banks.

Barrallier's first attempt at surmounting the Blue Mountains had ended in failure, but he was determined to try again. Before Barrallier's second attempt had been underway a week, Caley again wrote to Banks expressing the opinion that this attempt was also doomed to failure, for Barrallier insisted upon using bullocks as transport rather than the horses which Caley proposed. Barrallier set out from Parramatta with four soldiers and five convicts. During the westward march Barrallier noted in his journal the species of trees they encountered—mostly blue gum, yellow gum, ironbark, and stringybark—and recorded the general fertility of the soil. He collected specimens of plants and on 9 November was shown by a group of Aborigines portions of what Barrallier called a 'monkey' and the Aborigines called a 'colo'. Barrallier wished to obtain the head of the animal, but it had disappeared. He did manage to barter for the two paws which were preserved in alcohol and taken back to King. The 'monkey' was probably one of the first koalas (*Phascolarctos cinereus*) seen by Europeans in New South Wales.

Continuing westward the next day, Barrallier located a deposit of slate containing fossils of ferns and leaves; in close proximity was found a body of iron ore. Following a river that same day, Barrallier noted an abundance of fish, bivalves, and gastropods but concluded that the flora was much the same as that found in the Sydney region. During the next few days they encountered 'pheasants' (lyrebirds) and later in the journey came across a lizard which so confounded Barrallier with its distinctive red stomach that he determined to skin it and return it to Sydney. Unfortunately in his attempt at preserving the skin, Barrallier destroyed the specimen.

By 26 November, just when they thought that they had finally achieved their goal in crossing the Blue Mountains, they found a higher ridge of mountains ahead of them. Barrallier led his party on, noting sandstone replete with fossil shells, some trees he called figs, and another tree with fruit much like a cherry. Finally, lack of food and the exhuastion of his men forced Barrallier back without attempting the ridge they had seen. Barrallier, however, was still fresh enough to look for aquatic insects along a riverbank while his men nursed their weariness. By 24 December the party had returned to Sydney; the passage through the mountains remained an enigma for many years to come. By his own estimate, Barrallier had trekked 137 miles (250 kilometres) along the mountain range, all to no avail.

Caley made one more short attack on the mountains but was away only a brief time before giving up the attempt. His horses were no better for the purpose than had been Barrallier's bullocks. Concomitant with the inland exploration, King continued to sanction exploration by sea, as much to thwart any French plans for the colonisation of Van Diemens Land as for the purpose of gaining geographic knowledge. In November he sent the colonial vessel, *Cumberland* to Kings Island in Bass Strait and then to Port Phillip to survey and comment on its natural productions. A gardener was included in the ship's company, and it is probable that this was James Fleming. Earlier that month in a dispatch to Lord Hobart who had taken over direction of the colonies from the Duke of Portland, Governor King discussed the prospects of exportation from New South Wales, including such likely exports as whale oil, seal skins from Bass Strait, coal from Coal River or the Hunter River as it was increasingly being called, and fustic for dyeing. The Home Office was vitally interested in any return that could be made from its continual investment in the colony.

Back in Europe the fauna of New Holland was in great demand. In 1800 Louis Defresne, one of the French naturalists who had sailed as far as China on the ill-fated expedition of La Perouse in 1785, travelled to London to purchase animals for the Museum d'Histoire Naturelle de Paris where he was then employed. In 1802 he returned to England for much the same purpose. This time he was able to buy live kangaroos which he brought back to Paris along with a specimen of the platypus, received from Joseph Banks as a present for the Museum. Charles Blagden, a friend of Banks then touring France, had earlier written to Banks suggesting to him that a pair of live kangaroos would be a handsome present for Napoleon Bonaparte, the first consul of France, in return for Bonaparte's efforts to advance science. There was also some interest in the idea of introducing kangaroos into France as a game animal, but this quixotic idea came to naught.

The year 1802 saw the publication of the second supplement to John Latham's *A General Synopsis of Birds*. This supplement contained numerous birds of New Holland, specimens which Latham had never seen. The origin of the descriptions of many of these birds were a series of drawings, most of them executed in the 1790s by Thomas Watling. The original drawings were borrowed from A. B. Lambert who presumably had acquired them from John White. In a letter to Lambert in 1800, Latham admitted that he was not sure of the genus of many of the birds; he needed more information than could be obtained from the drawings. Latham went on to comment:

> The names I have given are such as struck me to be best adapted, but I am not solicitous to impose them on the world, especially as some persons seem to take pleasure in altering the names of previous describers.[2]

Latham was roundly criticised for his habit of describing birds from paintings or drawings, and it is an interesting feature of Australian natural history that a number of bird and mammal species were described from illustrations rather than specimens.

The controversy over the platypus continued to rage. Everard Home published 'A Description of the Anatomy of *Ornithorhynchus paradoxus*' in the *Philosophical Transactions of the Royal Society* in 1802, describing male and female specimens lent to him by Joseph Banks. The paper also included details of the platypus' life-history written by ex-Governor John Hunter from observations he had made while resident in New South Wales. Home, a comparative anatomist, was astounded by the platypus. The female had no mammary glands that he could find—a central feature of the mammals—and this led him to closely examine the species' reproductive system which only confused him more. The female platypus' reproductive system,

'*Ornithorhynchus hystrix*'
Home. *Philosophical Transactions of the Royal Society*. 1802.
Tachyglossus aculeatus

instead of having oviducts uniting to form a uterus, opened into a cloaca similar to the features found in ovoviviparous lizards and dogfish. Caley was soon to send corroborating evidence to Banks on this point for the next year he reported that an Aboriginal had told him that the platypus lived underground and laid eggs. Home could only envisage the bizarre animal as an intermediate link between the mammals, the birds, and the amphibians. The *Edinburgh Review* published an anonymous review of Home's article the following year in which Home was thoroughly criticised. The unknown author accepted the anatomical features described by Home, although he was inclined to taxonomically correlate the platypus with the Amphibians, but castigated the arrangement of the paper:

> The chain of connection which Mr. Home appears to have followed in this instance, might be excusable in a common-place book, but can hardly be admitted in a book of science . . .[3]

He concluded that the disarray of the paper must have resulted from 'want of time, or want of inclination'[4]. Home also published a 'Description of the

Anatomy of the *Ornithorhynchus hystrix*' that same year detailing a description of the echidna and including William Bligh's drawing of the animal from 1792.

For his pains this paper by Home was also criticised in the previously mentioned article in the *Edinburgh Review*.

Further reports in the *Transactions of the Linnean Society of London* dealing with the flora and fauna of New Holland in 1802 included: a description of the lyrebird, a description of the lily genus, *Doryanthes*, by José Correa de Serra using specimens discovered by George Bass and others which had since been grown at Kew, and an article by James Edward Smith on the botanical characters of the Myrti, specimens of which

'*Doryanthes excelsa*'
Bauer. *Illustrationes Florae Novae Hollandiae*. 1813.
Doryanthes excelsa

had been collected by John White and David Burton.

The demise of the *Naturalist's Pocket Magazine* occurred after five years of publication. The last volume contained no less than thirteen organisms from New South Wales, including two insects and eleven plants. The perennial *Naturalist's Miscellany* continued publication and included other examples of the New Holland flora and fauna. Another publication of George Shaw's, *General Zoology*, reached its third volume in 1802, which dealt with the Amphibia and included a

Heath sculp.

'Long necked tortoise'
Shaw. *General Zoology*. Volume III, part I. 1802.
Chelodina longicollis

tortoise, a frog, five lizards, and two snakes from New
Holland, many of them illustrated from John White's
Journal of a Voyage to New South Wales. Shaw, unlike
Home, was convinced that the platypus was a mammal
and so had included it in an earlier volume dealing with
mammals.

In 1802 the second of the major scientific
expeditions of the decade to visit New Holland put into
Port Jackson; this was the French expedition under
Nicholas Baudin. While conceived in good faith as an
exploratory and scientific expedition, Baudin's voyage
was to be stigmatised both during its stay in Port
Jackson and on its return to Europe by the political
machinations of the nationalists on both the English
and French sides. Nicholas Baudin had from 1796 to
1798 commanded a scientific expedition to the West
Indies. On his return from the Caribbean, he proposed
to the Institut National an expedition to chart the
waters of New Holland. The proposal was not acted
upon until 1800 when it was approved by Napoleon
Bonaparte. It was presumably Bonaparte's advocacy of
the voyage that the English physician Charles Blagden
considered as an advance to science when suggesting to
Joseph Banks that a present of live kangaroos should be

made to the first consul. Whether the approval resulted
from political or military interest in the southern
hemisphere is open to speculation, but among Baudin's
orders were instructions to ascertain whether there
were any British settlements in Van Diemens Land.
Other orders committed Baudin to survey the south-
eastern coast of Van Diemens Land, Bass Strait, and the
southern, western, and northern coasts of New
Holland.

A committee from the Institut National oversaw the
preparations for the voyage. Influential members of the
committee included Lacépède, de Jussieu, and Cuvier.
They chose to inundate the expedition with some
twenty-two scientific personnel, among them astronomers,
hydrographers, zoologists, botanists, mineralogists,
gardeners, and artists. Four botanists headed by Louis
Leschenault de la Tour and four zoologists under René
Maugé de Cely were chosen for the expedition. At the
last moment a young medical student, Francois Péron,
embarked, possibly to take the place of the German
explorer and scientist Alexander von Humboldt who
hoped to join the expedition but failed to gain approval
for his passage. Two of the naturalists, Maugé de Cely
and Anselme Riedlé, had previously sailed with Baudin
on his voyage to the West Indies. A pair of ships were
chosen for the expedition, *Le Géographe* and *Le
Naturaliste*, large 350-ton vessels that drew 5 metres of
water, a draught that was to be crucial in their attempts

to chart the inshore waters of the continent.

Preparations for the voyage were extensive: the two ships were packed with equipment, including a large library containing many of the journals of former mariners voyaging to New Holland from William Dampier to Cook, Phillip, Bligh, and La Billardière. As could be expected numerous texts on botany and zoology completed the library. *Le Géographe* and *Le Naturaliste* sailed on 19 October 1800, having obtained passports from the British government to guarantee their safety at the hands of the British Navy. The wait was worthwhile for they were intercepted by an English frigate soon after leaving the French coast. The long and tiresome voyage around the Cape of Good Hope and on to Mauritius took its toll on the optimism of both the crew and the scientists. Baudin, a strict disciplinarian who used both his crew and himself unstintingly, clashed frequently with his own officers and the scientists. At Mauritius twenty officers and scientists were left ashore either of their own volition or on Baudin's orders. Included among these withdrawals were a number of the appointed artists which caused the helmsman of *Le Géographe*, Charles Lesueur, to assist the remaining official artist, Nicholas Petit, with the natural history draughtsmanship during the voyage.

The coast of New Holland was sighted on 27 May 1801, close to Cape Leeuwin. Delays in the outward journey and the probability of winter storms caused Baudin to ignore his orders to survey Van Diemens Land first and he turned north to examine the west and north-western coasts of New Holland. This decision was to cost him the discovery and survey of a major portion of the south coast of New Holland. Within hours of sighting the coast, a dredge was heaved overboard, despite the 130 metres of water, and after half an hour it was returned to the deck with a wide variety of organisms enmeshed in it—algae, coral, sponges, and other invertebrates. Péron and Lesueur spent that night classifying and sketching the myriad specimens, and even the dour Baudin enthusiastically recorded details of the finds in his journal. The dredge was to be put over several more times in the following four days, always with rich rewards, before the two vessels anchored in Geographe Bay. On 30 May Riedlé, the gardener, and Depuch, one of the mineralogists on the expedition, were given the honour of making the first forays ashore and returned with detailed reports of the surrounding district, its flora, fauna, and geology. On 4 June the rest of the impatient naturalists were given their chance ashore, resulting in Riedlé collecting a large assemblage of plants including wild garlic and celery, Maugé concentrating on the collection of birds, and Péron locating fossils in addition to the only insects he could find, the ubiquitous ants. As recompense for the plants he pillaged, Riedlé planted a garden of European fruits and vegetables. The ships remained at

anchor for over a week, during which time specimens were accumulated from forays ashore as well as from dredging the sea floor:

> Amongst the various objects of Natural History that we collected, there was nothing very curious, except some sponges and several jellyfish. One of the latter was extremely beautiful and no doubt quite novel to those interested. The dredge brought up several starfish that were unknown to us and will be to many others.[5]

Strong winds eventually forced the two ships from their exposed anchorage, and here they were separated. Despite attempts to locate each other, *Le Naturaliste* and *Le Géographe* pursued separate routes until they met in Timor three months later.

Baudin, after a short search for *Le Naturaliste*, took *Le Géographe* north to Shark Bay, arriving off Dirk Hartog Island on 23 June. Here Riedlé and Péron went ashore, returning with twelve to fifteen new plants, two lizards, seven birds, and several turban shells. Four days later the ships ventured into Shark Bay, Péron commenting on the numerous cnidarians he observed from *Le Géographe*. Sea snakes were also numerous, and after watching them chase small schools of fish, and finding fish in their stomachs, Péron concluded that the sea snakes were predominantly fish eaters. The snakes in turn were presumed to have been eaten by sharks for several sharks which Péron dissected had sea snakes in their stomachs. With the sea snakes' rapid swimming ability aided by their flattened, oar-like tail, Péron could only assume that sharks caught the snakes while they were sleeping on the surface of the water, an occurrence he noticed frequently.

The 28 June saw Péron and the other naturalists ashore on one of the Barren Islands where the gardeners found a type of grass that they considered might be useful in stabilising the eroding sands of Cadiz and Bordeaux if taken back to France. Other finds included fossils of marine organisms, particularly shells, which were often located inland and became a major problem for naturalists of the nineteenth century. The most facile explanation of their location inland was to attribute it to the biblical Deluge, commonly accepted among theologians as occurring in 4,004 B.C. Geological evidence, however, indicated that the short duration of the Deluge would not suffice for the deposition of the various sedimentary rock strata with their enclosed fossils. Attempts to overcome the problem of time were not always fully successful. The French historian-philosopher Voltaire concluded that ammonites were not sea creatures at all but the petrified remains of coiled snakes, while other theoreticians postulated as many as twenty-seven separate creations. The neptunian theories of Werner allowed sufficient time for the deposition of the rock strata and fossils,

NOUVELLE-HOLLANDE: Île Bernier.

'Kanguroo à bandes'
Lesueur and Petit. *Voyage de découvertes aux Terra Australis.*
1824.
Lagostrophus fasciatus

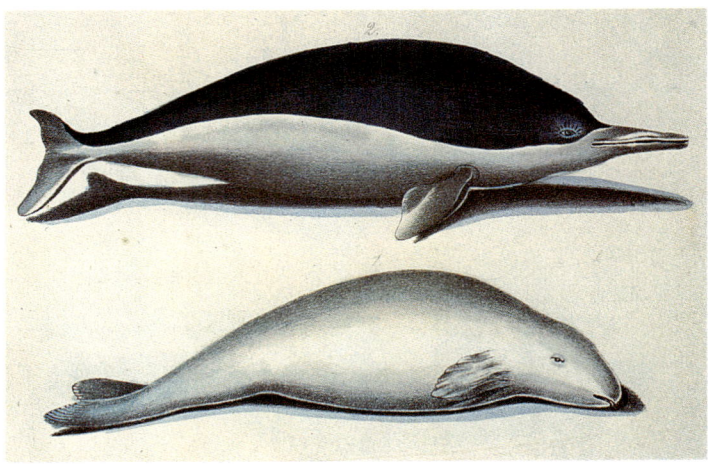

'Le Dauphin de Péron'
Lacépède. *Histoire Naturelle des Cétaces.* 1804.
Lissadelphis peronii

even if it did require numerous inundations of the earth to deposit both on the higher elevations of land, but James Hutton's plutonian theory came closer to current thought.

On the Barren Islands Péron also detected a small, striped kangaroo which he named '*Kangurus faciatus*', now known as *Lagostrophus fasciatus*. With twelve to fifteen narrow reddish stripes traversing its back and tail, Péron considered it to be the most beautiful of the kangaroo genus. He found the species on Dirk Hartog Island and other islands off Shark Bay but not on the mainland, and in this he felt he detected a pattern, that the various kangaroo species were all separated by geographic boundaries. If Péron had had occasion to penetrate further inland, he would have found that supposition to be incorrect. Several young kangaroos of this species were caught to be taken aboard *Le Géographe*, but most soon succumbed; only one survived to reach Timor where it died by an accident.

The next day Péron was off again, trekking over one of the islands, and in his enthusiasm he separated from his companions. Evening fell without him regaining their company, and he was forced to spend the night in the open. He was located the next day but this was not to be the last occasion that Péron became lost in the Shark Bay area; his absent-mindedness infuriated Baudin. The rest of the scientific party were more careful about straying but were equally enthusiastic about the bountiful assemblages of new specimens. Riedlé gathered new plants while Maugé noted a species of eagle that appeared to live on fish and shellfish—not surprisingly he named it the fishing eagle. Baudin in his journal summarised the natural history results from Bernier Island: Riedlé had located seventy species of plants, while Maugé had collected ten species of birds, ten species of insects, four or five species of shellfish, two guanos (lizards) described by Dampier in addition

to two other species, kangaroos, and many marine invertebrates. Péron also compiled a list of specimens obtained at the island, but this list was heavily biased towards marine invertebrates. He noted two portunid crabs, terrestrial and marine molluscs, coral, and two species of echinoderms, one of which was luminescent at night. While the French certainly attended to birds and mammals, the vast majority of their collections were marine invertebrates, a tradition carried on by subsequent French expeditions to New Holland. Péron considered that no other country of the world was as rich in fish species as was the Shark Bay region, where he found six types of fish undescribed by science. Of land animals Péron mentions the insects, reptiles, and varied bird species.

On 14 July *Le Géographe* sailed north from Shark Bay and spent the next month surveying the coast north to the Bonaparte Archipelago. The deep, 5-metre draught of *Le Géographe* and the lack of a small tender precluded extensive exploration of the inshore regions, and few landings to oblige the naturalists were made. Depuch Island was one of these infrequent landings, but Péron recorded that there was little of interest on land, and most of his time was taken up with the marine organisms obtained by trawling: medusae of amazing size which showed phosphorescence, and a species of fish that Péron thought new and named '*Balistapodus wittensis*'. It is now classified under the name *Balistapus undulatus*. The coast that they were now cruising was dry and inhospitable. Péron was astounded that New Holland should be so sterile when just to the north in the East Indies nature was so lavish and profligate. Provisions on board *Le Géographe* were beginning to run low and fresh water had been hard to locate on the coast of New Holland, so Baudin decided to sail for Timor, arriving there on 20 August.

The second vessel of the expedition, *Le Naturaliste*, had also sailed from Geographe Bay after separating

'Dasyure à longue queue'
Lesueur and Petit. *Voyage de découvertes aux Terra Australis.*
1824.
Dasyurus maculatus

from *Le Géographe* but did not make immediately for Shark Bay. First Hamelin, the captain of *Le Naturaliste*, took his vessel to Rottnest Island where his officers surveyed the island and the nearby Swan River estuary. On Rottnest Island the naturalists found two small species of kangaroo, one of which was later shown in Timor to Péron, who concluded that it was a new species. Seals, probably *Neophoca cinerea*, were abundant on the shores, and further inland they found many specimens of a 1·5-metre long reptile. While surveying the Swan River, eagles, 'red bellied green parrots', oystercatchers, pelicans, and black swans were found in plenty.

When Hamelin finally sailed north to Shark Bay he expected to find *Le Géographe* there—but he had missed Baudin by just a few days. Hamelin charted a portion of the bay and then followed Baudin north to Timor, arriving almost a month after *Le Géographe*. The stay in Timor, as it had been for so many other expeditions, proved fatal for many of the crew and scientists. On 21 October Riedlé died of dysentery and was buried alongside David Nelson, the gardener of William Bligh's *Bounty* expedition. Baudin was later to write that he thought Riedlé, whose position wàs only that of a gardener, was a much better botanist than the officially-appointed botanists to the expedition. In this Baudin might have been biased for Riedlé had accompanied Baudin on his prior expedition to the West Indies. La Billardière, when he finally published the botanical results of his earlier expedition to New Holland, commemorated Riedlé with the species *Macrozamia riedlei*. The death toll was to rise much higher for when the expedition sailed south-west from Timor for Van Diemens Land in November two more naturalists, Le Villain, a zoologist, and Sautier, the second gardener, died.

As they closed on the Van Diemens Land coast,

Péron described several new species of birds including a gull, '*Larus melanopterus*', and two terns, '*Sterna melanosema*' and '*Sterna caspiodes*', in addition to the black-muzzled dolphin which Lacépède was later to name '*Delphinus peronii*' (*Lissadelphis peronii*). Péron also noted a giant squid on the surface of the ocean, with tentacles which he estimated to be approximately 2 metres long. The 13 January 1802 saw the vessels double South West Cape and sail into D'Entrecasteaux Channel. Here Péron, along with his colleagues, went ashore and recorded:

> Innumerable flights of parrots, cockatoos &c. with the most varied and beautiful plumage . . . and the tom-tit, with a beautiful ultramarine blue ring round its neck . . . innumerable legions of black swans.[6]

While Lesueur collected a dozen species of birds including three types of parakeets and the tom-tit, Péron refused to limit himself to any group of animals— he collected omnivorously. Alert to the possibilities of the region, he recorded in his journal eating an undescribed species of mussel and finding within it an undescribed species of pinnothereid crab. Other animal groups to which he paid attention were lizards, molluscs, and insects. On 20 January Péron went fishing near Bruny Island and returned with twenty new species of fish and twelve to fifteen new or rare shells, including '*Trigonia antarctica*'; up until then this genus had been known only from fossils. Upon Péron's return to *Le Géographe* with his specimens, Maugé, who had been limited to shipboard activities by his declining health, wept at the lost opportunities and determined to go ashore the following day himself. Scarcely had Maugé landed on the beach than he collapsed and had to be carried back aboard the ship. He died several days later. '*Dasyurus maugei*', the Tasmanian native cat, was later named for him, although it has since been synonymised with *Dasyurus viverrinus*. Before the vessels left the D'Entrecasteaux Channel, Péron collected geological specimens, lichens, mosses, and a variety of plants. Lesueur, who had assumed part of the burden of collection as well as the illustration of the animals, obtained other new species of fish and some ten undescribed species of birds.

On 17 February the expedition moved closer to South West Cape and here Péron gave rapturous descriptions of the forests of Van Diemens Land:

> Divers kinds of beautiful grass made a pleasant verdant carpet: the Melaleuca, the Correa, the Fagara, the Conchyum, the Styphelia, the Metrosideros &c. here and there formed pleasant thickets, above which appeared loftly globulous Eucalyptus, the immense Leptosperma, the Exocarpus with leaves like cypress, the fibrous Casuarina, the Banksia with silver and a number of other trees peculiar to the southern climates.[7]

On the banks of the rivers stretching inland, Péron saw species of *Limodorum*, *Daucus*, *Richea* and *Apium*. Off the coast of Maria Island, the naturalists found enormous shoals of the seaweed '*Fucus gigantinus*', some specimens of which stretched 80 to 90 metres in length. The Linnaean genus, *Fucus*, under which the samples were classified, was one of only three genera of algae that had been formulated by Linnaeus, and during the early nineteenth century it encompassed a wide spectrum of the Chlorophyta, Rhodophyta, and the Phaeophyta. All the thick-bodied algae were lumped into the genus *Fucus*, the hair-like algae were assigned to the genus *Conferva*, while the flattened paper-like algae were accorded the name *Porphyra*. The adherence to the natural Linnaean orders of taxonomy was beginning to break down by the early 1800s, and the numerous specimens of algae brought back by this and subsequent French expeditions to New Holland contributed to the creation of new genera to separate the diversity of species.

On Maria Island itself the only mammal to be found was *Cercartetus nanus*, the eastern pygmy possum, but the surrounding waters were filled with dolphins, whales, and seals, and many new invertebrates were recorded. Sailing north *Le Naturaliste* and *Le Géographe* were once again separated while looking for a small boat overdue in returning from an inshore survey. Baudin fell sick, Henri Freycinet assumed command, and after fruitlessly searching for *Le Naturaliste* and the small boat, *Le Géographe* headed into Bass Strait to continue the charting of the southern coast of New Holland. Baudin soon recovered and resumed command of *Le Géographe* as she began to work her way westward from Wilsons Promontory on 28 March. Baudin and his officers charted the coastline but not in any great detail for they failed to note the entrance to Port Phillip Bay. Further to the west, when a sail was sighted, Baudin thought that he had relocated *Le Naturaliste*; instead it soon became apparent that it was a British vessel, the *Investigator* under Matthew Flinders. Flinders had just completed surveying most of the area that Baudin had been instructed to chart. The time he had lost on the north-west coast of New Holland, most of which was already known from older Dutch charts, had robbed Baudin of the honour of discovering and naming the south coast of the continent.

Nevertheless Baudin continued on after his meeting with Flinders, but in a desultory fashion. There was little opportunity for the naturalists to go ashore, and they had to content themselves with the description of marine organisms. Péron, busy as ever, collected and described another new species of '*Fucus*' in addition to a new crab, '*Portunus cyanophthalmus*', probably the blue crab *Portunus pelagicus*, as well as other marine organisms gathered in dredges or trawls. Baudin con-

tinued further west, stopping briefly at Kangaroo Island, but soon scurvy was rife in his crew and this outbreak, combined with the lack of fresh water and the deteriorating state of the provisions, forced *Le Géographe* back to the east. South West Cape of Van Diemens Land was rounded on 19 May, and after a short stay at Adventure Bay *Le Géographe* sailed for Port Jackson, arriving on 29 June 1802. By this time Baudin's crew were so weak that only four sailors were fit enough to man the vessel. Crews from Port Jackson, among them one from the *Investigator*, had to be sent out to the heads to help Baudin bring his boat to anchor.

Le Naturaliste, after her separation from *Le Géographe*, had located the lost boat and then searched for *Le Géographe*. After sailing as far west as Western Port she made for Port Jackson, arriving there 24 April. Resupplied, *Le Naturaliste* set off to the south, whether to continue her search for *Le Géographe* or to make for Mauritius is uncertain, but she was soon driven back to Port Jackson by contrary winds and arrived shortly after *Le Géographe*.

While the crews of the vessels recovered from the ravages of dysentery and scurvy, *Le Géographe* and *Le Naturaliste* lay at anchor in Port Jackson until 18 November; these were five months that the scientific party put to good use in exploring the immediate neighbourhood of Sydney. The mineralogists, Depuch and Bailly, travelled the basin of the Hawkesbury River where they found fossil ferns in shale, indicating to them that coal might be found nearby. They also examined iron ore found near Sydney but pronounced it to have too little iron content to be useful for smelting.

While the French ships were at anchor, *Le Géographe* was robbed of canvas by convicts in collaboration with the French crew, so a guard boat was ordered to patrol the area around the French vessels until their departure. Pains were also taken to ensure that no convicts tried to escape the colony by stowing away on the French vessels when they left. At Port Jackson Baudin purchased a 30-ton cutter built of native wood in the colony and named the *Casuarina*. The small cutter was to be used for inshore exploratory work, answering a pressing need of the French when the survey of the shores of New Holland was resumed.

The naturalists, those that still remained with the expedition after the hardships and disease, were far from idle. Lesueur and Péron, who had now taken on the bulk of the zoological collecting, roamed the Sydney area. Péron solicited the opportunity to join one of Barrallier's unsuccessful attempts to cross the Blue Mountains but was denied permission. He did travel as far as Parramatta where he saw the garden of George Caley full of specimens awaiting shipment to Joseph Banks. Péron wrote that:

An enlightened botanical professor, who combines modesty with indefatigable exertion, had just arrived from Europe at the time of our visit, to superintend the garden at Parramatta.[8]

This could hardly be considered a description of Caley.

Accompanied by William Paterson, Péron visited Castle Hill for the collection of insects and reptiles, and the next day they moved on to Parramatta where Caley joined them for more field work. Species that Péron was not able to locate were contributed from the collections of Caley or Paterson. George Suttor, who was also at Parramatta, noted that as Caley spoke no French and Péron no English they tried to communicate in Latin but their pronunciation was so different that they had little success. In the Sydney area, Péron managed to obtain over 150 species of insects including some forty butterflies. Two new species of frogs were detected which Péron named 'Rana pollicifera' and 'Rana pustulosa', two undescribed toads, and both marine and freshwater invertebrates. In considering the gecko that Shaw had named 'Gecko platurus', Péron decided that it appeared very different from other geckos and renamed the genus 'Geckoides'. Lesueur, not to be outdone, killed and preserved 200 birds and sixty-eight quadrupeds from the Sydney district.

The expedition of Baudin prolonged its stay in Port Jackson for astronomical observations on the transit of Mercury. It had been decided that due to the depleted state of the crew of the two vessels all the healthy individuals would be combined as the crew of Le Géographe for another year of exploratory work while the debilitated crew members and scientists would take Le Naturaliste back to France. Le Naturaliste was also to carry back the scientific collections gathered during the first part of the voyage, and extensive collections they were: 40,000 animals had been collected by the zoologists, filling thirty-three large packing cases. The botanical collections were likewise immense. Along with the preserved specimens, Le Naturaliste was to transport live plants and animals to the botanical gardens and menageries of France. Depuch, the mineralogist, was thought too ill to continue aboard Le Géographe and so was transferred to Le Naturaliste while Leschenault, the botanist from Le Naturaliste, moved aboard Le Géographe. Depuch was not to survive the voyage of Le Naturaliste back to France.

Le Géographe, Le Naturaliste, and Casuarina, left Port Jackson on 18 November. Two days out on the way south, they were hailed by a schooner they had met with before in Van Diemens Land. The captain of the vessel had a large wombat for Baudin who had previously requested him to watch for any interesting natural productions. The transfer of the specimen accomplished, Baudin sailed for King Island at the western end of Bass Strait, arriving there on 7 December.

Despite the precautions taken by both the administration of the colony and the French themselves, convicts were found to have stowed away on both Le Géographe and Le Naturaliste. Wanting nothing to do with such troublesome fellows, Baudin resolved to put them ashore on King Island. Le Naturaliste parted company from the two other vessels to make her way to France, while Le Géographe and the Casuarina continued to survey the southern coast of New Holland. At King Island Baudin was able to purchase emus, a tame kangaroo and several wombats from the resident fishermen. Here, the sniping between Baudin and the scientific party continued, Baudin noting in his journal that the scientists never moved anywhere without pomp and magnificence. To have shipped all the scientists back to France in Le Naturaliste would have pleased Baudin; from his point of view they only slowed the expedition down, always wanting to spend further days ashore to complete their collections long after he had finished his surveying tasks. The naturalists further persisted in filling all the cabins with foul-smelling specimens. The atmosphere aboard Le Géographe was not helped by the rigidity of Baudin's attitudes which continually clashed with the undoubted arrogance of young men such as Péron.

It was while the French ships were at King Island that the political implications of the voyage became manifest. After Baudin's departure from Sydney, rumours pervaded the settlement that several French officers had intimated that they were going to claim part of Van Diemens Land for France. On hearing this Governor King hastily dispatched the colonial schooner, Cumberland, to claim Van Diemens Land for Britain and raise the British flag over the French tents on King Island. King also intended to form a settlement on Van Diemens Land as soon as possible to further establish the validity of the British claim. Despite the British flag flying ridiculously above their tents, the French remained at King Island until the end of December before sailing westward. Péron employed his time on the island in collecting—and annoying Baudin.

> . . . all returned at about nine o'clock except for Mr. Péron, who seeing nothing but molluscs at every step, had amused himself by missing the first boat.[9]

On 2 January 1803, Le Géographe and Casuarina sighted Kangaroo Island and, after some initial seaborne surveying, landed on 6 January. Kangaroo Island was to prove a paradise for the naturalists: Péron made a collection of 800 species of animals and among these were specimens of the Kangaroo Island dwarf emu, a now extinct species much smaller than the mainland emu. During Péron's stay on the island, the dwarf emus existed in vast flocks, and the scientific party managed

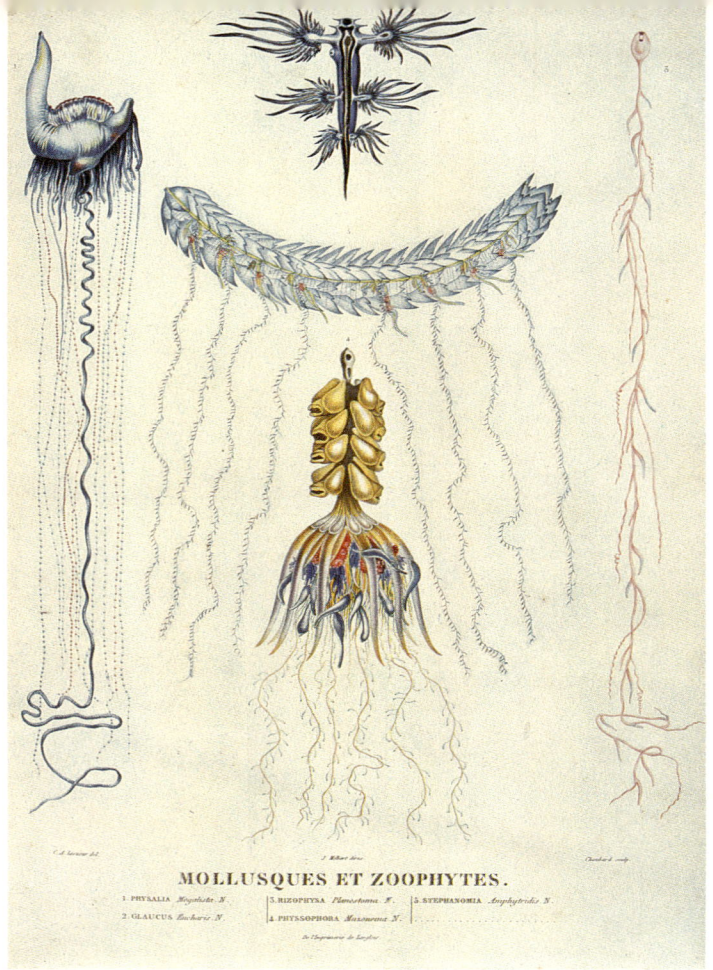

MOLLUSQUES ET ZOOPHYTES.

1. PHYSALIS *Megaliste N.*   3. RIZOPHYSA *Planctonia N.*   5. STEPHANOMIA *Amphytridis N.*
2. GLAUCUS *Eucharis N.*   4. PHYSOPHORA *Muzonoma N.*

C. A. Lesueur del.   J. Milbert direx.

NOUVELLE-HOLLAND

LE WOMBAT. *(Phascolomis Wombat*

114

NOUVELLE-HOLLANDE : ILE DECRÈS.

ABOVE:
'Casoar'
Lesueur and Petit. *Voyage de découvertes aux Terra Australis.* 1824.
Dromaius novaehollandiae

TOP LEFT:
'Mollusques et zoophytes'
Lesueur and Petit. *Voyage de découvertes aux Terra Australis.* 1824.

TOP CENTRE:
'Ornithornique brun, Ornithornique roux'
Lesueur and Petit. *Voyage de découvertes aux Terra Australis.* 1824.
Ornithorhynchus anatinus

BOTTOM LEFT:
'Wombat'
Lesueur and Petit. *Voyage de découvertes aux Terra Australis.* 1824.
Vombatus ursinus

to capture several live specimens in addition to ten kangaroos placed on board *Le Géographe*.

On Kangaroo Island Péron also described the seal *Neophoca cinerea* under the name '*Arctocephalus cinereus*'. Beside two species of kangaroos and the Kangaroo Island dwarf emu, other zoological finds included lizards, such as the black skink, the ocellated skink, the 'Decres Island iguana' (Decres Island was Baudin's name for Kangaroo Island), and a number of fish species. Péron was able to add 136 invertebrates to his collection, including new molluscs and polychaetes.

On 1 February *Le Géographe* sailed for King George Sound. Three days out from Kangaroo Island, two of the live kangaroos died from the constant dampness and, to correct the situation, Baudin evicted Leschenault and Ransonnet, a naval officer, from their cabins in order to house the remaining kangaroos away from the water. At further stops along the coast, Baudin would send boats ashore to collect grass for the animals, although along that barren coast the foraging parties were not always successful. From an island inshore of St Francis Island, the collecting parties brought aboard live 'short tailed opossums' and kangaroo rats. At King

George Sound the zoologists were not as overwhelmed as previous botanists who had visited the area. Lesueur shot several musk ducks, *Biziura lobata*, but Péron thought that birds in general were rare at the sound. As could be expected the botanists had more success: the gardener, Guichenot, collected 150 species of plants and brought aboard *Le Géographe* sixty-eight pots of live plants. Baudin as usual criticised Péron and Leschenault for what he thought was their lack of work, although Leschenault assembled a collection of over 200 plants from the district. Baudin somewhat sarcastically noted that Péron had collected a couple of cases of broken shells which should help him establish the age when New Holland had risen from beneath the sea.

By the beginning of March, the expedition was sailing from King George Sound for Rottnest Island and Shark Bay. At Shark Bay Baudin recorded in his journal that he had always thought it highly unlikely that Dampier had found part of a hippopotamus in a shark's stomach when he landed at Shark Bay in 1699—but Baudin's men brought back the teeth and the description of an animal that seemed very similar to the hippopotamuses Baudin had seen in Africa. Baudin retained the teeth to show to the savants of Europe, but he need only have asked his naturalist, Péron, who correctly identified the teeth as belonging to the dugong, a herbivore with teeth similar to the hippopotamus.

Leaving Shark Bay, Baudin rounded the north-west coast of New Holland, intending to chart the Gulf of Carpentaria, but *Le Géographe* had only reached as far as Melville Island before the easterly winds in combination with the implacable deterioration of the crew's condition forced him to run for Mauritius. By this time Baudin was very ill himself and survived *Le Géographe*'s arrival in Mauritius on 7 August by less than two weeks. *Le Géographe* limped home to France arriving on 24 March 1804.

The years of the expedition had taken a tremendous toll on the scientific party. Few remained aboard to return to France, most had either left the expedition early or died during its course. Those that did survive brought back with them an immense collection of plants and animals. Live specimens included emus, wombats, parakeets, and kangaroos (two of which were presented to the Empress Josephine), along with a pair of black swans, hundreds of species of live plants, and over 600 species of seeds. The real wealth of the expedition, however, lay not with the live specimens but in the more than 100,000 dried or preserved organisms comprising 2,500 new species.

The years following the expedition's return to Europe were to take their toll on the personnel of the voyage as surely as the perils that they had earlier encountered. Péron lived only a few years longer and published little of the scientific results of the voyage; what was published included short papers on the causes of phosphorescence in the ocean, the morphology and biology of the tunicate *Pyrosoma atlanticum*, the zoology of the Southern Hemisphere, a treatise on seals, the medicinal use of the betel nut, and the maintenance of zoological collections.

Before Péron died he did publish a narrative of the voyage, a volume that was both egotistical and vindictive. In it he heavily criticised Baudin, and even worse in the eyes of British readers, claimed the discovery of the entire south coast of New Holland for France. With Flinders, who could claim the original survey of the coast, interned on Mauritius, the British were doubly angered, but they were hardly without blame concerning the harassment of scientific expeditions. *Le Naturaliste*, covered by the passport issued to Baudin in 1800, had been seized by British warships in the English Channel in 1803 while returning to France. A difference in the tonnage from that stated in the passport convinced the British that the vessel was not *Le Naturaliste*, a mistake later rectified. Another French vessel, *L'Union*, was not so fortunate. *L'Union*, carrying the naturalist Louis Deschamps and his specimens, was also intercepted in 1803. Deschamps, a companion of La Billardière aboard *La Recherche*, had been interned with him in Java. On his release from confinement, Deschamps remained in Java to make additional collections before returning to France in *L'Union*. On the pretext that any material on a vessel captured by a warship becomes the property of the crew for prize money, the specimens on board *L'Union* were never returned to Deschamps despite the intervention in the dispute by Joseph Banks. The time when science was considered removed from the consequences of war was fast fading.

Results of the expedition other than Péron's few papers were eventually published in piecemeal fashion, but many of the specimens were never closely examined. In time the labels were misplaced and locations of specimens became uncertain. Many of the ornithological specimens were described by Jean-Pierre Vieillot from 1807 to 1819, while the marine algae were treated in part by Jean-Baptiste Lamarck and Jean Lamouroux. Other sections of the material were described in *Nouveau Dictionnaire d'Histoire Naturelle*. Baudin's expedition was to be the last French penetration into New Holland until Louis de Freycinet, one of Baudin's officers, returned in *L'Uraine* in 1818.

Chapter Seven

SETTLEMENT AND EXPANSION IN VAN DIEMENS LAND: 1803–10

At the behest of Charles Greville, Joseph Banks had included a miner on board the *Investigator* when it left England to explore the coasts of New Holland. Even earlier in 1797 Governor Hunter had requested that the authorities in England send out a mineralogist to the colony but this request had been ignored. In the early 1800s, with coal and iron discovered in increasing abundance and other minerals of possible commercial importance awaiting discovery, Governor King took up the refrain of the usefulness of a person knowledgeable in economic mineralogy. A marginal note in King's submission suggested that a chemist would be of service to the colony also. The British government, or more accurately its scientific representative, Sir Joseph Banks, already had in hand requests from geologists to be allowed to travel to New South Wales. In 1801 for example, Baron de Fuerk the Chamberlain to the Duke of Mecklenburg wrote to Banks outlining his qualifications and desire to work in New South Wales in return for the government paying his expenses. Fuerk hoped to go aboard the *Investigator*, but Banks was interested only in sending a miner, not a qualified mineralogist. Fuerk was never to exercise his talents in New South Wales.

In 1803 Greville renewed his previous request and on this occasion succeeded in having a mineralogist sent out to the colony. Just as Banks as a botanist was primarily interested in furthering the botanical knowledge of the colony, so Greville, whose interest was predominantly geological, sought to increase the mineralogical knowledge of New South Wales. The collection of minerals made by Robert Brown during the *Investigator*'s sojourn on the coasts of New Holland had been made primarily to satisfy Greville.

In February 1803, Adolarius W. H. Humphrey was offered the post of mineralogist in the territory of New South Wales. Later that month a letter from Lord Hobart to Governor King informed King that Humphrey would be embarking for the colony in the near future on the vessel *Ocean*. Humphrey was to break his journey briefly at Port Phillip to evaluate the geology of that region, as the British government proposed to site a settlement there, before progressing to Sydney to place himself at the disposal of King. Similarly to the other naturalists then resident in New South Wales, Humphrey was to be allowed to ship to England duplicate specimens of minerals to sell to dealers or collectors. Humphrey came from a family of natural history dealers so that this provision was important to him, especially in light of his relatively low salary.

March of that year saw John Lewin corresponding with Dru Drury about the problems faced by collectors in New South Wales.

> . . . I must inform you about this country, and you will find that Insects not to be got here as att home, for in all my trialls with the Sheet by beating I never could get Ither Caterpillars or full-Boddyed Moths for the trees are so exceedingly high that it is but few that you can reach with a long pole.[1]

Lewin initially could find few insects until he discovered that the majority gnawed a hole into the bark of the trees and hid themselves there, a strategy that Lewin attributed to intense predation on most insects by mantises. Lewin managed to complete twenty drawings of moths, three of which were enclosed for Drury's perusal. When Lewin finished the paintings of the moths, he intended to combine them into a book on the butterflies and moths of New South Wales, the publication of which he requested Drury to help arrange. He had also been working on paintings of native birds which he envisioned as making up a volume on the birds of New Holland. Drury had obtained for Lewin an associate membership in the Linnean Society, so in addition to the role of patron, Drury was also Lewin's

Pl. 9.

Publish'd as the Act directs Octo 24 1803 by J.W.Lewin New South Wales

scientific sponsor. Unfortunately this relationship was to be terminated before the publication of Lewin's proposed manuscripts, for Drury died early the next year.

On 5 March 1803, the first newspaper to be printed in the colony, the *Sydney Gazette and New South Wales Advertiser*, published its initial edition. The *Sydney Gazette* was to contain many items of natural history interest in its formative years; in the first month of publication it catered to the interest of naturalists in the colony by publishing 'Directions for collecting and preserving quadrupeds', an article reprinted from the British publication, *The Bee*. A second article on the collection and preservation of birds appeared on 19 June. During its first year it recorded the detection of: 'A Parrot of a species perfectly distinct from any hitherto found . . .', 'the Buzzing Squirrel', 'a native Owl', and 'a Kangaroo of a species perfectly distinct from any hitherto taken'.[2]

European journals also maintained an interest in antipodean events and in April the *Edinburgh Review* published a review of David Collins' *Account of the English Colony of New South Wales* in which the reviewer, contrary to most observers' opinions, thought that the discovery of coal in New South Wales was in fact a disadvantage. Inhabitants of the colony would use the coal for fuel instead of cutting down timber, a process which would have simultaneously cleared the land for agriculture.

Caley was not idle in 1803. In April he sent Joseph Banks a box of dried plant specimens, a box of living plants, 238 packages of seeds, sixty-five waratah pods, almost eighty bird skins from the Hawkesbury and Grose Rivers, specimens of minerals, timber, and gum, as well as detailed descriptions of all the specimens. Caley did not limit his observations to the natural history of the colony, for in 1803 he published a pamphlet entitled *A Short Account Relative to the Proceedings in New South Wales, from the Year 1801–1803, With Hints and critical Comments*, in which there was little natural history but a great deal of criticism of the administrative running of the colony. Caley's excursion into political commentary was probably less than favourably received by Governor King, but when in May Caley wrote to King requesting permission to go with the *Porpoise* to Bass Strait, the request was readily granted, either to gratify Caley's patron, Joseph Banks, or more probably to remove Caley from King's vicinity. Caley soon changed his mind about the journey, writing to Banks that the *Porpoise* was too small and that King had already found someone else to collect specimens on the voyage. A

'*Bombyx banksiae*'
Lewin. *Prodromus Entomology*. 1805.
Danima banksiae

paranoid Caley had apparently concluded that the governor was jealous of him and was determined to sabotage his efforts. Despite Caley's frequent shipments of specimens to Banks, which were freely acknowledged and paid for, Banks sympathised with Governor King stating in a letter about Caley: 'Had he been born a gentleman, he would have been shot long ago in a duel'.[3]

Before the *Porpoise* sailed, Caley had yet another change of heart and embarked. The effort was fruitless, as contrary winds kept the vessel from her destination. She returned to Sydney in early July, at which time Caley informed Banks of his lack of success, especially in procuring the echidna that Banks desired. Caley promised to try to obtain both the echidna and kangaroo skins on a forthcoming expedition he intended to take to the Blue Mountains.

Despite Caley's lack of success Banks continued to receive other specimens. In May, Paterson wrote to Banks lamenting his lack of free time to work on his natural history interests, but he was able to send Banks a specimen of the giant lily. That same month the ship, the *Glatton*, sailed from Port Jackson for England bearing on board cases of live plants sent by Governor King for Banks as well as dried specimens for Woodford of the War Office. Placed aboard the *Glatton* to care for the plants was James Fleming, praised by King as a clever gardener. Fleming had previously participated in a survey of Kings Island and Port Phillip on the colonial schooner, the *Cumberland*, and was highly recommended to Banks despite his convict background. Fleming's duties included the maintenance of the collection aboard the *Glatton* and on his arrival in England the selection of a collection of economic plants he would then escort back to New South Wales. On reaching England Fleming called on Banks and suggested to him that he would be willing to write a gardener's calendar for the colony, something much desired by the residents. Banks must not have been receptive to the idea as he later wrote to King that he did not know what had become of Fleming but thought that he had probably obtained a position which he liked better than New South Wales, although Banks was uncertain as to the legality of the employment. Banks' lack of faith in human nature was unwarranted in this case as it was later reported that Fleming had found an appointment to a botanical garden in the West Indies.

On 9 June the *Investigator* limped back into Port Jackson, having been found unseaworthy in the Gulf of Carpentaria. Two days after she arrived, Peter Good, the gardener of the expedition, died of dysentery. Brown, Bauer, and the miner, John Allen, decided to stay in New South Wales while Flinders went to England to procure another vessel to complete the survey. During his residence in New South Wales, Brown wrote to Banks about his decision to stay in

Sydney, complaining of his lack of success in his natural history collection. Mineralogy was a barren field, zoology the same, and even botany had not met his expectations, although Brown did admit to collecting over 2,000 species, of which 700 to 800 were undescribed. In this letter to Banks written in September 1803, Brown also reported the discovery of a new species of animal which he termed a '*Didelphis*'. Called by the Aborigines 'coloo' or 'coola' the animal seemed to Brown to be similar to the wombat. Brown had not been able to examine a specimen closely but did not think it was necessary for him to provide Banks with a detailed description as James Inman was endeavouring to send a pair of the animals to England. By the same vessel Governor King sent a message to Banks despairing of the animals reaching Europe alive, for they appeared to eat only fresh eucalyptus leaves. King enclosed a rough drawing made by John Lewin of the curious animal, promising a more accurate drawing on which Ferdinand Bauer was even then employed.

This mysterious animal had been reported a week before in the *Sydney Gazette* where the editor, George Howe, had remarked: 'the graveness of the visage, which differs little in colour from the back, would seem to indicate a more than ordinary portion of animal sagicity', a comment that has probably never been repeated about the koala since.[4] Six weeks after the initial report of the koala in the *Sydney Gazette*, the paper published another item, recording that the animals brought into Sydney fed chiefly on gum leaves but could also be induced to eat bread soaked in milk or water. William Paterson, in a letter to Banks in March 1804, claimed that a soldier he employed to collect specimens had been the first to find the koala and had obtained a specimen which Paterson later gave to John Hunter. After the initial discovery of the koala, a number were soon brought in to Sydney. One of a pair which Paterson domesticated was fond of tea. Both died before Paterson could send them to Banks, who did, however, receive the skins of the animals, while Paterson forwarded the skeletons to Everard Home.

In December Robert Brown embarked on the *Lady Nelson* to complete his proposed journey to Van Diemens Land. Before they arrived, foul weather forced the *Lady Nelson* to seek shelter in the Kent Group of islands, time which Brown used to examine the flora and fauna of the group. He found twelve undescribed plants to add to his collection but little else of interest. Brown was on his way to the new settlement that had recently been established on the Derwent River in Van Diemens Land to forestall the suspected French attempt to claim part of Van Diemens Land for France. Nine months previously King had authorised the establishment of the settlement under John Bowen, and Bowen had arrived at the Derwent on 12 September.

At about the same time, the British government commissioned David Collins, the former advocate-general of New South Wales, to establish a colony at Port Phillip. He sailed on the *Calcutta* from England on 29 April accompanied by the *Ocean*. Collins was very unhappy with the siting of the colony at Port Phillip, and as soon as he secured permission from King, he removed his settlement to the Derwent where he took over command from Bowen.

Included in Collins' party was Adolarius Humphrey, the mineralogist sent out by the British government. At Port Phillip Humphrey engaged in assembling collections of shells and minerals to forward to his father but seems to have pursued little of his governmental duties before the settlement was moved to a more suitable site. When that transfer was proposed, Humphrey went with the *Francis* to examine Port Dalrymple, one of the alternative locations that Collins considered before settling on the Derwent. Encountering the storm that had forced the *Lady Nelson* with Robert Brown aboard to seek shelter in the Kent Islands, the *Francis* sought the same sanctuary. The *Lady Nelson* was impressed for the survey of Port Dalrymple, and Humphrey and Brown spent the next several months in each other's company, first at Port Dalrymple and later at the Derwent River.

During the month of January 1804 both Humphrey and Brown continued to collect in the Port Dalrymple area until the 19th, when the *Lady Nelson* sailed for Port Phillip with both men aboard. There Brown was able to collect the specimen of *Pezoporus wallicus*, the ground parrot, which was later described by Vigors and Horsfield in 1827. Towards the middle of February the settlement at Port Phillip was abandoned and moved *en masse* to the Derwent River. Brown and Humphrey continued to make short excursions together in the Derwent River district, examining various rivers in the area and climbing Table Mountain, since renamed Mount Wellington. Brown remained in the region until 9 August, writing home to Joseph Banks that he had intended to be away from Sydney for only eight to ten weeks but had remained longer as he could not obtain transport back to New South Wales. As usual he managed collections of plants in addition to a few bird skins, but Brown was uncertain as to whether Baudin's botanists had already collected most of the species in the region. Brown later reported to Banks that he had assembled a collection of more than 540 species of plants from Van Diemens Land, about 100 of them undescribed. The French naturalists had reported beasts of prey in the Derwent region, presumably either the thylacine or Tasmanian devil, but Brown was unable to confirm the reports.

Humphrey collected both molluscs and minerals in Van Diemens Land for his family's natural history business. In letters to his father, Humphrey wrote of coal found near the Derwent River, 'delicately-crystallised alum', fossil wood, green garnet, and other mineralogical discoveries. With the example of the industrious Robert Brown before him, Humphrey pursued his geological interests ardently, a passion that he was to relinquish with Brown's departure for New South Wales. Humphrey's subsequent lack of enterprise may have been partially attributable to lack of equipment, about which he complained to his father, but probably was due to his increasing interest in commercial ventures. In early March Governor King wrote to Lord

'Ground Parrot'
Lewin. Unpublished. Courtesy of Mitchell Library.
Pezoporus wallicus

Hobart about the possibility of workable iron ore in New South Wales, intending that after Humphrey had finished his work in Van Diemens Land he should repair to New South Wales to occupy his time with mineralogical surveys between the Nepean River and the Blue Mountains. Despite King's interest in his presence, Humphrey was not to reach Port Jackson until the following year.

In March Lieutenant-Governor David Collins proclaimed protection for the black swans on the Derwent estuary, particularly during the nesting season. Collins was concerned not so much about the reduction in numbers of the graceful bird for its own sake, but that the swans as a valuable food resource would not be

squandered. Also in March the natural philosopher Humphrey Davy in England wrote a report on the tanning properties of bark from the trees of New South Wales. Davy considered that some of the bark might be of value if it could be brought to England cheaply enough either as raw bark or as an extract. For some years the use of tanning extracts from New Holland was considered as a possible item of export, but eventually the idea was discarded.

George Caley, having spent a relatively sedate year with little exploration, now intended a trip to Cow Pastures to the south-west of Sydney. He started on 11 February and was away until the 20th, finding items of neither geographic nor botanical interest. A month later he was able to send Banks a collection of 400 dried plant specimens, 162 packages of seeds, a number of kangaroo skins, a box of insects, and detailed notes on the whole collection. He also felt that his task was reaching an end:

> I am now pretty certain that the colony has been upon the whole well exposed in the Botanic department. What now remains may be called the gleanings.[5]

It is unclear whether Caley referred to his own collections or included those of the interloper, Robert Brown; Brown at least had a high opinion of Caley as a naturalist, naming for him a genus of orchids, *Caleana*, as well as *Banksia caleyi*, and *Grevillea calei*.

On his return to Parramatta Caley was soon off again, this time in the company of Ferdinand Bauer and Lieutenant Menzies to the settlement at Newcastle. Away for several months, Caley was able on his return to send Banks another shipment of bird and kangaroo skins, dried plants, and seeds.

In a dispatch to Lord Hobart in August, Governor King saw some gain in the wreck of the *Porpoise* on the Barrier Reef. It had been noted then that there existed quantities of bêche-de-mer or trepang on the reef which could possibly be exploited. A letter from King to Banks of the same date enclosed a sample of the holothurian, or sea slug, as well as an evaluation of its gastronomic merit. Also forwarded was a box of coal specimens mined at Newcastle for evaluation of their combustible qualities by European engineers, qualities of which the colonists were already aware.

In September the *Sydney Gazette* satirised the many amateur naturalists in the colony with the following anecdote:

> On Sunday last a bird, shot by a boatman, was presented as a new discovery, to a professed amateur, under the whimsical appellative of Sky-scraper. He was too much the connoiseur also to be easily duped, but at length fell into the deception, merely because a handsome sum had been tendered for it,—he flew to his Natural History,

expecting to find himself master of a rara avis, but was mortified and disappointed when from its description he had every reason to conclude himself Gull-ed.[6]

But for all its mockery, the *Gazette* continued to report items of natural history interest, including articles reprinted from English journals and accounts of native animals.

In August Robert Brown was finally able to return from Van Diemens Land to Sydney but almost immediately embarked on the colonial schooner, *Resource*, to visit the Hunter River district. Here he collected about fifty species of plants as well as specimens of birds. Caley, not to be outdone, was preparing another of his expeditions to try to cross the Blue Mountains, this time in the company of three other men. For twelve days they traversed valleys with almost perpendicular walls until they reached the base of the mountain that Caley called Mount Banks after his benefactor. Here Caley left his fatigued men to rest while he scaled the heights. The summit revealed nothing but further steeply rising ground, so yet again Caley abandoned the task. Six days later back in Parramatta, Caley wrote to Banks that the ruggedness of the country just traversed defied description. Even so, for an avid collector such as Caley, the journey was not a complete loss, as he procured some new plants. Even Governor King, who had frequently suffered the rough edge of Caley's tongue and vexatious temperament, could write of Caley's efforts, 'Few possess the bodily strength and enthusiastic mind which Cayley does to encounter such researches.'[7]

At the close of 1804 Robert Brown renewed his correspondence with Joseph Banks, detailing his travels of the past year, reporting on the possibility of the spice *Wintera* occurring in New Holland, in addition to mentioning his own ill health and the success of Ferdinand Bauer in locating new species of orchids. King also wrote to Banks denigrating the rumoured finds of auriferous rock in the colony as a hoax perpetrated in the expectation of quick profits. Governor King in one of his obligatory dispatches to Lord Hobart still held out hopes of Humphrey successfully using his mineralogical knowledge for the production of iron, but was now pessimistic about the export of coal as potential markets for the fuel were languishing.

Several publications of interest to the colony appeared in 1804. John Mawe published a pamphlet in England entitled *A Short Treatise addressed to gentlemen visiting the South Seas, and all Foreign Countries*. Mawe, a dealer in natural history collections, gave advice to amateur collectors setting off for unknown regions of the world. Primarily concerned with conchology, Mawe's pamphlet also included a section on mineralogy. Mawe offered to supply information and instruction to any gentleman setting out for that fifth division of the globe, New Holland, in addition to purchasing their collections on their return from parts exotic.

The fourth and fifth volumes of *General Zoology*, published by George Shaw in 1803 and 1804 respectively, were devoted to Pisces and contained a great many descriptions of fish from New Holland, fish taken as far back as Cook's voyages as well as specimens collected by George Tobin and John White. Described species included the 'foliated pipefish' which far exceeded

> . . . all the rest of the genus in the singularity of its appearance, which is such as at first view rather to suggest the idea of some production of fancy than of any real existence.[8]

The organism that Shaw described as the 'foliated pipefish', now known as the common seadragon, *Phyllopteryx taeniolatus*, was first collected by Joseph Banks on Cook's first voyage to the southern hemisphere.

Before the year 1804 was out the initial volume of James Edward Smith's *Exotic Botany* was placed on the market. Smith intended the work to include figures and descriptions of all the plants that he deemed worthy of introduction into the gardens of England, which would therefore embrace many of the New Holland flowers that had so attracted the attention of horticulturalists. Material for the work included a series of sketches forwarded to England by John White and subsequently loaned to Smith by Lambert, items from the collection of Joseph Banks, and a number of figures painted by James Sowerby from hothouse specimens grown in Britain.

By the end of 1804 the colonial administration had decided to colonise the northern side of Van Diemens Land to ensure British dominion over Bass Strait. After David Collins removed his abortive settlement from Port Phillip, the decision was made to found a settlement at Port Dalrymple, a site Collins had decided against, preferring the already established base on the Derwent. The job of organising the settlement at Port Dalrymple fell to Lieutenant-Colonel William Paterson, fellow of the Royal Society, resident naturalist of New South Wales, and correspondent of Joseph Banks. Shortly after taking up his duties at Port Dalrymple, Paterson wrote to Banks on the prospects of the region. Concerning the mineral kingdom he considered that there were both copper and iron ore close to the settlement, while as for zoology he had observed three species of kangaroos, bandicoots, native cats, opossums, kangaroo rats, musk ducks, black swans, and parrots that he thought much different from those of the Sydney area. Paterson had also collected seeds and live plants which he sent on to Banks.

Concurrently Paterson wrote to his immediate superior, Governor King, forwarding him specimens of the local iron ore in addition to a satchel of seeds which he desired King to forward to the Kennedy and Lee nursery in London—other seeds were to go to Charles Greville and General Bentham. A month later in a second letter to King, Paterson sent a specimen of an insect which he feared would be a particularly destructive agricultural pest. Paterson also informed King that some of the inhabitants of his small settlement had reported seeing the 'Devil', not the clerical nemesis, but the Tasmanian devil, however until that time they had been unable to catch one. Paterson lamented the fact that in his rude settlement he would have no access to either books on natural history or the services of a natural history draughtsman. Nonetheless, he continued his natural history exertions by conducting an experiment on the toxicity of snake venom. He placed a captured seagull into a barrel with a Van Diemens Land snake thought to be venomous. The gull died.

Collections continued to flow from New South Wales to England as evidenced in the *Sydney Gazette*. The vessel, *Aeolus*, carried with her flying foxes and parrots when she sailed in February of 1805, and even that archetypal capitalist, Robert Campbell, took a small collection of natural curiosities to England by the *Lady Barlow* early in that year. On 21 April the *Gazette* was able to record that an animal of 'Truly remarkable description' had been killed by dogs the previous month at Port Dalrymple, and William Paterson kindly forwarded a description to the Sydney paper. The animal looked very much like a hyena, and Paterson thought it to be the only powerful carnivore in New Holland. With a mention of stripes across its back, Paterson's description could only have been of the thylacine, *Thylacinus cyanocephalus*. The French reports of a beast of prey in Van Diemens Land had proved factual.

Under the questioning letters of Governor King, Humphrey had been forced to emerge from the Derwent River settlement and sail for Port Jackson, arriving in April. King was optimistic, he thought that there was little doubt of Humphrey making important and useful discoveries. On his arrival in Sydney Humphrey set about sorting through 10 tonnes of iron ore sent from the Port Dalrymple region by Paterson in order to select samples to be shipped to England. These samples were never to reach the mineralogists in England for the vessel in which they were loaded sank while rounding the coast of New Guinea. Rather than searching out his own specimens in New South Wales, Humphrey seems to have been content to examine the material brought in by others, including rock samples obtained by Barrallier on his penetration of the Blue Mountains. Mindful of his own interests, Humphrey pressed his claims on Governor King for 200 hectares of land near the settlement on the Derwent River, Hobart.

Meanwhile, Robert Brown and Ferdinand Bauer, having completed their final collections in New Holland, had been preparing to return to England. The formerly condemned *Investigator* was sufficiently well repaired to make the journey first to Norfolk Island and then back to Europe. It had been found that although the upper works of the hull were indeed rotten, the bottom was sound. Brown, when not collecting, had been at work integrating his several disparate assemblages of plants into one collection and writing up descriptions of some 1,000 species. Brown was also concerned with the shipment of the botanical specimens to England, and tried to obtain boxes sealed with pitch to prevent deterioration of the plants from the everpresent dampness found on board a vessel at sea. The problem was quickly settled, for Governor King had no desire to antagonise Joseph Banks by being responsible for the ruin of a collection destined for him. In addition to Brown's botanical, zoological, and mineralogical collections which the *Sydney Gazette* of 26 May gratuitously described as acceptable to amateurs of natural history, the *Investigator* carried several other specimens. These included a skin of the undescribed carnivore found by Paterson at Port Dalrymple, the thylacine; seeds from the same location; samples of sandalwood, and a box of gum from which Paterson thought varnish might be produced. Many of Brown's live plant specimens were left in the garden at Parramatta under the care of George Caley for shipment to England at a later date. The *Investigator* sailed on 23 May, not reaching England until 13 October; what Brown termed a tedious and uncomfortable voyage.

The sight of Brown and Bauer making preparations for their return to England must have aroused similar ambitions in George Caley. He wrote to Banks in April reiterating his desire to return to England. Caley explained that he had explored as much of the country as could be done by a single individual without great expense.

King also corresponded with Banks indicating that he thought Caley was ready to escort the plants that Brown had left in the colony back to England. The plants were intended to be shipped on the vessel *Sydney* along with the iron ore specimens from Van Diemens Land. Before departing for Europe, the *Sydney* sailed first for Van Diemens Land, Caley aboard her. He remained in Van Diemens Land for about a month, collecting plants, a wombat, and an echidna that Banks had specifically requested before returning to Port Jackson aboard the *Sydney* at the end of 1805. Caley changed his mind about accompanying the vessel as it sailed north, a fortunate decision as the *Sydney* sank off New Guinea with the loss of the mineralogical samples but not the plants that would have travelled under Caley's care.

Caley's change of heart about his intended return to England may have been instigated by the news that his imagined persecutor, Governor King, had been recalled to England. King had applied to the Home Office as early as 1803 to be allowed to return to England, but a successor was not chosen until 1805. Caley had always felt that King had never rendered him the assistance he required for his collecting efforts. Perhaps he was inclined to believe that he would fare better under the new governor, William Bligh, who had been appointed through the perennial influence of Joseph Banks.

While George Caley served as Banks' chief collector in the colony, John Lewin was not idle. Two years previously, Lewin had written to Dru Drury indicating that he expected to finish the illustrations for a volume on butterflies and moths of New South Wales in the near future. During 1803 and 1804 Lewin did finish the illustrations and engraved copper plates of them for the printing process. The *Sydney Gazette* of 3 March 1804 reported that Lewin intended to send part of the proposed work to England for printing on the vessel *Calcutta*. In 1805 this work, *Prodromus Entomology*, was published in London. Dedicated to Lady Arden, who had helped Lewin secure passage to New South Wales, the preface of the volume indicated that the work was published to afford the artist the means of returning to England. Lewin, like Caley, obviously thought that he had spent enough time in the isolated colony. *Prodromus Entomology* contained eighteen plates in which male and female moths or butterflies, the caterpillar stage, and the structure of the cocoon were all depicted against the species of plant on which the caterpillar fed.

Adjacent to the plates were taxonomic descriptions of the insects along with meagre notes on the species' natural history. Scientific names were applied to the insects but not by Lewin. His brother Thomas, who edited the volume, asked James Edward Smith to supply names for the plants illustrated while Alexander Macleay, then secretary of the Linnean Society and who was later to reside in New South Wales, described the insects.

While Lewin's work illustrated only eighteen species of insects from New Holland, that same year the English naturalist Edward Donovan's *An Epitome of the Natural History of the Insects of New Holland, New Zealand, New Guinea, Otaheite* covered considerably more ground. One hundred and fifty-three species were described, the majority from New Holland and most for the first time. The specimens used by Donovan came from: his own collection ultimately derived from John White, from Joseph Banks' entomological collection, from Bayly the astronomer on Cook's second voyage to the southern hemisphere, and from the collections of Drury and Macleay which probably originated with John Lewin.

In the beginning of the year 1806, William Paterson made further shipments of specimens from Port

ABOVE:
'*Sphinx ardenia*'
Lewin. *Prodromus Entomology*. 1805.
Cizara ardenia

BELOW:
'*Hemiptera*'
Donovan. *An epitome of the natural history of insects*. 1805.

ABOVE:
'*Coleoptera*'
Donovan. *An epitome of the natural history of insects*. 1805.

BELOW:
'*Papilo erecthus*'
Donovan. *An epitome of the natural history of insects*. 1805.
Papilo aegeus

Dalrymple to Joseph Banks. Besides the usual plants and seeds that he knew would interest Banks, Paterson included the skeleton and skin of a new opossum, two skulls of the Tasmanian devil, the hides of native cats and kangaroos, and specimens of crabs, coral, and minerals. Later that year in July, Joseph Banks was to write an extraordinary document dealing with the importation of items from New South Wales to England. Banks proposed that England claim only New South Wales and Van Diemens Land, leaving the greater part of New Holland open to the enterprise of any European country that might wish to establish colonies there. Banks did, however, add the rider that in the event of war the foreign settlements would certainly fall into British hands. Even so, in view of the strenuous efforts made by both the local colonial administrations and the Home Office in London to prevent foreign encroachment on New Holland, Banks' proposal was truly surprising. Banks was even reluctant to accept a name such as Australia as proposed by Flinders for the continent, as it might imply a claim for the entire continent by the British. Banks took this stand despite George Vancouver already having claimed part of the western and southern coast of New Holland in the name of the monarchy. Matthew Flinders, in the previous year, while still incarcerated in Mauritius, had advocated the name Australia for the continent in his letters to Banks, but it was not until 1817 that Governor Macquarie began to use the term Australia in his official correspondence. It is perhaps curious that although the continent had been called *Australis incognita* and *Terra Australis* at various times prior to 1800, the first reference to the term Australia was in George Shaw's *Zoology of New Holland* published in 1794.

In July 1806 the Leverian Museum was sold by auction in London. The museum compiled by Ashton Lever had proved too costly to maintain and had been offered by Lever as the prize in a one guinea lottery in 1797, a lottery won by James Parkinson. Parkinson attempted to preserve the collection as a museum but by 1806 found the burden too much, and so auctioned the contents in a sale lasting sixty-five days. Among the exotica, such as the scalp of a celebrated Indian chief and the copy of the ten commandments written by a man with no hands or legs, were more mundane items such as kangaroos and kangaroo rats, shells from New South Wales, and several species of parrots from New Holland. Some of the items had been collected on Cook's first voyage in 1770.

With the successful printing of *Prodromus Entomology* in 1805 Lewin embarked on his next project, the illustration of the birds of New South Wales.

In the 14 September 1806 edition of the *Sydney Gazette*, Lewin advertised his proposal for publishing by subscription *Birds of New South Wales*, an imperial quarto for the price of two guineas.

During the year 1806 Adolarius Humphrey, the government mineralogist, had done little to call himself to the attention of the authorities in the colony—with the exception of becoming involved in a court case concerning Harriet Sutton, a girl who was to follow him to Van Diemens Land when he returned there in 1807. Despite the insistence of Governor Bligh that Humphrey should return to New South Wales after prosecuting his studies in Van Diemens Land, Humphrey was not to leave Van Diemens Land again while employed by the government. However, on 27 July 1807 there arrived in Sydney a man who might have vastly overshadowed Humphrey's lethargic efforts in geology. That day the *Duke of Portland*, bearing Dr Robert Townson, dropped anchor in Port Jackson. Townson, the author of *Philosophy of Mineralogy* and *Tracts and Observations in Natural History*, both published in 1799, arrived complete with a comprehensive library and an assortment of chemical apparatus. Governor Bligh saw it as his object to promote Townson's scientific endeavours, but he was doomed to failure; Townson had evidently forgone his interest in science and was far more concerned with the size of the land grant he could obtain in New South Wales than with the unexplored and unexplained geology of the region.

Early in 1807 Philip Gidley King turned over the governorship of the colony to William Bligh and returned to England. Bligh was to demonstrate in the coming years that he was not the most affable of men, but he and Caley seem to have been quite compatible; a much better relationship existed between the two than the tenuous relations Caley had maintained with King. Caley limited himself to short excursions during 1807, and, much to Robert Brown's disgust, was very reluctant to ship to England the remaining live plants left in the garden at Parramatta.

During 1807 two papers appeared in the *Transactions of the Linnean Society of London* on the natural history of New Holland. The botanist-antiquary Edward Rudge published a 'Description of Seven New Species of Plants from New Holland' while the botanist Aylmer Bourke Lambert produced a 'Description of a New Species of *Macropus* from New Holland'. Although the collectors and settlers of New South Wales had known for years that there were many species of kangaroo on the continent, this knowledge was only now penetrating the cloistered halls of European zoology.

One of the most divisive episodes in Australian history occurred in 1808, with the arrest and imprisonment of Governor William Bligh by the officers of the New South Wales Corps. The deposition of Bligh directly affected the individuals concerned with natural history in the colony—and three individuals in particular: George Suttor, George Caley, and William Paterson.

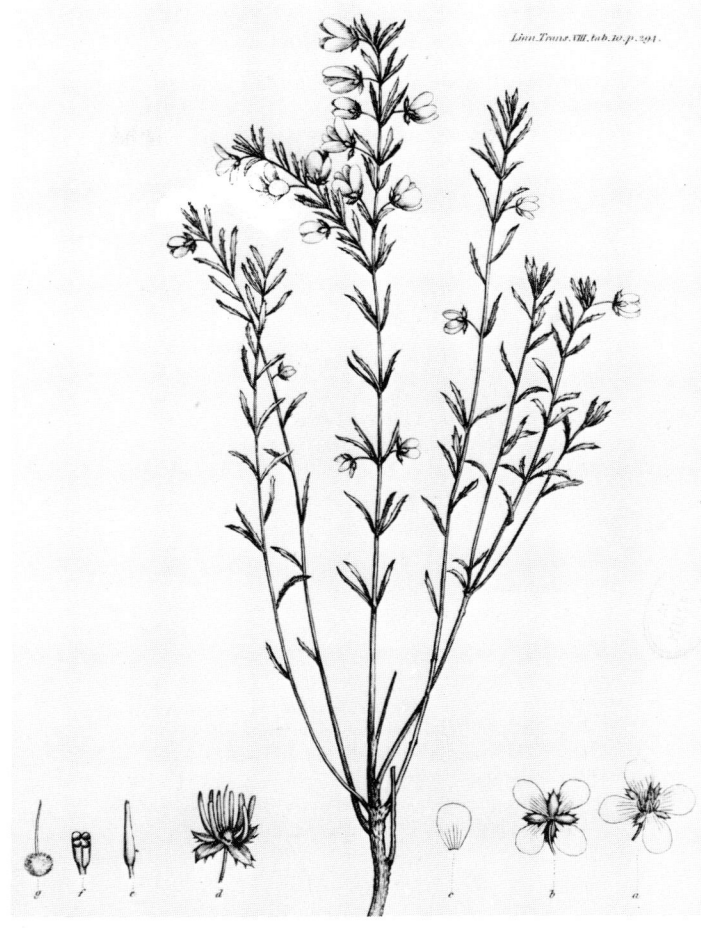

TOP LEFT:
'*Styphelia amplexicaulis*'
Rudge. *Transactions of the Linnean Society*. 1807.
Leucopogon amplexicaulis

TOP RIGHT:
'*Tetratheca glandulosa*'
Rudge. *Transactions of the Linnean Society*. 1807.
Tetratheca glandulosa

BOTTOM RIGHT:
'*Macropus elegans*'
Lambert. *Transactions of the Linnean Society*. 1807.
Macropus parryi

George Suttor had not been active as a collector or botanist since his arrival in the colony in 1800; he contented himself with pursuing the agricultural employment for which he had been trained. Suttor became well respected in the Hawkesbury region and upon Bligh's overthrow wrote lengthy petitions to the government in England in addition to reassuring Bligh of his loyalty to the ousted administration. When Lieutenant-Colonel Joseph Foveaux, on his arrival from England, took over the administration of the colony from the usurper George Johnston, and ordered all land owners to attend a muster, Suttor ignored it. Committed for trial for not attending the muster, Suttor denied the legality of the trial itself as not properly constituted under the sanctioned colonial government. The court,

consisting of officers of the New South Wales Corps and their sympathisers, sought to crush Suttor's 'rebellion' by sentencing him to six months' jail. When Bligh eventually returned to England to present his case against Major Johnston and the rest of the rebellious New South Wales Corps, Suttor travelled to England to present evidence on Bligh's behalf.

George Caley, although not having obtained the support for his exploratory ventures that he had hoped for from Bligh, nevertheless also backed Bligh against the refractory officers. Caley could or would do little against the prevailing powers except to write to Banks and attend the incarcerated governor, who was restricted to Government House. Caley wrote to Banks that he thought Bligh was unfit for the duties of the governor of New South Wales, deriding Bligh's fondness of flattery, his acceptance of several farms from Governor King at the government's expense, and his lack of judgement. But he was even more critical of the men behind the usurpation. Caley opined that John Macarthur was behind all the mischief, a belief that gained ready acceptance with Joseph Banks who had previously clashed with Macarthur over the introduction of merino sheep into the colony. Banks had earlier tried to prevent Macarthur from returning to New South Wales (subsequent to his return to England after his duel with Paterson), while Macarthur in turn, according to Caley, disdainfully called Banks 'an old debauched character'.[9]

William Paterson, the senior officer of the New South Wales Corps, was at the time of the rebellion in charge of the settlement organised at Port Dalrymple. After the usurpation, he was requested by most of the parties involved to return to Sydney as soon as possible, and several times vessels were dispatched to collect him. Paterson put off his return to Sydney with claims of ill health, but he almost certainly did not want to involve himself in the struggle between his own New South Wales Corps and the overturned colonial administration. He was content to remain in Port Dalrymple for almost a year after the critical event — avoiding the unpleasantness at the cost of being considered a weak and ineffectual person.

For all the traumatic events of the year, the residents of the colony proceeded with their own petty concerns. Dr Robert Townson wrote to Viscount Castlereagh complaining that Bligh would not give him the land he had been promised, a ready excuse for leaving the promise of his scientific endeavours unfulfilled:

> . . . otherwise I might have been comfortably settled on my farm and beginning to enjoy a portion of leisure which I expected when I invited (conjointly with the Hon. C. F. Greville) Mr. Windham to send out with me a laboratory and a small collection of books, that as a man of science I might be of use to the settlement; but, alas! all my pleasing prospects of this nature are gone,

and if I can save myself from ruin this is all I can now expect.[10]

The colony was obviously not ready for established naturalists such as Robert Townson who needed all the accoutrements of established society and science in order to undertake their work. George Caley, for all his infuriating conduct and demands and his ungentlemanly manners, could and did achieve much more than many Robert Townsons. But even Caley's stamina and enthusiasm could not last forever, and in July he again wrote to Banks about his intention to return to England. Due to lack of governmental support, he would have to leave the exploration of most of the colony to others: 'But the misfortune is, they who study geography are very indifferent botanists, and vice versa.'[11]

Caley anticipated that he would return to England with Bligh and he awaited only Banks' consent to his return. He proposed no new explorations to seek specimens but whiled away his time readying the plants that he had assembled for shipment and protecting his garden of specimens from the deprivations he thought sure to occur with the decline of lawful government since Bligh's arrest. He continued to ship specimens to Banks including two new species of *Boronia* and a dingo pup.

Writing on 25 August 1808, Banks told Caley:

> I have grown of late years very infirm. My eyes fail me much and I have not, of course, the pleasure I us'd to have in the pursuit of natural history. I have not, therefore any longer occasion for your services in the extensive manner in which you have employ'd yourself of collecting great quantities of articles.[12]

Banks indicated to Caley that in view of his services he would settle upon him a £50 annuity for life. The letter reached Caley late in 1809.

William Paterson, ensconced in Port Dalrymple away from the tumultuous events of Sydney, was still maintaining his interest in natural history although he wrote to Banks that due to his poor health and the troubles of government he had secured no new plant specimens that year. His collection amounted to some fossils and an insect that produced manna, called by Paterson the 'locust' of Van Diemens Land. Paterson wrote a short treatise on the insect, which appeared in its thousands in November, congregating on the narrow-leaved eucalyptus trees. Here it produced enormous quantities of manna, the sweet substance that could be collected and used as a sugar substitute, in quantities that Paterson estimated at over twenty pounds (9 kilograms) per tree. Paterson had noticed a similar insect in New South Wales but it did not seem to produce manna. He promised Banks that he would send him specimens of

the larvae, the immature, and the mature insect along with samples of the manna and the eucalyptus that the insect fed upon. Paterson showed notable interest in an obscure problem of natural history while the government of New South Wales floundered, yet perhaps there was some substance to Paterson's plea of ill health, for he was to die less than two years later.

Late in 1808, on 20 November, John Lewin advertised in the *Sydney Gazette* that the first volume of his work *Birds of New Holland* would be arriving by the next vessel from England. Lewin, as had the other Banksian protégés, supported Bligh against the New South Wales Corps but not in such a flagrant fashion as George Suttor. Lewin and his subscribers in New South Wales were destined to be disappointed for apparently no copies of the book ever reached the colony. The only extant copies remained in England, leading to the supposition that the copies bound for New South Wales were somehow destroyed, either in a fire at the printery or on the journey itself.

Birds of New Holland was to be the first volume of a multiple-volume set in which Lewin hoped to include all the birds of New Holland. The eighteen birds represented in the prints were common to the Sydney region; several had appeared before in the paintings of Watling, Hunter, and Raper, and prior descriptions of others had been published in John Latham's second supplement to his *General Synopsis of Birds*. As with his *Prodromus Entomology*, Lewin lacked the scientific training to accurately classify the birds, as he was primarily an illustrator and collector rather than a taxonomist. The names and descriptions of the birds were probably applied by John Latham at the request of Thomas Lewin, who again edited his brother's work. Thomas Lewin, in the preface to the volume, states that he cut down the descriptions because:

> Sure we are that such a body of dry description as usually accompanies the little quantity of useful Natural History which is generally given with each Species, is both tedious and disgusting, and so unmeaning to the general Reader as to make Ornithology appear pedantic . . .[13]

The list of subscribers to the work included many of the foremost individuals in the colony: Governor Bligh,

TOP:
'Mountain bee-eater'
Lewin. *A Natural History of the birds of New South Wales.*
1822.
Merops ornatus

BOTTOM:
'Crested shrike'
Lewin. *A Natural History of the birds of New South Wales.*
1822.
Falcunculus frontatus

Didelphis ursina.

Didelphis cynocephala

Philip Gidley King, William Paterson, Reverend Samuel Marsden, Gregory Blaxland, and even Adolarius Humphrey, while the subscribers in England seem to have been limited to Lewin's sponsors: Lady Arden, Lady Wilson, Joseph Banks, and Alexander Macleay.

In 1808 the formal scientific description appeared of the new marsupial that Paterson had described in the *Sydney Gazette* in 1805. The description was written by George Prideaux Harris, the deputy-surveyor of Van Diemens Land who had accompanied David Collins to Port Phillip and later to Hobart. Harris, who was a reasonable natural history draughtsman, had delineated much of the fauna found in Van Diemens Land and forwarded written descriptions and illustrations of two of the unique animals of the island to Joseph Banks who had them inserted in the *Transactions of the Linnean Society of London* in 1808. The powerful carnivore described by Paterson was given the name 'Didelphis cynaocephala' by Harris but was commonly known to the settlers as the 'zebra wolf', or 'zebra opossum'. Because it posed a threat to animal husbandry, the thylacine was eventually hunted to extinction. The second species described in the paper 'Description of two new species of *Didelphis* from Van Diemen's land' was the Tasmanian devil, *Sarcophilus harrisii*.

One of these 'native devils', as they were called by the populace, had been sent alive to Joseph Banks but did not survive the journey. The Tasmanian devil was also said to be destructive to poultry, but as Harris mentioned in his paper, they furnished the convicts with fresh meat tasting not unlike veal. Harris was later to send Dr William Leach samples of the cicada, '*Tettigonia harrisii*' (*Psaltoda harrisii*), from Van Diemens Land which Leach subsequently named for him.

Harris, in a letter to Banks, indicated that he proposed to prepare a volume 'Illustrations of the Zoology of Van Diemen's Land'. He had already completed over 150 drawings of quadrupeds, fish, birds, and insects for the work, but it never appeared.

In 1808 Everard Home published 'An Account of some peculiarities in the anatomical structure of the Wombat, with observations on the female organs of generation' in the *Philosophical Transactions of the Royal Society*. Home related that Robert Brown had brought him a live wombat which lived with him for two years. Included in the report was the description of what he thought to be another species of wombat, the koala. This taxonomic linking of the koala with the wombat in early work on Australian marsupials has since been accepted, although they are probably not as closely related as earlier envisaged.

The opening of the year 1809 continued the hiatus

'Didelphis cyanocephala, Didelphis ursina'
Harris. *Transactions of the Linnean Society*, 1808.
Thylacinus cyanocephalus, Sarcophilus harrisii

that the entire colony seemed to have undergone since the usurpation of Bligh's administration. Despite a year having passed since the event, no instructions had been received from the Home Office in England and the colony waited, more or less at a standstill, until orders were forthcoming. William Paterson finally summoned up the resolution to travel to Sydney where, as he feared, he clashed with the still incarcerated Bligh. Eventually Bligh agreed to leave the colony and seek redress in England. Others may have been making preparations to leave New South Wales, for during February and March a number of private natural history collections were offered for sale in the *Sydney Gazette*: four collections of botanical seeds on 5 February, five emus and a collection of parrots on 12 February, and a 'superb small beautiful collection of insects' on 5 March.

During 1809 George Caley continued to regale Joseph Banks with letters, but letters of a more reflective nature than had been sent previously. They were less simple descriptions of the plants, animals, and general nature of the country than his reflections on the problems of collecting and classifying species, on the explorations undertaken, and the opportunities missed. In one of these letters, Caley wrote that he thought that Paterson had been lost to botany, no doubt a reference to Paterson's increasing involvement in what both Caley and Paterson regarded as the tiresome politics of the colony. Paterson was indeed lost to botany, for after assuming control of the affairs of the colony until the arrival of newly-designated Governor Lachlan Macquarie, Paterson took passage for England in the same convoy that bore Bligh home. Caley thought that on his assumption of power Paterson changed from a good man to a dangerous one, for in Caley's opinion Paterson pandered to the officers of the New South Wales Corps. Caley's letters are very much taken up with the political crisis in the colony and how it affected him. At times he broke out:

> Curse upon the envious and ambitious designs of unbridled men, for they have greatly retarded my success in my natural pursuit.[14]

In Europe, as Banks commented to Caley, botany was no longer as fashionable as it had been in the past. During the late eighteenth century naturalists had envisioned that they would be able to collect and catalogue every species of plant on the earth's surface, but with the ever-increasing number of specimens pouring in from all quarters of the world, the naturalist philosophers saw that such a task had no prospect of fulfilment in the immediate future.

Late in 1809 Dr Joseph Arnold arrived in the colony on board the *Hindostan*. A surgeon with a keen interest in botany, Arnold found that as a doctor in the Royal Navy, both medicine and natural history could be combined successfully. Arnold travelled to New South Wales in the convoy that brought Lieutenant-Colonel Macquarie as the new governor. While in Port Jackson Arnold was often able to go into the surrounding countryside to collect insects and seeds; the insects he thought were particularly beautiful. In a letter to the

Top:
'*Tettigonia harrisii*'
Leach. *Zoological Miscellany*. 1814.
Psaltoda harrisii

Bottom:
'Alcedo, Three-toed Kingfisher'
Harris. Unpublished. Courtesy of Mitchell Library.
Alcyone azurea

Facing Page:
'Falco, Van Diemen Hobby'
Harris. Unpublished. Courtesy of Mitchell Library.
Falco sp.

English physician William Crowfoot some months after his arrival in New South Wales Arnold lamented:

> And I cannot sufficiently regret that I neglected to bring out with me books on the different departments of Natural History. For all that I discover is as strange to me as if I had become an inhabitant of the moon.[15]

Arnold thought to bring many of these curiosities back to England on his return but found that the colonists extracted a fearful price for them, a price usually paid for in rum of which Arnold had none. A far-sighted lieutenant from the *Hindostan* who had brought with him a hogshead of rum was able to fill the ship with kangaroos, parrots, opossums, and mollusc shells. While in New South Wales, Arnold compiled a description of the Tasmanian devil, *Sarcophilus harrisii*, which he hoped to use to obtain an introduction to Joseph Banks and perhaps secure his patronage.

Naturalists continued to quibble about the taxonomic status of the platypus. The French naturalist Etienne Geoffroy Saint-Hilaire, in 1803 had created the new order Monotremes for the platypus and the echidna, while Lamarck used the class Prototheria, to encompass the two. Lamarck felt that since the two animals apparently lacked mammary glands they could not be mammals, they could not be classified with the birds as they had an incompatible lung structure with that group and obviously lacked even vestigial wings, and could surely not be reptiles for they did not possess a four-chambered heart. Two years later Illiger placed the platypus as an intermediate between the mammals and the reptiles, while the following year the French physician-naturalist Henri de Blainville, noting their resemblance to the marsupials, placed the platypus and echidna in a separate order of the mammals.

The public of England by now had the opportunity to view some of these curious animals from Australia. Bullock's Museum in Liverpool had a large variety of the Australian flora and fauna including the platypus, echidna, kangaroo, kangaroo rat, opossum, black swan, emu, and other assorted birds and plants. Both the kangaroo and kangaroo rat had been kept for some years in England and were reproducing in the Royal Domain at Richmond.

The first day of 1810 saw a restoration of the sanctioned administration to New South Wales, for that day Lachlan Macquarie stepped ashore to assume the governorship. To uphold the authority of the powers in England, Macquarie had orders to reinstate Bligh, who had still not returned to England, as Governor for a period of twenty-four hours and then to relieve him. In Macquarie's commission he was charged with administering the colony within the limits of Cape York (10° 37'S) to South Cape (43° 39'S) and as far west as 135°E, a line connecting the Eyre Peninsula with Arnhem Land.

When Bligh finally left the colony in the *Hindostan* in May of 1810, he took with him most of the individuals who had dominated natural history in the colony for the past decade. George Caley, obedient to Banks' orders, ceased his sojourn as a collector in the colony and returned to England as a witness for Bligh against the malfeasance of the New South Wales Corps. Also aboard in the same role was George Suttor. William Paterson, returning to England with his regiment, sailed in the accompanying convoy of vessels.

Paterson died on the return voyage; Suttor appeared as a witness for Bligh at the court martial of Major Johnston, then returned to New South Wales to continue his agricultural endeavours; and although Caley was tempted to return to the colony he never did. The cold weather of England distressed Caley to the extent that he sought a more congenial climate in the West Indies where he was appointed superintendent of a botanical garden. Caley remained in the Caribbean for seven years but not without demonstrating the irritability for which he had become notorious in New South Wales. Eventually he returned to England in 1823 where he died six years later. His name and indeed his contributions to botany in Australia have been preserved in the various species named for him. Robert Brown, surely one of the most eminent botanists of the period, commended Caley as a competent botanist—high praise indeed from the somewhat dour Scot.

Chapter Eight

PENETRATING THE INTERIOR: 1811–18

The previous decade had seen Joseph Banks dispatch a cohort of naturalists to New South Wales for the collection of specimens for both the Royal Gardens at Kew and himself. Of these collectors, only one, George Caley, fulfilled his patron's expectations, and Caley was withdrawn in 1810 due to Banks' increasing age and the press of duties in England. Although there still existed vast areas of Australia yet to be explored, the entire interior remained untouched. Many of the obvious zoological and botanical curiosities had now been gathered, either by Caley and Brown or their predecessors. The blush of the new was over, but there still remained the more prosaic task of collecting and classifying the myriad organisms on the continent, a task that remains unfinished to this day.

The early years of the second decade of the nineteenth century were a period of dormancy for the natural history of Australia. The year 1811 was typical of this somnolent period; the few naturalists resident in the colonies of either Van Diemens Land or New South Wales drew attention to themselves by their extra-curricular activities rather than their additions to the store of knowledge of the country. The previous year the mineralogist, Humphrey, had brought himself under the scrutiny of the new governor by a report on a sample of salt. Macquarie's subsequent investigation of the lack of discernible work by the government mineralogist extended to Humphrey's moral turpitude, and he directed the commandant of Hobart to inform Humphrey that Harriet Sutton, a girl living in Van Diemens Land with Humphrey since 1806 despite her father's disapproval and a government edict for her return, must be sent back to Sydney and her father's house. Macquarie had already verbally requested Humphrey to comply with this demand, but Humphrey seems to have responded to neither the written or verbal admonishment. The rest of 1811 passed undramatically. Dr Robert Townson continued to inundate English friends with letters of complaint about his treatment in New South Wales but with little apparent effect. John Oxley, one of the future crop of the explorers of the interior of Australia, returned to England from his military duty in New South Wales and while in England petitioned for the position of surveyor in the colony.

In England, the ebb of the affairs of the colony was also evident. However the period did see William Westall's collection of bird skins, gathered while on Matthew Flinder's voyage, donated to the Linnean Society by A. B. Lambert, while George Perry commenced publication of the serial work *Arcana*. Among the organisms figured and described were a number from Australia, many of them represented before in other publications but others quite new. Perry used individual animals to make a specific point about natural history or their position in the 'great chain of Being'. Animals from Australia made up a significant proportion of the animals described, disproportionate to their importance or numbers. The legacy of the numerous natural history paintings arising from the early years of the colony continued to assure the flora and fauna of Australia a dominant part in the natural history volumes of the day.

Arcana is representative of the increasingly schizophrenic attitude adopted by individuals concerned with natural history while remaining devout Christians. The contradictions arose from the disparity between the findings of geology and the accepted dogma of the established churches. In a discussion of the natural history of the platypus, Perry argued that the animals of Australia were very different from the animals found in other regions of the world and this could:

> . . . be considered as the strongest natural proof to a reasoning mind, that the Flood or Diluvian Overflux of the Ocean, was not universal, for if so, it would be

GREEN PARROTT.

G. Perry del.

S

WOMBACH.

TOP LEFT:
'Green parrot'
Perry. *Arcana*. 1811.
Pezoporus wallicus

TOP RIGHT:
'Foliated pipefish'
Perry. *Arcana*. 1811.
Phyllopteryx taeniolatus

ABOVE:
'Wombach'
Perry. *Arcana*. 1811.
Vombatus ursinus

RIGHT:
'Koalo'
Perry. *Arcana*. 1811.
Phascolarctos cinereus

T.L.Busby sc.

impossible to account for the restoration, of each individual species to each particular climate.[1]

Perry extended the argument by postulating that animals must therefore have been created where they are presently found. Although careful to affirm his belief in the biblical creation of disparate species, Perry had nevertheless trespassed on theology by denying the universality of the Flood. Having reduced the Deluge then from the religious to the scientific, Perry continued his heresy by proposing a scientific explanation of the Flood, an explanation that he felt accounted for the peculiar animals found in Australia and at the same time explained marine fossils found on the peaks of the highest mountains. This theory, which conveniently ignored contradictory evidence, placed Perry as one of the first catastrophists willing to attribute phenomenal upheavals of the earth's surface to the close passage of a comet.

Briefly, Perry postulated that a comet's path had brought it near to the orbit of the earth, resulting in a sudden or gradual change in the inclination of the earth's axis of rotation. The modification of the earth's inclination would result in the redistribution of the oceans, some rushing over the face of the continents and eliminating the resident flora and fauna while leaving millions of marine organisms stranded on the land,

organisms which eventually mineralised to become fossils. Parts of the earth, however, would escape the havoc of the onrushing water. Perry thought that those continents farthest from the Equator would be spared— these would have included Australia, parts of Africa, Asia, and America. Such untouched areas would retain their original flora and fauna while the denuded continents would be recolonised from elsewhere; thus he accounted for Australia's very different plants and animals. As further proof of his theory, Perry offered as evidence the fact that no marine fossils had been found in Australia, demonstrating that it had been untouched by the flooding oceans set in motion by the change in the earth's inclination. Here Perry's use of data was selective, for reports from many of the seaborne expeditions to Australia had mentioned the marine fossils found well inland. Perry was not to be the last to involve the 'cometary theory' in an explanation of the Deluge, for it was to resurface in the work of Peter Cunningham in 1827.

Despite proposing an alternative to the biblical explanation of the Deluge, Perry stated quite categorically in *Arcana* that all species were created by God and could not be ascribed to the processes advocated by naturalists such as Lamarck twenty years previously; alterations such as would be possible 'to make from the same individual an apparently different species.'[2] Yet even here Perry edged towards evolutionary thought for in other sections of *Arcana* he accepted the idea of chemical change in geological formations. The acceptance of geological evolution was to form an important precursor to acceptance of biological evolution.

Perry, in a section of his work dealing with the recently discovered koala, presages the theory of ecological niches, albeit in somewhat different terminology:

> . . . they (the koalas) have little either in their character or appearance to interest the Naturalist or Philosopher. As Nature however provides nothing in vain, we may suppose that even these torpid, senseless creatures are wisely intended to fill up one of the great links of the chain of animated nature . . .[3]

The year 1812 continued the hiatus in the extension of knowledge of natural history in Australia. With a dearth of field collectors, the flow of specimens to Europe languished; even 'His Majesty's Mineralogist' sought permission to resign his commission, permission which was readily granted as of 30 June. The colony had lost its first official mineralogist, but in light of the amount of scientific work he completed, his loss was minimal, a point made by Governor Macquarie when he wrote back to England of Humphrey's indolent nature and lack of useful or important discoveries. Humphrey remained in Van Diemens Land as a settler, and having married Harriet Sutton went on to hold a number of administrative posts in the colony.

With the withdrawal of Humphrey from his official duties, Earl Bathurst recommended to Lachlan Macquarie that a convict, named Hutchinson, assume any mineralogical duties required; Macquarie in vain implored Bathurst to send to New South Wales a person properly skilled for the task. Subsequent dispatches from Macquarie to Bathurst detailed the attempts made by Macquarie to induce Hutchinson to conduct scientific research. Hutchinson was directed to examine the timber of the colony in order to assess its potential for the extraction of dye. On receipt of this order, Hutchinson complained that to pursue such studies to the satisfaction of the government he would need various chemicals and chemical apparatus which Macquarie declined to supply due to the expense involved. Hutchinson claimed that he himself had brought out much of the necessary equipment but that it had been usurped by Simeon Lord with whom he had entered into a business arrangement after receiving a conditional pardon. Finally Hutchinson was directed to make what practical research into the natural productivity of the land he could with simple tools and instruments. He limited himself to the extraction of dyes from plants. Macquarie continued to inveigh Bathurst to send to the colony a competent mineralogist, for Macquarie felt that while Hutchinson had a rudimentary knowledge of practical industry, his knowledge was much over-rated.

In 1813 the impetus for exploration of the unknown parts of the continent was revived. It was this year that saw the formidable barrier to expansion west in New South Wales, the Blue Mountains, breached, first by the party of Blaxland, Lawson, and Wentworth, then again that same year by a party led by the Colonial Surveyor, George William Evans. Although both parties lacked a recognised naturalist and little knowledge of the natural productions to the west of the mountains was gained, Wentworth listed a number of the plants that he noticed on the initial journey and returned with rock specimens resembling white marble flaked with yellow veins, and samples of the native timber. During the second passage of the mountains, Evans noted a species of 'trout' in the Fish River, surely the first reference to the Murray cod, *Maccullochella peelii*.

In 1813 the printing of the first natural history book in the colony itself occurred, although it appears to be a somewhat enforced printing. As mentioned previously, copies of John Lewin's *Birds of New Holland* printed in England never reached New South Wales, leaving the subscribers residing in the colony unsatisfied. In 1813 Lewin published a locally printed edition of the work slightly changed in title to *Birds of New South Wales* and with a number of changes to the original eighteen illustrations. This later edition involved the substitution of one bird species and the inclusion of new figures for other species. Unlike the earlier English edition, the volumes printed in New South Wales by George Howe, the proprietor of the *Sydney Gazette*, lacked the scientific names that had been appended to the 1808 London edition, further substantiating the suspicion that Lewin lacked the scientific training to adequately classify the birds. The 1813 edition, as might be expected from the conditions in which it was produced, was a rather rough reproduction. Inserted into several copies was a 'Panegyric, on an eminent artist' by the convict-poet and agitator John Grant including the verses:

> Nature! Where dwells in these Australian lands
> Thy faithful Copyist? Whose art expands
> Thy novel beauties o'er our ancient Globe?
> Who to far distant Climes thy Charms derobe?
>
> Modest, laborious, steady in his Plan
> I view, admire, venerate the Man;
> And lest neglect a tender Genius blight,
> Cheer, Muse! his patience, usher Him to light.
>
> Lewin! rare, beauteous plant in Genius's Vale
> Painter! Engraver! Naturer's Wooer! hail.
> Courage, the labours consecrate thy Fame
> Ages to come shall venerate thy name.[4]

Although Lewin was to publish no other natural history works during his life, he continued to paint the flora and fauna of the colony until his death in 1819. His illustrations from *Birds of New South Wales* were reprinted by George Howe in the *New South Wales Pocket Almanac* for 1821, and another edition of the work was published in England in 1838, probably at the instigation of his wife when she returned to England subsequent to Lewin's death.

The year 1813 saw the compilation of another work on the natural history of Australia, although one which was doomed never to see a printing press. Thomas Skottowe, a lieutenant in the 73rd Regiment, compiled a manuscript of 'Selected Specimens from Nature' while he was stationed at Newcastle where he had been assigned in 1811. Skottowe wrote descriptions, natural history notes, and provided Aboriginal names for a variety of animals which were accompanied by illustrations painted by T. Browne, a somewhat elusive figure who variously signed his work T. R. Browne, and I. R. Browne. The majority of the manuscript dealt with birds, over twenty species receiving attention, but also covered marsupials, such as kangaroos, native cats, and opossums. Thirteen species of fish also received descriptions, and there were several plates of insects and one of snakes.

Skottowe was no naturalist, he admitted as much in

the manuscript. He was an amateur and some of his ideas were clearly wrong, including the identification of a bird he called the 'ant killer' which he believed foraged among the trees for ants. The bird was a honeyeater. Nevertheless, Skottowe recognised at least five different kinds of kangaroos, a distinction that other more professional naturalists did not make. In his description of the butterflies in the volume he wrote:

> Many nice Critics I have no doubt will dispute the Existence of the most of them; and put them down as the visionary subjects of a traveller, who thinks he may snugly laugh at the Credulity of those who have not seen so much of the World as himself.[5]

But Skottowe insisted that all his vivid butterflies existed.

Of Browne, who painted the illustrations, little is known. He was probably a convict who served some of his time at Newcastle where Skottowe acquired his services to draw natural history subjects, but if he ever produced any other natural history illustrations, they are unknown.

A relapse into somnolence of natural history in Australia occurred in 1814. John Lewin continued to sketch and paint the plants and animals around him, but there appears to have been very little other activity in the colony.

By 1815 a renewal of the itinerant visits of officer-naturalists occurred. Joseph Arnold, who had visited the colony briefly in 1810, returned, this time as a medical superintendent on the female convict ship, *Northampton*. Arnold apparently owed his appointment on the *Northampton* to the intervention of Alexander Macleay, then secretary of the Board of Transport in England. That Macleay was indeed Arnold's patron is indicated by Macleay also standing as one of Arnold's proposers as a fellow of the Linnean Society that same year. When the Northampton called at Rio de Janeiro en route southward, Arnold collected insects, probably for Macleay. Arnold, who on his first voyage to Australia had lamented neglecting to bring with him some natural history reference texts, this time brought a copy of Robert Brown's *Prodromus* to while away the long hours of the voyage. On his arrival in Sydney on 18 June, Arnold expected to settle in New South Wales, but soon found to his dismay that the high cost of living combined with the rather cold welcome he received from the colonial administration changed his outlook. Arnold's reception by the colonial government became the subject of a number of exchanges between Governor Macquarie and Earl Bathurst, Bathurst censuring Macquarie for his treatment of such valuable prospective settlers as surgeons. Macquarie in turn complained of Arnold's 'pertinacious and lofty' demands. While Arnold certainly requested rations while in the

colony and passage back to England, these requests were commonplace.

Before he had passed three weeks in the colony, Arnold revised his plans to settle in New South Wales and took passage to Batavia, Java. Prior to leaving Port Jackson, he made further collections of insects and other natural history specimens, all to no avail. While anchored off Batavia, the vessel caught fire and sank, destroying his collections of insects, shells, and parrots in addition to his books and papers. An enthusiastic naturalist, Arnold was a less-than-sympathetic individual. On the voyage out to Sydney on the convict ship he wrote to his brother:

> The Newgate birds on board the ship behave tolerably well. When they kick up any riots I hand cuff them and put them in the coal-hold.[6]

Arnold was later to accompany Sir Stamford Raffles on his explorations in Sumatra, and here Arnold died in 1818 without having returned to Australia.

In 1815 Governor Macquarie received a request from Earl Bathurst that the person in the colony assigned to collecting natural history specimens be issued with a sufficient quantity of rum or other spirits to preserve samples of female platypuses and the reproductive organs of female kangaroos of differing ages. The request had been initiated by the Royal College of Surgeons of England which wished to complete studies on the natural history of the two animals. Behind the request from the College of Surgeons was undoubtedly Everard Home who was still working on the comparative anatomy of the marsupials. Whoever the collector was, unless fired by the enthusiasm of a Caley or Brown, he would have thought it a great waste of rum to use it to preserve kangaroo parts.

Opportunities for collection of specimens in New South Wales increased in 1815, for after Blaxland, Lawson, and Wentworth had shown in 1813 that the scarp of the Blue Mountains was no longer impassable, Macquarie ordered that a road be constructed across the mountain chain to open up the pastoral country to the west. By 1815 this was complete, and in April the governor, accompanied by a party that included John Lewin, George Evans, and John Oxley, set off from Sydney to view the newly opened country. In his record of the journey, Macquarie noted items of interest such as the animal then known as the 'paradox', a reference to the now discarded specific name of the platypus, '*paradoxus*'. Macquarie also recorded the large numbers of fish in the rivers that he thought resembled perch; this was the Murray cod that Evans had seen in the same area two years before.

The year 1816 was a fortuitous one for botany in Australia, for as well as the arrival of a botanical collector of the calibre of Allan Cunningham, it also marked the organisation of the Sydney Botanic Gardens. Although the site of the Botanic Gardens had been in continuous use as an experimental farm from the first days of Arthur Phillip's settlement of Sydney Cove, the sandy soil and the prevalence of rust had limited the productivity of the garden. The government farms were soon moved to the more fertile land surrounding Parramatta. However the Sydney Cove site was maintained as a vegetable garden for the governor, simultaneously acting as a trans-shipment garden both for exotic Australian flora on its way to either Joseph Banks or the nurserymen of London and for receiving plants of agricultural importance shipped to the settlement. Previously in 1808 Governor King had listed among the assets of the garden such an exotic enclosure as a pinery where pineapples were grown under glass.

Just as the formal organisation of the Botanic Gardens is traditionally given as 1816, so the first superintendent of the garden, Charles Fraser, is supposed to have begun his work that year. Fraser himself in a letter to the colonial secretary in 1820 stated that he was placed in charge of the Botanic Gardens at the termination of Oxley's expedition of 1818, while the formal appointment of Fraser to the position of colonial botanist was not until 1 January 1820. The date of 1816 for the organisation of the gardens may therefore be premature.

Regardless of the organisational date of the Botanic Gardens, the real impetus to botany in Australia in the second decade of the nineteenth century was given by the arrival of Allan Cunningham on 16 December 1816. Cunningham was another of the innumerable Scots in botanical employment throughout the world. Son of the head gardener to Earl Spencer at his home in London, Allan Cunningham was given an adequate education and then a fortunate apprenticeship at the Royal Gardens at Kew in 1810 or 1811 when he was about twenty years old. Kew, under the control of Joseph Banks, at this time had expanded to such a degree that it was thought desirable to issue a revised edition of *Hortus Kewensis*. William T. Aiton, then head gardener of the Royal Gardens, found that Allan Cunningham with his combination of botanical skills and education was an ideal assistant for the task; Cunningham's brother Richard was later to join the work as well. In 1814 Banks, who had four years earlier written to Caley that he could no longer justify the need for a full-time collector, at the instigation of William Aiton set about sending botanical collectors abroad again. This time the naturalists would not be in Banks' personal employment as had been Caley; they were to be employed by the Royal Gardens, paid by the Treasury, and would be under the nominal control of Aiton. When the possibility of naturalist positions becoming available was mooted, Allan Cunningham, along with another Kew assistant, James Bowie, applied. Both were appointed and initially were to be sent to Brazil.

140

Banks, in view of the problems he had had with past collectors such as Caley, (although possibly also because he was growing older and more conservative), pedantically lectured the young men on the need for his field-workers to exemplify a formidable list of traits, such as honesty, sobriety, diligence, activity, humility, and civility before they left England, and furnished them with extensive instructions about their expected duties.

Cunningham and Bowie landed in Brazil with the intention of remaining only a short time, but unable to find transport to the Cape of Good Hope, they were to spend almost two years in the country. This time, however, was well spent in gathering the native flora and perhaps more importantly in the training that was so necessary for a naturalist in the field. Their work, even if their plant specimens did not often survive the sea voyage back to England, sufficiently impressed Aiton and Banks. In September of 1816, both left Brazil for the Cape of Good Hope by different vessels, Bowie remaining at the Cape to continue the work of the English botanist Francis Masson while Cunningham proceeded further to New South Wales to continue the tradition of Banks, Burton, Caley, and Brown. During the outward journey, Cunningham learned the rudiments of celestial navigation and pored over a manuscript copy of Brown's *Prodromus* in preparation for the rigors and challenges of the land he was approaching.

Cunningham had barely stepped ashore before he became involved in his first exploratory excursion. During their initial interview Governor Macquarie alluded to the organisation of an expedition to explore the district west of the Blue Mountains, beyond the area discovered by Evans in 1813. Macquarie recommended that Cunningham make the journey, for there would be ample opportunity for the collection of undescribed species in such virgin country.

Cunningham had received no specific orders from either Banks or Aiton as to the nature of his duties on arrival in New South Wales, so he was in a quandary as to whether or not he should join the expedition. Cunningham finally concluded that he would be wasting a precious opportunity if he failed to venture west, a decision made easier no doubt by the knowledge that no botanist had previously crossed the Blue Mountains. He would be investigating unknown territory and so might hope to equal his predecessors, Caley and Brown.

Macquarie, in searching for a leader for the exploratory party, hit upon John Oxley. Lord Bathurst had hoped that Macquarie would be able to select a knowledgeable botanist or mineralogist to lead the party, but Cunningham was too new to the colony for such responsibility, and as there were no other suitable candidates then resident, Macquarie settled on Oxley, the surveyor-general. The best that Macquarie could do for the forthcoming expedition was to provide the party with the naturalists he had on hand—Allan Cunningham and the botanist-soldier, Charles Fraser. Fraser, another Scot, had arrived in New South Wales as a soldier in the 46th Regiment and was probably subsequently assigned to Macquarie's 73rd Regiment to facilitate his secondment to botanical duties. Fraser certainly had some botanical skills, probably gained through prior experience as a gardener, and Macquarie was aware of these. The reason for Fraser's inclusion on the list of personnel for the expedition seems to stem from a request Macquarie received from Bathurst shortly before the expedition was conceived, a request to ship to England seeds of the choicest plants. The prince regent wished to present the seeds to the emperor of Austria as a gift.

To ensure that the necessary information about the country west of the Blue Mountains was elicited, Bathurst wrote a detailed set of instructions to be given to the explorers. These instructions stated that a detailed journal must be kept of all pertinent facts, which in addition to the general appearance of the country, its soil, flora, fauna, and minerals, was to detail the climate and relevant facts about the Aborigines. Oxley, as leader of the expedition, was given orders by Macquarie to trace the headwaters of the Lachlan River. The party of thirteen accompanying him included Cunningham, Fraser, George Evans—who had crossed the mountains in 1813 and was appointed second-in-command of the expedition—and William Parr, described as a mineralogist but listed in the early civil records of the colony as a commissary clerk. Macquarie authorised the issue of acid from the medical dispensary to Parr for testing minerals and metal ores during the expedition.

While the party was being organised, Cunningham lived at Parramatta and began his systematic collection of plants. On 31 March 1817, Cunningham received word from Oxley to hold himself ready at Parramatta on 3 April, and from there they departed the following day.

Even during that first day on a route that had been covered many times before, Cunningham was busy collecting. Not surprisingly he found the plants to be similar to those with which he had already familiarised himself at Parramatta. In the next few days, as they travelled over Coxs Road across the mountains to Bathurst, Cunningham continued to collect, and although most of the plants had already been described by Brown, they were new to Cunningham. He also noted white cockatoos and flying squirrels in his wanderings away from the road in search of plants. By 9 April the party reached the cairn of stones thought to be erected by George Caley to mark his farthest penetration into the Blue Mountains, and five days later they were in Bathurst. In the two years since 1815, when Macquarie had visited the undeveloped site, houses had been constructed and stock was now run in the surrounding district. For six days the expedition remained at Bathurst completing preparations for the journey, days that Cunningham used to expand his collection. On 20 April the exploratory party started westward towards a forward supply depot that had earlier been established for them on the banks of the Lachlan River. Cunningham was kept busy by the continuous supply of botanical species new to him. Many he had seen before, but there were a far greater number with which he was unfamiliar. He had then been in the colony a scant four months. The vista spread before him was very different from that he had so recently traversed in the wet rainforests of Brazil. Here, instead of crowding masses of luxuriant vegetation, he saw sparse dry brush. In South America the trees were festooned with attractive epiphytes and parasitic creepers, but here few such plants existed. On 23 April Cunningham noted in his journal, almost with relief, that he saw a species of *Loranthus* parasitising a eucalypt. There were other new sights though, for he soon saw several specimens of that wonder of Australian zoology, the platypus, in a series of pools by the river. Mineralogical investigations kept pace with the zoological novelties—experimentation produced lime from a limestone outcropping when the rock was placed in a fire overnight. More significantly for the colony, the land the party traversed was admirably suited to grazing and agriculture.

Following their arrival at the forward depot, the expedition commenced preparations for descending the Lachlan by boat. Cunningham fossicked about the area collecting specimens when he was not changing the paper in which he pressed his samples, a necessary step to hasten the dehydration of the plants. Often the two botanists, Fraser and Cunningham, collected in each other's company. Fraser seems to have possessed an adequate botanical knowledge and had already spent a month at Bathurst collecting specimens for the emperor of Austria and the nascent Botanic Gardens in Sydney. In the list of personnel drawn up by Macquarie for the expedition, Fraser was already described as the 'colonial botanist', a title he was not to gain officially for another four years, as opposed to Cunningham who was styled as the 'king's botanist'.

The party left the forward depot on 28 April and descended the Lachlan with boats portaging the heavier supplies, the main party following on horseback. Cunningham regarded the journey as the 'grand Western Expedition' and he continued to procure both known and unknown species of plants. He noted that to the west of the Blue Mountains the brown gum disappeared and was replaced by the blue gum and stringybark. Days later Cunningham detected a new species of lily which he named '*Pancratium macquaria*' for the governor. The expedition soon passed the limit of prior exploration and began carefully charting the ground. Due to the often swampy nature of the land and the need for numerous surveying sites, they found that they could average no more than 15 kilometres each day. On 6 May, it was Oxley's turn to be commemorated, for that day Cunningham named the species '*Tecoma oxleyi*' for him. Oxley was able to return the compliment almost immediately as a distant mountain was that same day named Mount Cunningham. During this stage of their journey, the salted provisions were relieved by the Murray cod which abounded in the river. Beyond Mount Cunningham they encountered a plain which Oxley named for Barron Field, at that time the judge of the New South Wales Supreme Court. Here they chanced upon numerous emus which assuaged the monotony of their diet, especially with Cunningham's recommendation that the meat be stewed with the leaves of *Rhagodia*. The marshy country through which they were now travelling contained prolific waterfowl, native companions (brolgas), black swans, and myriad other birds.

The Lachlan soon degenerated into a series of meandering channels and marshes, so Oxley determined to break away to the south-west. If the Lachlan indeed flowed westward to Spencers Gulf as was thought likely, then the party should come upon it further west. They left the river and boats on 18 May and pressed south-west for the coast on horseback. Within two days they had exchanged the marshy lands for unwatered scrub so dry that there was soon little water for either themselves or their horses. They continued on, however, through brush that Cunningham thought dismal, although at least he had the consolation that it afforded him new species of plants. On 3 June the party came upon an elevation which Oxley named Mount Caley for his predecessor in the colony, noting that Mount Caley possessed a grand and majestic bluff front, a fact that would have appealed to Caley's vanity. That day the party penetrated as far to the south as they were to reach. All the horses were then showing signs of weakness from the lack of fodder, and the men were tired and weak, so with no relief from the sterile conditions in sight, Oxley turned north. Even the animals seemed to have deserted this barren land; the party saw only a few kangaroo rats, which they caught and ate, and some black cockatoos.

On 3 June Cunningham planted peach and quince seeds near Mount Brogden, a habit he continued throughout the expedition and on his subsequent journeys, in the hope that some of the fruit would eventually provide a meal for native or settler. Oxley was less optimistic, despairing that the region would ever be visited again by civilised man. The meticulousness of Cunningham throughout the journey was demonstrated by such small exercises as the planting of seeds and his constant repacking and redrying of specimens in an effort to maintain them in the best possible condition.

The party continued to travel northward, but it was not until 23 June that they again sighted running water. Oxley was uncertain as to whether it was the Lachlan that they had quitted five weeks previously but resolved to follow it downstream nevertheless. Along the river banks their rapidly diminishing supplies were supplemented with the fish in the river and the animals that dwelt upon its banks; one of the latter was described as an animal of the kangaroo family, with a long tail notable for its flat formation at its tip, possibly the bridled nail-tail wallaby *Onychogalea frenata*. On 3 July several flocks of a new species of pigeon were sighted and two shot. They displayed brown wings, a green breast, and a small topknot of black feathers. Also in evidence were galahs, which when tried as food were found to be unpalatable. Much to Oxley's disgust, the river again lost itself in a maze of swamps, and here Oxley terminated travel westward. The party turned back upstream, continuing past the point where they had intercepted the river earlier. Following the river far enough upstream to ascertain that it was indeed the Lachlan, Oxley then headed north-east away from the Lachlan and toward the Macquarie River.

Of the animals that they observed on their journey to the north-east, Cunningham said little; he was primarily concerned with botanical specimens, apparently much more so than previous collectors who, while interested in plants, had also kept a wary eye out for unique animals. Oxley, in his published journal, listed the animals seen as similar to those found at Bathurst with the exception of a new species of red kangaroo, a second smaller kangaroo species, and the two birds already mentioned, the pigeon and the galah.

Crossing overland between the two rivers, the land, which had been barren and desolate, took on a fertile appearance. The vegetation resembled that close to

J.C.Whichelo.del.

T.L.Busby.sculp.

'Nonpareil parrot'
Perry. *Arcana*. 1811.
Platycercus eximius

144

'Crested pigeon'
Sturt. *Two expeditions into the interior of southern Australia.* 1833.
Ocyphaps lophotes

Bathurst. Reaching the Macquarie River on 20 August, the party travelled downstream as far as was possible in one day before turning their direction toward civilisation or at least Bathurst. On the return trip they encountered a seam of limestone which they thought to be a continuation of the limestone reef they had discovered directly to the south many weeks before, and so tested its quality with the acid brought for that purpose. With little in the way of provisions left, the party hurried toward Bathurst where they arrived on 29 August, having been absent from that settlement for nineteen weeks on a journey that Oxley reckoned at 1,200 miles (2,000 kilometres), a good portion of them—as many as 750 (1,200 kilometres) covered on foot. From Oxley's viewpoint the expedition had ended in failure. The promising route of the Lachlan River to the southern coast of Australia had ended in marshy swamps far distant from any coast. Cunningham, whose hopes centred around the collection of new plant specimens, thought the expedition a success. He had collected more than 400 plant specimens, often with duplicate samples, and brought back 150 packets of seeds, all of which would please his employers Joseph Banks and William Aiton. Perhaps more importantly for Cunningham, he had familiarised himself with some of the flora of eastern Australia and successfully withstood the hardships of exploration, enough so that future expeditions could be faced with confidence. At the termination of the expedition Cunningham's journal was surrendered to Oxley for transmission to Macquarie.

Of the botanical activities of Charles Fraser during the expedition there is little record, except for meagre mention in the journals of Cunningham or Oxley. Oxley refers to him by name three times in his journal, managing to spell his name differently each time—even his title seemed in a state of flux. Sometimes he was the 'botanical soldier' while at others the 'colonial collector' or 'colonial botanist'. When Fraser reported to Macquarie about the expedition on 9 September, he brought with him a month-old emu, obtained on the banks of the Macquarie River, as a present for Macquarie's wife.

Cunningham returned across the Blue Mountains from Bathurst to Parramatta on 1 September, walking a considerable part of the way so that his horse could carry his specimen collection. In the seven leisurely days he spent on the journey to Parramatta, Cunningham continued to add to his plant collection. On 9 September Cunningham attended an interview with Macquarie to report on the expedition. At this time he was informed of a proposed voyage of exploration to the north and north-western coasts of Australia to finish the survey that the leaky *Investigator* had cut short for Matthew Flinders and Robert Brown. In letters that Macquarie handed him from Joseph Banks, Cunningham found a suggestion that he join the proposed seaborne expedition.

Cunningham of course wrote to his patron, Banks, during this period. In a letter of 20 September 1817 he reported on the inland expedition, at the same time disparaging those who called the range of hills behind Sydney the Blue Mountains. Cunningham commented that they were nothing in height compared to the range behind Rio de Janiero, but Cunningham might have been less disdainful had he forged his own route across the escarpment instead of merely travelling Coxs road. Other comments by Cunningham dealt with the similarity between the botany of the Blue Mountain region and that of the coastline, the upland flora forming a diversified transition zone between the coastal vegetation and the considerably different flora found to the west of the mountains.

While Cunningham set about preparing his specimens for shipment to Kew and organising his affairs for the forthcoming voyage, a disagreement arose between himself and Macquarie. Macquarie had authorised the use of a horse by Cunningham during Oxley's expedition, and on 18 September the government superintendent of stores requested its return. Cunningham in turn wrote to Macquarie asking to be allowed to retain the use of the horse for future excursions, but Macquarie disallowed the request on the grounds that even medical officers of the colony were not provided with horses, and advised Cunningham to apply to his employers in England for money to purchase a horse. Cunningham made little mention of the incident in his daily journal, although this might be attributable to the knowledge that the journals were liable to confiscation by the governor at any time, but the issue continued to fester. Cunningham, in a letter to Banks sent with a shipment of plant specimens, indicated some dissatisfaction with the reception that Macquarie had given him in terms of material help. Complaints by Cunningham included the poor quality of specimen packing cases, his meagre ration, and the return of the horse. News of this letter reached Macquarie, and when Cunningham next called upon the governor before leaving on the voyage to northern Australia, Macquarie accused Cunningham of having written divisive comments concerning the governor's person. Cunningham defended himself by protesting that anything he had written was merely a justification of his expenses, but Macquarie refused to accept the excuse. Both men subsequently submitted explanations to Banks, Cunningham stating that he was driven by the purest of motives, while Macquarie savaged Cunningham in a letter marked by its vehemence. Macquarie accused Cunningham of ingratitude and, more harshly, of ill-breeding, terms hardly justifiable in view of the issues involved. Banks could only wonder if he was forever doomed to be making peace between his collectors in New South Wales and the colonial administration, for the furore resembled nothing so much as prior confrontations between George Caley and previous governors.

Banks defended Cunningham both directly to Macquarie and in more subtle ways, such as provoking Bathurst to direct Macquarie to provide the king's botanist with all assistance possible. Banks could have done no less than support Cunningham, for contained among the directives issued to Cunningham by Banks before he left for New South Wales was the instruction to make known to Banks the conduct of the governor towards the employee of Kew. While Charles Fraser and Allan Cunningham remained friends, although they were not above sniping at each other's abilities on occasion, their respective patrons, Governor Macquarie and Joseph Banks, were jealous of their prerogatives. Banks felt that Macquarie over-favoured the colonial botanist to the extent of allowing him to send to England specimens for the benefit of nurserymen in London, specimens that Cunningham had not been able to collect for Kew. No doubt it galled Banks that commercial enterprises should obtain specimens while his beloved Kew went without.

The matter of illicit trade of live plants and seeds was of great concern to Cunningham. Some of the convicts that had accompanied the Oxley expedition had spent their free time in gathering plants, intending to sell them to wealthy colonists who would dispatch them to England. Cunningham, in apprising Banks of the existence of several sources of plant specimens, was apprehensive lest Banks think he was the source supplying the English market.

Despite the recriminatory statements made by both Macquarie and Cunningham, arrangements were proceeding apace for Cunningham to embark on the northern cruise. Lieutenant Phillip Parker King, son of Philip Gidley King, earlier governor of the colony, had been appointed to the command of the expedition with authorisation to procure a suitable vessel in New South Wales. Unable to find a satisfactory vessel initially, King was finally able to purchase a small cutter, the *Mermaid*, newly built in India.

Specifically, King's instructions directed him to examine and survey the hitherto unexplored coasts of New Holland from Arnhem Bay near the western side of the Gulf of Carpentaria as far westward and southward as North West Cape. He was to maintain a vigilant lookout for any navigable rivers that might lead into the interior of the continent, for the great hope of both the colonial administrations in Sydney and London was still that there would be located a river highway into the sought-after fertile regions occupying the interior of Australia, a dream that was to persist for many years to come. Included in King's supplemental instructions were orders to receive on board his vessel Allan Cunningham for the purpose of making botanical collections, as well as any other person in the colony

that could display a competent knowledge of natural history. The ship chosen to fulfil this variety of tasks, the *Mermaid*, was not the ideal vessel for the purpose but was the best that King could obtain in the colony. Only 84 tons and measuring 18 metres long, the *Mermaid* was practical for inshore survey work but extremely small for nineteen men to live and work in for many months at a time. On 23 September 1817 Cunningham spoke with King about the projected departure date of the voyage but found that it had not been finalised and was still some time off. Cunningham spent the remaining time in preparing and repapering his specimens and writing a fair copy of his journal. Despite the *contretemps* with Macquarie, Cunningham also assisted him with the shipment to England of the plant specimens that Fraser had collected on Oxley's expedition. Four of the plant specimens were so striking that Macquarie determined to have paintings made of them 'by the Masterly hand of Mr. Lewin'.

Bathurst, in an earlier dispatch, had suggested that John Lewin might be prevailed upon to undertake the voyage on the *Mermaid* in the position as naturalist, but Lewin had declined due to the necessity of supporting his family. Macquarie arranged for Lewin to paint the four botanical specimens, paintings that Macquarie transmitted to Bathurst. Macquarie also had illustrations prepared of the two species of birds that had been obtained on the expedition, 'Leadbeater's cockatoo' (now known as the pink, or Major Mitchell's, cockatoo), *Cacatua leadbeateri* and the bar-shouldered dove, *Geopelia humeralis*, which were also dispatched to English naturalists. Macquarie suggested to Bathurst that Lewin's artistic talents were such that he might be usefully employed exclusively in the service of the government. Lewin was already in the employment of the government: appointed the coroner of Sydney in 1814, he had derived only a meagre living from that position. Concomitant with the paintings of plants and animals that Macquarie forwarded to England were shipped packets of seeds from which Joseph Banks was to choose an assortment for Monsieur Goum, superintendent of the king's garden in Paris, and for the emperor of Austria.

On 1 December Cunningham spoke with King again and learned that the *Mermaid*'s projected sailing date was about ten days off. The next several days were busy ones, spent overseeing Lewin's work on the figures of the botanical specimens and completing his own preparations for the sea voyage. The *Mermaid* tried to get away on 21 December but contrary winds forced her back into the harbour. She set out again the following day, this time successfully. Part of King's instructions were to accurately survey the area around Cape Leeuwin, and with the westerly monsoon already setting in to the north King decided to commence his survey at its western limit, sailing for Cape Leeuwin by way of Bass

'*Angophora intermedia*'
Lewin. Unpublished. Courtesy of Mitchell Library.
Angophora floribunda

Strait. Despite a battering by a gale off Twofold Bay, the *Mermaid* passaged Bass Strait and crossed the Australian Bight before arriving at King George Sound in the middle of January. There Cunningham found the character of the vegetation to be much different from that on the eastern coast of Australia. Plants that he had only seen in cultivated gardens in England, or in Sydney, he now saw growing wild. While King and his crew watered the vessel, Cunningham botanised in the area that had previously afforded such pleasure to Menzies, La Billardière, and Brown. Cunningham found a wealth of *Banksia*, *Dryandra*, *Epacris* and other plants, such that before he left he noted that the area was 'a rich botanical depository of sterling worth'. He found a terrestrial example of the genus '*Loranthus*' with vivid orange flowers and assumed that this was the plant that La Billardière had called '*Loranthus flori-bundus*'. Later, before he left the region, Cunningham found a species of the plant genus that James Edward Smith had named for La Billardière, *Billardiera*. Before the *Mermaid* proceeded to sea, Cunningham sought the pitcher plants that had been reported in the boggy ground near the sound but was disappointed in finding none. While Cunningham was concerned almost

'*Xylomelum pyriforme*'
Lewin. Unpublished, Courtesy of Mitchell Library.
Xylomelum pyriforme

exclusively with the plants of the district, Phillip Parker King had time to observe the huge nests of the sea eagles, a species of cockatoo he thought similar to the black cockatoo of New South Wales, and to collect shells and minerals. In February the *Mermaid*'s anchors were hauled and she rounded Cape Leeuwin and ran north along the coastline. While coasting north the crippling disease of every expedition, dysentery, struck, severely depleting the crew and effectively preventing any survey work. On this leg of the journey Cunningham noted the turtles, sea snakes, and dolphins that invariably were mentioned in the journals of the naturalists who had preceded him.

Rounding North West Cape and heading eastward from Exmouth Gulf, King began his survey in earnest. The barren, sterile land gave Cunningham little in the way of additions to his collection, but he noted in his journal the presence of a species of kangaroo rat and was astounded by the anthills rising 2·5 metres in height. Cunningham found that when these structures were abandoned by the constructors they formed nurseries and sanctuaries for a variety of wildlife. At one such site Cunningham and his companions chased a 1·5 metre lizard until it took refuge in an abandoned anthill. Behind the foreshore Cunningham noticed fragments of coral and shells scattered over the flat plain, stimulating him to consider that the sea must once have covered much of the area. King continued to collect mineral samples and shells on the beaches of the north-west coast of Australia as well as on the numerous offshore islands that complicated his survey. As they progressed further north-east, the *Mermaid* anchored off the island which Dampier had named Rosemary Island for the plant he obtained there and illustrated in his journal. Here, Cunningham was pleased to gather specimens of the plant for his own collection. Continuing through the Dampier Archipelago and farther east, the barren, sandy coastline gradually gave way to muddy foreshores, the land rimmed by mangroves that advanced to meet the water's edge.

At Depuch Island a change in the wind pattern caused King to take the *Mermaid* further offshore. After running north-east he turned landward making the coast somewhat to the east of the Cobourg Peninsula and Port Essington. Here King reversed his direction. Working his way back to the west, he encountered and named Raffles Bay, then Port Essington. Cunningham thought that Port Essington would offer shelter and protection to any number of ships but concluded that the land was too overgrown with mangroves and too destitute of fresh water to be of much use for agriculture. King felt somewhat differently, for that although the soil did not seem particularly rich, every kind of plant thrived here, indicative of its potential. Landward excursions revealed no fresh water, but from the large number of Aborigines living in the area, King was convinced that it must exist in abundance. With its superior harbour, its proximity to the Molucca Islands, centre of the spice trade, and its location on the route from Sydney to India, King felt that Port Essington had a promising future. King's opinion was obviously considered by the mandarins at the Home Office in London for it was not long before an attempt was made to establish a settlement at Raffles Bay. Perhaps it would have been wiser to consider Cunningham's opinion in conjunction with Lieutenant King's, for Cunningham foresaw most of the problems which were later to lead to the demise of the settlement on the northern coast.

'*Hibiscus radiatus*'
Britten. *Illustrations of the botany of Cook's voyage round the world in HMS Endeavour.* 1900–05.
Hibiscus radiatus

Continuing around the coast, the *Mermaid*'s crew surveyed the shores of Van Diemens Gulf and the entrance to the Alligator River. In naming the Alligator River, King mistook the resident crocodiles for alligators. Rowing up the river King and Cunningham had ample opportunity to observe the flora and fauna, but Cunningham found a dull uniformity to the mangroves that was enlivened only by the yellow flowers of *Hibiscus*. The presence of numerous crocodiles disinclined Cunningham from exploring the river banks for new

specimens. White cockatoos were seen, as well as a:

> Large bird of the Anas family with very long necks, some perfectly white, others very dark, and even of a black colour

which built its nest in the mangroves, possibly the magpie goose, *Anseranas semipalmata*.[7]

Several times during the following weeks they pursued indentations in the coastline that they thought might herald the long-sought river into the interior, but each inlet brought only disappointment as it dwindled into mangrove swamp. Provisions quickly became depleted, so King gave the order to sail for Timor on 31 May, arriving there five days later. Cunningham took the opportunity to botanise on the island for the two weeks while the *Mermaid* was resupplied. From Timor they paused briefly at Barrow Island then sailed for Port Jackson via Cape Leeuwin and Bass Strait, arriving in Sydney Cove on 29 July. In a letter to Bathurst later that year, Macquarie summed up the expedition: King had made no discovery of importance, meaning that the voyage had not found the rivers into the interior that all thought and hoped would exist.

Before the return of the *Mermaid*, Macquarie had sent a shipment of live plants to England. Included were a collection of choice and rare flowers for Queen Charlotte Sophia of England, a collection for the emperor of Austria, and a third collection for Prince Leopold of Saxe-Coburg, king of the Belgians. Among the specimens sent were giant lilies, rock lilies, and Norfolk pines. The plants were placed under the care of Alexander Colley, a convict gardener to whom Macquarie granted a pardon for his service in caring for the plants on the voyage to Europe.

While King and Cunningham were still off the northwest coast of Australia, Macquarie decided on another expedition into the interior of New South Wales, or the 'western country' as it was often called. The Lachlan River had been shown to lose itself in interminable swamps in the interior, but the size of the other river named for the governor, the Macquarie, along which Oxley's expedition had travelled in the return portion of his first journey, gave rise to expectations that it might contribute its waters to either the ocean on the northwest coast of Australia or to a large inland sea.

Again Macquarie appointed Oxley to the command of the expedition, and again Evans was his second-in-command. With Cunningham not yet returned from King's expedition, Macquarie assigned Charles Fraser to collect botanical specimens during the journey. Remembering the problems with the private collections gathered on Oxley's first expedition, Macquarie issued orders that with the exception of Fraser's plant gathering and Oxley's mineral sampling, all other collecting of natural history specimens was prohibited. The expedition left Bathurst on 25 May 1818, and travelled north west down the Macquarie River. Almost immediately they caught in the Macquarie a new species of fish with:

> . . . four smellers above and four under the mouth; the hind part of it resembled an eel; it had one dorsal fin, and four other fins, with a white belly . . .[8]

This must have been the freshwater catfish, *Tandanus tandanus*. The party journeyed through open plains and scant forest noting limestone outcroppings and collecting mineral samples of agate, iron-stone, jasper, and flint. They remained well fed on the abundant game close to the river: swans, the kangaroo that A. B. Lambert had denominated '*Macropus elegans*', and fish. To Oxley's eye, the plants bore a great resemblance to those found along the return route of the previous expedition. Fraser continued to collect assiduously, though many of the plants were identical to those he had seen the previous year. Fraser left no record of the journey so only Oxley's published comments can be recorded. Birds were seen but only at such a distance as to render it impossible to identify them, with the exception of 'Leadbeater's cockatoo' and the bar-shouldered dove seen the previous year on the Lachlan River.

Further downstream the party encountered two hills of granite, one of which Oxley named for Surgeon Harris who accompanied the expedition as a volunteer. Oxley surmised that the mountains had to be of volcanic origin as they reared up out of the alluvial plain far distant from any other mountain chain. Soon Oxley was to suffer the disappointment of the Macquarie degenerating into a swampy morass, much as the Lachlan had been found to do the preceding year. Oxley was at this point certain that he had reached the shores of an inland sea, but when he published his journal in 1820 he was no longer optimistic of the inland sea existing. Thwarted from progressing further westward along the river banks by the increasingly wet nature of the country, Oxley led his party overland to the east. Even here the ground proved miserable for travel, consisting of quicksand and bog alternating with barren hills. The sole consolation of the area was that it produced many new plant species for the travellers. In his journal Oxley wrote that just as the geological features of New South Wales seemed to have a north–south orientation, so did the productions of the vegetable kingdom, especially plants such as *Banksia*. Crossing the northern section of the Liverpool Plains and later the Peel River, Fraser found platypuses and many examples of undescribed orchids. The character of the country had now changed appreciably. Lush and verdant vegetation abounded and the presence of *Casuarina* indicated to Oxley that they were nearing the sea, even though they were yet 110 kilometres distant from it. At one site Fraser detected over fifty species of plants, some of which he hoped

would be undescribed genera. From a mountain top on 23 September, the party sighted the sea in the distance, but it was not until 8 October that they camped on the shore at an embayment and river mouth they called Port Macquarie, adding the governor's name to yet another geographical feature. Oxley led the party down the coast as far as Port Stephens where they were taken off by boat and transported to Sydney.

The grand design of tracing the Macquarie to its terminus had failed, but the botanical efforts of Charles Fraser were entirely successful. He returned with some 300 or more specimens of plants, descriptions of the plants, the nature of the soil in which they grew, their time of flowering, and other data about their habitat. The author of a review of Oxley's published journal in the *Quarterly Review* years later concluded that Oxley's two expeditions settled two major points: that the colonisation of New South Wales beyond 30 kilometres from the coast was never very likely and that it was improbable that either the Lachlan or the Macquarie Rivers ever reached the coast. In fact the reviewer thought it extremely unlikely that there were any major rivers on the continent of Australia. He was to be proven wrong in both his conclusions as greater knowledge of the country was amassed. If Oxley's expeditions were characterised by the lack of success in attaining their geographic goals, they proved entirely the opposite from the botanist's point of view. Vast new areas had been opened for them to seek specimens to expand their collections, and credible returns had already been gained from much of the region. Governor Macquarie once again employed John Lewin to illustrate specimens that Fraser brought back from Oxley's second expedition. Eight paintings were forwarded to Earl Bathurst in March 1819.

Throughout the latter part of 1818, after his return from King's voyage, Allan Cunningham resided in Parramatta working on his specimen collection. Employed in producing a fair copy of his journal and arranging shipment of his specimens to England, he still found time for short excursions in the immediate environs of Sydney and Parramatta. Early in October he met with Phillip Parker King, who indicated that his second voyage to the north-west coast would not commence before December. With several months in hand, Cunningham made application to Macquarie for a government horse and cart for a trip he planned to the Illawarra region. After some time had elapsed with no answer from Macquarie, Cunningham probably reflected on the disadvantages of antagonising the powers that be. On further application he found that Macquarie had not bothered with a written reply but had verbally authorised the superintendent of stores to supply Cunningham's needs. Even this did not end Cunningham's problems, for he found that in order to obtain any supplies from the government stores he had to specify every item in detail; perhaps Macquarie thus obtained a measure of quiet revenge for their earlier confrontation.

Cunningham was away by 19 October with his horse and cart and spent several weeks in the Illawarra or Five Islands region. He delighted in finding many orchids, which from the time he had spent in Brazil had occasioned a special interest for him. He was forced by the rocky terrain to leave his cart at a farmhouse and spend several days either on foot or horseback collecting the seeds, plant specimens, and bulbs that he wished to return to Parramatta. His journal also recorded finding a possum, with its cub, in a tree. An Aboriginal travelling with Cunningham killed the parent while Cunningham attempted to keep the cub alive but with what success is unknown. During this trip Cunningham collected and named the Illawarra flame tree, *Brachychiton acerifolius*, although he described it under the name '*Sterculia acerifolia*'.

Returning to Parramatta Cunningham dried his new specimens and planted his bulbs in the garden of a friend, as he was unable to locate a vessel returning directly from Port Jackson to England and feared that the bulbs might not survive a protracted ocean voyage. Cunningham was not above professional jealousy. Writing to Aiton in 1818, Cunningham recorded the appointment of Charles Fraser as the colonial botanist. While acknowledging that Fraser had made extensive collections on Oxley's second inland expedition, Cunningham disparaged the collection as consisting predominantly of species that he, Cunningham, had already obtained. The bulbs in Fraser's collection he thought to duplicate species that Cunningham had previously dispatched to the gardens at Kew. Even if not styled the colonial botanist, Cunningham could at least no longer complain about the asperity of the colonial administration. He now received everything he had asked for: drying paper, specimen boxes, even a horse and cart.

Although Cunningham and Fraser were the only professionally trained naturalists in the colony, if employment in the gardens of England could be considered professional training, wealthy residents of New South Wales had occasion to utilise less qualified individuals to collect curiosities of natural history. A member of the colonial gentry, Sir John Jamison, employed Thomas Jones as his collector of natural history productions. In the latter part of the decade, Jones made a number of minor excursions, either in the company of his employer or more usually in the company of Aborigines, to verify details of local geography or to collect specimens. Jamison's records indicate that he directed Jones to keep a detailed diary on these excursions including items such as the collection of fossils, the geology of the area, and observations on bird species.

When Cunningham returned from Illawarra, he found that King had changed his plans for the voyage north. Rather than sail via Cape Leeuwin to the western coast of Australia and work his way east as he had attempted previously, King now proposed to sail north via Cape York then westward, running before the prevailing easterly winds. The wind pattern would not shift to the east until March, so King proposed a voyage to Van Diemens Land in order to survey Macquarie Harbour. Cunningham accompanied the *Mermaid* when she sailed on 25 December, and after a brief stop at Hobart King pressed on to Macquarie Harbour. Here Cunningham was able to describe the cones of the Huon pine, previously unobserved due to their minute size. Cunningham placed the Huon pine in the genus *Dacrydium* where it remains today as *Dacrydium franklinii*. While he waited at Macquarie Harbour for King to complete his survey, Cunningham compiled a chart of the various types of timber to be found there, a chart that King later published in his narrative of his journeys for the benefit of those seeking timber in Van Diemens Land. The *Mermaid* arrived back in Port Jackson on 14 February 1819.

Chapter Nine

COASTAL EXPLORATION—
BRITISH AND FRENCH: 1819–21

The first two expeditions that Allan Cunningham undertook, one by land, the other a coastal survey by sea, were to inaugurate his principal activities for the next ten years. His inland exploration, except for short excursions to known areas of New South Wales, were held in abeyance and for the next several years his botanical skills were employed on a series of voyages to the north-west coast of Australia reminiscent of the one just undertaken with Lieutenant Phillip Parker King.

Three months after the *Mermaid* returned from Van Diemens Land to Port Jackson, Phillip Parker King was ready to embark on the next of his continuing series of explorations of north-western Australia. The *Mermaid* sailed from Sydney on 8 May in company with the *Lady Nelson*. On board the latter travelled John Oxley, who was to prepare a survey of Port Macquarie and the Hastings River, both discovered on his last inland journey. At Port Macquarie King helped Oxley with the survey of the river mouth while Cunningham botanised in the district. Cunningham determined that about three-quarters of the plant species at Port Macquarie were common to the Illawarra district, and so found few new species there. Eleven days after their arrival, the *Lady Nelson* parted company with the *Mermaid*— the *Lady Nelson* returning to Sydney, the *Mermaid* destined for Cape York, then westward. The *Mermaid* ran north anchoring inshore only occasionally to obtain fresh water. Cunningham had little opportunity to observe and collect, but on those chances to go ashore he noticed a great similarity between the flora south of Port Bowen and that found at Port Macquarie. Further north, once they had passed the Whitsunday Islands, Cunningham observed a change in the flora, which began to resemble the vegetation of the Indies. He was startled to find a South American plant genus in the

region but would have been even more amazed to learn of the reason why South America and Australia have certain similarities in flora and fauna, having once been connected via Antarctica. At Cape Cleveland, where Cunningham was able to procure a number of plants and seeds, both he and King noticed that the stems of the *Xanthorrhoea* were covered with a species of butterfly. The English naturalist William Sharp Macleay, who later described the insects collected on King's voyages, named the butterfly '*Euplaea hamata*', a species closely resembling a butterfly found on the coast of India as well as in Indonesia. At Fitzroy Island, Cunningham went ashore and recognised a specimen of the nutmeg, described as '*Myristica cimicifera*' in King's journal, in addition to two species of his personal favourite, the orchids, one *Dendrobium canaliculatum*, the other undescribed.

By 27 June, King was able to anchor in the Endeavour River at much the same site that had proven a safe haven for Cook and his leaking *Endeavour* almost fifty years before. Here Cunningham collected specimens that had occupied the attention of his patron, Joseph Banks, and Cunningham was to write to Banks of his enthusiasm for collecting plants with such historic associations. He gathered duplicate specimens to refurbish the herbarium at Soho Square and collected bulbs to be shipped back to England, one set a species he thought to be *Crinum angustifolium*, named by Robert Brown from specimens he had collected on this same coast. On one of his excursions, Cunningham fell in with a group of Aborigines and, seeing a kangaroo, indicated it with the name that Cook had obtained from the Aborigines. The Aborigines did not appear to understand, leaving open the question as to whether the word kangaroo actually was the Aboriginal name for the animal. Soon less peaceful confrontations with Aborigines put an end to Cunningham's solitary rambles in the bush, and his collecting was much reduced by the time the *Mermaid* sailed from the Endeavour River on 11 July.

Before leaving the Endeavour River district, King made an inventory of his mineralogical observations; he found that the base geological formation was granite overlain by quartzite. Coal was detected near the river, a fact that King had difficulty in accounting for until, in reading a version of Cook's narrative, he noted that Cook had landed his stores of coal there while repairing his vessel. The mystery was explained.

Eleven weeks out of Port Jackson with the major portion of the voyage still ahead, the *Mermaid* rounded Cape York. King crossed the Gulf of Carpentaria and made for the western edge of Arnhem Land to begin the survey that had been left unfinished the previous year. Taking up the charting of the unexplored northern coast and still seeking the illusive river into the interior, King and a party penetrated a short distance up the Liverpool River. They detected a profusion of egrets, brolgas, and crocodiles, but unfortunately Cunningham was struck by illness on the excursion. While the *Mermaid* proceeded on past Port Essington then southward to Cambridge Gulf, Cunningham, still weak from his illness, had little opportunity for natural history, his only observations being on the numbers of medusae, (which Phillip Parker King opined might be the '*Medusa panopya*' of Péron), and the occasional turtle.

By the time that King initiated his survey of Cambridge Gulf, Cunningham had recovered sufficiently to again participate in excursions ashore, but now King found it difficult to complete his survey, weakhanded as the *Mermaid* was due to illness among the crew and the continual struggle to locate potable water. Prolonging his survey only a little while longer, King was forced to sail for Timor to seek the necessary fresh water and provisions. Arriving there in early November, King was told that the rival French exploratory corvette, *L'Uranie*, had anchored at Coepang the previous October before sailing into the Pacific. The *Mermaid* stayed only nine days in Timor before sailing for Port Jackson via Cape Leeuwin and Bass Strait, arriving on 12 January 1820. Although absent from that port for more than thirty-five weeks, much of the survey remained incomplete. Cunningham had had more success: his collection from the voyage included 400 specimens, 200 packets of seeds, and fifty-five bulbs.

While King's survey was taking place, Charles Fraser, Cunningham's erstwhile rival, was still active in Sydney. He opportuned Macquarie to procure a number of botanical texts for his edification, and Macquarie forwarded the request to Lord Bathurst, indicating his compliance. The books that Fraser desired were the Dutch botanist Christian Hendrick Persoon's *Synopsis*, Brown's *Prodromus Florae Novae Hollandiae* and Aiton's *Hortus Kewensis*, the volume that Cunningham had helped revise. In the request for the books, Fraser was styled as the acting colonial botanist, so by 1819 his position must have been official, at least from Macquarie's point of view.

In July of 1819 the *Edinburgh Review* printed a review of James O'Hara's *History of New South Wales* which had been published the previous year. The review passed into farce when describing the natural productions:

> Nature . . . seems determined to have a bit of play and to amuse herself as she pleases. Accordingly, she makes cherries with the stone on the outside; and a monstrous animal, as tall as a grenadier, with the head of a rabbit, a tail as big as a bedpost, hopping along at a rate of five hops to a mile, with three or four young kangaroos looking out of its false uterus to see what is passing. Then comes a quadruped as big as a large cat, with the eyes, colour and skin of a mole, and the bill and web-feet of a duck—puzzling Dr. Shaw, and rendering the latter half of his life miserable, from his utter inability to determine whether it was bird or beast.[1]

If George Shaw was to be lampooned, Joseph Banks was not ignored:

> . . . and a bird of such monstrous dimensions, that a side bone of it will dine three real carnivorous Englishmen;— together with the many other productions that agitate Sir Joseph, and fill him with mingled emotions of distress and delight.[2]

Amid the buffoonery, there was a statement that was to be prophetic of much of Australia's history:

> And great indeed must be the natural resources, and splendid the endowments of that land that has been able to survive the system of neglect and oppression experienced from the mother country, and the series of ignorant and absurd Governors that have been selected for the administration of its affairs.[3]

Late in 1819 yet another of the numerous French expeditions that sailed the Pacific during the late eighteenth and early nineteenth centuries called at Port Jackson. This was the corvette, *L'Uranie*, commanded by Louis de Freycinet, one of the officers on Baudin's expedition of 1800 and the author of the nationalistic narrative of that expedition. Bathurst had informed Governor Macquarie of the expedition's intent to put into Port Jackson and as the French and British were not engaged in their seemingly perennial warfare, Macquarie was instructed to give every assistance in the way of supplies and repairs to Freycinet. King, on his two expeditions to the north-west coast of Australia, had kept a wary eye open for the French vessel, anxious that the French not rob him of the honour of surveying portions of that coast. Cunningham noted in his journal on the first of King's expeditions that they had seen no evidence of the French presence but had left sufficient signs of their own passing that the French would know they had been forestalled in charting the region. Cunningham need not have worried as, unlike the Baudin expedition, the French had little intention of charting any of the Australian continent—the majority of their time was spent surveying Pacific islands.

The first of the expedition's two stop-overs in Australia occurred in September 1818 when *L'Uranie* spent two weeks at Shark Bay. Although the break was primarily to replenish their fresh water stocks and to gather geographical data, collections of natural history were also made. Unlike the major French expeditions of the past, Freycinet took no civilian scientists aboard *L'Uranie*; he relied solely on his officers for completion of the scientific studies undertaken. Having sailed on Baudin's expedition and seen the strife caused by the conflicting interests of the scientific and naval parties, Freycinet sought to alleviate the problem by dispensing with the scientific party. Much of the work of the expedition was indeed of the type that could be done equally well by trained naval officers; it included the investigation and collection of meteorological, magnetic, and hydrographic data. Collections and descriptions of natural history were undertaken principally by the two naval surgeons and the pharmacist aboard *L'Uranie*.

Jean René Constant Quoy and Joseph Paul Gaimard, the surgeons, collected and named many of the organisms found on the coastal fringe of Australia, and it is commonplace in studying the fauna of Australia to find their names linked as the progenitors of the original description. The pharmacist of the expedition, Charles Gaudichaud, took on the additional duty of botanist, while the appointed draughtsman, Jacques Arago, was helped by a midshipman, J. Alphonse Pellion in depicting zoological and botanical specimens. Although these individuals fulfilled their duties as naturalists extremely competently, Nicholas Vigors, when reviewing the zoological results of the voyage in 1828, castigated the French government and Freycinet for the exclusion of a professional scientific party on such an important expedition.

Despite Shark Bay having been scoured by a number of previous expeditions, including that of Baudin, the two surgeons were able to claim the discovery of several undescribed species of animals. On Dirk Hartog Island, they detected a large species of the bandicoot *Perameles* which had not been recognised before due to its propensity to disappear at the slightest commotion, in addition to the banded hare-wallaby *Lagostrophus fasciatus* previously described by Péron and Lesueur. Another of the islands in Shark Bay revealed a second small species of *Perameles* that was as yet undescribed, and they later illustrated and described it in the *Zoological Atlas* of the expeditions as *Perameles bougainville*.

Two species of birds were seen for the first time, the white-winged fairy-wren, *Malurus leucopterus* of which they discovered the rarer black-and-white form rather than the common blue-and-white form, and the thick-billed grasswren, *Amytornis textilis*, but many other birds were seen or collected, including sea eagles, honeyeaters, and bronze-wing pigeons. The type specimens of these two new species of birds were lost in the later shipwreck of *L'Uranie* in the Falkland Islands; the plates by the artist, Arago, now form the first record of the species.

Just as Baudin had been plagued by his naturalists becoming lost on their short excursions ashore, Freycinet suffered the same behaviour from his surgeon-naturalists. With more effective command over them, however, he was able to limit their adventuring to reasonable distances, thus reducing the possibility of them becoming lost.

The expedition left Shark Bay on 26 September but not before grounding briefly on a sandbank, presaging *L'Uranie*'s eventual loss. From this brief stop in Australia, Freycinet sailed for Timor and on into the Pacific. More than a year later, on 13 November 1819, *L'Uranie* sighted the coast of New South Wales and put into Port Jackson for two months for rest and replenishment. The artist, Arago, perhaps affected by the two years of shipboard life, or succumbing to poetic licence, described Sydney in euphoric terms:

> Magnificent hotels, majestic mansions, houses of extra-ordinary taste and elegance, fountains ornamented with sculptures worthy of the chisel of our best artists . . .[4]

This description would certainly have amazed many of the town's inhabitants. The French were made welcome, a house allocated for their astronomical observations, and supplies made available. The French were feted and enjoyed the hospitality of many residents of the colony including explorer-naturalists such as Oxley, who attended them and described his journeys into the interior.

Cunningham was still away on King's second voyage but the French naturalists interacted with Charles Fraser. In fact Fraser, described by Quoy as the botanist-director of the government garden, gave Quoy and Gaimard an undescribed species of kangaroo distinguished by a very large tail which he had obtained on Oxley's second expedition near Port Macquarie. Named and described in the zoological volume of the Freycinet voyage as '*Kangurus laniger*', it is now known as *Macropus rufus*, the red kangaroo. Before they left Port Jackson, the naturalists were given a specimen of an undescribed species of *Perameles* which they proposed to call '*Perameles lawson*' after the commandant of Bathurst, but they had the misfortune to lose the specimen in the wreck of *L'Uranie*.

It remains unrecorded whether the residents of New

MÉRION NATTÉ: *(MALURUS TEXTILIS . N .)*

MÉRION LEUCOPTÈRE: *(MALURUS LEUCOPTERUS . N .)*

TOP:
'Scinque jaune et noir'
Freycinet. *Voyage autour du monde*. Zoological Atlas. 1824.
Tiliqua nigrolutea

BOTTOM:
'Loriot Prince-régent'
Freycinet. *Voyage autour du monde*. Zoological Atlas. 1824.
Sericulus chrysocephalus

TOP:
'Péramèle bougainville'
Freycinet. *Voyage autour de monde*. Zoological Atlas. 1824.
Perameles bougainville

BOTTOM:
'Mérion natté, Mérion leucoptère'
Freycinet. *Voyage autour du monde*. Zoological Atlas. 1824.
Amytornis textilis, Malurus leucopterus

South Wales were shocked by the presence of Freycinet's wife on board *L'Uranie*, but she was included in the hospitality offered the French. Rose de Freycinet had clandestinely boarded *L'Uranie* against all naval rules before the vessel left France, purportedly to nurse her husband's health. The French naval authorities turned a blind eye, but at some of the ports of call on the voyage the authorities were less forgiving and the presence of a woman on board a naval vessel away from France for years was bound to cause some dissension. French voyages acquired a history of such illegal passengers for women were to be found on both Bougainville's voyage of 1766, and d'Entrecasteaux's voyage of 1791. The English were not immune from such behaviour, and, before Joseph Banks chose not to

156

'Potoroo white'
Freycinet. *Voyage autour du monde*. Zoological Atlas. 1824.
Aepyprymnus rufescens

'*Dasyure maugé*'
Freycinet. *Voyage autour du monde*. Zoological Atlas. 1824.
Dasyurus viverrinus

BOTTOM:
'*Perruche érythroptère*'
Freycinet. *Voyage autour du monde*. Zoological Atlas. 1824.
Aprosmictus erythropterus

participate, it was rumoured that he intended to arrange for a female 'valet' to be smuggled aboard the second of Cook's voyages.

Despite the lavish entertainment accorded the French, there was still a little time left for the naturalists to do some useful work. Gaimard collected at Botany Bay while Quoy, Pellion, and Gaudichaud travelled by Coxs Road as far as Bathurst to increase their collections. They left Sydney on 27 November 1819, on horseback, laden with collecting gear and paper for pressing plants. Barely two hours out of Parramatta, Pellion dismounted to shoot birds, only to have his horse shy at the noise of the gun and bolt. The horse disappeared taking much of their equipment. On this trip they were accompanied by the explorer and pastoralist William Lawson, who shot many bird specimens for them along the road as well as helping them collect plant specimens. The group stayed a night at Sir John Jamison's home and for his kindness named one of the birds they encountered for him, a pigeon which unfortunately for Jamison had previously been described as *Columba melanoleuca* by John Latham in 1801 and has since been renamed the Wonga pigeon, *Leucosarcia melanoleuca*. They saw numerous other birds such as bellbirds, cockatoos, parrots, honey-eaters, and the kookaburra on the trip, but the one that impressed them as most singular was the lyrebird. Quoy was hard-pressed during the journey to preserve all the specimens that they collected. Unfortunately most of them were to be lost in the subsequent wreck of *L'Uranie*. The vertebrates they saw comprised the rufous rat kangaroo, *Aepyprymnus rufescens*, native cats, and squirrel-gliders, as well as kangaroos.

As they travelled towards Bathurst, it struck the French naturalists, just as in previous years it had astonished Allan Cunningham, that in comparison to the noisy populated forests of South America the woods of Australia were strangely silent, the only noise that of their horses' hooves. This concept of silent desolation

was to occur often in accounts of the Australian bush. By 3 December, the party reached Bathurst and left to return to Sydney two days later. Throughout the trip, Quoy noticed that certain of the Australian birds, parrots and cockatoos in particular, now seemed to frequent the farms in the area, probably as they found the grain planted on the farms an ideal source of food, much to the disgruntlement of the farmers.

When *L'Uranie* pulled her anchors free of the harbour and sailed out of the heads on 25 December 1819, she took with her live specimens of many of Australia's natural curiosities—kangaroos, black swans, parrots, emus and possums, but these gradually sickened and died as they sailed southward into the Antarctic weather off Cape Horn. Those surviving the rigours of the voyage would have died at the Falkland Islands when *L'Uranie* struck a rock and although beached in time, was damaged beyond repair. In the wreck, eighteen cases of natural history specimens were lost, many of them obtained at Shark Bay or near Port Jackson.

Not all was lost, for the report made to the Academy of Sciences in Paris on Freycinet's voyage by such well-known scientists as Humboldt, Cuvier, and the French chemist Joseph-Louis Guy-Lussac praised the efforts of the surgeon-naturalists and Gaudichaud, listing twenty-five species of mammals, 313 species of birds, forty-five of reptiles, 164 of fish and numerous invertebrates received in France beyond what was lost in the wreck. Of these four mammals, forty-five birds, thirty reptiles, and 120 species of fish were new to science. Among them were numbered many Australian species. Three thousand plant species were brought back, of which some 1,200 were undescribed; again, many originated from Shark Bay and New South Wales. Quoy and Gaimard published their observations both in the zoological volume of the narrative of the voyage and in smaller papers delivered over a number of years.

Years later, when he was writing the narrative of the voyage, Freycinet was to correspond with Governor Macquarie's wife requesting answers to some questions about New South Wales. He advised her that among the thirteen drawings given him in the colony was one of a dove unknown to naturalists. He had an illustration produced of the dove for the *Zoological Atlas* of the voyage and named it the 'Macquarie dove', '*Columba macquarie*' (diamond dove, *Geopelia cuneata*).

In 1819, Judge Barron Field published a slim volume of poetry, *First Fruits of Australian Poetry*, so slim that it contained only two poems. The first poem 'Botany Bay Flowers', a eulogy to the Australian flora, especially *Eparis grandifolia*, contained Field's opinion of the new scientific spirit that was invading natural history:

> Tho' thousands of thy vegetable works
> Have, by the hand of Science (as 'tis call'd)
> Been gather'd and dissected, press'd and dried,
> Till all their blood and beauty are extinct;
> And nam'd in barb'rous Latin, men's surnames,
> With terminations of the Roman tongue.[5]

The second poem 'The Kangaroo' echoes the then current idea that the Australian continent was geologically younger than other continents:

> Kangaroo, Kangaroo!
> Thou Spirit of Australia,
> That redeems from utter failure,
> From perfect desolation,
> And warrants the creation
> Of this fifth part of the Earth

> Which would seem an after-birth,
> Not conceiv'd in the Beginning.[6]

In England, William Elford Leach published *The Zoological Miscellany* a compendium of curiosities of natural history with illustrations drawn by Frederick Nodder. The animals from Australia were numerous, ranging from molluscs to echidnas, but predominantly involved insects from Alexander Macleay's collection, and birds.

Of interest is the claim by Leach that there existed two species of platypus, '*Ornithorhynchus fuscus*' and '*O. rufus*'. '*O. rufus*' differed from '*O. fuscus*' in the colour and texture of the hair and in having a narrower beak with the nostrils set closer to the end. The source of this information was the report of the Baudin expedition which listed both species in the zoological illustrations of the voyage.

Although the origin of the Botanic Gardens in Sydney is commonly dated from 1816, it is obvious that the Botanic Gardens evolved gradually, rather than suddenly being created. The original vegetable garden to supply the first convicts and their warders also gradually took on the function of a temporary garden for plants that were either on their way to Europe or were brought from Europe for the colonies' benefit.

Charles Fraser, although referred to by Macquarie as the colonial botanist for some years in his dispatches to the Colonial Office, was finally appointed to that position on 1 January 1820. In a letter to the Colonial Secretary the following month, Fraser made it clear that he had already been responsible for the Botanic Gardens for some years, indicating that he had been placed in charge of the garden at the termination of Oxley's expeditions. During these expeditions, he had collected bulbs and seeds for the Gardens, so he had probably had some connection with it before the first expedition in 1817.

In June 1820 when Commissioner John Bigge was making his investigation into the colony, Allan Cunningham directed a communication entitled 'General hints on the formation of a Botanic Garden in New South Wales' to Bigge after pursuing the subject with him earlier in February. This communication would appear to be an effort to have the Home Office in England sanction the steps already taken toward forming a botanic garden, for it called for the cultivation of indigenous plants, establishment of communication with nurserymen in England, exchange of native Australian plants for European agricultural plants, the appointment of an experienced practical director of the garden, and the comparison of imported grasses with native grasses to determine that most suitable for grazing. Many of these steps had already been undertaken under the guidance of Charles Fraser. Cunningham also suggested that the Botanic Gardens reduce its demands for colonial revenue by selling surplus seeds and trees to colonists.

Of the natural history works produced in 1820, the most outstanding was a set of botanical studies done by Joseph Lycett, possibly for Governor Macquarie. Lycett had arrived in the colony in 1814 and was another in the series of convicts who had been transported to New South Wales convicted of forgery. Almost all these men had been trained as artists in England and subsequently thought to turn their hand to a more profitable venture than art by forging notes. These individuals supplied the colony with considerable artistic talent, and Joseph Lycett was no exception. In New South Wales Lycett soon saw the chance to again ply his adopted trade— forgery—but again was caught and convicted, this time sentenced to the harsh life in Newcastle. Here he refrained from illegal activities, probably more from lack of opportunity than from inclination and on the commandant's recommendation received a conditional pardon and began to apply his artistic skills in earnest.

When Lycett eventually was granted a full pardon and returned to England, he produced a portfolio, *View of Australia* published in England in 1824. In the preface to the work Lycett described himself as employed by the governor as an artist, refraining from mentioning the circumstances behind this somewhat enforced servitude. In the same preface, Lycett indicated that he planned to publish a subsequent work on the natural history of Australia, but for unknown reasons this follow-up folio never appeared.

Next in the continuing series of European scientific expeditions that reached Australia's shores during the early nineteenth century was a Russian expedition. Since the close of the eighteenth century Russia had rapidly expanded both its naval capabilities and its interest in its eastern frontier. Many Russian vessels were to stop at Port Jackson during the 1820s as it formed a convenient break in the journey to the east, but only one of the expeditions pursued much natural history during their time on the Australian coast.

A fleet of four Russian vessels left Kronstadt in July 1819, two of the vessels, the *Blagonamerenny*, and the *Otkrytie* to search for the fabled North West Passage, while the *Vostok* and the *Mirnyi* were commissioned to explore the Antarctic regions. As the latter expedition was intended to increase the existing body of information on natural history, two German scientists, Mertens and Kuntze, were appointed to the expedition—both were to join the vessels at Copenhagen. Neither of the Germans made the rendezvous, declining on the grounds of insufficient time to prepare for the voyage, so it was left to the officers of the vessels to make what observations they could. Thaddeus von Bellingshausen, the commander of the expedition and captain of the *Vostok*, was particularly annoyed at this development, as two Russian students of natural history had desired

to participate in the voyage but had been passed over in favour of the Germans. While obtaining navigational instruments in London on the outward leg of the voyage, Bellingshausen sought to obtain replacements for the naturalists with the help of the aging Joseph Banks but was unsuccessful in the short time of their stay in England. The official instructions for the expeditions included directives to procure zoological, botanical, and mineralogical specimens.

The four vessels set out from European Russia simultaneously, but the northern expedition of the *Blagonamerenny* and the *Otkrytie* preceded the other two vessels to Port Jackson arriving on 28 February 1820. Friedrich Stein, one of the expedition's surgeons, and the artist, Karneev, obtained permission to cross the Blue Mountains as far as Bathurst with William Lawson to guide them as he had previously escorted Quoy and Gaimard from the *L'Uranie* expedition in 1819. Allan Cunningham, who had been generously treated by the Russian consul in Brazil, was anxious to return the favour and successfully sought Macquarie's permission to accompany the party. Foul weather cut short the excursion before the party reached the mountains but did not prevent the surgeon-naturalist, Stein, from pursuing geological studies. Although Stein was not enabled to visit much of the environs of Port Jackson, by the judicious use of the formations he did observe and the conversations he undoubtedly engaged in with Lawson and Cunningham, he wrote a report on the geology of the area. Stein was considered by Cunningham to be a disciple of Werner and viewed the geological structures in the district through the Neptunian mist. He was reported to have detected gold in the Sydney area, but there seems to be no basis for this rumour. On 1 April the two vessels sailed out of Port Jackson for the Arctic.

Less than two weeks after their departure, one of the vessels of the second expedition, the *Vostok* under Bellingshausen, sailed into Port Jackson. Eight days later, on 19 April, the second Russian vessel, the *Mirnyi*, came to anchor in Port Jackson, having separated from the *Vostok* to look for a reported island that they concluded did not exist. Governor Macquarie gave the expedition every facility just as he had obliged their compatriots weeks before. An area was set aside for an astronomical observatory for calibrating the ship's chronometers, and Lieutenant Phillip Parker King presented the expedition's officers with maps of the Australian coast. The Russian's natural history endeavours on this call were severely limited; they seemed to consist of a collection of the local fauna obtained by Lieutenant Alexei Lazarev. On 19 May, five weeks after the *Vostok* had arrived, she sailed in company with the *Mirnyi* for the Antarctic.

Although much of the original European interest in the Australian flora and fauna had diminished with its

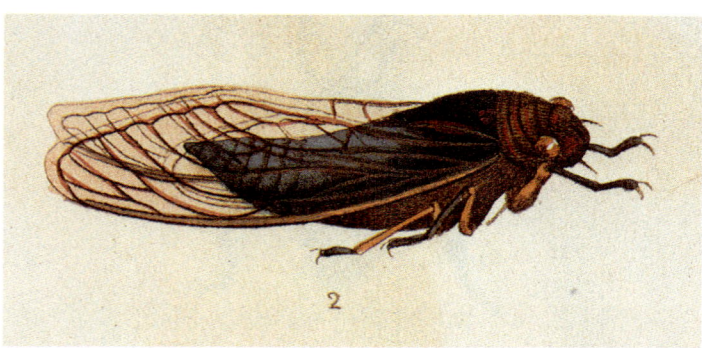

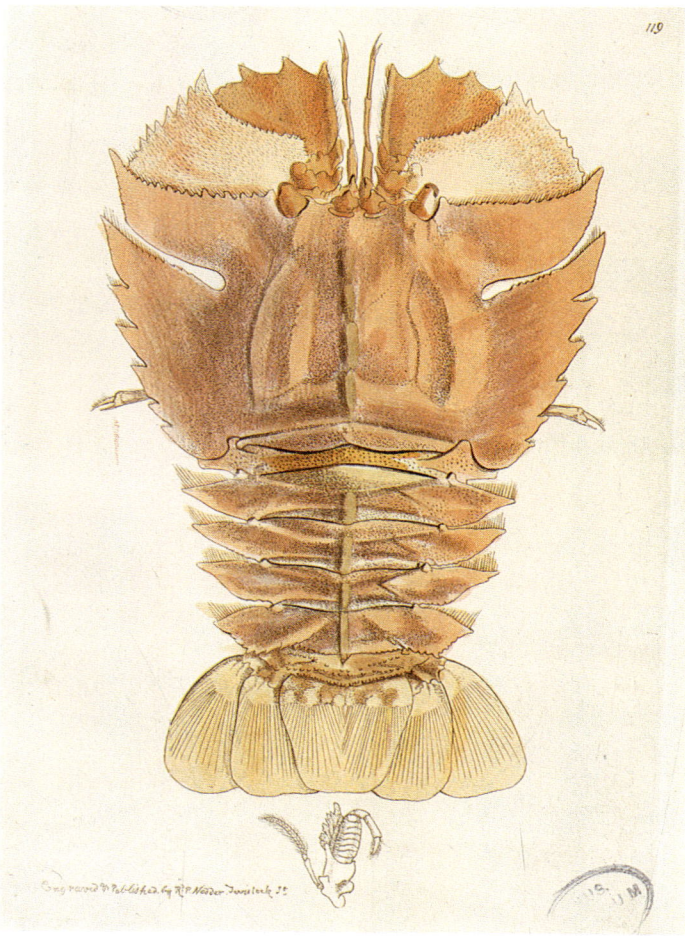

increasing familiarity, vessels proceeding from the colony to Europe still carried extensive shipments of live animals. As the flamboyant convict James Hardy Vaux recalled in his memoirs on returning home in 1819, his ship transported:

> . . . almost every natural production of New South Wales, with some very fine specimens, of which our ship was at first literally crowded, so as to resemble Noah's Ark. There were kangaroos, black swans, a noble emu, and cockatoos, parrots, and smaller birds without number . . .[7]

Unfortunately most of these animals did not survive the voyage, for with the exception of one cockatoo that was carefully watched over by its mistress and half a dozen black swans from Van Diemens Land that were carefully nurtured, the other animals succumbed to the severity of the storms encountered rounding Cape Horn. On arrival in England, the surviving black swans were presented to the Royal Menagerie in Kew Gardens, and Vaux observed that the English commoner had more interest in these natural curiosities than in the state of the colony of New South Wales which was thought of only as a place to be avoided.

In June of 1820 there occurred an event that was to mark the end of an era for natural history in Australia: on 19 June Joseph Banks died. Although his active interest in the natural history of New South Wales had been waning for years as his health declined, the collectors now in the colony being employees of Kew Gardens rather than his personal employees, Banks' continued concern about the colony had done much to forward its advancement. Banks' reputation as a scientist has undergone extreme fluctuation. At times he has been regarded as one of the eminent scientists of the age, while at others he has been labelled as a mere dilettante. The truth lies somewhere in the middle of the spectrum. Banks can hardly be considered as one of the foremost scientists of his era, for he indulged in little science himself although for much of his life he surrounded himself with some of the best scientific minds in England. The one time that he prosecuted natural history alone was on an expedition undertaken

Top:
'Colombe macquarie'
Freycinet. *Voyage autour du monde*. Zoological Atlas. 1824.
Geopelia humeralis

Centre:
'Gryllus australasiae'
Leach. *Zoological Miscellany*. 1814.

Bottom:
'Ibacus peronii'
Leach. *Zoological Miscellany*. 1815.
Ibacus peronii

to Newfoundland when quite young, and here his work consisted only of collecting specimens and writing rudimentary descriptions. He was enthusiastic in his collecting but never rose beyond that. Subsequent to this voyage to Newfoundland, Banks associated with names such as Carl Solander and Robert Brown, men who, while in his employ, far surpassed him in scientific acumen. Banks was a collector, and it must be remembered that by far the majority of the scientists then extant were no more than collectors and describers; few were of the calibre of Solander and Brown, attempting to impose order on the collections in a systematic way. Perhaps the best comparison with Banks is James Edward Smith, often described as Banks' protégé. Blessed with much the same financial and societal position as Banks, Smith pursued a more scientific career. Joseph Banks' position as president of the Royal Society is reminiscent of Smith's similar position in the Linnean Society. Smith, however, regularly published scientific papers describing new specimens or attempting to redefine genera. Possibly Banks' contribution to natural history should be seen more in light of the example he set for encouraging the inclusion of natural history in the itinerary of exploratory expeditions and in his encouragement and patronage of naturalists everywhere. Despite his lack of active participation in natural history, it cannot be doubted that Banks possessed a sound grasp of the science of the day; his letters to scientists range over a wide array of subjects.

After the death of Banks but before it could possibly be known in the colony, Phillip Parker King and Allan Cunningham set out on their third voyage to the north-west coast of Australia. Also on board this voyage was a surgeon, James Hunter, who volunteered to join the expedition. Hunter collected many insects on the expedition which found their way into various private English collections such as those of the Reverend Frederick William Hope as well as the British Museum. A number of the specimens were later figured and described by the zoologist George Robert Gray in his *The Entomology of Australia* published in 1833.

Before sailing, King tried to rid the *Mermaid* of the ever present rats and cockroaches by temporarily sinking the vessel in Port Jackson, this extreme measure proved ineffective as both rats and cockroaches soon returned to torment the crew, albeit in considerably reduced numbers. Departing from Port Jackson on

'*Diura titan*'
Gray. *The Entomology of Australia*. 1833.
Acrophylla titan

'*Extatosoma tiaratum*'
Gray. *The Entomology of Australia*. 1833.
Extatosoma tiaratum

13 July, King was inclined to proceed as quickly as possible to the north-west coast to once again resume his unfinished survey, but on 20 July as they entered Port Bowen on the voyage along the Barrier Reef the *Mermaid* took the ground on a sandbank. After being warped off into deeper water she was found to have sustained some damage, but how much was not to become evident until much later in the voyage. The next day, Cunningham was able to venture ashore and begin his collection of plants for this circumnavigation of Australia. The *Mermaid* carried on to the north and by 27 July was anchored at Endeavour River where Cunningham gathered more seeds and bulbs including the readily obtainable and popular *Crinum angusti-folium*, cabbage palms and a species of yam labelled by Cunningham '*Caladium macrorrhizium*', which were used as vegetables. Hunter, the surgeon, shot a number of birds including the Blue Mountain parrot, '*Psittacus haematodus*' (rainbow lorikeet); a crane-like bird similar to '*Ardea antigone*', probably the white-faced heron *Ardea novaehollandiae*, was seen but not caught. Pushing on, King took the *Mermaid* to Lizard Island and then on to Cape York which they doubled on 15 August.

Off the entrance of Van Diemens Gulf they sailed through 'sea saw-dust' which, when gathered by

Drawn by H. C. Field, Fel. Coll. Surg.

Published by John Murray Albemarle Street. March

Cunningham and put in a bottle, soon putrified and tinged the water crimson. By 3 September the *Mermaid* had arrived at the spot where the previous year King had left off his survey; however, the *Mermaid* was already showing the effects of her encounter with the sandbank—a noticeable increase in water seepage through the hull. The water leaking into the *Mermaid* had reached such proportions that King had no choice but to careen her to try to effect repairs, enabling Cunningham to spend three weeks in the region of Prince Frederick Sound. Here Cunningham discovered an enormous species of *Capparis* whose soft trunk reached almost 10 metres in circumference despite its

height of less than 8 metres. Cunningham had seen such trees before in Cambridge Gulf but never of the same proportions. The fauna sighted at the careening site was limited to a native cat similar to those of Port Jackson, a few pigeons, and a curious lizard with a thin membrane extending from the head to the front legs. Cunningham later sent home a specimen of the lizard to the Royal College of Surgeons of England where it was described and named *Chlamydosaurus kingii*.

Repairs to the *Mermaid* were not effective so King decided to abandon the survey yet again and sail for Port Jackson which he did via Cape Leeuwin and Bass Strait. The *Mermaid* arrived and dropped anchor in Port Jackson on 6 December, though not without a moment of apprehension when the vessel struck a rock off the southern head of Botany Bay. Cunningham had been back for less than two weeks before he was writing to Governor Macquarie requesting a horse that he could retain for as long as he continued in the colony. Obviously in receipt of information from Banks, Cunningham obliquely referred to recent instructions that Macquarie may have received from the Colonial Office to that effect. Macquarie was nothing if not consistent and the request was refused. In addition to receiving a report of Banks' death some six months after the event, Cunningham also obtained the final letter Banks had written him, a letter in which Banks repeated his satisfaction in Cunningham's work and the diligence with which he was pursuing it. Banks went on to suggest that rather than continue on the series of circumnavigations of Australia with King that Cunningham should perhaps turn his attention to exploration inland. Cunningham was to follow this advice, but not before one last voyage with King during the coming year. As Cunningham was later to point out to William Aiton, he was reluctant to miss out on a chance to visit an area that perhaps might not see another expedition for many years.

While Cunningham was away on King's third voyage, his colleague, Charles Fraser, continued his work as the colonial botanist. In March Fraser visited Van Diemens Land to collect specimens, later in October Fraser accompanied John Bigge on a trip to Bathurst. Appointed by the British Government as commissioner to enquire into the state of the Colony of New South Wales, with the added responsibility of investigating the conduct of officials of the colony, Bigge was to be instrumental in the replacement of Cunningham's adversary, Governor Macquarie, by Thomas Brisbane. It must be noted, however, that Macquarie had submitted a request to be allowed to resign long before Bigge arrived in the colony.

'*Chlamydosaurus kingii*'
King. *Narrative of a survey of the intertropical and western coasts of Australia*. 1826.
Chlamydosaurus kingii

'*Jasia australis*'
Swainson. *Zoological Illustrations*. 1820–33.
Polyura pyrrhus sempronius

'*Heleona fenestrata*
Swainson. *Zoological Illustrations*. 1820–1833.

Late in the year of 1820, the Russian vessels, the *Vostok* and the *Mirnyi*, returned to Port Jackson, having spent several months cruising the Pacific. On 9 September Bellingshausen dropped anchor in the spot he had occupied during his previous visit. In his published journal of the voyage, Bellingshausen included a short section entitled 'Short Notes on the Colonies of New South Wales' which recorded among the myriad other details of the colony some natural history notes. Bellingshausen enumerated the principal timbers of the colony, fifty-nine flowers and trees from Port Jackson's shores, and another eighteen from the governor's garden. Bellingshausen himself collected specimens of the flora around Port Jackson, and the specimens were examined by the naturalists Eichenwald and Fischer on his return to Russia. Bellingshausen also made a collection of birds, including both live specimens obtained from the Aborigines in exchange for alcohol and on which he later made observations on moulting, and dead specimens obtained from the guns of his officers.

The officers of the vessels visited the Botanic Gardens, synonymous with the governor's garden, and Bellingshausen sent ashore live specimens of plants that

he had obtained in Tahiti. Among the minerals in the colony of New South Wales, Bellingshausen noted that there appeared to be an abundance of iron ore, that gold and copper had recently been found, although this record of the discovery of gold is questionable, and that there was sure to be an abundance of metals and precious stones to be found in the interior. He thought that Australian topaz was much finer than the American variety and rivalled diamond in its beauty. The animals that Bellingshausen listed included possums, kangaroos, kangaroo rats, dingoes, wombats, great numbers of birds, and the platypus, which, when a specimen was dissected, was found to have eggs. The eggs combined with its bird-like bill caused Bellingshausen to ally it with the birds.

When the two Russian vessels left Port Jackson on 31 October, they took with them a menagerie of birds and a tame kangaroo that had the run of the deck and played with the sailors. Among the eighty-four live birds on board were cockatoos, lories, Blue Mountain and 'royal' parrots, and doves, all of which were brought on deck during fine weather. Bellingshausen later related how a black cockatoo, one of their prized possessions, died when it tried to eat a stuffed specimen

'*Scaphella maculata*'
Swainson. *Exotic Conchology*. 1834–35.
Amoria maculata

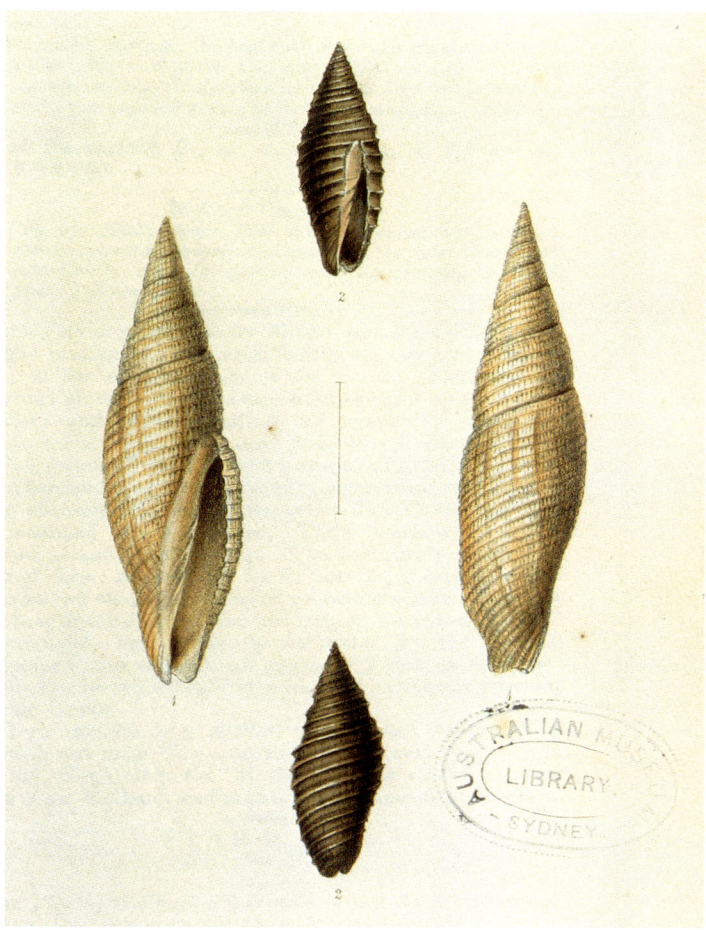

'Mitrana'
Swainson. *Exotic Conchology*.

of a kookaburra. In light of the distance that Bellings-hausen penetrated into Antarctic waters and the severe cold experienced by the vessels, it is remarkable that any of the birds reached Russia alive.

That year the under-secretary of the Colonial Office approved Governor Macquarie's request for the botanical books desired by Charles Fraser. In his letter of approval for the purchase of the books, Goulburn acknowledged Fraser as the acting colonial botanist. Whether the Colonial Office had any real need to concern itself with Fraser's appointment is question-able; he was paid out of the Police Fund whose money was obtained from customs' fees and other taxes paid in the colony.

In the previous decade, George Shaw had dominated the production of lavishly illustrated natural history publications in England, publishing *The Naturalist's Miscellany* and *Museum Leverianum* among others. Shaw died in 1813, so in the 1820s William Swainson adopted Shaw's mantle with *Zoological Illustrations* and *Exotic Conchology*; both publications contained figures of Australian animals.

On 1 January 1821 Charles Fraser, who had long laboured in the interest of botanical science in the

colony and who had occupied the position of colonial botanist since the first of Oxley's inland expeditions in 1817, was finally officially listed as such in the Returns of the Colony by the colonial secretary and at the same time appointed as the superintendent of the Botanic Gardens. His annual salary of £200 was paid out of the Police Fund.

Macquarie was still sending plant specimens to England: further sets of plants for the emperor of Austria and Prince Leopold as replacements for those sent previously but lost in the wreck of the *Lady Castle-reagh*. The plants were under the charge of John Richardson, a gardener. A set of geological samples was to accompany the plants, presumably duplicates of those also lost on the ill-fated *Lady Castlereagh*. Both plants and minerals had been collected by Charles Fraser on Oxley's second expedition inland.

Earlier samples returned from this same expedition had been the subject of a paper written by the Reverend William Buckland and published in the *Transactions of the Geological Society of London* in 1821. Buckland determined that the samples could be separated into two types: primitive rocks, which included granite, mica-slate, clay-slate, and serpentine; and trap rocks, which were represented by jaspers, limestone, quartzose, and sandstone. The samples were all from west of the Blue Mountains, but there was no indication of the specific collection localities or of any fossils, both inadequacies which Buckland lamented. The samples also gave no indication of valuable metal ores or precious stones. Buckland had access to the geological specimens collected by Robert Brown during his time in Australia twenty years earlier and, on the basis of these two fairly localised collections, Oxley's and Brown's, Buckland speculated on the similarities between the coal formations and the marine fossils found in the limestone of Van Diemens Land and those occurring in England. He concluded that geological formations in the southern hemisphere were basically the same as those in its northern counterpart, both in the primary rock formations as well as the secondary sedimentary strata.

Phillip Parker King, after his last unsuccessful trip in the *Mermaid*, was still anxious to finish his charting of the north-west coast of Australia. The *Mermaid* had been surveyed on her return and declared as unseaworthy—therefore a 170-ton brig was purchased and renamed the *Bathurst*. The vessel was more than twice the tonnage of the *Mermaid* and so would offer a greater degree of comfort. Allan Cunningham was again to join the expedition to complete the botanical characterisation of the northern flora. The *Bathurst* sailed from Port Jackson on 26 May and headed north for Torres Strait. Stopping to take on water and wood at some of the islands along the coast, flights of cockatoos and parrots were seen, and a few shells were collected, but Cunningham had limited opportunities for botanising. Cape York was rounded and by the middle of July the *Bathurst* was involved in surveying the north-west coast. The long periods at sea were often broken by towing a net, employed to collect samples of pelagic crustaceans and cnidarians. Specimens of sea snakes were obtained as well as the occasional shark. As on the previous trip, much of the time Cunningham was sick, remaining on board the *Bathurst* while King and his officers sought specimens for him on their trips ashore. The banks of the rivers that were surveyed were covered with *Pandanus* and the prolific *Hibiscus*, but otherwise the land was sterile and arid. Cunningham wrote in his journal: 'This miserable line of coast . . . assumes all the extremes of sterility so obvious during our former stay'[8]. In the rivers, crocodiles were in evidence, while '*Chironectes*', the amphibious fish seen by King 'sporting about' on the mudbanks using its strong pectoral fins to propel itself over the mud, was abundant on the estuarine shores. It was probably one of the mudskippers now classified in the genus *Periophthalmus*. After several months of surveying during which Cunningham was content to obtain a limited number of plant species, King took the *Bathurst* to Mauritius arriving on 26 September for replenishment of supplies.

For almost six weeks the *Bathurst* lay in Mauritius, time which Cunningham used to good effect in collecting plants from that island as well as obtaining specimens from the Botanic Garden. King sailed for the Australian coast on 15 November, and by 23 December the *Bathurst* was anchored in King George Sound. Cunningham was again onshore collecting plants, gathering *Banksia grandis*, *B. coccinea*, and *B. attenuata* as well as a *Pimelea* species which he rejoiced upon as the most beautiful of the wildflowers in the district. As before he made a point of locating pitcher plants and this time was rewarded with specimens of *Cephalotus follicularis*, but all were in poor shape and he could find none in flower. Cunningham was unable to decide if the fluid in the pitcher plant was a secretion of the plant as Robert Brown believed or just trapped rain water, but he inclined to think that it was a secretion similar to that of the pitcher plant of India. King on the other hand concluded that the dead insects in the pitcher were deposited inside by a carnivorous insect which used the pitcher as a storage site, while the fluid served as a water supply for the plant. It is now known that the fluid is indeed a secretion. Other plants collected included the wild parsley, *Apium prostratum*, and the orache, *Atriplex*, both edible and used by the crew as vegetables, as well as plants which were later to form the specimens from which Robert Brown described the new genus *Kingia*, named in honour of Captain Phillip Parker King. King George Sound was then probably one of the botanically best known sites in Australia, for since its original discovery by Vancouver with the botanist Menzies on board, it had been visited by a succession of botanists all of whom collected assiduously. Yet in 1821 the area still had no permanent settlement, although within five years that lack was to be rectified.

After two weeks at the sound, the *Bathurst* sailed for Rottnest Island. The kangaroos which had been so evident to de Vlamingh were not to be seen here although their presence was obvious from dung, nor were Péron's kangaroo rats seen. Cunningham was surprised that on an island so close to the coast of Australia there should be no representative of the Proteaceae or the Acaciae which were abundant almost everywhere on the Australian coastline. While the botanical takings were meagre on the island they were able to collect a wide variety of shells.

Sailing northward through the Abrolhos, the *Bathurst* anchored off Dirk Hartog Island on 20 January 1822. Here Cunningham continued his harvest of plants including species originally noticed by Dampier in 1699. Despite the historical ties of the island, Cunningham thought that no part of the coast that they had visited so far could exceed the barren appearance of Dirk Hartog Island. Sailing further northward, King continued his intermittent charting, occasioning

Cunningham infrequent chances for collecting. As well as the plants he obtained, members of the crew brought back various insects and shells, and on one occasion a flying fox. By the time that they had reached Cygnet Bay, the need for rest and replenishment determined King to return to Port Jackson. They arrived on 25 April having spent almost a year away.

Whatever the merits of the surveying work of the voyage, and although he spent four years and four voyages charting portions of the north-west coast, King failed in his primary objective—to either discover the hoped-for navigable river into the interior of the continent, or to conclusively disprove its existence. The voyages reaped considerable natural history knowledge, but that was secondary to the primary geographical purpose of the journeys. In 1827 when King published the edited journal of the voyages, *Narrative of A Survey of the intertropical and Western Coasts of Australia*, it contained two appendices, one a description of the flora and fauna collected, the other concerning the geology of the voyage. Of the larger animals, the identifications and descriptions of which were provided by J. E. Gray of the British Museum, only a few had been returned to England due to the very limited space aboard the *Mermaid* and the *Bathurst* and the lack of materials to preserve the specimens. Included were: the flying fox; dingo (of which a living specimen was brought back and given to Everard Home); seal, the '*Otaria cinerea*' of Péron and Lesueur obtained on the south-west coast of Australia (now *Neophoca cinerea*); sugar squirrel (or yellow-bellied glider); '*Petaurista sciurea*' (now *Petaurus australis*); pygmy opossum (or feather-tail glider), *Acrobates pygmaeus*; and the dolphin, '*Delphinorhynchus pernettenis*' (now *Delphinus delphis*). The reptiles, also described by Gray, included the new genus *Chlamydosaurus* (the specimen obtained by Cunningham was given the specific name *kingii*) as well as two other new genera.

Gray contributed descriptions of seven fish and 111 molluscs to the appendix. The limited collection of birds that resulted from the voyage were identified and described by Nicholas Vigors, and subsequently the collection was presented to the Linnean Society by King. Only two of the fourteen birds were considered by Vigors to be new species, '*Sterna pelecanoides*' and '*Larus georgii*'. The collection of insects was extensive, probably due to the presence of James Hunter, the surgeon-naturalist on the third of the voyages. When this collection was reviewed by William Sharp Macleay he described 188 insects, many of them new genera or new species. One of the new genera was *Carpophagus* of which a figure was included in King's *Narrative*. Other invertebrates received cursory mention.

Both Allan Cunningham and Robert Brown wrote segments for the flora section of the natural history appendix. Brown contributed a description of the

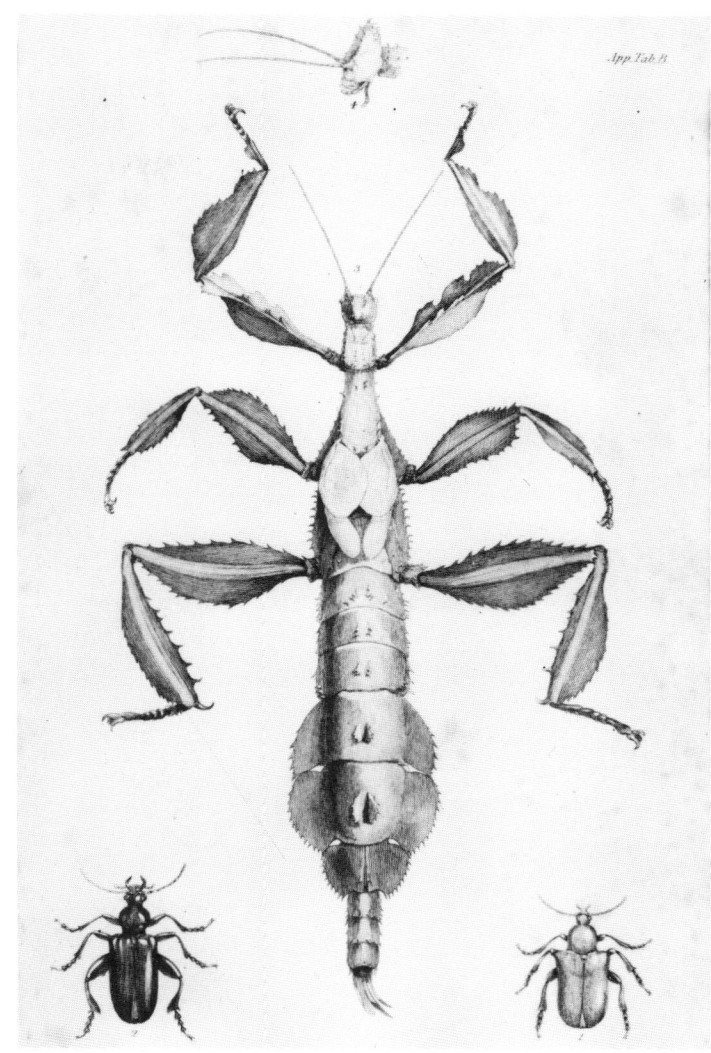

'*Carpophagus banksiae, Megamerus kingii, Extatosoma tiaratum*' King. *Narrative of a survey of the intertropical and western coasts of Australia.* 1826.
Carpophagus banksiae, Megamerus kingii, Extatosoma tiaratum

previously undescribed genus *Kingia* which Brown named after the father and son combination Philip Gidley King and Phillip Parker King, both of whom had been of service to botanists collecting in Australia.

Kingia was named for them at the request of Allan Cunningham. Cunningham himself wrote *A Few General Remarks on the Vegetation of Certain Coasts of Terra Australia, and more especially of its North-western shores*. While acknowledging that he followed in the footsteps of his mentor Robert Brown in many of the collecting sites and indeed the classification of the plants, Cunningham was still able to claim a collection of almost 1,300 species, less than one-half of which could be attributed to previously described species. The species were not described in detail, rather Cunningham made comments on the general nature and geographic distribution of the various groups of plants including the palms, pines, eucalypts, and banksia.

The final section of the appendix on the geology of

the expedition was written by the English geologist William Fitton from specimens that King gave to the Geological Society of London. Fitton also used geological specimens collected by Robert Brown when he was in the colony, in addition to some supplemental information from the French voyages, to complete his analysis of the geological features of the country. As Buckland had years earlier, Fitton thought that the correspondence between the sandstones of England and Australia, and between the calcareous breccia of Sicily and those of Australia was remarkable. Much of Fitton's paper is taken up with the possible origin of the calcareous breccia and its position often over 100 metres above sea level. The most likely explanation for the phenomenon, Fitton reasoned, was elevation of the sea floor by earthquake. Fitton concluded his exposition with a set of instructions for collecting geological specimens on the grounds that collectors are often unpractised in geology and have been given no instruction in how to do so. Like Buckland, Fitton thought that the discovery of fossils was of great importance and that particular attention should be paid to it.

With the termination of Phillip Parker King's fourth and final voyage, Cunningham was able to turn his attention to inland excursions, probably a welcome relief, for during much of the last two voyages he had been unable to work, debilitated by sickness. The next few years were to see Cunningham rejecting the role of an appendage to exploratory missions and assuming control of his own discoveries, both botanical and geographical.

Chapter Ten

THE INFRASTRUCTURE OF
NATURAL HISTORY: 1821–28

The years 1821–28 were to herald a singular change in the development of Australian natural history: an increasingly large role was played by colonial residents, not simply in the collection of specimens but in the extension of knowledge about the flora and fauna of the country. Many of these early attempts at the genesis of a local natural history structure were abortive, doomed to failure by the dearth of scientific personnel in the colony and the fractious political climate that tended to dominate all events in New South Wales, but they were to lay a foundation that could be built upon successfully at a later date.

Subsequent to the departure of the *Bathurst* on Phillip Parker King's fourth and final exploratory voyage of Australian waters, the first of the inchoate attempts to establish a scientific society in Australia, the Philosophical Society of Australasia, occurred. On 4 July 1821 Barron Field, John Oxley, the surgeon James Bowman, Frederick Goulburn, doctor of medicine Henry Douglass, Captain Francis Irvine, and the merchant Edward Wollstonecraft, the founding members of the society, held the initial meeting at which a stringent set of bylaws was adopted which included: a requirement that each member read a paper to the society, the subject matter to preclude religious dogma and political expositions, fines payable for non-attendance of meetings, and a subscription fee of £5 due on acceptance of membership in the society. To uphold the sobriety of the society's meetings a bylaw was enacted stating that no refreshments other than tea or coffee were to be allowed at meeting.

The Philosophical Society inaugurated its existence with such commendable intentions as the use of the subscription fees of the members to establish a museum and library in a room provided by the colonial secretary,

Frederick Goulburn, and undertaking correspondence with scientific societies abroad. However the society was soon to be bogged down in minutiae such as the exact wording of a plaque to be set up at the Botany Bay site of Cook's first landing to commemorate that event, or the format of a circular announcing the existence of the newly established society to other scientific institutions. The inability of the society to rise above such trivia was to plague its short existence, but initially such problems were ignored as other leaders of the community were invited to take membership in the society: the merchant Alexander Berry, surgeon Patrick Hill, Samuel Marsden, William Howe, and Lieutenant Phillip Parker King. When on 7 November 1821, Major-General Thomas Brisbane arrived in Sydney to relieve Lachlan Macquarie as governor of the colony, he was promptly requested to accept the presidency of the society, an invitation that Brisbane acceded to. These first few months of the society's existence were also devoted to obtaining specimens for its embryonic museum; members were asked to obtain specimens of the soil from districts in which they resided. Various collections of minerals that were thought to be available were sought, and colonial officers in other settlements were requested to forward specimens of different strata of coal, timber, or natural history to the museum, requests that carried considerable weight given the membership of both the governor and the colonial secretary in the society. Late in December Wollstonecraft informed the society of the reported existence of a 'manatee or hippopotamus' in Lake Bathurst and was authorised by the society to obtain a specimen of the said animal. The attempt was futile, no such animal existed, but the idea that hippopotamuses existed in Australia was to survive for some years to come.

As might be expected the requirement that each member of the society must deliver a paper before the society was gradually relaxed—members found more pressing duties. Nevertheless a number of papers were read, the first by Barron Field on the 'Aborigines of New Holland and Van Diemen's Land', later another by Alexander Berry on the 'Geology of the Coastline between Newcastle and Bateman's Bay'. Phillip Parker King produced a paper on the 'Maritime Geography of Australia', and Charles Rumker read a paper on astronomical observations in the southern hemisphere. Rumker, an astronomer and mathematician, arrived in the retinue of Thomas Brisbane to set up and run an astronomical observatory at Parramatta for Brisbane. Rumker, the magistrate Donald Macleod, and Robert Townson were all honoured with invitations to join the society.

Despite the founders' good intentions, the Philosophical Society of Australasia lasted only a year before succumbing to 'the baneful atmosphere of distracted politics', as Barron Field was to write of it several years later. Antagonism between the principals over events in the colony soon had a debilitating effect on the society, but scientific disagreements were also to result in declining membership. Friction between Thomas Brisbane and Charles Rumker over work at the astronomical observatory resulted in Rumker leaving Brisbane's employment, and in his non-attendance at meetings of the society.

Perhaps the most curious characteristic of the Philosophical Society was that despite its stated intentions of 'collecting information with respect to the Natural State, capabilities, productions and resources in Australasia', with the exception of Charles Rumker, there were no active scientists included among its membership. Possibly the most worthwhile candidate for membership would have been Allan Cunningham, but he was never mentioned in the minutes of the society's meetings nor issued an invitation to join. Although Cunningham was often away from Sydney on collecting expeditions, he was away no more than Phillip Parker King who was elected a member. The answer to Cunningham's exclusion may lie in the background of the individuals who made up the Philosophical Society: its members were chosen from the surgeons, judges, colonial administrators, and military officers of the colony, the only exception being Charles Rumker who was probably elected on the recommendation of Thomas Brisbane while the two were still on congenial terms. It was hardly surprising that these individuals would ignore the merits of Cunningham who was, after all, only the paid employee of Kew. Likewise, Charles Fraser, who was even then styled the colonial botanist, was not seen as a candidate for membership. The irony remains that Allan Cunningham was to establish a reputation in Australian science to which none of the members of the Philosophical Society could ever aspire. Although the Philosophical Society passed out of existence in 1822, in 1825 Barron Field published a number of the papers presented before the society under the title *Geographical Memoirs on New South Wales*.

The year 1822 was a year of consolidation of previous work in natural history rather than the launching of new activity, a pause between explorations. Allan Cunningham returned from Phillip Parker King's fourth voyage at the end of April, and it was another five months before he again ventured on another round of exploration and plant collecting. During these months, as he curated his collection of dried plants and prepared both living and dried specimens for shipment to Kew, Cunningham planned for the future. He envisioned his position as king's botanist in New South Wales as lasting only until 1826, so he was anxious to maximise the territory he could cover in that time. He anticipated spending most of his time on expeditions crossing the Blue Mountains but wished to include trips further afield to Van Diemens Land and New Zealand before he finally returned to England. With his proposed inland excursions in mind, Cunningham wrote to Colonial Secretary Frederick Goulburn indicating that an integral part of his duties as transmitted from William Aiton was the collection of living plants for conveyance to Kew. In order to fulfil this task he would need the use of a horse and cart, which he respectfully requested be supplied to him. Cunningham obviously thought to renew his attempts to secure a horse and cart now that Macquarie had been replaced by Thomas Brisbane as governor. Brisbane, as might be expected from an occasional scientist, was more forthcoming than the administrator Macquarie, and Cunningham soon had his horse and cart.

Although the Philosophical Society of Australasia was in the process of disintegration in the middle of 1822, another, wider based society came into existence, although it was less concerned with scientific questions. The Agricultural Society of New South Wales held its first meeting on 5 July 1822; the society was to last fourteen years. Concerned only with agriculture, it was able to attract many more members than the select group who had formed the Philosophical Society and was less liable to the factionalism that had led to the downfall of that society. The Agricultural Society was, however, dominated by members of the Philosophical Society.

By late 1822, with his newly obtained means of transportation, Cunningham was ready to begin his collections west of the Blue Mountains. In September he left Parramatta, crossed the mountains slowly, delaying several days to search for plants, and then based himself at Bathurst. From here he was able to explore westward, having the good fortune to obtain specimens of the orchids in which, despite years in Australia with its comparatively impoverished flora of the Orchidaceae, Cunningham had not lost his joy. On 18 November he set out on a more prolonged journey north of the Cudgegong River, but the inadvertent loss of the horses for which he had exchanged his cart prematurely ended the excursion. He continued short forays into the immediate neighbourhood of Bathurst before returning to Parramatta at the end of the year, having collected 200 plant specimens.

Others in the colony also made the journey to Bathurst. Barron Field travelled there in October of 1822, noting in his journal the floral novelties that caught his attention. Although he was adept with botanical names, Field was no botanist; it was the picturesque which attracted the poet in him as he had previously recorded in *First Fruits of Australian Poetry*, not the botanical wonders to be found in the country-side that he so disparaged:

> New South Wales is a perpetual flower garden, but there is not a single scene in it of which a painter could make a landscape, without greatly disguising the true character of the trees.[1]

Indeed, in support of his view, Field quoted James Edward Smith, one of the English botanists most familiar with Australian plants:

> New Holland seems no very beautiful or picturesque country, such as is likely to form, or to inspire, a poet . . . There seems, however, to be no transition of seasons in the climate itself, to excite hope, or to expand the heart and fancy.[2]

These were attitudes that pointed out the difference between the view of natural history as exemplified by the membership of the Philosophical Society and the business-like attitudes of collectors Allan Cunningham and Charles Fraser, who could have had little time for such sentiments as they continuously expanded their collections with untold new genera and species. Field reiterated the observation made by a number of earlier explorers of Australia that both the geological structure and the biogeography of the continent appeared to change with divisions of latitude, an observation which posed for him the question of whether the Deity recognised the artificial measurements of mankind.

Towards the end of the year, Phillip Parker King returned to England. On the return voyage he put into King George Sound and collected dried plant specimens for transmission to Kew. At the sound he also procured a number of living plants, the prize specimen of which was the pitcher plant, *Cephalotus follicularis*, which had so intrigued the botanists who had frequented King George Sound in the past. The pitcher plants were the only survivors of King's trip back to England and eventually became well established at Kew. Over previous voyages King had collected a small herbarium separate from that of his usual companion, Allan Cunningham, and on his return to England he gave this collection to A. B. Lambert.

During 1822, George Evans, former surveyor of Van Diemens Land, published his *A Geographical, Historical and Topographical Description of Van Diemen's Land* with a prefacing note that many of the passages of his work appeared to be the same as those published by Lieutenant Jeffreys in *Geographical and Descriptive Delineations*. The cause of this evident plagiarism was attributed to Evans having once been a passenger on a ship under Jeffreys' command and having discovered portions of his own manuscript in the hands of Jeffreys' clerk. Evans' observations concerning the botany and zoology of Van Diemens Land centred around the fact that there appeared to be little difference between the flora and fauna of the mainland of Australia and Van Diemens Land. The only exceptions being that Van Diemens Land had the Huon pine and an animal of the panther tribe, presumably the thylacine, while lacking the cedar, mahogany, rosewood, and dingo found on the mainland. As for mineralogy, Van Diemens Land was rich in copper, iron, alum, limestone, asbestos, coal, and basalt, and close to Launceston there appeared to be entire mountains of iron some of it reckoned to be as much as 70 per cent pure.

In England in 1822 William Swainson published a catalogue for the auction of the shells in the collection of Mrs Bligh, wife of Admiral William Bligh. As might be expected from a family that had at one time resided in New South Wales even if under stressful circumstances, the collection contained a wide variety of Australian shells. In an appendix to the sale catalogue, Swainson appended a description of several undescribed shells including '*Haliotis glabra*' (*Mitra glabra*), '*Mitra carbonaria*', '*Voluta maculata*' (*Amoria maculata*), and '*Mitra nivosa*' (*Mitra nubila*), all from Australian waters. Swainson seemed little concerned that the catalogue of an auction might be unfitting for the original scientific descriptions of species.

That same year Coenraad Jacob Temminck published an account of a number of new species of parrots and pigeons acquired by the Linnean Society and deposited in their museum. Many of the specimens had been collected by Brown and Westall during the voyage of the *Investigator* more than twenty years earlier. Temminck dedicated the species '*Psittacus brownii*' (*Platycercus venustus*), brought back from Arnhem Land by the *Investigator*, to Robert Brown, and the species '*Psittacus baueri*' (*Barnardius zonarius*), to Ferdinand Bauer, Brown's artist companion. Temminck read the paper describing the birds before the Linnean Society in 1819, but due to delays in publication of the *Transactions of the Linnean Society* the paper did not receive formal publication until 1822. In 1820, Kuhl described the same birds and because his written descriptions appeared first, Kuhl's names have priority; thus Temminck's '*Psittacus brownii*' has been given the specific name *venustus*.

The early months of 1823 found Allan Cunningham preparing his most recently collected specimens for shipment to Kew, concomitantly planning and preparing for further excursions to the west of the Blue Mountains. By now Cunningham was determined to find a pass through the Liverpool Range to the Liverpool Plains and, with Governor Brisbane's approval, organised an expedition to leave Bathurst in the middle of April to accomplish this purpose. Initially attempting to find a crossing too far to the east, Cunningham's party was forced westward by the mountain range, and here he found the sought-after passage to the plains. Romantically, Cunningham named the gap Pandora Pass, having found the pass at the bottom of a box canyon much as the mythological Pandora had found Hope. Without sufficient supplies to force a passage across the pass out on to Liverpool Plains, Cunningham had to content himself with charting its location and returning to Bathurst on 27 June. Throughout the remaining months of 1823, Cunningham employed himself in short journeys across the Blue Mountains in search of plant specimens and seeds. In the forested country he was now inspecting, he was able to add another twenty-five species to his orchid collection as well as completing a study of the tree fern, *Dicksonia antarctica*.

Cunningham's sometime rival and colleague, the superintendent of the Sydney Botanic Gardens, suffered a private setback in 1823. Fraser had participated in Oxley's expeditions of 1817 and 1818 on the pay of a soldier. He was later presented with £75 from the Police Fund for this work but in addition Macquarie, who seems to have favoured the colonial botanist over the king's botanist, allotted Fraser a grant of 220 hectares for his services on the expeditions. In 1823 Fraser applied to Colonial Secretary Frederick Goulburn to take up his land allotment to establish a garden. By that time Macquarie had departed New South Wales for England and Goulburn sarcastically replied to Fraser that he himself had just returned from Bathurst having accompanied Governor Brisbane there—and when he received a grant of land to compensate him for his services then so would Fraser receive his grant. The pendulum had swung back, the king's botanist supplanted the colonial botanist under Brisbane's administration.

After the abdication of Adolarius Humphrey from his position as the colonial mineralogist in 1812 no further geological appointments were forthcoming until 1823. That year John Busby was assigned mineral-surveyor and civil engineer to the colony, however, only on a part-time basis of 200 days a year. One aspect of Busby's duties was to manage the coal mines at Newcastle, but Busby's time was predominantly spent in the construction of water supplies for Sydney, and aside from one report on the coal mines he had little to do with the geology or mineralogy of the colony for the duration of his residence in New South Wales.

Early in 1824 another of the many French scientific and exploratory expeditions put into Port Jackson for a period of rest and refurbishment. *La Coquille*, under the command of Louis Duperrey, had sailed from France in the middle of 1822, spending the intervening time on the coasts of South America and the islands of the Pacific. Duperrey, who had sailed under Freycinet in the *L'Uranie* expedition of 1817, continued the tradition of relying on naval officers to carry out the intended natural history studies rather than employing professional naturalists. Fortunately for the French scientific community the surgeons employed on the majority of these expeditions were of outstanding ability, resulting in the acquisition of prodigious amounts of information. Unhappily, all too often many of the collected specimens were lost in shipwrecks on the journey home, and the expedition of Duperrey was to be no different. Prosper Garnot, the senior of the two surgeons on board, left Duperrey's expedition on reaching Australian waters; he had contracted dysentery in South America and on arrival in Port Jackson sought to return to Europe. He and much of the expedition's collections obtained passage on the *Castle Forbes*, but the vessel was lost rounding the Cape of Good Hope in July 1824. Garnot survived the wreck but the accumulation of specimens did not, making Duperrey's the third French expedition fated to lose a portion of its collections.

While Garnot had concerned himself with the vertebrates, particularly the mammals and the birds, the botany and the entomology were under the care of Dumont d'Urville, a naval lieutenant who was later to command his own expedition to the Pacific. The second surgeon, René Lesson, undertook the burden of the zoological work after the departure of Garnot.

La Coquille arrived at Port Jackson on 17 January 1824 and stayed just over two months in that port before leaving on 20 March. During this time the surgeon-naturalists and d'Urville followed much the same pursuits as had their predecessors: discussions with Allan Cunningham, visits to the Botanic Gardens and Charles Fraser, an excursion over the Blue Mountains to Bathurst, and a visit to Botany Bay both to view Father Receveur's grave and to see the plate placed on the shores of Botany Bay by the Philosophical Society to commemorate Cook's landing.

The excursion to Bathurst was undertaken by Lesson and d'Urville and commenced on 29 January. At Parramatta they dined with Governor Brisbane and were treated to a tour of his astronomical observatory. In the park surrounding the governor's residence at Parramatta Brisbane had established a menagerie of animals: kangaroos, emus, black swans, and other birds, which the French naturalists were eager to examine, having had no acquaintance with such exotic creatures previously. A visit was paid to Allan Cunningham who was happy to show d'Urville his botanical specimens and provide Lesson and d'Urville with a detailed description of the botanical and geographical features they would observe on their forthcoming journey to Bathurst. On that well-worn path across the Blue Mountains Lesson was able to claim, as early as the Nepean River, that he had discovered undescribed animals and fresh water 'scallops' in addition to seeing many of the plants that Cunningham had described. Progressing further into the mountains, Lesson hoped to obtain specimens of the lyrebird, *Menura novaehollandiae*, but was able only to view a preserved specimen; the lyrebird was becoming increasingly rare in the district from overhunting. Lesson was more fortunate with other species and was able to observe or collect kookaburras, parrots, and other birds. The Frenchmen did not limit themselves to assemblages of birds and plants, and assiduously collected whatever they encountered— insects, lizards, and a specimen of the possum *Didelphis petaurus* that they were able to purchase. At Fish River they tried in vain to capture samples of the platypus; Lesson later attributed their lack of success to the creatures remaining in their burrows during long periods of dry weather.

In 1824 the platypus was again the centre of controversy over its precise taxonomic position, and no doubt Lesson was anxious to examine one himself. That year the German physician Johann Friedrich Meckel announced that he had found well-developed mammary glands in a female platypus which should have firmly established the animal as a mammal. Meckel found that the glands enlarged only when raising young, thus the normally shrunken glands had been overlooked by other anatomists. Lesson, on the other hand, had been assured by both Aborigines and colonists that the platypus laid eggs, hardly a typical mammalian feature. Others in Europe were still not convinced of the platypus' status. Étienne Geoffroy Saint-Hilaire and his son Isidore, long proponents of the view that the platypus was not a mammal, argued that the newly found mammary glands differed appreciably from those of other mammals and were possibly scent glands or accessories which aided in fur grooming. The Geoffroys argued that the Monotremes, as they called the platypus and echidna, should be separated taxonomically from the other mammals.

Besides the numerous mineral specimens that Lesson collected on the journey to Bathurst and the plants that d'Urville procured, much of the party's concentration was on ornithology. Parrots especially attracted their attention, and specimens of '*Psittacus pennanti*', '*P. haematodus*', '*P. personnatus*', and '*P. discolor*' all fell before their guns. They were presented with or bought specimens of '*Platycercus scapulatus*', '*Meliphaga chrysocephalus*', and the paradise rifle-bird. Lesson considered Australia rich in little-known animals and although he saw many of the species that had been described by past expeditions to the colony, especially

those figured in the *Zoological Atlas* of the Freycinet expedition, Lesson was disappointed that he never caught a glimpse of animals such as wombats or dasyurids. Before Garnot left the colony on the *Forbes Castle* the French naturalists procured a live echidna which Garnot took with him, but even if it survived to the Cape of Good Hope it surely perished during the wreck of the vessel there.

In common with so many observers, Lesson concluded that the vegetation of Australia was monotonous, dominated as it was by only two score species of eucalyptus. D'Urville, for all Lesson's monotony, found at least 360 species of plants, and his conversations with Cunningham must surely have awakened d'Urville to the diversity of the Australian flora.

Cunningham himself was not idle during 1824. Early in the year he prepared to set off on another of his exploration-collecting trips. Finding Thomas Brisbane more obliging regarding his requests for material help than Macquarie had ever been, Cunningham pushed hard for equipment and supplies. When given a cart and horse to pursue his explorations, Cunningham complained that the horse was too old to be of any use—and he was scarcely satisfied with the cart either. There were requests for the provision of pack saddles to hold his specimens, packing cases for shipment of specimens back to England, a second servant to help with his collections, and a general and permanent passport to investigate all parts of the colony. The passport was necessary because the colonial administration was still anxious to prevent squatters from moving into newly discovered territory. All the demands made by Cunningham were met by Brisbane, who was assuredly more sympathetic to the pursuit of natural history than had been his predecessors. From March to May Cunningham ventured south-west towards the Queanbeyan Valley. May saw him collecting in the rainforests of the Illawarra district, while in September he was off north, this time accompanying John Oxley to Moreton Bay where the government had decided to found a penal settlement.

As Oxley examined the area with a view to selecting a site for the settlement, Cunningham ranged over the lower reaches of the Brisbane River. Initially he found little of interest: the mouth of the river was clothed in blue gums and ironbark, the monotony broken only by the flowers of *Hibiscus heterophyllus*. But soon he came across a strand of hoop pine reaching heights of 30 metres or more. Cunningham was unable to obtain cones of the hoop pine and so was unwilling to classify the tree into any known genera. He was able to gather bulbs of *Crinum* and the orchids *Cymbidium suave*, *C. canaliculatum*, and *Dendrobium teretifolium* as well as other undescribed species. Farther upstream the land afforded Cunningham several other new species of plants, and upon further examination of fallen cones of the hoop pine Cunningham was able to assign it to the genus *Araucaria*, although it was a different species from the Norfolk Island pine. Cunningham described the hoop pine under the name '*Araucaria brisbanii*', but it has since been renamed *A. cunninghamii*. The other tall tree present that attracted his attention as a possibility for conversion into naval spars was *Flindersia australis*.

The Brisbane River Oxley found to be inhabited by the Murray cod, although in describing what is presumably the same fish, Allan Cunningham insisted that it was a fresh water shark. The discrepancy arose because neither individual was able to obtain a fresh specimen of the animal; they only observed it swimming in the river and examined a partially eaten specimen proffered by Aborigines.

Oxley's party returned to Sydney in the middle of October with reports on the area sufficiently encouraging to induce Brisbane to visit the district before the end of the year. On Brisbane's return to Sydney, he sent specimens of the hoop pine to England for evaluation as naval timber.

During 1824 Fraser, at the Botanic Gardens in Sydney, continued with the work of acclimatising European plants to Australian conditions and maintaining a garden of indigenous plants. The pastoralist William MacArthur contributed samples of seeds sent to him from England to the Botanic Gardens, praising Fraser for his open-handed dispensing of plants:

> Mr. Fraxier deserves much praise for his industry and liberality unlike most of his profession he makes a point of giving to everyone who will promise to take care of them, whatever plants can be spared without injury to the Garden.[3]

Deprived of his immediate patron, Macquarie, the colonial botanist seemed to have fared less well than the king's botanist, but even Brisbane was full of praise for him:

> Mr Fraser, Botanist, highly qualified to do every justice to his appointment, from zeal, talent, and enthusiasm.[4]

Brisbane also remarked on the 3,000 varieties of plants that had been introduced to the Botanic Gardens during Fraser's tenure as Superintendent. Fraser continued to try to acclimatise European plants to Australia as witnessed by an attempt to introduce flax, thwarted, however, by the opposing growing seasons in the northern and southern hemisphere. Later efforts by Fraser to cultivate cotton in the colony resulted in the Agricultural and Horticultural Society of New South Wales awarding him a gold medal.

During 1824 yet another botanist sought exotic flora around the coasts of Australia, this time in private

'*Correa pulchella*'
Sweet. *Flora Australasica*. 1827–28.
Correa pulchella

employ. William Baxter, engaged by F. Henchman, a nurseryman in England, collected at both Kangaroo Island off the coast of South Australia and later that year at King George Sound. Many of the seeds he dispatched to England were germinated, producing plants that were described in 1827 and 1828 by Robert Sweet in his *Flora Australasica*. *Flora Australasica* was designed primarily as an adjunct for those wealthy gentlemen who maintained gardens luxuriant in Australian plants. A richly illustrated, costly book, the text indicated conditions for successful growth of each species in addition to supplying botanical descriptions. The majority of the plants were relatively well known, many originally described by either Robert Brown or James Edward Smith and subsequently found adorning the gardens of London. In addition to the seeds collected by Baxter, other plants illustrated in the work were

derived from seeds collected by either Allan Cunningham or Charles Fraser.

In 1824, en route to England from India where he had long served as an officer in the artillery, Thomas Hardwicke touched at Van Diemens Land. Here he collected the specimens that were to form the basis for J. E. Gray's description of 'Hardwicke's snipe', '*Scolopax hardwickii*' (Latham's snipe, *Gallinago hardwickii*). Hardwicke later became well-known for his assemblage of paintings published as *Illustrations of Indian Zoology*. When he bequeathed more than 1,700 bird illustrations to the British Museum, among them were seventy-six paintings from New South Wales and Van Diemens Land said to have been drawn by John Lewin.

Also in 1824, Thomas Hobbes Scott, brother-in-law to John Bigge, and who had accompanied Bigge to New South Wales as his secretary, submitted a paper to the *Annals of Philosophy* on the geology of New South Wales and Van Diemens Land. The coast of New South Wales, as examined by Scott, from Cape Howe to Port Stephens consisted of a series of coal strata occasionally surfacing, as at Illawarra, through the sandstone overburden. The coal seams overlay old red sandstone as indicated by the Blue Mountain escarpment, where it in turn was underlain by primitive or igneous rock. Scott felt that the geological structure of Van Diemens Land was very similar, both Hobart and Georgetown resting on coal formations.

Allan Cunningham continued to prosecute his botanical and geographical researches during 1825 and strove to reach Pandora Pass, which he had discovered in 1823, and cross into the Liverpool Plains. Setting out in March, he attained his objective. Later that year he travelled north-east from Bathurst toward the Cudgegong River where he added considerably to his collection of orchids which he now maintained in greenhouses back in Parramatta.

Another French expedition sailed into Port Jackson on 1 July of that year, *La Thétis* and *L'Espérance* under the command of Hyacinthe Bougainville. Again there were no professional naturalists on board, the purported explanation being that preparations were made so quickly for the voyage that there had been no time to recruit any naturalists. Again the surgeon was suborned as naturalist. François Busseuil accumulated a variety of specimens on the voyage but died before describing them, leaving the collection to be described intermittently by other authorities.

TOP:
'*Banksia dryandroides*'
Sweet. *Flora Australasica*. 1827–28.
Banksia dryandroides

BOTTOM:
'*Hovea purpurea*'
Sweet. *Flora Australasica*.
Hovea longifolia

175

In 1825 that governor sympathetic to the sciences, Thomas Brisbane, was recalled to England. His replacement was Ralph Darling. Frederick Goulburn was also superseded as colonial secretary, and his successor was to be Alexander Macleay, fully as sympathetic to science as Brisbane and, as colonial secretary, possibly in a position to do more about it. Macleay had held the position of secretary of the Linnean Society for many years and during that time had amassed possibly the foremost private entomological collection in England, initially through his own collecting but later through the purchase of other collections as they came under the hammer. Macleay already possessed a large number of Australian insects obtained on voyages as far back as that of Cook in 1770, but most of his material had come from more recent sources. Always ready to sponsor naturalists abroad, Macleay had contributed funds to John Lewin to outfit him for his emigration to New South Wales in 1800; Lewin had repaid the debt by sending specimens to Macleay. Macleay took up his posting as colonial secretary in 1825 and brought to the colony his extensive entomological collection. Like so many scientifically oriented gentlemen of his day, Macleay was primarily an accumulator of specimens; he contributed very little to the systematisation of insect taxonomy. There is no indication that Macleay embarked on any scientific endeavours during his residence in New South Wales. Perhaps more importantly, he contributed his patronage and his organisational abilities to various scientific institutions which were to begin life during his tenure as colonial secretary and later, while he was Speaker of the Legislative Council.

During 1825 Barron Field edited and published a number of the papers delivered before the defunct Philosophical Society of Australasia as well as official descriptions of exploratory journeys. Included in the collection, printed under the title *Geographical Memoirs on New South Wales*, were geographic papers by Cunningham and Phillip Parker King, Charles Rumker on the astronomy of the southern hemisphere, and Frederick Goulburn and Thomas Brisbane on the meteorology of the colony. Natural history was represented by a paper on geology by Alexander Berry, a treatise on botany by Cunningham, and a rather inadequate list of the flora and fauna by Field.

Alexander Berry's paper, entitled 'On the Geology of part of the Coast of New South Wales' was primarily descriptive, although in one significant paragraph Berry revealed his sympathies in the debate between the Huttonians and the Wernerians:

> Dr. Hutton would have given much for a single day's walk along this shore. Here we see at one glance the progress of some of the most interesting operations of nature — the work of many ages. It appears as if the crust of the earth had been broken, and a bold and regular

section forced upwards and presented to our examination.[5]

Allan Cunningham's contribution, a paper on the indigenous botany of Australia, was similar to his work included as an appendix to Phillip Parker King's narrative, and surveyed a number of plant groups in terms of biogeography. Cunningham's special interest, the orchids, also received mention. He suggested that although there were possibly over 100 species of orchids to be found in Australia, they were comparatively rare here, as opposed to other continents in the tropics such as South America. There were fewer dense forests in Australia providing the shade and moisture necessary for orchid growth.

Barron Field's appendix, with its limited survey of the flora and especially the fauna of the colony, reinforced Field's plea in the preface to the book:

> Australia is the land of contrarieties, where the laws of nature seem reversed; her zoology can only be studied and unravelled on the spot.[6]

Field thought that it was a national disgrace for England that she should maintain sovereignty over Australia only to have other countries, (presumably France), claiming much of the glory of zoological discovery. He suggested that the British government should appoint a public zoologist, much as botanists had been supported in New South Wales for some years. Field went on to coyly suggest that such a person might be the author of *Horae Entomologicae*. This, of course, was William Sharp Macleay, the son of Alexander Macleay and a noted entomologist.

In England that year considerable attention was paid to Australian ornithology. William Swainson described a new species of parrot, the 'rufous headed parrot', '*Psittacus fieldii*' (red-cheeked parrot, *Geoffroyus geoffroyi*), sent to him by Barron Field, in addition to contributing a paper that concentrated on the taxonomic re-arrangement of the pigeons, the Columbidae. In the first article Swainson referred to Nicholas Vigors' arrangement of the parrots according to the 'quinary system', a new taxonomy devised by William Sharp Macleay. The quinary system, or the natural affinity system as it was alternately called, adopted by both Vigors and Swainson in their taxonomic studies of Australian birds involved splitting animal groups into subdivisions based on the number five, thus the term quinary. Each of the five subdivisions grouped animals with shared traits, these characteristics forming a transition with those subdivisions classified adjacent thereby illustrating their natural affinities. The fifth subdivision in the series merged smoothly with the first subdivision to form a circular arrangement. Claims for the merit of the system centred around the fact that it professed to be a natural classification, rather than an

'*Phebalium aureum, Fieldia australis*'
Field. *Geographical memoirs on New South Wales.* 1825.
Phebalium squamulosum, Fieldia australis

'*Anthocercis albicans, Grevillea acanthifolia*'
Field. *Geographical memoirs on New South Wales.* 1825.
Anthocercis albicans, Grevillea acanthifolia

artificial classificatory scheme such as the then prevalent Linnean system. The basis of this claim was the intent of Macleay and his disciples to establish a connection between an animal's form and the function of its various organs and appendages. Although the quinary system enjoyed some initial success, it was later discarded and declared an aberration, becoming an example of the convoluted theorising that naturalists were taught to abhor. The Linnean system which it was to replace continues to function in a limited sense even now.

The work on parrots by Vigors, referred to by Swainson in his article, was then unpublished, but Vigors serially presented the work to the Zoological Club of the Linnean Society. It included his revision of the rosella group, removing them from the genus 'Psittacus' and placing them in the genus Platycercus where they remain today. Either Vigors or the writer of the accounts of the Zoological Club was an incipient evolutionist, for Vigors' work was described as having:

> . . . pointed out the adaptation of such characters (wings) to habits of life, and the natural station of the birds in which they are found.[7]

This more than thirty years before the publications of Darwin or Wallace.

Also during the year 1825 at the Zoological Club, Phillip Parker King, having returned to England after his exploratory voyages to the north-west coast of Australia, exhibited various birds and fish collected in Australia; he later presented the specimens to the Linnean Society Museum.

At one of the meetings following the discussion of Australian birds, King, in an effort to uphold honours due to his father, Philip Gidley King, pointed out that the bird described by Lewin as 'Meliphaga chrysocephalus' was commonly called King's oriole or honeysucker. Similarly 'Platycercus scapulatus', called the King parrot, was originally called King's parrot.

Little that was new in the way of natural history occurred in the year 1826 in Australia. Allan Cunningham spent the initial months of the year recovering from ill health brought on by his years of living under primitive field conditions. He was never to completely recover his former robust strength and future explorations were to extract a high toll on his constitution. Nevertheless, he managed two short journeys to collect seeds and orchids, first in the Blue Mountains then later in the Illawarra district. His free periods were spent curating his herbarium, sending off specimens to Kew, and tending his orchids in his greenhouses. Increasingly Cunningham was coming to rely on convicts assigned to him as servants to seek out the plants he desired. Late in the year a combined project to the Liverpool Plains with the astronomer Rumker came

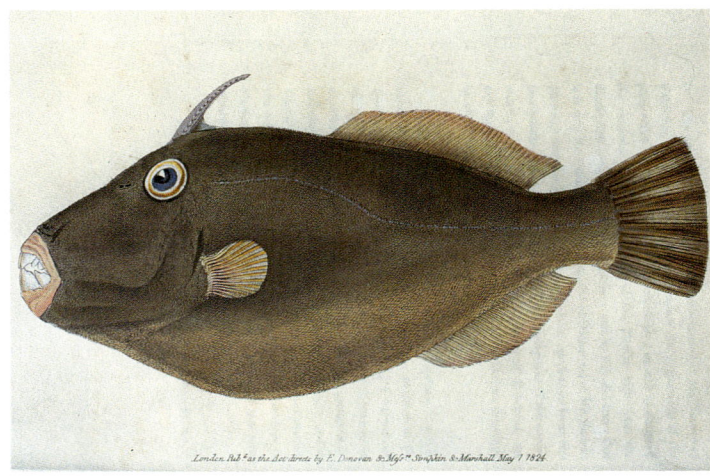

'Balistes australis'
Donovan. Naturalists Repository. 1825.
Navodon australis

to naught when the colonial government declined to provide the astronomer with the proper instrumentation necessary for taking a measurement of the arc of the meridian. As an alternative Cunningham was able to take passage to New Zealand for several months of travel and botanical collecting. Possibly Cunningham was galvanised to visit New Zealand by the knowledge that Charles Fraser had been there the previous year and returned with a rich haul of plants. Leaving Port Jackson in August of 1826 Cunningham was not to return until the following year.

The year 1826 also saw another of the interminable series of French expeditions to the shores of Australia; this time the main participants on the voyage had all visited Australia previously. The vessel was the former La Coquille, which had been in Australia two years before, and was now renamed L'Astrolabe. Her commander, Dumont d'Urville, had been second in command on the earlier voyage as well as contributing much of the botanical work of that expedition. His work appeared in Annales des Sciences Naturelles in addition to a monograph printed by the Linnean Society. On board L'Astrolabe were: the surgeon-naturalists Quoy and Gaimard, who had been to Australia as part of L'Uranie expedition in 1817; Pierre Lesson the brother of René Lesson who had accompanied La Coquille two years previously; Achille Richard, a botanist like Lesson; and Charles Jacquinot, another naturalist and the first-lieutenant of the vessel. With d'Urville also a botanist of some repute, the officers of the voyage had a decidedly scientific cast. The expedition's initial call on 7 October 1826, was at King George Sound where they remained for two-and-a-half weeks. Here they found an abundance of undescribed bird species, including the

'Psittacus tabuensis'
Donovan. Naturalists Repository. 1825.
Alisterus scapularis

western yellow robin, *Eopsaltria griseogularis*; the white-breasted robin, *E. georgiana*; the splendid fairy-wren, *Malurus splendens*; and the red-eared firetail finch, '*Zonaeginthus oculatus*' (*Emblema oculata*). Quoy also considered that two new species of parrots were detected, but one turned out to be a mature specimen of the red-capped parrot which had previously only been seen and described as a juvenile, while the other was the twenty-eight parrot, now considered to be a geographic race of the Port Lincoln ringneck, *Barnardius zonarius*, rather than a separate species in its own right. Quoy attributed their success at finding so many undescribed species in an area that had been frequently visited previously to his expedition's extensive excursions inland away from King George Sound, but it may just have been that former expeditions had concentrated heavily on botany. Not that botany was ignored on d'Urville's expedition—d'Urville spent much of his time ashore for the purpose of collecting. Before *L'Astrolabe* sailed, Quoy and Gaimard shot an undescribed species of kangaroo that they named '*Kangurus brachyurus*', now known as *Setonix brachyurus*.

Sailing eastward from King George Sound, *L'Astrolabe* next called at Western Port where the vessel spent a week at anchor. Here Quoy and Gaimard found the beach strewn with shells, some of which they recognised as '*Trigonia pectinata*' the so-called living fossil pelecypod. Despite much searching, the two zoologists could find no live specimens of the mollusc, but their disappointment was later assuaged when they dredged a small live specimen from Bass Strait.

After leaving Western Port, *L'Astrolabe* called at Jervis Bay for three days before finally arriving at Port Jackson on 2 December. Here the usual rounds of ceremonial courtesy were performed, although the French were looked upon with considerable suspicion concerning the expedition's motive, suspicion enough for Governor Darling to dispatch a party of convicts and soldiers to form a settlement at King George Sound as a provision against any French aspirations on the western coast of Australia. A stay of only seventeen days in Port Jackson left the naturalists little time for the customary journey to the Blue Mountains, and they had to content themselves with accepting a gift from Charles Fraser of plants gathered in the Blue Mountains, Moreton Bay, Port Macquarie, and Melville Island.

L'Astrolabe sailed for New Zealand and then the East Indies, but before the end of the next year became the first French naval vessel to visit Hobart since its settlement. Again the French stayed less than a month, but in that time Quoy obtained another new species, the dusky robin, or '*Muscicapa vittata*' as he named it, although it is now known as *Melanodryas vittata*.

The scientific results of the voyage were extensive, published in the usual sumptuous French fashion—the pictorial *Zoological Atlas* was the equal of any natural history draughtsmanship ever inspired by Australia's natural productions. Comparatively little time was spent in Australian waters, so the Australian portion of the final results was small. As was typical of the French scientific personnel, the naturalists spent much of their time working on marine invertebrates rather than the more eye-catching mammals and birds.

In 1826 Samuel Stutchbury, a young man with little formal education but several years experience behind him as an assistant at the Museum of the Royal College of Surgeons of England developing his knowledge of mineralogy and palaeontology, visited Australia. He left his position at the Museum of the Royal College of Surgeons to join an expedition, organised by the Pacific Pearl Fishing Company, to scour the Pacific for pearls. When the expedition put into Port Jackson on 17 December 1825, Stutchbury spent several months in the environs of Sydney collecting mineralogical specimens. He was also reputed to have dredged Port Jackson for molluscs, turning up specimens of '*Trigonia*', samples of which had previously been obtained by Péron over twenty years earlier and by Péron's compatriots Quoy and Gaimard in the same year as Stutchbury. Stutchbury left Sydney on 8 March 1826 but was to return to Australia in 1851 as a government mineralogist during the upsurge of interest in gold, copper, and lead in New South Wales, South Australia, and Victoria.

Forty years after the colony of New South Wales had been founded, the export of natural history specimens was still being carried out at a furious rate. In early 1827 George Harper, who had arrived in Australia in 1820 bearing recommendations from Sir Walter Scott, returned to England and took with him a cargo of over 1,600 bird skins. Many of the skins were later acquired by William Jardine or by the Edinburgh Museum. Harper also carried with him two live emus and two cases of mineralogical specimens.

The year that George Harper chose to return to England, James King, newly arrived in New South Wales from England, dispatched a letter to the *Edinburgh Journal of Science* under the title of 'Observations on the Climate and Geology of New South Wales'. King did not limit himself to the narrow fields included in the title but querulously complained of the foolish and despotic captain he had been forced to endure on the voyage out to New South Wales and castigated the colonial government for the importation of salt when abundant supplies could be obtained locally. This dearth of wisdom on the part of the colonial administration King attributed to the lack of a practical mineralogist in the colony. Only John Busby, Alexander Berry, and of course himself, could tell the difference between basalt and bloodstone, which conveniently excluded Robert

Townson and A. Humphrey in Van Diemens Land. King felt that the government encouraged botany for the benefit of a few individuals in Europe while dismissing mineralogy which would have been of immediate advantage to the entire colony. King was to contribute to mineralogical knowledge by his discovery that the beach sand around Sydney was ideal for the production of glass. His worth was never realised, however, for while he considered that such a useful discovery should be rewarded financially, the colonial administration offered him only a land grant for his efforts.

Despite King's criticisms botany continued to receive support from the colonial administration. Colonial Botanist Charles Fraser continued to develop the Sydney Botanic Gardens, and in 1827 a government garden was declared in Parramatta with John Ayers appointed as superintendent. Fraser, like his colleague Allan Cunningham, never ceased to journey to various parts of the colony to obtain plant specimens, and in 1827 seized the opportunity to take passage aboard a vessel bound for the Swan River region on the western coast of Australia. In the years before 1826 Britain had acknowledged none of the prior claims to the territory west of 135°E, but recent French expeditions calling at King George Sound excited British attention. King George Sound was occupied at the end of 1826, and in 1827 Governor Darling ordered Captain James Stirling to survey the Swan River with a view to establishing a further settlement there. The colonial botanist was to accompany Stirling to report on the prospect of the area for agriculture. Travelling on board the vessel *Success* the party reached the Swan River area on 5 March. Fraser was immediately struck by the myriad wildflowers for which south-western Australia was to become so well-known, and the luxuriant vegetation on the land immediately behind the beach amazed him. Further inland he found *Eucalyptus*, *Leptospermum*, *Banksia*, *Dryandra*, *Grevillea*, and *Goodenia*. Despite the presence of the plants *Banksia* and *Xanthorrhoea*, which in New South Wales were considered indicative of poor soil, Fraser concluded that the land was fertile. He was able to collect a number of undescribed species in addition to samples from a petrified forest.

The animals of the Swan River district Fraser recorded as being similar to those of New South Wales. Most of his references were to birds: the black swan which had so amazed early Dutch explorers of the coast, and a parrot, possibly the pink cockatoo, *Cacatua leadbeateri*, which he believed fed upon the roots of orchids that it scratched from the ground. While at Swan River Fraser heard a bellowing which he attributed to the dugong reported by earlier French expeditions. William J. Hooker, in a footnote to Fraser's published report on the area in *Botanical Miscellany*, disagreed, pointing out that the bellowing was probably from seals that Fraser had noted in the area, especially as the dugong was only found much further to the north.

After a two-week survey, the *Success* rerounded Cape Leeuwin and anchored in King George Sound where it remained for twelve days. The land surrounding the Sound seemed to Fraser to have great potential because of its abundance of limestone and water, good fertility of the soil, and its situation on the routes from Sydney to India, the East Indies, and the Cape of Good Hope. Like so many other botanists, Fraser was fascinated by the pitcher plants, but rather than accepting its carnivorous habits he concluded that the pitcher was an adaptation for storing water. He surmised that the lid of the pitcher opened during rainfall to trap the moisture and closed to prevent evaporation until the water was needed during the dry season.

Fraser compiled a number of reports on the Swan River area, one of which appeared in Hooker's *Botanical Miscellany* in 1830, while another was read to the Linnean Society. In one of these reports Fraser stated:

> In giving my opinion of the land seen on the banks of the Swan River, I hesitate not in pronouncing it superior to any I ever saw in New South Wales east of the Blue Mountains.[8]

For statements such as this Fraser was to be subjected to heavy criticism in later years, for the soil in the Swan River district was soon shown to be infertile. Fraser had based his comments on the luxuriance of the tree growth instead of testing the fertility of the soil directly (by attempting to grow agricultural crops in the soil, which he could then have returned to the Sydney Botanic Garden).

While Fraser was away at Swan River Allan Cunningham set out on another of his explorations. Cunningham had returned from New Zealand early in 1827 and by April was on his way north from the Hunter Valley. Unlike most of his previous journeys, where botany had always played a part, Cunningham regarded this excursion as purely for geographical discovery. Geographic discoveries were made in plenty, the rich fertile lands of Darling Downs were crossed, and Cunningham caught a glimpse of a gap through the Great Dividing Range eastward to Moreton Bay, a gap for which he would later search from the other side of the mountain range, eventually finding the pass that now bears his name. On his return from the journey, Cunningham had little time for exploration the rest of that year, contenting himself with writing reports of his trip and maintaining his collections of live and preserved plants.

Although that great patron of botanists in Australia, Joseph Banks, had died in 1820, the demand for Australian flora continued unabated. William J. Hooker had been appointed to the directorship of the Royal Gardens at Kew upon Banks' death, and in addition to

1 GOBE-MOUCHE À GROS BEC........
2 GOBE-MOUCHE À BANDE........

3 GOBE-MOUCHE DE MANADO........
4 GOBE-MOUCHE GEORGIEN........

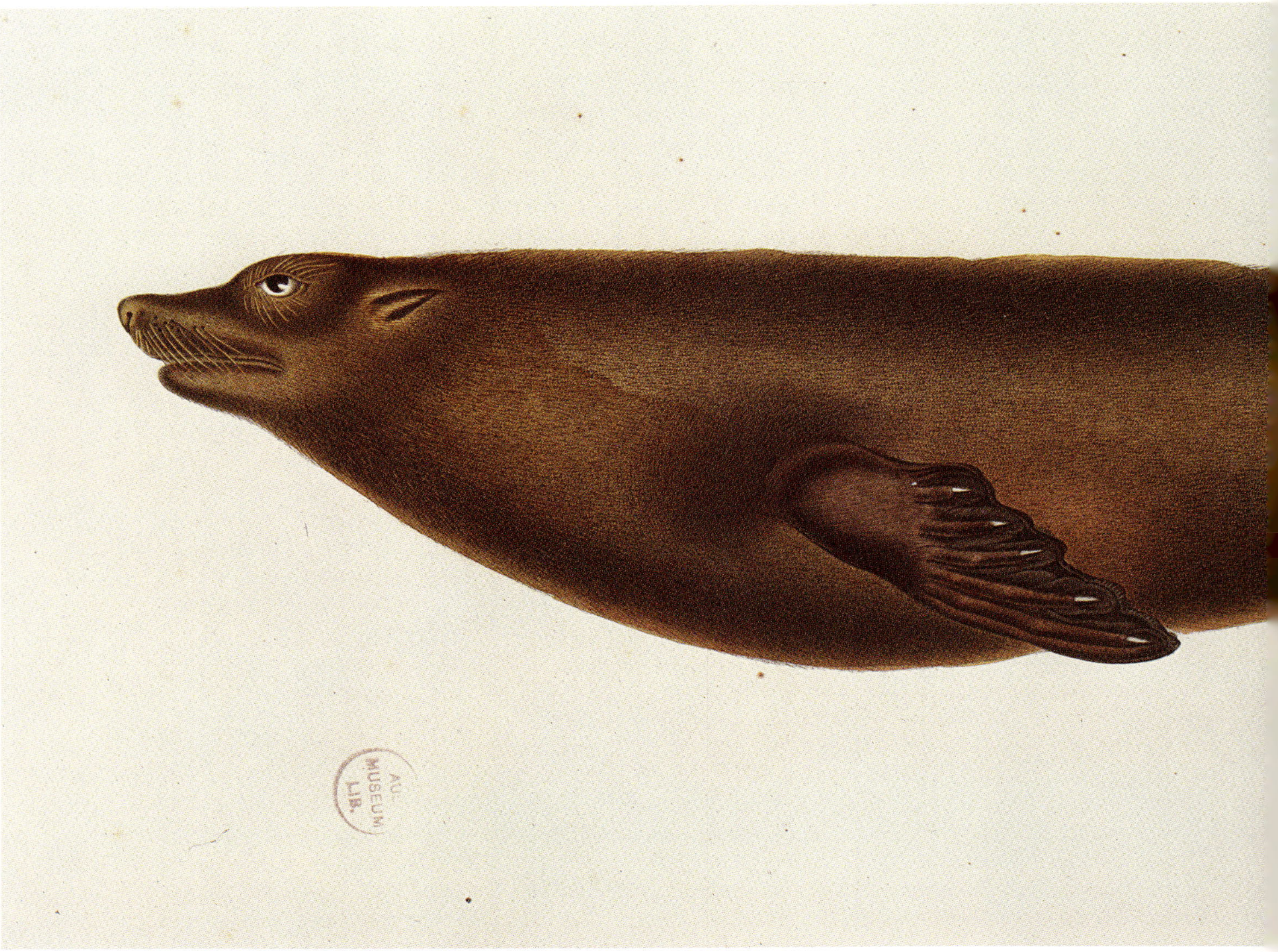

dealing with the specimens returned by Cunningham and Fraser, Hooker sought collectors in other parts of the colony, particularly Van Diemens Land. As early as 1823 Hooker sent drying paper and collecting instructions to possible collectors, one of whom was Thomas Scott, a merchant in Launceston. Scott proved less than a success as a botanical correspondent for it was over four years before he replied to Hooker, even then sending only a few packages of seeds. Scott was apprehensive about even that small consignment arriving safely in England, for in the accompanying letter to Hooker he implied that the captain of the vessel transporting them might appropriate them for his own use. Although Scott was never to be the botanical correspondent that Hooker desired, he was instrumental in introducing to Hooker other Van Diemens Land collectors who were more appropriate for the role.

During 1827 Nicholas Vigors and T. Horsfield published their major work on the ornithology of Australia. The subjects of their treatise were contained in the collection of the Museum of the Linnean Society— the majority had been collected by George Caley and Robert Brown. The list of species was long and included the kookaburra, which Vigors and Horsfield reported from Caley's field notes as the 'Hawkesbury Clock', as it was among the first birds to announce the day. As mentioned previously the paper included a revision of the parrots, splitting the all-encompassing genus 'Psittacus' into a number of separate genera. This reclassification of the parrots quickly came under attack from the French zoologist, Desmarest. Desmarest criticised the subdivision of the Psittacidae on the grounds that the parrots formed a natural Linnean genus and that there was no need to divide them into separate genera, especially on the basis of minute differences that could mean very little to the animal itself. Vigors was unwilling to accept that his reclassification was based on minor differences and that same year defended his several genera in the *Zoological Journal* on the basis that Linnaeus' genus had been devised before numerous new species were obtained from Australia. These new species rendered the genus unwieldy. To subdivide a genus was not necessarily to disunite it, and the new taxonomic system allowed the close affinities of each of the new genera to be expressed. Vigors went on to admit a point often ignored in taxonomy: the formation of genera was an operation imposed by man upon organisms and did not necessarily always reflect valid relationships. The argument of Vigors and Desmarest was really one between the conservative naturalists, who insisted on retaining the original Linnean taxonomy and forcing the increasingly large numbers of established species into that framework, and the more radical naturalists who were willing to dispense with Linnaean genera when they deemed it necessary. In this case Vigors triumphed, and many of

his new genera remain valid today, even if the theoretical framework that he sought to establish, the quinary system, was ignominiously discarded.

In 1827 James King had claimed that he, John Busby, and Alexander Berry had formed the triumvirate of competent geologists in the colony. Although King's assertion was an exaggeration, the ranks of recognised geologists were swollen by the arrival of the Reverend Charles P. N. Wilton late in that year. Soon after his arrival in New South Wales, Wilton was to begin his geological researches on one of the more fascinating phenomena in New South Wales, the Burning Mountain. Early in 1828 a settler in the upper Hunter Valley noted smoke arising from the side of a mountain and on ascertaining from the Aborigines that it was not a fire set by them, investigated more closely. He returned to Sydney bearing reports of a volcano, reports of interest to the geologically inclined for, if true, they would support earlier observations of volcanic rock in Australia by the French mineralogists Depuch and Bailly on the 1800–1804 Baudin expedition. The account of smoke issuing from a fissure in the ground excited Wilton's interest, and he began a series of visits to the Burning Mountain, formally named Mount Wingen, an Aboriginal word for fire. Wilton's conclusions were published in a variety of sources ranging from the *Sydney Gazette* and the *Australian Almanac* to the *Philosophical Transactions of the Royal Society*. Wilton determined after a number of visits, as did Thomas Mitchell who mapped the region in February of 1829, that the smoke was due to a buried burning coal seam rather than volcanic action. Wilton found that the candescent rocks around the openings of the fissure were sandstone; no trace of lava or other volcanic rock was present. The rocks surrounding the openings, and there were several fissures due to the advance of the combustion through the coal seam, were covered with crystals deposited from the sulphur-laden smoke. Depending on the contaminants, the crystals were either red-orange from iron impurities or pale straw-coloured from alum impurities. In his writings on the subject, Wilton noted that these sulphur crystals had been put to beneficial use by the local pastoralists to successfully treat scab in sheep.

Thomas Mitchell, then surveyor-general of the colony, ascribed the ignition of the coal seam to a phenomenon described by William Buckland and the English geologist Henry de la Beche for a similar occurrence in England, in which the combustion was effected by the action of rain water on iron pyrites when in conjunction with coal or bituminous shale. Mitchell's map of the region showed numerous rents or fissures opened by the subterranean combustion, and from the evidence of mature trees established in old extinguished vents, Mitchell concluded that the fire had been burning for a considerable length of time.

By the winter months of 1828 Allan Cunningham

and Charles Fraser were working together for the first time since Oxley's initial expedition to the Lachlan River in 1817. Fraser had been busy earlier in the year, his duties including the shipment of cotton seed from the Botanic Gardens to Norfolk Island, which the government had decided to reconstitute as a penal colony, and visits to Port Stephens with Macarthur, presumably in connection with evaluation of land for the Australian Agricultural Company. On the journey to Port Stephens, Fraser was admonished by Alexander Macleay to 'learn something about the Eggs of the *Ornithorhynchus*, which I am told abounds there'.[9]

The object of the expedition combining the talents of Fraser and Cunningham was once again the exploration of the Moreton Bay area to which the party was borne at the beginning of July by the vessel *Lucy Ann*. Three weeks passed without any attempt at inland exploration, Cunningham collecting in the immediate area of the mouth of the Brisbane River while Fraser fulfilled his orders to establish a public garden, observe the soil and timber for agricultural purposes, and collect samples of the local vegetation. His collections included the staghorn fern, *Platycerium grande*, along with seeds which were sent to W. J. Hooker at the Glasgow Botanical Garden; the then undescribed Moreton Bay chestnut, *Castanospermum australe*, with its nuts that the Aborigines knew to roast before eating, unlike the Europeans who suffered sickness for their ignorance; the undescribed Bell fruit tree of the genus *Codonocarpus*, in addition to the orchids that Cunningham so assiduously collected.

On the 23 July a party under the command of Captain Patrick Logan, which included both Fraser and Cunningham, set off to the south-east to determine the position of various geographical features. Pushing through the gums and the undergrowth of honeysuckle, Fraser and Cunningham extracted a toll in new species from the countryside. The party reached Mount Barney before Fraser, prompted by a desire to return his collection of living plants to the safety of the Botanic Garden in Sydney, chose to accompany Logan back to Moreton Bay and embark for Port Jackson.

Cunningham determined to remain in the area and pursue geographic discoveries, particularly the discovery of a pass through the mountain range to the west. Having sighted such a pass from the other side of the mountains the previous year, he was sure that a passage to the Darling Downs existed. After sending to Moreton Bay for a replenishment of supplies, Cunningham parted company with Logan and Fraser and headed north with a party to the Bremer River. From here the party journeyed south-east, arriving on 24 August at Mount Mitchell from where Cunningham caught sight of a gap through the Dividing Range to Darling Downs which was later to be named Cunninghams Gap. Although Cunningham did make some collections of

plants on the journey, he was clearly more interested in geographic discovery than in adding to his plant collection. Much of the territory he covered during his search for the pass would have had similar vegetation to the area he had scoured in company with Fraser during the previous two months. On his return to the Bremer River Cunningham observed a set of hills: '. . . one rather elevated and of remarkable figure I named Mount Fraser, after my friend and fellow-traveller.'[10] Before he returned to the Brisbane River Cunningham traced the Bremer River to its confluency with the Brisbane. He departed Moreton Bay for Port Jackson on 21 October.

Cunningham could well be satisfied with the results of his foray inland from Moreton Bay: he had established a pass over the Great Dividing Range which would open up Darling Downs to agriculture and he had collected numerous new species of plants unknown further to the south. These included the silky oak, *Grevillea robusta* called by Cunningham '*Grevillea excelsa*' and considered by him to be excellent timber for furniture; the coral tree with its brilliant scarlet flowers; and the macadamia tree, *Macadamia ternifolia*, which Cunningham thought might prove useful to farmers. In addition Cunningham collected geological samples, the skins of several rare birds, and, at the request of Everard Home, the skull of a female Aboriginal from an Aboriginal gravesite where Cunningham turned grave robber. Firmly established now as the king's botanist, Cunningham was no longer reluctant to send seeds of exotic plants to friends a practice against which he had earlier been admonished by Joseph Banks. In a letter to Charles Felfair, a botanist in Mauritius, he enclosed a packet of seeds from the Moreton Bay area including those of the Moreton Bay chestnut.

Fraser, who had long since returned home to Sydney to resume his duties at the Botanic Gardens, was in November making arrangements to receive plant specimens from King George Sound. William Baxter, an occasional botanical collector in the colony, gained an interview with Fraser and proposed that he go to King George Sound for botanical collections. In return for passage to the sound, where a regular garrison had been established some years past, as well as rations and an outfit of collecting equipment, Baxter promised to supply the Botanic Gardens with one half of all of his collections, the other half to be shipped to his patrons in England. On Fraser's recommendation, Governor Darling approved the arrangement and Baxter took passage to King George Sound on the *Lucy Ann*. Initially the arrangement appeared to progress well: the following March Baxter wrote to Fraser that although he was surprised to find seeds ripening so late in the season, he had been able to collect every plant that had ripened that year. The pitcher plants so favoured by botanists had not yet ripened, nor had the *Banksia*, but he intended to make every effort to secure their seeds on maturity. Baxter was unable to supply any preserved plant specimens or living plants yet, for the season had been too dry to permit him to collect any acceptable samples. Although at this time Fraser had received little from Baxter he could not have been worried, for the commandant of the King George Sound garrison had sent the reassuring news that Baxter was diligent in his collecting duties. When Baxter eventually returned by boat to Sydney in 1829, he proved unwilling to fulfil his side of the arrangement. Having already enjoyed passage to and from King George Sound, rations, housing, and the use of a convict servant while there, Baxter declined to divide his collection between the Botanic Gardens and his private employers. On hearing Baxter's excuses and evasions for not releasing the Botanic Gardens' share of the collection and learning that Baxter had previously given orders that several bags of seeds were to be retained for his personal disbursement, Fraser promptly sent the collector of customs on board the vessel to secure the government's due. Baxter in turn physically threatened the customs collector and attempted to throw a portion of the plants overboard. The constabulary calmed the antagonists, and after Baxter left the vessel Fraser was able to divide the collection as originally envisioned. According to Fraser Baxter was later heard to boast that he had cheated the government of the best specimens and had poisoned some of the rest, but this last claim may be discounted for by that time many of the seeds were growing under Fraser's careful scrutiny in the Botanic Gardens. Little more is known of William Baxter but he apparently died in 1836, no doubt without any further government assistance for his botanic studies.

Despite the explorations of Oxley, Cunningham, Hume, and Hovell, there existed very little knowledge of the land farther inland than the Blue Mountains. Oxley's expeditions of ten years previously had led him to believe that a large lake or marsh occupied much of the interior of Australia, while Phillip Parker King still considered that the rivers draining the western side of the Blue Mountains ran north-east to outlets on the small portion of the north-west coast of Australia that he had left uncharted. In this conjecture King was supported by Cunningham, who argued that a portion of the interior of the continent was covered by an inland lake, drained by a large river which ran to the north-west coast. This argument was sustained despite the distance the water would have to flow, propelled by the slight gradient from the differences in elevation of the two areas. Interest in the hypothetical river was enormous, for if it existed it was thought to provide the best means of penetrating the interior of the continent and would open up extensive land for agriculture on its banks. In 1828, after two years of drought, it was felt that the marshes which had denied Oxley the chance of pushing further westward in 1818 might be dry enough to allow another expedition success, and Governor Darling appointed Charles Sturt to command the expedition. Sturt had arrived in the colony the previous year and came reasonably close to the ideal of a military officer for leading inland explorations as suggested by Earl Bathurst as far back as 1816.

Sturt assembled his exploratory party in the Wellington Valley. Accompanied by Hamilton Hume and ten others, Sturt left this departure point on 7 December 1828. Pushing north-west along the Macquarie River, they soon passed the few outlying stations before swiftly approaching bush dominated by *Acacia pendula*, an indication of marshy grounds—although due to the drought conditions many of the former marsh areas were completely dry. As they progressed down the Macquarie River toward Mount Harris, members of the party were able to shoot crested pigeons, *Ocyphaps lophotes*; the galah reported by Oxley's expedition, *Cacatua roseicapilla*; and the little lorikeet, *Glossopsitta pusilla*, but Sturt felt that most of the birds they saw were similar to those found at Melville Island and were therefore migratory birds.

After various excursions to the east and west of the Macquarie, the party passed through the swamps which had halted Oxley and by the end of January 1829 reached D'Urbans Group, a sandstone formation that Sturt envisaged as having been surrounded by the ocean in the not-too-distant past. Further to the north-west the party encountered the river that Sturt named in honour of Governor Darling, but much to the disappointment of both the men and their horses the water in the river proved unpalatable due to salt springs. Travelling some distance down the Darling River, Hume shot a cockatoo ornamented with a yellow and scarlet crest, probably the pink cockatoo, *Cacatua leadbeateri*, before the party's lack of water necessitated turning back to the east. Later attempts to explore westward were again thwarted by the Darling River and lack of water, so the expedition returned to the Wellington Valley. While finding land which could only be described as barren, Sturt's expedition had shown to all but the most stubborn that the fabled inland sea, if it existed at all, had to lie much further inland, and the chance of any of the rivers running from the western slopes of the Blue Mountains to the north-west coastline was indeed remote. While the botanical and zoological results of the journey were minimal, Sturt had collected a variety of mineral specimens.

In his general remarks on the colony prefacing the published narrative of his journey, Sturt noted that the barrier ranges near the coast were all composed of sandstone but beyond Coxs River gave way to igneous granite, or primitive rock as it was then called. Limestone formations outcropped in many areas, and usually within these formations could be found caverns, some-

'Rose cockatoo'
Sturt. *Two expeditions into the interior of southern Australia.*
1833.
Cacatua roseicapilla

times filled with bones or fossils.

The Reverend Charles Wilton, who only arrived in Australia in 1827, was quick to contribute to the organised structure of Australian natural history. At the beginning of 1828 he commenced publication of *The Australian Quarterly Journal of Theology, Literature, and Science.* Unfortunately for natural history, the arguments about any particular phenomenon were often weighed in the order of the disciplines listed in the title of the journal. This, however, should scarcely come as a surprise in any journal published in the early 1800s by a clergyman.

Wilton was obviously aware of the tension that was growing between naturalists, especially geologists, and the doctrines of the established church, for the lead article written by Wilton in the first edition of the journal was entitled 'On the connection between Religion and Science'. Wilton attempted in the article to justify an interest in geology, especially his own interest, by claiming that it was man's duty to exercise and improve his mind by investigating the world that

had been created by God for his use and instruction. This interest could then be utilised in the defense of religion:

> The Geologist, in observing the several stratifications of the Globe, and the various petrified remains of what once formed part of animated nature, beholds the exact accomplishment of Scripture, and is enabled, by adducing the strongest evidences of a universal Deluge, to put to silence the Infidel and the Sceptic. Surely then Religion and Science may well go hand in hand together . . .[11]

In the eyes of many, religion and science could travel together, especially geology and the verses of Genesis. In the early part of the nineteenth century, a school of geology which staunchly advocated 'Mosaic' or 'Diluvial' geology rose to prominence in England. The principal feature of this school was the use of geological data to substantiate the Genesis mythology. In England the prime spokesman for Mosaic Geology was the Reverend William Buckland, who in future years was to play an important part in the analysis of Australian fossils, while locally, in the colony of New South Wales, Charles Wilton was a willing disciple of the movement. Wilton was in fact a much stricter creationist than Buckland who had conceded that the evidence of geology made nonsense of the claim by theologians that only 6,000 years had past since the creation of the earth. In order to allow for the time needed for the manipulation of the earth's surface by geologic processes, Buckland postulated two arguments. The first point was that the phrase 'in the beginning' did not explicitly introduce a time scale and may have been an undefined period of great length. The second point argued that the six days of creation and the seventh day of rest as specified in Genesis need not be thought of as days of twenty-four hours duration but merely as long, successive periods of time. In combination these two arguments allowed for the extension of the age of the earth to whatever period was necessary to embrace current geological concepts. While considering that Genesis might be an abstract statement not necessarily tied to specific time periods, Buckland was conservative in his belief that geology revealed many proofs of the existence of God, the most positive of these was the Deluge or Flood as evidenced by fossils buried in rock strata.

If Buckland chose to be a revisionist and argue for an abstract version of Genesis, Charles Wilton would have none of those heretical statements. In two articles published in the *Australian Quarterly* late in 1828 Wilton argued strenuously for a strict interpretation of the Genesis account; if the bible recorded a day it meant a twenty-four hour day and nothing else. Reproving those tempted to apostasy, Wilton harangued his readers with fire and brimstone (or sulphur as a geologically-minded cleric would appreciate):

Instead of indulging in wild and visionary theory respecting the mode of first formations . . . give implicit credit to the facts, however mysterious, recorded in the Scripture and to bow down with awful submission before the plentitude of power revealed in its pages.[12]

Before Wilton could elucidate his reconciliation between Genesis and the revelations of geology the *Australian Quarterly* ceased publication.

Before the demise of the *Australian Quarterly* Wilton set himself one other target. In 1827 Peter Cunningham (no relation to Allan Cunningham), a ship's surgeon who had made several trips out to the colony of New South Wales, published a volume titled *Two Years in New South Wales*. Many of the ideas contained in the book were inimical to Wilton, and he attacked them in a review of the book published in the *Australian Quarterly*. Peter Cunningham subscribed to the theory that a large astral body or comet passing sufficiently close to the earth's surface induced immense effects on wind and water which had produced the changes that had hitherto been attributed to the Deluge. Wilton could obviously not accept such a viewpoint and rebutted its points in his review, thundering to the conclusion that the Deluge was punishment visited on mankind for his wickedness, and that theoretical concoctions of comets causing floods could have no basis in reality.

Never was the contrast greater between two proponents of natural history in Australia than between the other Cunningham—Allan—and Charles Wilton. Cunningham the field collector, a diligent worker intent on the meticulous collection of all the species he encountered, working within a theoretical framework of Linnaean taxonomy and Wilton, representing an individual rarely encountered in the colony up to this point, an individual strongly committed to the support of a theoretical structure, in this case creationism. So strong was Wilton's commitment that he used natural history solely to validate his chosen theoretical construct. Yet the two individuals could exist easily in the colony together; Allan Cunningham never published cosmological speculations as did his namesake Peter Cunningham and therefore did not incur the wrath of Wilton. The grounds were laid, however, for the conflict between the empirical observers of nature as exemplified by Cunningham and the defenders of the established theological structures such as Wilton. While the conflict was never to undermine the foundations of Australian society to the extent that it did in Europe, the mere fact that such an argument existed in a colony torn from the wilderness just fifty years previously records the advances made in the life of the colony.

Epilogue

Fifty years of European occupation of the continent of Australia had brought about remarkable advances in the status of natural history. Prior to settlement and during the first difficult years of the colony's existence in New South Wales considerable effort was put into furthering natural history, but only at the level of the collection of specimens for dispatch to Europe; the collectors saw themselves in the colony for only a limited time. In the early 1800s, natural history in the colony gained an increasing local input. Certainly most of the analysis of the flora, the fauna, and the minerals was still carried out in Europe, but an infrastructure began to develop in the colony to support the natural history aspirations of the long-term residents. A volume on natural history printed in the colony, the development of a Botanic Gardens, the formation of a scientific society, the initiation of a rudimentary museum, the recording of a portion of the flora and fauna pictorially, all took place within twenty years. If some of these activities proved abortive, it merely indicated that too few naturalists resided in the colony to support such high-minded activities. Later attempts were to prove more successful, but the foundations had clearly been laid by the 1830s.

The year 1829 was to prove a turning point in the development of natural history in Australia. Until 1829 the colony in New South Wales had dominated the continent. Natural history collectors travelled on occasion to Van Diemens Land, Moreton Bay, or King George Sound, but the focal point of natural history, as it was for all sectors of the colony be it agriculture or administration, was Sydney. In 1829 this dominance began to erode. The Swan River colony was established and included resident naturalists, while in Van Diemens Land organised natural history in terms of scientific societies and publications began an advance that was soon to overtake similar efforts in New South Wales.

The replacement of New South Wales as the centre of natural history was neither abrupt nor planned, it came about through lapses in the replacement of individuals interested in natural history as they either left the colony or died. Institutionally Sydney continued to progress: in 1829 the Botanic Gardens had expanded to the point where the colonial administration felt it necessary to appoint an assistant colonial botanist, in part because Charles Fraser was away so frequently on collecting expeditions of many months' duration. With application that was to presage the impoverished collectors of the Australian Museum, Fraser would often strip off his clothing for use in carrying specimens rather than forego opportunities. Fraser's salary was increased, but before confirmation of the increase arrived, Fraser fell ill on a collecting expedition in 1832 and died that year.

In Sydney Allan Cunningham was beginning to think of his return to England. Originally Cunningham had intended to stay in Australia no longer than 1826, but before he could be satisfied with his collections and explorations there had been so many new areas to visit. In 1828 Cunningham requested permission from Kew to terminate his activities in New South Wales and return to England, but with the delays in the transmission of dispatches, it was 1830 before his request was granted and Cunningham was informed. He sailed for England early in 1831 and remained in England for six years before eventually returning to Australia again, only to die two years later. The Botanic Gardens had continued under the stewardship of various botanists until the present day.

Just as the Botanic Gardens in Sydney evolved out of gardens that occupied the site prior to the Gardens' formation, so another institution in Sydney, the Colonial Museum, later to become the Australian Museum, evolved from another admittedly minor museum. It will be recalled that the Philosophical Society of Australasia founded a small museum during its brief lifetime, predominantly to display mineral specimens from outlying settlements. The museum which had been housed in a room in the colonial secretary's office probably continued its existence when that office was transferred to Alexander Macleay in 1826. Macleay, having been a former secretary of the Linnean Society of London, would no doubt have been sympathetic to the cause of a museum in Sydney, and Governor Darling received a dispatch from Earl Bathurst in 1827 about the desirability of the establishment of such a museum, including Bathurst's approval for the sum of £200 per annum for that purpose. The dispatch from Bathurst and subsequent suggestions for a museum which appeared in the *Australian Quarterly* and the *Sydney Gazette* had the desired effect on Darling, and in June 1829 he appointed William Holmes as the colonial zoologist. Holmes, who appears to have had little training for the position, may have owed his selection to the influence of Charles Wilton who had emigrated to Australia on the same vessel as Holmes. His tenure in the position was brief, he died in 1831, but the museum of which he assumed charge continues to this day.

On the opposite side of the continent, the Swan River colony had been organised. The reports of James Stirling and Charles Fraser had encouraged backers of the proposal to found a colony on the western coast of Australia, and it had not been long before the vessel *Parmelia* brought 150 settlers to the area. Included among them was James Drummond who held an honorary appointment as government naturalist. Most of the animals that the settlers at Swan River encountered had been described before, the black swans, the kangaroos, the emus, and the parrots, but there still remained the occasional fearful report of large animals in the interior lagoons, animals that although forever proving mythical, had troubled natural history on the western coast of Australia since the time of Dampier. In those first few years of the Swan River colony, few settlers had time to worry about whether the quokka on Rottnest Island or the Dama wallaby on Garden Island had been described by naturalists; the animals were seen only as sources of food or pests to agriculture.

The flowering of natural history in Van Diemens Land saw the establishment of the Van Diemens Land Society in 1829, a society dedicated to the collection and publication of information peculiar to that island. Although the society was able to enrol over 100 members, few of them had any claim to expertise in natural history. The enthusiasm could not last and soon the society faded from existence having lasted little longer than its New South Wales' forerunner, the Philosophical Society. Natural history, however, did not fade in Van Diemens Land, and its resurgence by the end of the 1830s established it as the leading scientific centre in Australia.

Notes

INTRODUCTION pp. 1–8

[1] G. Shaw, *Zoological Lectures* (George Kearsley, London, 1809), p. 13.

[2] W. Wood, *Zoography* (Cadell and Davies, London, 1807), p. IX.

CHAPTER ONE pp. 9–22

[1] W. Dampier, *A Voyage to New Holland* (J. Knapton, London, 1703) p. 122.

[2] Dampier, *Voyage to New Holland*, p. 123.

[3] N. Witsen 'Observations in New Holland', in *Philosophical Transactions of the Royal Society* (C. and R. Baldwin, London, 1809), vol. IV (abridged), p. 316.

[4] Dampier, *Voyage to New Holland*, p. 140.

[5] J. Banks, *The Endeavour Journal of Joseph Banks*, ed. J. C. Beaglehole (Trustees of the Public Library of New South Wales, Sydney, 1962) vol. I, p. 33.

[6] S. Parkinson, *Journal of a Voyage to the South Seas* (S. Parkinson, London, 1773), p. 136.

[7] K. Lemmon, *The Golden Age of Plant Hunters* (Phoenix House, London, 1968), p. 12.

[8] Banks, *Endeavour Journal of Joseph Banks*, vol. II, p. 84.

[9] *ibid.*, vol. II, p. 84.

[10] Parkinson, *Voyage to the South Seas*, pp. 144–5.

[11] Banks, *Endeavour Journal of Joseph Banks*, vol. II, p. 94.

[12] Linnaeus, *A Selection of the Correspondence of Linnaeus and other Naturalists*, ed. J. E. Smith (London, 1821), vol. I, p. 267.

[13] *ibid.*, vol. I, pp. 230–2.

[14] Furneaux's Narrative, in *The Journals of Captain James Cook on his Voyages of Discovery*, ed. J. C. Beaglehole (for Hakluyt Society, by Cambridge University Press, Cambridge, 1961), vol. II, *The Voyage of the Resolution and Adventure*, p. 734.

[15] Anderson's Journal, in *The Journals of Captain James Cook on his Voyages of Discovery*, ed. J. C. Beaglehole (for Hakluyt Society by Cambridge University Press, Cambridge, 1967), vol. III, part 2, *The Voyage of the Resolution and Discovery*, p. 792.

CHAPTER TWO pp. 23–40

[1] K. Lemmon, *The Golden Age of Plant Hunters* (Phoenix House, London, 1968), p. 95.

[2] J.-J. de La Billardière, *Voyage in Search of La Perouse* (Stockdale, London, 1800) English translation, p. 324.

[3] G. Tobin, Journal and sketches on HMS Providence 1791–1793, (original manuscript, Mitchell Library), catalogue number A562, vol. I, p. 41.

[4] *ibid.* vol. I, p. 99.

[5] *ibid.* vol. I, p. 99.

[6] I. Lee, *Captain Bligh's Second Voyage to the South Seas* (Longmans, Green and Co., London, 1920), p. 20.

[7] E. Home 'Description of the Anatomy of the Ornithorhynchus Hystrix', in *Philosophical Transactions of the Royal Society*, 1802 (G. and W. Nicol, London, 1802), part 2, p. 357.

[8] *ibid.*, p. 361.

[9] Lee, *Captain Bligh's Second Voyage*, p. 27.

[10] Letter from G. Tobin to F. Bond, 15 December 1817 (Mitchell Library), catalogue number AG60.

[11] G. Vancouver, *A Voyage of Discovery* (Robinson and Edwards, London, 1798), p. XV.

[12] *ibid.*, pp. 12–13.

[13] La Billardière, *In Search of La Perouse*, p. 98.

[14] *ibid.*, p. 101.

[15] *ibid.*, p. 119.

[16] *ibid.*, p. 274.

CHAPTER THREE pp. 41–62

[1] Banks, *Endeavour Journal of Joseph Banks*, vol. II, p. 122.

[2] A. B. Smyth, *The Journal of Arthur Bowes Smyth: Surgeon, Lady Penrhyn, 1787–1789*, (Australian Documents Library, Sydney, 1979), p. 58.

[3] J. White, *Journal of a Voyage to New South Wales* (Debrett, London, 1790), p. 137.

[4] Anonymous, *The Voyage of Governor Phillip to Botany Bay* (J. Stockdale, London, 1789), p. 59.

[5] *ibid.*, p. 91.

[6] 'Lieutenant Watts Narrative', in *Voyage of Governor Phillip to Botany Bay*, p. 225.

[7] A. Phillip to Lord Sydney, 15 May 1788, in *Historical Records of Australia: Series I, Governors Despatches to and from England*, ed. F. Watson (Library Committee of the Commonwealth Parliament, Sydney, 1914), vol. I, 1788–1796, p. 24.

[8] J. Lee, 'Rules for collecting and preserving seeds from Botany Bay' in *James Lee and the Vineyard Nursery Hammersmith*, E. J. Wilson (Hammersmith Local History Group, London, 1961), p. 2.

[9] W. Tench, *A Narrative of the Expedition to Botany Bay* (J. Debrett, London, 1789), p. 119.

[10] *ibid.*, pp. 122–6.

[11] Anonymous, August 1790, in *Historical Records of New South Wales: Phillip 1783–1792*, ed. A. Britton (C. Potter Gov't Printer, Sydney, 1892). vol. I, part 2, pp. 399–400.

[12] Hill to Wathen, 26 July 1790, in *Historical Records of New South Wales*, vol. I, part 2, p. 366.

[13] D. Burton to J. Banks, January 1791, Bradbourne Collection of Banks Papers; Australia and South Sea Islands, 1774–1809 (Mitchell Library), catalogue no. A83, p. 3.

[14] D. Blackburn to R. Knight, 19 March 1791 (Mitchell Library), catalogue no. Ab163.

[15] A. Phillip to Lord Grenville, 14 December 1791, in *Historical Records of Australia*, Series I, vol. I, p. 319.

[16] D. Burton to A. Phillip, 24 February 1792, in *Historical Records of New South Wales*, vol. I, part 2, pp. 599–600.

[17] D. Collins, *An Account of the English Colony in New South Wales* (T. Cadell and W. Davies, London, 1798–1802), vol. 1, p. 206.

[18] *ibid.*, p. 205.

[19] W. Paterson to J. Banks, 1 May 1792, in Bradbourne Collection of Banks Papers: Botanical and Horticultural, 1789–1796 (Mitchell Library), catalogue no. A81.

CHAPTER FOUR   pp. 63–82

[1] J. Hunter, *An Historical Journal of the Transactions at Port Jackson and Norfolk Island* (J. Stockdale, London, 1793) p. 57.

[2] White, *Voyage to New South Wales*, p. 183.

[3] Daniel Southwell Papers; extract from his journal 1787–1791, in Bonwick Transcripts Box 57 (Mitchell Library, original in British Museum), pp. 275–6.

[4] T. Watling, *Letters from an exile at Botany Bay to his aunt in Dumfries* (A. Bell, Penrith, 1794) p. 20.

[5] *ibid.*, p. 10.

[6] *ibid.*, p. 16.

[7] J. Banks to J. Hunter, 30 March 1797, in *Historical Records of New South Wales: Hunter, 1796–1799*, ed. F. M. Bladen (C. Potter Gov't Printer, Sydney, 1895), vol. III, p. 202.

[8] Collins, *The English Colony in New South Wales*, vol. II, p. 62.

[9] Anonymous, 'Journal into the interior of the country New South Wales' in *Historical Records of New South Wales*, vol. III, p. 821.

[10] M. Flinders, *A Voyage to Terra Australis* (G. and W. Nicol, London, 1814), vol. I, p. cxxxiii.

[11] Collins, *The English Colony in New South Wales*, vol. II, p. 158.

[12] Anonymous, *The Naturalist's Pocket Magazine* (Harrison, Cluse and Co., London, 1799), vol. I, Preface.

[13] *ibid.*, vol. I, Preface.

[14] *ibid.*, vol. I, Preface.

[15] G. Shaw, *Naturalist's Miscellany* (no publisher given).

CHAPTER FIVE   pp. 83–104

[1] J. Banks to P. King, 22 June 1801, King Papers vol. 8 (Mitchell Library), catalogue no. A1980 2 p. 47.

[2] G. Caley, *Reflections on the Colony of New South Wales: George Caley*, ed. J. E. B. Currey (Lansdowne Press, Melbourne, 1966), p. 44.

[3] G. Shaw, *General Zoology* (G. Kearsley, London, 1800), vol. I, p. 175.

[4] Anonymous, *Naturalist's Pocket Magazine* (Harrison, Cluse and Co., London, 1800), vol. V.

[5] J. Grant, *The narrative of a Voyage of discovery performed in HMS Lady Nelson* (T. Egerton, London, 1803), p. 112.

[6] Caley, *Reflections on the Colony of New South Wales*, p. 46.

[7] P. King to J. Banks, 21 August 1801, in *Historical Records of New South Wales: Hunter and King, 1800–1802*, ed. F. M. Bladen (C. Potter Gov't Printer, Sydney, 1896), vol. IV, p. 356.

[8] M. Flinders to J. Banks, 6 September 1800, Bradbourne Collection of Banks papers: Australia and South Sea Islands, 1774–1809 (Mitchell Library), catalogue no. A83.

[9] Anonymous to J. Banks, undated, *Historical Records of New South Wales*, vol. IV, p. 348.

[10] R. Brown, 'General remarks, geographical and systematical, on the Botany of Terra Australis', in *A Voyage to Terra Australis*, M. Flinders (G. and W. Nicol, London, 1814), p. 539.

[11] J. D. Hooker, *The Botany of the Antarctic Voyage of HM Discovery ships Erebus and Terror in the year 1839–1843* (Lovell Reeve, London, 1860), vol. I, part III, *Florae Tasmania*, p. cxiv.

CHAPTER SIX   pp. 105–116

[1] P. King to J. Banks, September 1803, in *Historical Records of New South Wales: King 1803–1805*, ed. F. M. Bladen (W. Gullick Gov't printer, Sydney, 1897), vol. V, p. 229.

[2] J. Latham to A. Lambert, 26 January 1800, in *Austral Avian Record*, ed. G. M. Matthews (Witherby, London, 1922), vol. V, p. 25.

[3] Anonymous, *Edinburgh Review* (A. Constable, Edinburgh, 1803), vol. II, no. 4, p. 430.

[4] *ibid.*, vol. II, no. 4, p. 430.

[5] N. Baudin, *The Journal of Post Captain Nicholas Baudin*, trans. and ed. C. Cornell (Libraries Board of South Australia, Adelaide, 1974), p. 191.

[6] F. Péron, *A Voyage to the Southern Hemisphere* (R. Phillips, London, 1809), translation, p. 173.

[7] *ibid.*, p. 206.

[8] *ibid.*, p. 283.

[9] Baudin, *Journal of Post Captain Nicholas Baudin*, p. 452.

CHAPTER SEVEN   pp. 117–34

[1] J. Lewin, in *Documents on Art and Taste in Australia: The Colonial Period, 1770–1914*, ed. B. Smith (Oxford University Press, Melbourne, 1975), p. 19.

[2] Anonymous, *Sydney Gazette and New South Wales Advertiser*, 7 August 1803, vol. I, no. 23, p. 2b; *ibid.*, 21 August 1803, vol. I, no. 25, p. 2a; *ibid.*, 11 September 1803, vol. I, no. 28, p. 3b; *ibid.*, 2 October 1803, vol. I, no. 31, p. 2c.

[3] J. Banks to P. King, 29 August 1804, in Caley, *Reflections on the Colony of New South Wales*, p. 99.

[4] Anonymous, *Sydney Gazette and New South Wales Advertiser*, 21 August 1803, vol. I, no. 25, p. 3b.

[5] G. Caley to J. Banks, 18 August 1804, in Caley, *Reflections on the Colony of New South Wales*, p. 105.

[6] Anonymous, *Sydney Gazette and New South Wales Advertiser*, 9 September 1804, vol. II, no. 80, p. 2c.

[7] P. King, 2 August 1805, in *Historical Records of New South Wales: King 1803–1805*, ed. F. M. Bladen (W. Gullick Gov't Printer, Sydney, 1897), vol. V, p. 726.

[8] G. Shaw, *General Zoology* (G. Kearsley, London, 1804), vol. V, part II, p. 456.

[9] G. Caley to J. Banks, in *Historical Records of New South Wales: King and Bligh, 1806–1808*, ed. F. M. Bladen (W. Gullick Gov't Printer, Sydney, 1898), vol. VI, p. 691.

[10] R. Townson to Viscount Castlereagh, 2 April 1808, in *Historical Records of New South Wales: King and Bligh, 1806–1808*, vol. VI, p. 573.

[11] G. Caley to J. Banks, 7 July 1808, in *Historical Records of New South Wales*, vol. VI, p. 695.

[12] J. Banks to G. Caley, 25 August 1808, in *Historical Records of New South Wales*, vol. VI, p. 704.

[13] J. Lewin, *Birds of New Holland* (White and Bagster, London, 1808), Preface.

[14] G. Caley to J. Banks, 16 February 1809, in *Reflections on the Colony of New South Wales: George Caley*, p. 176.

[15] J. Arnold to W. Crowfoot, 28 February 1810, Dr. Arnold's Diary and Letters, vol. II (Mitchell Library), catalogue no. A 1846, p. 494.

CHAPTER EIGHT pp. 135–52

[1] G. Perry, *Arcana; or The Museum of Natural History* (J. Stratford, London, 1811), p. 37.

[2] *ibid.*, p. 38.

[3] *ibid.*, p. 65.

[4] J. Lewin, *Birds of New South Wales* (G. Howe, Sydney, 1813).

[5] T. Skottowe, Select Specimens from Nature (Mitchell Library), catalogue no. PXA 555.

[6] J. Arnold to E. Arnold, 12 March 1815. Dr. Arnold's Diary and Letters vol. II (Mitchell Library), catalogue no. A 1846, p. 605.

[7] A. Cunningham, Journal, 20 September 1816–14 February 1819, (unpublished manuscript, State Archives of New South Wales), catalogue no. SZ 7, p. 278.

[8] J. Oxley, *Journals of Two Expeditions into the Interior of New South Wales* (J. Murray, London, 1820), part II, p. 214.

CHAPTER NINE pp. 153–68

[1] Anonymous, *The Edinburgh Review*, July 1819 (A. Constable, Edinburgh, 1819), p. 30.

[2] *ibid.*, p. 31.

[3] *ibid.*, p. 28.

[4] J. Argo, *Narrative of a Voyage around the world* (Treuttel, Wurtz and Richter, London, 1823), part II, p. 163.

[5] B. Field, *First Fruits of Australian Poetry* (privately printed, Sydney, 1819), p. 2.

[6] *ibid.*, p. 7.

[7] J. Vaux, *Memoirs of the First Thirty-Two Years of the Life of J. H. Vaux* (J. Murray, London, 1819), p. 205.

[8] A. Cunningham, Journal 8 May 1819–27 August 1822 (State Archives of New South Wales), catalogue no. SZ 8.

CHAPTER TEN pp. 169–88

[1] B. Field, 'Preface', in *Geographical Memoirs on New South Wales*, ed. B. Field (J. Murray, London, 1825), p. v.

[2] B. Field, 'Journal of an excursion across the Blue Mountains of New South Wales, October 1822', in *Geographical Memoirs on New South Wales*, p. 442.

[3] W. Macarthur to J. Macarthur, 16 January 1824. Macarthur Papers, vol. 39 (Mitchell Library), catalogue no. A 2935.

[4] T. Brisbane to Earl Bathurst, 18 March 1825, Transcripts of the missing despatches from the Governor of NSW: 1823–32 (Mitchell Library), catalogue no. A 1267, part 4, p. 46.

[5] A. Berry, 'On the Geology of Part of the Coast of New South Wales' in *Geographical Memoirs on New South Wales*, p. 235.

[6] B. Field, 'Preface' in *Geographical Memoirs on New South Wales*, p. viii.

[7] Anonymous, *Zoological Journal*, (W. Phillips, London, 1826), vol. II, April 1825, p. 135.

[8] Anonymous, *Quarterly Review*, (J. Murray, London, 1829), vol. XXXIX, January–April 1829, p. 325.

[9] A. Macleay to C. Fraser, 1828, Macarthur Papers, Australian Agricultural Company Letters (Mitchell Library), catalogue no. A 4330, p. 71.

[10] A. Cunningham, 'Report to Governor Darling, 16 December 1828', R. Darling's Despatches 1828 (Mitchell Library), catalogue no. A 1203.

[11] C. Wilton, 'On the connection between Religion and Science', in *The Australian Quarterly Journal of Theology, Literature, and Science*, (G. Eagar, Sydney, 1828), vol. I, January 1828, p. 4.

[12] C. Wilton, 'Geology', in *The Australian Quarterly Journal of Theology, Literature and Science*, (A. Hill, Sydney, 1828), vol. 4, October 1828, p. 377.

Scientific Index

* Organisms named by Peron in his "Voyage de decouvertes" but not formally described.

195

ANIMALIA

* Organisms named by Peron in his "Voyage de decouvertes" but not formally described.

* Organisms named by Peron in his "Voyage de decouvertes" but not formally described.

* Organisms named by Peron in his "Voyage de decouvertes" but
  not formally described.

* Organisms named by Peron in his "Voyage de decouvertes" but not formally described.

General Index

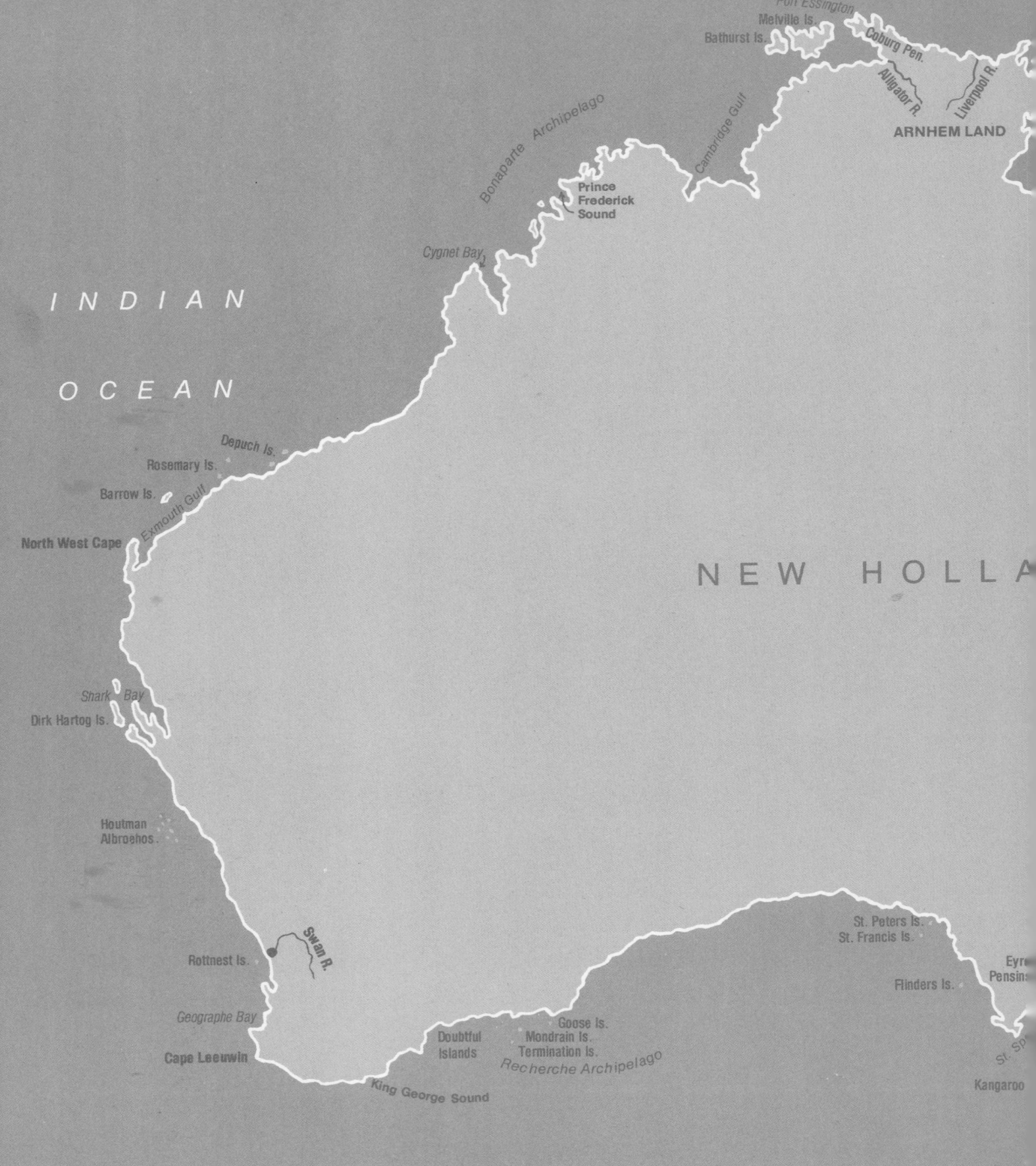

INDIAN

OCEAN

Bonaparte Archipelago

Port Essington
Melville Is.
Bathurst Is.
Coburg Pen.
Alligator R.
Liverpool R.
ARNHEM LAND

Cambridge Gulf

Prince
Frederick
Sound

Cygnet Bay

NEW HOLLA

Depuch Is.
Rosemary Is.
Barrow Is.
Exmouth Gulf
North West Cape

Shark Bay
Dirk Hartog Is.

Houtman
Albroehos.

St. Peters Is.
St. Francis Is.

Eyre
Pensins

Flinders Is.

Swan R.
Rottnest Is.

Geographe Bay

Cape Leeuwin

Doubtful
Islands

Goose Is.
Mondrain Is.
Termination Is.
Recherche Archipelago

St. Sp

Kangaroo

King George Sound

SOUTHERN

OCEAN